Adventure Tourism: The New Frontier

Adventure Tourism: The New Frontier

Rakesh Kumar Sah

RANDOM

RANDOM PUBLICATIONS

NEW DELHI (INDIA)

Adventure Tourism: The New Frontier

ISBN 978-93-5111-325-6

Published in 2014 in India by

RANDOM PUBLICATIONS

4376-A/4B, Gali Murari Lal, Ansari Road
New Delhi-110 002
Phone : +91-11-43580356, +91-11-23289044
e-mail: randomexports@gmail.com, sales@randompublications.com, info@randompublications.com

Type Setting by : Keystoneprintads, Delhi-110051
Printed at : Thomson Press (India) Ltd

Preface

Since the earliest explorers, adventure travel has been part of the world's culture. According to the National Tour Association, adventure tourism is a "tour designed around an adventurous activity such as rafting, hiking, or mountain climbing." Be it fueled by sport, riches or escape from tyranny, exploration and adventure tourism continues to thrive, change and grow every year. Modern adventure travel was born with the first planned trek to the Himalayas in Nepal decades ago. The first commercial rafting trips in Ethiopia were made in the early 1970s. As political climates, natural disasters and the taste of the adventurer change, so does the adventure travel industry. Floating the Egyptian Nile and climbing Mount Ararat were popular in the 1980s. In the 90s that interest turned toward the Swiss Alps and diving in Thailand. On the Edge magazine claims that the most popular adventure tours today are taking place in the Central America region, such as kayaking in the Dominican Republic or trekking through Costa Rica.

The term "adventure" means something different to everyone. For some, sleeping outdoors may be an adventure. For others, it may be a multi-day whitewater rafting trip that is both exciting and physically challenging. Adventure tourism can be accomplished in many environments, from scuba diving in Belize or Australia to mountain climbing in Bhutan or Nepal. Traditionally, adventure travel includes some type of sport. However, depending upon an individual's physical abilities and desires, adventure tourism can include a number of more passive activities, including guided tours, mystery and murder-mystery tours.

I thank all members of my team who have helped in the preparation of the book. My special thanks go to "Random Publications" who have published the book.

—Rakesh Kumar Sah

Contents

1

Adventure Tourism Related Activities

LAND BASED ACTIVITIES

MOUNTAINEERING

- Application: These Basic Minimum Standards (BMS) will apply specifically to commercial operators attempting 6000m or other comparable peaks, which offer to guide or accompany climbers above Base Camp and also to operators who offer more limited facilities. However, it will also concern operators who supply transport etc to Base Camp, and also supply Base Camp services and High Altitude porters.
- Information to Clients: A variety of organisations offer to take clients on 6000m or other comparable peaks. They vary from those which provide a full service to the summit or nearly to the summit, to those where there is minimal support for clients above Base Camp. However at the present moment it is difficult for clients to deduce from brochures exactly what is offered in terms of guiding and support, and whether it corresponds to their needs. These Basic Minimum Standards will supply clients with pointers to assist them to make an informed choice.
- Danger awareness: Mountaineers climbing at very high altitude, especially above 6000m are at considerable stress to their mental and physical powers and may not be capable of assisting others as has always been traditional in mountaineering. This fact is of particular importance to mountaineers of limited experience, who rely on professional guides to bring them safely up and down 6000m+ peaks. They should be made aware that the risks involved in climbing at altitudes are such that a degree of self-reliance is necessary.
- General Guidelines for Mountaineering:
  - All such operators will have to be registered with Adventure Tour Operators Association of India and Ministry of Tourism.

- The leader or chief guide and as many as possible of the uides should have high altitude experience appropriate to the altitude of the peak to be climbed. He must have been a member of three climbing expeditions above 6000 m and must have completed the Basic Mountaineering Course with an 'A' grade or an equivalent from abroad. He/She must be qualified on first aid and cardiopulmonary resuscitation (CPR) certification.
- The guiding and porter staff on the mountain and the material supplied must be adequate for the aims of the party and stated level of service offered.
- An experienced doctor in the party is desirable but at the very least advance arrangements must be known for medical help. Advance arrangements must also be made for evacuation assistance in case of emergency.
- The minimum safety equipment available is recommended walkie-talkie radios and recommended medical supplies.
- Advertising must give a true picture of all the difficulties and dangers involved, and avoid promising the impossible. If an expedition is commercially launched by an operator, then the Biographical information about the guiding team should be included.
- The client must truthfully reveal his experience, supported by documentation/photograph, medical history etc to the organiser so that the organiser can make an informed choice about the potential client.
- Information supplied in advance will include a clear statement of the guiding, porterage and equipment which will be supplied by the organiser, together with details of the clothing and equipment to be supplied by the client. This is not in context of the operators assisting expeditions with logistics alone.
- All equipment on which life is dependent must be Union International de Alpine Association (UIAA) or European Union (EU) certified. (j) Knowledge of low impact environmental expeditioning must be undertaken, pledging to environmental guidelines of Union International de Alpine Association (UIAA)/ Himalayan Environment Trust (HET) etc.

TREKKING

- The leader or chief guide and as many as possible of the guides should have experience appropriate to the difficulty of the route being attempted The trip leader must have completed at least two trekking trips in general and must have completed the Basic Mountaineering Course or equivalent with an 'A' grade. He/She must be qualified on first aid and cardiopulmonary resuscitation (CPR) certification.

- The guiding and porter staff for the trek and the material supplied must be adequate for the aims of the party and stated level of services offered.
- Adequate arrangements must be made known in advance for medical help available in the area. Advance information must also be made for evacuation assistance in case of emergency. Minimum first aid medical supplies must be carried on the trip. In case of a helicopter requirement for rescue operation, it is recommended that the Accreditation Committee be empowered to authorize the rescue.
- Information provided to clients must give a true picture of all the difficulties and dangers involved, and avoid promising the impossible. Biographical information about the guiding team should be included.
- The client must truthfully reveal his experience, medical history etc to the organiser so that the organiser can make an informed choice about the potential client.
- Information supplied in advance will include a clear statement of the guiding, porterage and equipment which will be supplied by the organiser, together with details of the clothing and equipment to be supplied by the client.

WATER BASED ACTIVITIES

RIVER RUNNING

- Any company operating river running trips or commercial white water rafting trips must be registered with Indian Association of Professional Rafting Outfitters/Adventure Tour Operators Association of India and Ministry of Tourism.
- All trips on white water for tourists will be conducted with at least one qualified guide on each craft. A senior guide or trip leader must be present and supervise the activity at all times.
- The Guide accompanying the trips should:
  - Be at least 18 years of age;
  - Be able to swim;
  - Hold a valid first aid and cardiopulmonary resuscitation (CPR) certificate or equivalent.
- Training: Guide trainees should complete a course (or equivalent training) that equips them with the necessary skills and knowledge to safely and competently guide a raft. A guide training course should include the following topics:
  - Skills -rafting techniques, crew training and management, emergency and rescue techniques.
  - Knowledge - equipment, safety and emergency procedures, rapid theory, leadership, signals, environment protection

- Recognition Experience: Guides should:
  - have guided a raft under the supervision of and to the satisfaction of a Trip Leader on at least ten white water runs within the past two years in rapids of the same class or higher than the run they intend to guide on;
  - complete a familiarization run on any new stretch of white water they intend to guide on;
  - maintain a log book recording each run and signed by the Trip leader as proof of experience;
  - should have good communication skills in Hindi and English
- Special Requirements for Trip Leaders: Trip Leaders should:
  - have been qualified guides for at least two years;
  - have a high level of guide skills and knowledge;
  - have a thorough knowledge of trip planning, white water rescue techniques, emergency procedures and advanced first aid;
  - have guided a raft as a qualified guide on at least twenty white water runs within the past two years in rapids of the same class or higher than the run they intend to lead on;
  - complete a familiarization run and know the evacuation routes on any new stretch of white water they intend to lead on;
  - should have excellent communication skills in Hindi and English.
- Single Raft Trips: Some of the worst accidents in river running internationally have occurred where there has been only one raft. There should always be at least two crafts on the water i.e, two rafts or kayaks or a raft and a safety kayak. This may be relaxed for float trips (maximum grade II) in the case of rafts. For kayaks a minimum of two or preferably three is always recommended. Safety Kayaks must be mandatory on technical rapids grade IV and beyond. In case on continuous white water sections, one should look at a minimum of one kayak per raft, if not more.
- Kit: All trips must carry a well- equipped first Aid kit (it must have triangular bandages, sterile pads, gauze roller bandages, pressure bandages, first aid adhesive tape, splints, scissors as bare minimum), a repair kit (it must contain approx. half meter of repair material, a sufficient amount of flue and accelerator, sand paper or roughing tool and waterproof repair tape/ duck tape). Oar rafts must carry at least one spare oar. All rafts must have a safety line going all around the raft, a bow- line and preferably a stern line as well. All rafts must have a throw bag and a bailing bucket (in case of non self bailer bucket boats). A flip line is recommended for all big drops.
- Personal River Equipment: All rafters/ kayakers must have a life jacket on all times while on water. This includes the guides also.

The life jackets must have adequate buoyancy (minimum of 6.14 kgs, and preferably 9 – 10 kgs.), must be the proper type (U.S. coast Guard Type III or V) with a provision of ensuring a snug fit by straps etc. and the life jacket must be worn correctly. Inflatable life jackets and the 'keyhole' type jackets should not be allowed. Guides must ensure that the life jackets are on in a secure manner before the trip starts and above all major drops. Helmets are mandatory on all rapids and it is recommended that helmets be kept on throughout the trip. The helmet should be properly strapped. Rafts must be of good condition with no leakage or compartment damage. A baffle / compartment inflation check must be carried out at regular intervals to ensure that each compartment is air tight with no leaks. A minimum of 14 – 16 feet boats are recommended for commercial rafting. Self bailing rafts are recommended.

- Age Limit: Fourteen years on all stretches except float trips (grade II and below), where it may be relaxed to ten years.
- Non Swimmers: Non swimmers should not be allowed on any serious rapid (grade III +/IV)/ or hard section.
- Safety Briefing: Guides/ trip leader must ensure that a thorough safety briefing covering all pertinent details for that particular trip is given before each trip. The trip leader must ensure that clients are in suitable attire (bulky clothes, sarees, neck ties, long skirts and three piece suits should not be permitted). People suffering from any serious ailments, weak heart conditions, epilepsy and expecting mothers should not be allowed. Non- swimmers should be allowed to body surf only with rope back up. Shoes/appropriate sandals/ booties are a must for rafting. Appropriate clothing must be worn during winter/ on glacial melt rivers with cold air temperatures. For such rivers, dry suits/ wet suits are recommended. If not, light woolens/synthetic clothes are a must. Trips must be timed carefully to finish at least an hour before sunset.
- Alcohol and Drugs: Consuming alcohol in any form or quantity or illicit drugs at least six hours prior to the river trip must not be allowed.
- Familiarization Runs: One or two familiarization runs before operating commercially each season or on new rivers is recommended. Rivers should not be run commercially at flood levels.
- Foreign Guides: Foreign Guides must be aware of the Indian Safety Regulations before being allowed to operate. They must fulfill the required criteria and should do a few familiarisation runs on the river and equipment before being allowed to operate commercially. A valid first aid certificate is a must.
- Senior Guide: A senior guide must have spent at least three consecutive seasons on any of the above three rivers with a minimum

of sixty days on the river per season. He must have all requisite first aid and cardiopulmonary resuscitation (CPR) qualifications and must have a clean safety record. A senior guide must have river-running experience on at least three different rivers.

- Safety Kayaker: A safety and rescue kayaker must be thoroughly trained and experienced in all safety norms, river rescue and first aid/cardiopulmonary resuscitation (CPR) certification. A minimum of thirty days on the river is mandatory before kayaking with commercial trips.

AIR BASED ACTIVITIES

Aerosports need the highest skill requirements. They also have the highest risk element and anything that goes wrong hardly gives an opportunity for corrective action. Accordingly adherence to safety guidelines must be followed meticulously.

Generally the following principles need to be adopted:-

- The equipment used in each aero-sport must be defined in terms of its specifications, certifying agency and its life (shelf life and usage life), as defined by the manufacturer, who for the purpose must hold a valid authorization for manufacturing the particular aero-sport equipment.
- Instructor/operator qualification is very important. It is not enough to have an initial certificate or qualification. Currency and continued evaluation in terms of safety and skill needs to be carried out.

PARAGLIDING

Infrastructure

- Operator must have access to safe and open take off points in case of hill launches. The take off point should be free from obstructions in the take off path and should not have rock or crops which could injure the participant. Cliff take off points must strictly not to be used.
- The operator must have free and clear access to a designated landing ground free of obstructions such as tall trees, buildings, electric wires etc.
- First aid must be available at site with Qualified First aid Instructors (having additional knowledge of related accidents), with arrangements with a nearby hospital for quick emergency services.
- Wind conditions should be strictly monitored and the activity must be done within the weather conditions stipulated by the equipment manufacturer.

Equipment And Accessories

- Paragliding wings must have APCUL DHV or CEN certification.

Such certification should be stitched on the wing and visible for inspection. Harness should be with back protection and harness must be fitted with round type certified rescue parachute.

- Helmets and Ankle shoes must be compulsory.
- Proper log books must be maintained for all equipment.
- Annual inspection and certification of equipment for air worthiness must be carried out.

Operator Qualification

- In case of solo flights the pilot should have undergone two full days ground training consisting theoretical and practical training and instructor should satisfy himself of the first launch both in hill and winch launched paragliding. For first 15 launches height should be restricted to Max 500 feet and student should be radio guided. After demonstrated capability for 180 degree stable turns, five spot (20 Mtrs) landings and after the theory paper is cleared, the student may be allowed to carry out free fly. The student pilot must have a valid registration with a club recognised by the Aero Club of India.
- Tandem pilots must have a tandem pilots licence issued by the competent authority, which will be issued after the following:
  - 150 logged flights.
  - 35 h + logged.
  - Pass theory paper
- All instructors must be current pilots having sufficient knowledge and experience in the sport.

PARASAILING

- Operator Classifications: All operators shall be certified by the appropriate agency in terms of their capability to conduct the activity on land or water, specifically endorsed to allow multi-passenger flight operations.
- In Flight Floatation Devices and helmets: At all times passengers participating in parasailing activities over water, while in flight shall wear a properly fitted approved life jacket. Over land, the passengers must wear an ISI approved helmet.
- Assumption of Risk And Release of Liability Waiver: Without exception, all operators shall require ALL PARTICIPANTS of legal age or if a minor; a parent or legal guardian to read and sign an assumption of Risk and Release of Liability waiver prior to starting the activity.
- Passenger Safety Briefing: All parasail participants shall be required to view a Parasail Safety Briefing video and/or be given a written Parasail Safety Briefing handout. In addition, the crew shall give a

pre-flight verbal summary of the briefing before any parasail flight activities commence, which should include the following:

- A description of the activity itself.
- Safety precautions while underway and in-flight.
- Safety and life saving equipment locations.
- Warnings and Procedures for unexpected events, such as water landings, equipment malfunctions, and towline separation.
- Procedure in the event of an emergency onboard the vessel.
- The proper use of signals.
- Question and answer period.
- Exclusion of any participant that may be afraid or intimidated prior to participation.

• Proximity to Obstructions. Wind restrictions: Operator should have a wind measurement device and should not operate in winds exceeding 18 Kph. Operator shall at all times maintain a minimum operating distance from any surf-zone, shoreline, or fixed object, of not less than 500 feet. In addition, at no time shall a parasail vessel's operator allow a canopy to pass within the following distance from the shore while an onshore wind is present. (Onshore wind shall be defined as any wind direction that could potentially place a parasail vessel, canopy, or participant in contact with land in the event of the loss of vessel or systems power and/or line separation.).

• Responsibility of Vessel Sea worthiness and tow vehicle road worthiness: It shall be the responsibility of the first mate in charge to make certain that the vessel is maintained and is properly equipped in a sea worthy condition. A current written log shall be kept of all mandatory daily inspections and all routine maintenance performed on vessel. Under no circumstances shall the operator and/or crew utilize any equipment outside the parameters for which it was designed and must at all times adhere to manufacturers' specifications, requirements and/or recommendations. Similar conditions should apply for land based parasailing vehicles.

• Passenger Weight Restrictions: At no time shall a passenger be allowed to participate in parasailing activities unless they meet the manufacturers' recommendations or requirements in terms of weight. Passenger must be able to be comfortably and safely fitted into harness.

• Towline Length Limitations: At no time
  - shall any vessel's winch drum be equipped with more than 500 feet of towline, while conducting parasail flight operations. Similarly land based operations should not use more than 500 feet of rope.
  - Exceed a maximum of 300 feet AGL (Above Ground/ Water Level).

- Minimum Age Requirements: Children may participate in parasailing activities only after the operator has made reasonable prior judgment that wind and sea conditions are conducive to such activities and extreme caution should be exercised. Children under 12 are not to be allowed.
- Towline Inspection and Maintenance: Towline in its entirety shall be inspected daily for damage and/or wear and if necessary shall be immediately replaced. Towline shall be kept clean and maintained in accordance with manufacturers' specifications, requirements and/or recommendations.. A written log of such inspections and maintenance shall be kept at all times.
- Pre-Flight Weather Evaluation: It is the operators responsibility to evaluate and determine if weather conditions are favorable for parasailing. He shall use all means available to make such a determination. No operator shall knowingly parasail in rain, heavy fog or during a known lighting storm within 50 km from the parasailing area, in addition a daily weather log shall be maintained.
- Multiple Passenger Flights: Multi-passenger flights shall only be conducted under the following conditions and only after the operator has made reasonable judgment prior to each and every flight. Extreme caution shall be exercised:
  - At no time shall there be more than 2 passengers in any canopy.
  - Wind conditions must be adequate, stable and consistent.
  - Conditions must be conducive to such activities.
  - Commercial equipment specifically designed and professionally manufactured for multi-passenger flight operations must be utilised.
  - All equipment must adhere to manufacturers' specifications, requirements and/or recommendations.
  - Vessel's winch system must be equipped with a functional level-winder during all multi-passenger flights.

BUNGEE JUMPING

- Essential requirements: All parts of the jump line must be duplicated. This extends from the connection of the bungee to the jumper and the connection to the structure at the other end of the line. Normally the jumper should have an attachment to ankle straps, and another to a body or sit harness.
- Equipment (harnesses, karabiners) should be of sound construction and suitable for this use. Mountaineering equipment from reputable suppliers is appropriate. Karabiners should be of the screw gate type.
- Braided ropes: At least 2 braided ropes should be used and matched to the weight of the jumper; they should be to BS 3F 70 1991

specification for heavy duty braided rubber cord, or to a demonstrably similar standard.

- Unbraided ropes: Normally one unbraided rope is adequate because of the in-built redundancy from its structure of approximately one thousand individual strands bound together. Each rope should have an examiners certificate from an independent source and be selected according to the weight of the jumper.
- Rope log books should be kept, describing maximum load, and numbers of jumps and drop tests undertaken, and in the case of unbraided ropes, any other conditions required by the examiner (eg length of time in sunlight). Ropes have a finite life and operators should be able to demonstrate that this has not been exceeded.
- There should be a written operating procedure. If not written, elements will be more likely to be forgotten or short circuited. Both operators and enforcement officers should be able to check that safe procedures have been established and are being followed.
- The procedure should cover at least:
  - medical enquiry;
  - age verification - if under 18, parental consent should be required;
  - if under 14, they should not be allowed to jump;
  - weighing and rope selection: There should be a method of checking that the weight of the jumper has been correctly measured and recorded so as to ensure that the correct rope is selected for each jumper;
  - attachment of each part of harness and ropes, and the checking of each action by a second trained person;
  - briefing of jumper;
  - entry into and riding in cage;
  - re-instruction and jump; and
  - retrieval of jumper.
- Use of mobile cranes: Use of mobile cranes is not recommended allowed as this is too dangerous.
- Other important elements: Training of personnel is of paramount importance. Each job undertaken requires a different level of training and experience. Those in charge should be able to demonstrate that everyone who is carrying out a task has enough experience to do so, unless under direct supervision by another experienced person. There should be a proper training schedule showing how a person progresses from one level of competence to the next. The schedule of work should clearly state, who carries out every safety critical action and who checks it. Each person should know the tasks, which they are permitted to carry out and those which they are not

authorised to do. To date, all known fatal accidents world wide have resulted from human error.

- The person in overall charge should keep close control of the site. Arrangements should be made to exclude spectators from the jump zone for their own safety and to avoid distraction of the operators.
- Anyone in a cage should be securely attached to it. Spectator riding, especially by children, should be discouraged.
- There should be a dead-weight drop test of the whole line at the beginning of the day to ensure its integrity.
- Spares for all the components in the jump line should be kept on site so as to be available for immediate replacement of suspect components.
- An air bag should be used for jumps over land with unbraided ropes. The purpose of the bag is to prevent a jumper striking the ground if an incorrect rope selection is made. It is not to safeguard jumpers who fall due to a failure to properly connect them to the supporting structure. Braided ropes to BS 3F 70 have an outer covering which tightens when stretched. Unbraided ropes do not, so there is more risk of a jumper descending too far if a wrong rope selection is made. If a jump is made over water with an unbraided rope, relying on the water to perform the function of the airbag, steps should be taken to ensure that there are no obstructions under the water surface. In addition, suitable arrangements should be made for rescue from the water.

ENFORCEMENT AGENCY

- An ACCREDITATION COMMITTEE may be formed for operators and outfitters in one or several activities. The constitution of this accreditation committee should be as follows:-
  - Chairman (Designated by Ministry of Tourism, Government of India).
  - Members: Members must be proven specialists with actual experience of adventure activities, who meet the minimum criteria for guides and trip leaders.
  - Two members nominated by Adventure Tour Operators Association of India (ATOAI).
  - One member each nominated by National Institute of Water Sports (NIWS) and the Indian Association of Professional Rafters (IAPRO).
  - One member nominated by Parachuting Federation of India
  - One member nominated by Indian Mountaineering Foundation
- The committee may also appoint examiners, in consultation with relevant Adventure Trade Associations, who have proven experience in the activity to carry out inspection of the operator's facilities and

certify compliance to safety regulations. The appointed examiners must be individually capable of conducting the activity independently and must themselves meet the minimum requirements for trip leaders or instructors.

- This committee will also be empowered to look into any complaint against any adventure tour operator.
- This committee may further keep upgrading the guidelines and safety regulations, as and when required on a yearly basis.
- This committee may also do training programmes/refresher courses and coordinate any relevant issues impacting the smooth running of the adventure activities in India.

2

Types of Adventure Tourism

ADVENTURE TRAVEL

Adventure travel is a type of tourism, involving exploration or travel with perceived (and possibly actual) risk, and potentially requiring specialized skills and physical exertion. Adventure tourism is rapidly growing in popularity, as tourists seek different kinds of vacations. According to the U.S. based Adventure Travel Trade Association, adventure travel may be any tourist activity, including two of the following three components: a physical activity, a cultural exchange or interaction and engagement with nature.

Adventure tourists may be motivated to achieve mental states characterized as rush or flow, resulting from stepping outside of their comfort zone. This may be from experiencing culture shock or through the performance of acts, that require significant effort and involve some degree of risk (real or perceived) and/or physical danger.

This may include activities such as mountaineering, trekking, bungee jumping, mountain biking, rafting, zip-lining, paragliding, and rock climbing. Some obscure forms of adventure travel include disaster and ghetto tourism. Other rising forms of adventure travel include social and jungle tourism.

Access to inexpensive consumer technology, with respect to Global Positioning Systems, flashpacking, social networking and photography, have increased the worldwide interest in adventure travel. The interest in independent adventure travel has also increased as more specialist travel websites emerge offering previously niche locations and sports.

WILDLIFE TOURISM

Wildlife tourism can be an eco and animal friendly tourism, usually showing animals in their natural habitat. Wildlife tourism, in its simplest sense, is watching wild animals in their natural habitat. Wildlife tourism is an important part of the tourism industries in many countries including many African and South American countries, Australia, India, Canada, Indonesia, Bangladesh, Malaysia and Maldives among many. It has experienced a dramatic and rapid growth in recent years world wide and is closely aligned to eco-tourism and sustainable-tourism.

Wildlife tourism is also a multi-million dollar industry offering customized tour packages and safaris.

NEGATIVE IMPACTS

Wildlife tourism can cause significant disturbances to animals in their natural habitats. The growing interest in traveling to developing countries has created a boom in resort and hotel construction, particularly on rain forest and mangrove forest lands. Wildlife viewing can scare away animals, disrupt their feeding and nesting sites, or acclimate them to the presence of people. In Kenya, for example, wildlife-observer disruption drives cheetahs off their reserves, increasing the risk of inbreeding and further endangering the species.

Direct Impacts

The effect that wildlife tourism will have on wildlife depend on the scale of tourist development and the behavior and resilience of wildlife to the presence of humans. When tourists activities occur during sensitive times of the life cycle (for example, during nesting season), and when they involve close approaches to wildlife for the purpose of identification or photography, the potential for disturbance is high. Not all species appear to be disturbed by tourists even within heavily visited areas.

Disturbing Breeding Patterns

The pressures of tourists searching out wildlife to photograph or hunt can adversely affect hunting and feeding patterns, and the breeding success of some species. Some may even have long-term implications for behavioral and ecological relationships. For example, an increase in boat traffic has disturbed the feeding of giant otters in Manú National Park, Peru. Further disturbance to wildlife occurs when tourist guides dig up turtle nests and chase swimming jaguars, tapirs, and otters to give clients better viewing opportunities. On the shores of Lake Kariba in Zimbabwe, the number of tourist boats and the noise generated as disrupted the feeding and drinking patterns of elephants and the black rhinoceros - it is feared that further increases in boat traffic will affect their reproductive success.

Disturbing Feeding Patterns

Artificial feeding of wildlife by tourists can have severe consequences for social behavior patterns. Artificial feeding by tourists caused a breakdown of the territorial breeding system of land iguanas on the South Plaza in the Galápagos Islands. Territories were abandoned in favor of sites where food could be begged from tourists, and this has had a negative effect on the breeding success of iguanas. Artificial feeding can also result in a complete loss of normal feeding behaviors. In the Galápagos Islands, overfeeding by tourists was so extreme that, when stopped, some animals were unable to locate their natural food sources. Similarly, until the early 1970s, the diet of some grizzly bears in Yellowstone National Park consisted, to a large extent, of food wastes left by visitors at park refuse sites. When these sites were closed, the bears showed significant decreases in body size, reproductive rate, and litter size.

Disruption of Parent-offspring Bonds

Wildlife tourism also causes disruption to intra-specific relationships. Attendance by female harp seals to their pups declined when tourists were present and those females remaining with their pups spent significantly less time nursing and more time watching the tourists. There is also a risk of the young not being recognized, and being more exposed to predator attacks. A similar concern has been expressed over whale watching, whale calves normally maintain constant body contact with their mothers but, when separated, can transfer their attachment to the side of the boat.

Increased Vulnerability to Predators and Competitors

The viewing of certain species by wildlife tourists makes the species more vulnerable to predators. Evidence of this phenomenon has been recorded in birds, reptiles and mammals. Problems have occurred in breeding colonies of pelicans .

POSITIVE IMPACTS

- Habitat restoration by eco-lodges and other tourism operations: Many owners of eco-accommodation or wildlife attractions preserve and restore native habitats on their properties
- Conservation breeding: Many wildlife parks (e.g. David Fleay Wildlife Park, Gold Coast, Australia) and zoos breed rare and endangered species as a major part of their activities, and release the progeny when possible into suitable habitat.
- Financial donations: Some wildlife tourism contributes monetary donations to conservation efforts e.g. Dreamworld, Gold Coast, has a display of Sumatran tigers, and money from visitor donations and from their 'tiger walk' goes to Sumatra to assist in-situ conservation of wild tigers.
- Quality interpretation: A good wildlife guide will impart a deeper understanding of the local wildlife and its ecological needs, which may give visitors a more informed base on which to subsequently modify their behaviour (e.g. not throw out plastic bags that may be eaten by turtles) and decide what poiltical moves to support.
- Research and monitoring: Some wildlife tourism operations contribute to monitoring of wildlife numbers or general research relevant to conservation

- Anti-poaching: Bringing tourists regularly into some areas may make it more difficult for poachers of large animals or those who collect smaller species for the black market

VOLUNTEER TRAVEL

Volunteer travel, volunteer vacations or voluntourism is travel which includes volunteering for a charitable cause. In recent years, "bite-sized" volunteer vacations have grown in popularity. Volunteer vacations vary widely in scope, from low-skill work cleaning up local wildlife areas to providing high-skill medical aid in a foreign country. Volunteer vacations participants are diverse but typically share a desire to "do something good" while also experiencing new places and challenges in locales they might not otherwise visit.

There are also other types of traveling that engage people with scientific research and education to promote the understanding and action necessary for a sustainable environment. Participants cover a fee that would include expenses on the different sites worldwide, and engage in projects according to their interest or location.

HISTORY

Originally most volunteer vacations were undertaken by people with a direct connection to a particular cause and were considered more as short term, intense volunteer projects rather than vacations. Many of these organizations were long-standing international development assistance organizations which placed short-term volunteers on community development project sites.

Inception of volunteer travel can be linked to Volunteer services incoproated in 1958. These services and that of the U.S. Peace Corps, established in 1961 during the John F. Kennedy administration, have paved the way for volunteer travel and volunteer vacations throughout the world. However, some would argue, and with good reason, that the connection between travel and volunteering in the Modern Era can be traced back to the work of Herb Feith in Indonesia in 1951. Feith's contribution, the Volunteer Graduate Scheme, today known as Australian Volunteers International, may very well have paved the way for the connection between travel and volunteering that has evolved in the 60 years since.—During the 1960's and 1970's a movement of volunteerism and study abroad programs became popular among college age individuals.

The first known volunteer travel operation began with Earthwatch in 1971. Earthwatch wanted to engage the general public in the scientific process by bringing together individual volunteers and scientists on field research projects. This grouping of scientists and volunteers provided an alternative means to funding, as well as provide a dedicated labour force for field scientists

1990S

During the 1990s the travel industry developed niche products and firms to provide volunteer vacations to people who had no previous experience with a cause, and to cater to the increasing number of young people taking gap years. These providers expanded the market but also drew criticism for the impact of their methods. At the same time, the first edition of "Volunteer Vacations" by Bill McMillon was published, featuring under 200 non-profit organizations which facilitated such service opportunities. According to the Travel Industry Association of America, more than 55 million Americans have participated in a volunteer vacation, and about 100 million more are considering taking one.

VOLUNTEER BASE

Volunteer tourism appeals to a wide variety of travelers, but the majority of volunteers are made up of high school and college students. Many students use these trips to boost their resumes, travel with friends, and as a way to gain world experience and see new countries. Recently there has also been an increase in baby boomer volunteers. One possible explanation for the increase is that baby boomers are transitioning into a new stage of life and their focus may shift toward finding activities that give their life new meaning. Voluntourism is therefore appealing, as it is specifically targeted at travelers who want to make a positive change in the world, while still providing a tourist experience. People generally volunteer in order to increase their international awareness, to contextualize poverty and its effects, as an education opportunity, and to help people while having a morally rewarding experience. Many believe that the trip will change the way they think when they return home. However, others are just looking to give to others and do not believe that their experience will cause them to think twice about their lives back home.

Rebecca Tiessens recent work with Canadian gap year students suggests that volunteer experiences are becoming viewed as a commodity that can be bought for a price for use in future college or job applications. She also suggests a correlation between conspicuous consumption and volunteer work. People may do what they perceive as good deeds primarily for the recognition of their peers rather than out of good will.

Vacations have been hit hard by the recession. However, voluntourism has remained stable because it offers individuals the opportunity to take a guilt free vacation. As criticism for excessive, lavish spending increased, volunteer vacations have become an attractive option. As many volunteer vacations include tourist activities at the end of the trip, these vacations provide volunteers with an enjoyable vacation that has an enhanced value. Families participating in volunteer vacations may feel better about spending money on their trip while still enjoying the bonding time vacations provide.

A survey by CheapTickets.com of 430 US adults 18 and older found that half of their respondents would consider voluntourism for their next vacation. In addition, 55% of respondents would consider adding volunteer activities to an already planned vacation. While 48% had heard about volunteer vacations, only 5% of applicants had actually participated in one.

CONTROVERSY

While some experts on volunteering welcome the expansion of volunteer vacations as an opportunity to provide more resources to projects and to encourage a volunteer ethic in people, others have pointed out that the business methods used by tour operators, such as exclusivity deals, and catering to the needs of the volunteer rather than the volunteer project, exploit the communities the projects are intended to help. In many different provinces in these third world countries where voluntourism is most prominent, orphanages often take children out into the main city where they play in the streets with one another or play instruments, in an attempt to garner donations from tourists and volunteers. Many also invite potential and actual donors to visit the orphanage itself, and many then ask them to volunteer there. What these donors do not know, is that orphanages network themselves with volunteer organizations to ensure a steady flow of money and volunteers to their organizations. In addition, in order to ensure that such funding is never reduced and to promote additional donations, some orphanages are deliberately kept in decrepit conditions despite having adequate resources for dramatic improvements. Some news organizations have done inside reports on the volunteer industry finding exploitation.

Economic Effects on Host Countries

Claims by volunteer tourism organizations that these activities contribute to improving people's lives and contributing to development goals are yet to be evaluated in the vast majority of cases. It is true that many countries have greatly benefited from the influx of tourism. Local economies and businesses have benefited as volunteers stay in their hotels, eat at their local restaurants, unwind at local bars, and stroll the local markets. However, it is possible that volunteer travel might exacerbate existing problems in the host community. Dr Anna Mdee of Voluntourism.org contends that while there is still a lack of understanding of the direct impact volunteering overseas has on development activities, there is a much larger value that can be gained from working and living in another culture. Such value is often gained by the volunteer individually.

However, short term volunteer vacations may serve to strengthen the 'us and them' dichotomy instead of acting to bring people from different backgrounds together. While solidarity between the volunteers and recipients is part of the goal, the actuality may be that volunteers see a deeper divide between themselves and those they helped. In addition, voluntourism may help reinforce stereotypes and preconceived ideas rather than providing a deeper understanding of other cultures. This is especially likely to occur if volunteers lack knowledge about the country in which they are volunteering, and about how the policies and history of said country have affected poverty or development. In order to make a genuine change, it is essential that volunteers are qualified and reasonably well-informed.

Social and Psychological Effects on the Orphans

A Human Sciences Research Council report suggests that voluntourism companies treat orphans like commodities and that the projects can create "adverse emotional and psychological effects" on the children.

Abuse at Orphanages

At the beginning of 2011, the government of Cambodia began inspecting orphanages, almost all of which are privately operated and funded, due to claims that many orphans in fact had at least one living parent. More than 250 orphanages are under review after one study found that only 28% of the 12,000 children in these orphanages had actually lost both parents. UNICEF has publically expressed concern as the number of orphans has doubled in the past five years. Coincidentally, trips to orphanages have proven to be one of the most popular, and best-selling, volunteer vacations. In fact, "the rate of growth in the number of Cambodia's orphanages over the past five years matches the increase in the number of tourists visiting the country during that same period." In Ghana, a government study found that almost 90% of orphans had at least one parent and that only 5% of orphanages were licensed. UNICEF estimates that less than one-third of the money orphanages receive, through both income and donations, actually goes to child care.

SUSTAINABILITY

Much of the conflict regarding volunteer tourism is that these trips are not sustainable. There will always be groups who want to partner with international organizations and individuals who desire to spend their free time helping others, but the trips and projects these people choose should focus on development that both involves the locals directly and caters to their most important needs. Volunteer trips that benefit communities through the construction of new facilities and community spaces may or may not involve the help of locals. Those that do not prevent local workers from getting much-needed jobs and those that bring their own resources fail to support the local businesses and economy. Sustainability is especially important in cases where projects are initiated by volunteers and left in the hands of locals to finish. Volunteer groups should be certain before beginning a project that there is enough funding and support for the project to be completed once they leave, in order to avoid letting their hard work waste away as a pile of rubble or their supplies sit in storage unused.

For example, voluntourism blogger Alexia Nestora found a village in Kenya that had been significantly impacted by voluntourism. This village had approximately 500 residents and as a community had built a school and furnished it with the necessities, such as individual classrooms and blackboards. The village was using this schoolhouse when a well-funded NGO came in and decided to build the community a larger school, complete with a very expensive commercial kitchen. Volunteers flew in and the NGO purchased expensive building materials and built the second school right next to the first. The community then decided to use the second schoolhouse as their school, and now they use their original schoolhouse for storage. A second group then came in to build a third school and they began construction right next to the second school. However, they ran out of funding before it was even time to build walls and have not been back to complete their work. Talking to the locals in the village revealed that they never wanted a second, much less a third, school and had no need or desire for an expensive commercial kitchen. However, they could have benefited from new teachers or an additional source of funding in order to pay teachers already on staff. Many other villages in Kenya lack adequate structures for schooling and would have welcomed the help of these NGO and volunteer groups had they offered to build a school for them. In many projects like this one, NGO and volunteer organizations often overlook one of the most important steps – talking to the locals and asking what they need.

VAGRANCY (PEOPLE)

A vagrant or a vagabond is a person, often in poverty, who wanders from place to place without a home or regular employment or income. Other synonyms include "tramp," "hobo," and "drifter". A vagrant could be described as being "a person without a settled home or regular work who wanders from place to place and lives by begging"; vagrancy is the condition of such persons.

Both "vagrant" and "vagabond" ultimately derive from Latin word *vagari* "wander." The term "vagabond" is derived from Latin *vagabundus.* In Middle English, "vagabond" originally denoted a criminal.

HISTORY

In settled, ordered communities, vagrants have been historically characterised as outsiders, embodiments of otherness, objects of scorn or mistrust, or worthy recipients of help and charity. Some ancient sources show vagrants as passive objects of pity, who deserve generosity and the gift of alms. Others show them as subversives, or outlaws, who make a parasitical living through theft, fear and threat. Some fairy tales of medieval Europe have beggars cast curses on anyone who was insulting or stingy towards them. In Tudor England, some of those who begged door-to-door for "milk, yeast, drink, pottage" were thought to be witches. In some East Asian and South Asian countries, the condition of vagrancy has long been historically associated with the religious life, as described in the religious literature of Hindu, Buddhist, Jain and Muslim Sufi traditions. Examples include sadhus, dervishes, Bhikkhus and the sramanic traditions generally.

VAGRANCY UNDER THE LAW

Germany

In Germany, according to the 1871 Penal Code (§ 361 des Strafgesetzbuches von 1871), vagabondage was among the grounds to confine a person to a labor house.

In the Weimar Republic, the law against vagrancy was relaxed, but it became much more stringent in Nazi Germany, where vagrancy, together with begging, prostitution, and "work-shyness" (*arbeitsscheu*), was classified "asocial behavior" as punishable by confinement to concentration camps.

Russia

Tsardom of Russia

In the Tsardom of Russia, the legal term "vagrancy" was defined in another way than respective terms (vagabondage, Landstreicherei) in Western Europe. Russian law recognized one as a vagrant if he could not prove his own standing (title), or if he changed his residence without a permission from authorities, rather than punishing loitering or absence of livelihood. Foreigners who had been twice expatriated with prohibition of return to the Russian Empire and were arrested in Russia again were also recognized as vagrants. Punishments were harsh: According to Ulozhenie, a vagrant who could not elaborate on his kinship, standing, or permanent residence, or gave false evidence, was sentenced to 4-year imprisonment and subsequent exile to Siberia or another far-off province.

Soviet Union

In the Criminal Code of the RSFSR (1960), which came into force on 1 January 1961, systematic vagrancy (that which was identified more than once) was punishable by up to two years' imprisonment (section 209). This continued until 5th December 1991, when Section 209 was repealed and vagrancy ceased to be a criminal offence.

Modern Russia

At present, vagrancy is not a criminal offence in the Russian Federation, but it is an offence for someone over 18 to induce a juvenile (one who has not reached that age) to vagrancy (CC of RF, section 151).

United Kingdom

The first major vagrancy law was passed in 1349 to increase the workforce following the Black Death by making "idleness" (unemployment) an offense. By the 1500s the statutes were mainly used as a means of controlling criminals. In the 16th and 17th century in England, a vagrant was a person who could work, but preferred not to (or could not find employment, so took to the road in order to do so), or one who begs for a living. Vagrancy was illegal, punishable by branding, whipping, conscription into the military, or at times penal transportation to penal colonies. Vagrants were different from impotent poor, who were unable to support themselves because of advanced age or sickness. However, the English laws usually did not distinguish between the impotent poor and the criminals, so both received the same harsh punishments.

In 1824, earlier vagrancy laws were consolidated in the *Vagrancy Act 1824 (UK)* whose main aim was removing *undesirables* from public view. The act assumed that homelessness was due to idleness and thus deliberate, and made it a criminal offense to engage in behaviors associated with extreme poverty. The Poor Law was the system for the provision of social security in operation in England and Wales from the 16th century until the establishment of the Welfare State in the 20th century.

United States

In colonial America, if a person wandered into a town and did not find work, he/she was told to leave town or be prosecuted. In the U.S., vagrancy laws were vague and covered a wide range of activities and crimes associated with vagrants, such as loitering, prostitution, drunkenness, and associating with known criminals. Under the vagrancy laws, police arrested people who were suspected of crime, but who had not committed a crime. Eventually, punishments were changed to a fine, or several months in jail.

After the U.S. Civil War, the South passed Black Codes, laws that tried to control freed black slaves. Vagrancy laws were included in these codes. Homeless unemployed black Americans were arrested and fined as vagrants. Usually, the person could not afford the fine, and so was sent to county labor or hired out to a private employer.

In the U.S. of the 1960s, vagrancy laws were found to be too broad and vague, and in violation of the due process requirements of the Fourteenth Amendment to the U.S. Constitution, as citizens were not informed of which behaviors were illegal. Police had too much power in deciding whether or not to arrest someone. Vagrancy laws could no longer violate Freedom of Speech, such as when police use them against political demonstrators and unpopular groups. U.S. vagrancy laws became clearer, narrower, and more defined. Since then, the status of being a vagrant is punished by the vagrancy laws, while other actions are punished under other laws.

In *Papachristou v. Jacksonville,* 405 U.S. 156 (1972), the U.S. Supreme Court ruled that a Florida vagrancy law was unconstitutional because it was too vague to be understood.

Nevertheless, new local laws in the U.S. have been passed to criminalize aggressive panhandling activities by vagrants. In recent years, there has been an increase in laws criminalizing vagrancy and related activities in the United States, some under the rubric of sit-lie ordinances.

In the U.S., some local officials encourage vagrants to move away instead of arresting them. The word *vagrant* has been replaced by *homeless person.* Prosecutions for vagrancy are rare, being replaced by prosecutions for specific offenses such as loitering.

ULTRALIGHT BACKPACKING

Ultralight backpacking is a style of backpacking that emphasizes carrying the lightest and simplest kit safely possible for a given trip. *Base pack weight* (the weight of a backpack plus the gear inside, excluding consumables such as food, water, and fuel, which vary depending on the duration and style of trip) is reduced as much as safely possible, though reduction of the weight of consumables is also applied.

The terms light and ultralight commonly refer to base pack weights below 20 pounds (9.1 kg) and 10 pounds (4.5 kg) respectively. Traditional backpacking often results in base pack weights above 30 pounds (14 kg), and sometimes up to 60 pounds (27 kg) or more. Enthusiasts of ultralight backpacking sometimes attempt *super-ultralight backpacking* (SUL) in which the base pack weight is below 5 pounds (2.3 kg) and *extreme-ultralight backpacking* (XUL) in which the base pack weight is below 3 pounds (1.4 kg).

Ultralight backpacking was popularized by rock climber Ray Jardine, whose 1992 book *PCT Hiker's Handbook,* later retitled as *Beyond Backpacking* in 1999, laid the foundations for many techniques that ultralight backpackers use today. Jardine claimed his first Pacific Crest Trail thru-hike was with a base pack weight of 25 pounds (11 kg), and by his third PCT thru-hike it was below 9 pounds (4.1 kg).

An early pioneer was Emma "Grandma" Gatewood, who thru-hiked the Appalachian Trail in 1955 with only a duffel bag containing an army blanket, a plastic sheet, an umbrella, and other very simple gear much lighter than the heavy equipment common among *thru-hikers* in those days.

PHILOSOPHY

By carrying lighter and more multi-purpose equipment, ultralight backpackers are frequently able to cover longer distances per day with less wear and tear on the body. This is particularly useful when thru-hiking a long-distance trail.

The first way to reduce weight is by omitting unnecessary items. This often includes camping luxuries such as camp chairs, coffee makers, electronic gadgets, multiple items of clothing, etc. This is the initial step taken by any backpacker seeking less weight on their back.

The next method is reducing item weight. Modifying items to reduce superfluous weight, such as removing the handle from a toothbrush or cutting tags off of clothing is one example of reducing an item's weight. Replacing items manufactured using heavy materials with items made from lighter ones will help as well. For instance, Ripstop nylon can make a much lighter pack than canvas material. The fabrics Silnylon, spinnaker sailcloths and spectra-woven Cuben Fiber (UHMWPE) are regularly used in ultralight applications for their low ratio of weight to surface area. Exchanging fully featured items for minimalist (and therefore lighter) items will save weight as well. For instance an inflatable sleeping pad is more feature-rich and weighs more than a closed-cell foam pad, yet both serve the same purpose. There are many options, so reducing item weight has innumerable choices.

The final method is to use multi-purpose gear: one piece of gear which serves the purpose of two, thereby theoretically cutting the weight of the item in half. For example, a lightweight rain poncho which is modified with tie-outs (or tied out with sheet bends) also serves as a tarpaulin shelter. All these efforts can result in base backpacking weight that is under six pounds (3 kg), which was the weight of Francis Tapon's backpack during his round-trip on the Continental Divide Trail.

According to Ryan Jordan:

- The poncho-tarp is probably the lightest possible combination of shelter and raingear that can be carried by the ultralight backpacker.

Another example is an insulated sweater or jacket used in conjunction with a lightweight sleeping bag which boosts the efficiency of the lightweight sleeping bag while remaining a useful clothing item. By using an insulated sweater in conjunction with a lightweight sleeping bag a warmer rated sleeping bag may be made appropriate for the current weather. Warmer weather sleeping bags tend to be lighter and more compressible than colder weather sleeping bags.

BASE PACK

"Three Heavies" or "Big Three"

The rain shelter, sleeping system, and backpack are considered to be the three major items carried by backpackers. Consequently, reducing the weight of these will reduce overall pack weight. In ultralight backpacking the weight of the big three is reduced.

The most common rain shelter in use is the tent, but these are relatively heavy due to a number of reasons. They are often designed from two layers of fabric (to address the internal condensation problem), often require the use of metal poles, stakes, and sometimes include a separate ground cloth to protect the tent bottom. Replacing a double-wall tent with a simple tarp and bivy combination will reduce not only weight but also volume carried in a backpack. Other methods to reduce shelter weight include single layer tarp tent hybrids, hammocks, poncho-tarps, or the use of a bivy sack (*Alpine style*) as the sole shelter.

Reduction in weight of the second of the big three, the sleeping system, is achieved through reduction of the quantity of fabric used in its manufacture or through use of lighterweight materials in its construction. The use of down as an insulation material which is lighter by volume than currently available synthetic fibers will decrease bag weight but alternately suffer from its susceptibility to loft loss caused by moisture. Reducing the overall weight of a sleeping bag by eliminating superfluous material will reduce its weight. An example of this is the use of a sleeping quilt or top bag. A sleeping quilt is a bottom-less insulated blanket which has no insulation on its bottom side, relying on the user's sleeping pad to guard against conductive heat loss into the ground. A top bag is more like a conventional sleeping bag in that it wraps around the user's entire body but the bottom fabric contains no insulation. The philosophy behind these two alternatives is that insulation crushed under a person's weight is devoid of air and therefore useless. Some modern down sleeping bags are *through-baffled* and *under-filled* such that the user can shift all the insulation to the top of their body thereby maximizing its potential to retain heat. Ultralight hikers also tend to carry bags rated for warmer temperatures than traditional-weight backpackers, making up the difference on cold nights by wearing insulated clothing to bed, such as a balaclava or an insulated jacket. Proper camping site selection that avoids colder *hollows* (low points where cold air tends to collect) or that makes use of natural wind barriers such as thick vegetation or cliffs makes up the difference in heat lost by lighter gear.

With a lighter shelter and sleeping system, the backpack can consist of lighter material and a less bulky frame or no frame at all. The common ultralight alternative to an internal frame pack is a frameless pack made of ripstop nylon, silnylon, or Dyneema, with a carrying limit of 25 pounds (11 kg). An internal-frame pack can weigh upwards of 6 pounds (2.7 kg) with features such as hip belt stabilizers, lifter straps, sternum straps, and compression straps; ultralight frameless packs are commercially available in weights ranging from eight to fourteen ounces (200-400 g) and can consist of not much more than a sack with shoulder straps, a return to the simplicity of the rucksack. Jardine's book includes directions to make your own "ultralight pack".

Some backpackers choose to make their own gear. Advantages to such an approach include possible reduction of cost and the opportunity to customize the gear to the individual user. Additionally, if a homemade item were to break down, the hiker would be in a better position to repair it. Lastly, commercial manufacturers often choose heavier, more durable material for their products in order to reduce the amount of care and maintenance required of the user (and minimize returns of damaged gear). Given proper care, homemade lightweight gear can last as long as it is needed.

Examples

Jardine:

- Backpack: homemade "ultralight pack" (13.5 ounces (380 g))
- Sleeping system: homemade *polarguard* 2-inch (5.1 cm) thick quilt (33 ounces (940 g)); stowbag (1.75 ounces (50 g)); trimmed D_8-inch (9.5 mm) thick, 36-inch (91 cm) long, *closed cell polyethylene pad* (4.8 ounces (140 g)); *space blanket* ground sheet (1.25 ounces (35 g))
- Rain shelter: homemade 9-foot (2.7 m) by 7-foot (2.1 m) *silnylon* tarp (12 ounces (340 g)); 8 aluminum tent stakes and stowbag (2.6 ounces (74 g)); guyline cord (0.5 ounces (14 g))
- Total: 69.4 ounces (1.97 kg; 4.34 lb)

Jordan:

- Backpack: commercial "ultralight pack" (3.7 ounces (100 g))
- Sleeping system: commercial 2.25-inch (5.7 cm) loft down sleeping bag (15.2 ounces (430 g)); *spinnaker cloth* stuff sack (.5 ounces (14 g)); torso sized, D_8-inch (9.5 mm) thick, sleeping pad (1.9 ounces (54 g));
- Rain shelter: commercial *poncho-tarp* made of *spinnaker cloth* 5-foot (1.5 m) by 8-foot (2.4 m) (6.3 ounces (180 g)); *silnylon bivy sack* (6.2 ounces (180 g)); 6 titanium tent stakes (1.3 ounces (37 g)); 24 feet (7.3 m) *UHMWP* guyline (0.2 ounces (5.7 g))
- Total: 35.3 ounces (1.00 kg; 2.21 lb)

Other Gear

The remaining gear (such as ten essentials and survival kit) carried by an ultralight backpacker follows a similar philosophy of replacing traditional backpacking gear with lighter options. Replacements that some Ultralight hikers choose instead of traditional backpacking gear include:

- Making a fire instead of carrying a stove.
- Light weight alcohol stove such as a beverage can stove or solid fuel stoves instead of heavier gas stoves and a single cook pot ("billycan") with a single spoon instead of a traditional mess kit.
- Some ultralight hikers opt to not carry a stove and its associated paraphernalia at all, relying on no-cook meals for food.
- Trail running or running shoes (Grandma Gatewood used Keds sneakers) instead of hiking boots and lightweight nylon socks instead of heavy wool socks.
- The minimal amount of extra clothing safely possible.

- An ultralight hiker's first-aid kit and repair kit are often stored in plastic or silnylon bags instead of the conventional (and heavier) packaging that a traditional backpacker might carry. The contents can also be optimized, for example Jordan proposes a 5-ounce (140 g) kit.
- A 1 ounce (28 g) mini pocket knife instead of a heavier Leatherman style multi-tool or Swiss army knife.
- Chemical disinfectant water treatment (iodine tablets, chlorine dioxide) instead of heavier water filters. Some are known to carry no purification or filter and ingest untreated water straight from a wilderness source.
- Plastic Soft drink bottles instead of heavier nalgene or lexan bottles or Hydration packs.
- A 0.25-ounce (7.1 g) LED light instead of a heavy flashlight or headlamp.

CONSUMABLES

In addition to carrying equipment, hikers must also carry consumables such as water and food and in some cases fuel. Some ultralight backpackers save weight by resupplying these items more frequently. On long-distance trails with multiple access points, some ultralight hikers choose to place food caches or stop at stores to resupply consumables at frequent intervals, allowing just two or three days' worth of food to be carried in place of a larger load.

Water

1 litre (1.1 US qt) of water weighs 1 kilogram (2.2 lb), thus it is a significant contributor to pack weight.

Moderate activity in a moderate climate requires 2 litres (2.1 US qt) of drinking water per day, and in many regions hikers must carry their water from oasis to oasis. When traveling through an area with many springs and streams, some ultralight hikers can carry as little as 350 millilitres (12 US fl oz) of water, or none at all, provided the hiker is confident on how far away the next reliable water source is and the expected weather conditions (or is smart enough to double back before becoming dehydrated).

Some ultralight hikers reduce the weight of water purifying devices, carried to prevent waterborne diseases such as Giardiasis, Cryptosporidiosis and dysentery, by carrying lighter disinfectants as opposed to heavier filters. Ultra Violet (UV) treatment devices are also used. These devices deactivate DNA in viruses, bacteria, and protozoa rendering them non-infectious, if present. The devices weigh about the same as filters, but being electronic, require batteries. Boiling, disinfectants, UV devices and/or ordinary filters are not effective against chemical pollution.

Food

Once the *Big 3* and water are resolved, food becomes the biggest contributor to pack weight and an area where substantial gains over traditional backpacking can be made.

The Basal metabolic rate requirement of food calories (one food calorie is 1000 heat calories, thus sometimes labelled kcal) is approximately 1000 per day per 100 pounds of body weight. However exertion in the form of hiking consumes additional calories; for example the standard US Army field ration is 4500 calories per day for strenuous work. Thus depending upon type of food an average hiker carries, a hiker requires approximately 2 kilograms (4.4 lb) of food per day. Ultralight techniques can substantially reduce this weight, Jardine suggests 2.5 pounds (1.1 kg) per day for thru-hiking, Jordan suggests 1.25 pounds (0.57 kg) per day (at 125 calories per ounce, 4.4 calories per gram) for a 3-season 3-day backpack.

Many foods can be dried or dehydrated to reduce water weight. Dehydrated meals can be purchased or dehydrated at home. On the trail, rehydration can typically be performed by cooking in hot water. Some ultralight hikers reduce weight by not carrying a stove and rehydrating food in a container with water (although this method requires more time to rehydrate than the traditional cooking method). For example Ramen noodles, dehydrated refried beans (in powdered form), or dehydrated hummus can be put in a ziploc bag or lightweight microwave disposable plastic container with water to rehydrate. Oats (groats or rolled, granola or muesli) and barley also become soft enough with soaking to eat uncooked as a raw food. Tsampa is a simple, bland and lightweight dish made from flour used for centuries by the wandering Tibetan monks.

Weight in the form of food can also be reduced by choosing foods that have the highest ratio of calories per weight. Proteins and carbohydrates have approximately 4 food calories per gram whereas fat has 9 food calories per gram, thus carrying foods high in fat content can reduce weight, such as:

- Peanut butter (5.89 kcal/gram)
- Nuts (Pecans are 6.87 kcal/gram, toasted coconut is 5.92 kcal/gram)
- Pemican (5.7 kcal/gram)
- Dried whole egg (5.92 kcal/gram)

Clarified butter (anhydrous), which stores well unrefrigerated, is almost pure fat (8.76 kcal/gram), thus about 4,000 food calories per pound; however, it is also a potent bear attractant. Alternatively, so-called "energy bars" on average contain more protein and carbohydrates than fat, similar to a fig newton (3.68 kcal/gram), lowering their calorie to weight ratio relative to other choices.

Food Protection

In many areas, unprotected food has the potential of being eaten by wild animals. In many areas, food is hung in trees to keep it away from ground animals, but this is ineffective where animals have become accustomed to humans. In the U.S.A.'s Yosemite National Park where there are numerous black bears, hanging food is ineffective, and an approved bear-resistant food storage container is required. The conflict with the ultralight hiker philosophy is that approved bear-proof containers are both bulky to pack and can weigh between 1 lb, 9 ounces (879 g) at the lightest, to 3 lbs, 2 ounces (1.42 kg) at the heaviest.

TREKKING

A trek is a long, adventurous journey undertaken on foot in areas where common means of transport are generally not available. Trekking should not be confused with mountaineering. In North America the equivalent is backpacking, while New Zealanders use the word tramping.

The term derived from the Afrikaans word *trek* (noun), *trekken* (verb), (literally meaning to "pull, travel"), became a word in English language in mid 19th century, and means a long arduous journey, typically on foot.

TREKKING IN THE HIMALAYAS

The Himalayan routes are famous for attracting a large number of trekkers. Typical trekking regions in Nepal are Annapurna, Dolpo, Langtang, Manaslu, Kangchenjunga Mount Everest. Other popular trekking routes in India include Chandra Taal, Gomukh, Hemkund, Kafni Glacier, Kailash-Manasarovar, Kedarnath, Kedartal, Milam Glacier, Nanda Devi Sanctuary, Pindari Glacier, Richenpong, Roopkund, Sar Pass, Satopanth Tal, Saurkundi Pass, Singalila Ridge, and Valley of Flowers.

TRAMPING IN NEW ZEALAND

Tramping, known elsewhere as hiking, rambling, hill walking or bushwalking, is a popular activity in New Zealand. Tramping is defined as a recreational activity involving walking over rough country carrying all the required food and equipment. The term is generally used for trips that are of at least one overnight stay in the backcountry.

Alpine climbing as a recreational activity was taken up in the early days of European settlement and tramping became popular with the widespread use of motor vehicles. From the 1950s tracks, huts and bridges were built in the forested areas of New Zealand to allow easy access for hunters to cull the introduced deer which had become a threat to the biodiversity of New Zealand. As tramping became popular these facilities were increasingly used by trampers. In later years tramping has become popular for both local and foreign tourists.

Tramping clubs were formed in many towns, cities and universities with regular trips being organised. The clubs sometimes own a bus to transport club members to the tracks.

TRAMPING TRACKS

A network of tramping tracks has been developed throughout New

Zealand of varying length and difficulty. A small number of tramping tracks cross private land either in part or in full. All of the major tramping tracks are on public land that is administered by the Department of Conservation.

HUTS

There is a network of over 950 backcountry huts throughout New Zealand operated by the Department of Conservation (DOC) on public land. Some areas have privately owned huts on public land used for commercial tourism operations. The majority of the huts were built by the now defunct New Zealand Forest Service for deer culling operations. Other huts were built by alpine clubs, schools, ski clubs. Some of the buildings on public land that are readily accessible by vehicle, are generally "baches" or "cribs" built by private individuals when control of the use of public land was less stringent. These baches are not made available to the public. Some public huts are associated with a local club and volunteers from clubs will perform much of the maintenace on these huts.

In the Tararua Forest Park north of Wellington huts are managed in a partnership between DOC and various lower North Island clubs. In the eastern Southern Alps near Christchurch some huts are managed solely by the Canterbury Climbing Club and they rely on fees from these huts to help pay the cost of maintenance.

Amongst experienced trampers there is a strong culture of looking after huts. The phrase "hut etiquette" encompasses looking after any hut that is used and showing consideration for other hut users. Most huts on the conservation estate are open to the public and the state of a hut depends on the care by those who use it.

SAFARI

A safari /sY^fQ^ri/ is an overland journey, usually a trip by tourists to Africa. Traditionally, the trip was a big-game hunt, but today, safari often refers to trips to observe and photograph wildlife—or hiking and sight-seeing.

The Swahili word *safari* means *long journey*, originally from the Arabic meaning *a journey* The verb for "to travel" in Swahili is "kusafiri", the noun for the journey is "safari".

These words are used for any type of journey, e.g., by bus from Nairobi to Mombasa or by ferry from Dar es Salaam to Unguja. *Safari* entered the English language in the late 19th century, The person generally attributed to having used the word in English is Sir Richard Francis Burton, the famous explorer.

The Regimental March of the King's African Rifles was 'Funga Safari', literally 'tie up the March', or, in other words, pack up equipment ready to march.

- Funga safari, funga safari. Funga safari, funga safari. Hamri ya nani? Hamri ya nani? Hamri ya Bwana Kapteni, Hamri ya keyaa.

Which is, in English:

- Prepare to March, Prepare to March. On whose orders? On whose orders? On the order of the boss captain, On the order of the KAR.

On Kenya's independence from Britain, Funga Safari was retained as the Regimental March of the Kenya Rifles, successor to the K.A.R.

Today, many operators throughout the African continent offer various types of safari service, from lodge based tours, where clients travel between lodges or tented camps often by air, fly in safaris where clients meet the camps and staff after travel by plane or helicopter, to the true Mobile Safari operation where the clients travel with the Guides, staff and equipment from site to site.

The Mobile Safari offers guests a genuine safari experience, and they are often very ecologically friendly as they allow areas to regenerate and wildlife do not become as habituated to human presence as they may with a permanent lodge or tented camp.

HISTORY

In 1836 William Cornwallis Harris led an expedition purely to observe and record wildlife and landscapes by the expedition's members. Harris established the safari style of journey, starting with a not too strenuous rising at first light, an energetic day walking, an afternoon rest then concluding with a formal dinner and telling stories in the evening over drinks and tobacco.

LITERARY GENRE

Jules Verne's first novel *Five Weeks in a Balloon* published in 1863 and H. Rider Haggard's first novel *King Solomon's Mines* published in 1885, both describe journeys of English travellers on Safari and were best sellers in their day. These two books gave rise to a genre of Safari adventure novels and films.

CINEMA GENRE

The safari provided countless hours of cinema entertainment in sound films from *Trader Horn* (1931) onwards. The safari was used in many adventure films such as the Tarzan, Jungle Jim, and Bomba the Jungle Boy film series up to *The Naked Prey* (1966) where Cornel Wilde, a white hunter, becomes game himself. The safari genre films were parodied in the Bob Hope comedies *Road to Zanzibar* and *Call Me Bwana*. An instant 15-minute helicopter safari was shown in *Africa Addio* where clients are armed, flown from their hotel and landed in front of an unlucky and baffled elephant.

Out of Africa has Karen Blixen and Denys Finch Hatton travelling, with Denys refusing to abandon home comforts using fine china and crystal and listening to Mozart recordings over the gramophone while on safari trip. Tourists must also have appropriate clothing such as hats, long-sleeved shirts and blankets for when the night gets very cold.

SAFARI STYLE

There is a certain theme or style associated with the word, which includes khaki clothing, belted bush jackets, pith helmets or slouch hats, and animal skin patterns—like leopard's skin. There is also a term of *safari chic* that followed the film *Out of Africa*. This not only included clothing but also interior design and architecture.

MODERN SAFARI

Safaris have today diversified considerably from the initial fledgling expeditions of the pioneering European explorers and colonialists. Tourism is becoming an increasingly prevalent economic factor for many Eastern and Southern African nations, in several regions surpassing traditional industries such as agriculture. Lending to specific conditions such as relative infrastructure or inherent geography countries such as Tanzania, Kenya, Botswana, Zambia, Namibia, Uganda, South Africa, Democratic Republic of the Congo and Zimbabwe advertise locally specialised safari experiences ranging from guided safaris, mobile safaris, walking safaris and fly-in safaris to more niche concepts including elephant back safaris, river safaris, primate safaris, horseback safaris, balloon safaris photographic safaris, mobile tented safaris, and accessible safaris for those with disabilities.

Secondly: Safaris are a form of Eco tourism in which the public can become educated on the ecosystems and animal kingdoms of indigenous regions like Africa and Australia on expeditions by vehicles and stations. Through the use of professional guides tourists are provided safe transportation, certified educational services, discovery, photography and expanding the countries exploitation. The many common uses of Safaris are photography, video shooting, Eco and Adventure tourism, hunting, and discovery in which a customer cannot provide for themselves in the wilderness regions of places such as Africa or Australia.

ROGUE (VAGRANT)

A rogue is a vagrant person who wanders from place to place. Like a drifter, a rogue is an independent person who rejects conventional rules of society in favor of following their own personal goals and values. In modern English language, the term *rogue* is used pejoratively to describe a dishonest or unprincipled person whose behavior one disapproves of, but who is nonetheless likeable or attractive.

The word *rogue* was first recorded in print in John Awdely's *Fraternity of Vagabonds* (1561), and then in Thomas Harman's *Caveat for Common Cursitors* (1566).

In England, the 1572 Vagabonds Act defined a rogue as a person who has no land, no master, and no legitimate trade or source of income; it included rogues in the class of idle vagrants or vagabonds. If a person were apprehended as a rogue, he would be stripped to the waist, whipped until bleeding, and a hole, about the compass of an inch about, would be burned through the cartilage of his right ear with a hot iron. A rogue who was charged with a second offense, unless taken in by someone who would give him work for one year, could face execution as a felony. A rogue charged with a third-offense would only escape death if someone hired him for two years.

The 1598 Vagabonds Act banished and transplanted "incorrigible and dangerous rogues" overseas, and the 1604 Act commanded that rogues be branded with the letter "R" on their bodies.

ENTERTAINMENT

In the 2010 Jonah Hex film, Josh Brolin plays the protagonist Jonah Hex, who turns rogue and effectively becomes an outlaw after his general officer, Quentin Turnbull (played by John Malkovich), orders him to burn down a hospital. When Hex refuses to follow Turnbull's orders, Turnbull burns down Hex's house with his family inside.

Similarly to the enactment of the 1604 Vagabonds Act, Quentin Turnbull brands his initials "QT" on Jonah Hex's face with a hot iron.

Gaming

In many role-playing games, such as Dungeons & Dragons and other fantasy franchises, rogue is often considered a character class. The characters vary widely but are commonplace in the genre, and are considered a vital part of a balanced party. Rogues are typically dexterous and possess many skills, allowing them to excel in many areas of expertise. The rogue character's focus is often on finesse over raw strength, making them use wit and traps before direct confrontation in a fight, adept at picking locks, disarming and laying traps, use stealth and other unconventional approaches to accomplishing their goals.

ROGAINING

Rogaining is a sport of long distance cross-country navigation, involving both route planning and navigation between checkpoints using a variety of map types. In a rogaine, teams of 2-5 people choose which checkpoints to visit within a time limit with the intent of maximizing their score. Teamwork, endurance, competition and an appreciation for the natural environment are features of the sport. Championship rogaines are 24 hours long, however rogaines can be as short as 2 hours.

Rogaining can trace its roots back to 1947 when the first of many events with some of the features of rogaines was organized by the Melbourne University Mountaineering Club. The events from the 1940s eventually led to the birth of the sport of rogaining in April, 1976, in Melbourne, Australia. The sport was named, rules were adopted and the world's first rogaining association was formed (the Victorian Rogaining Association). Growth of the association and the sport occurred rapidly over the next decade.

The word rogaining is derived from the names of three of the founders, Rod Phillips, Gail Davis (née Phillips) and Neil Phillips (RoGaiNe, hence 'rogaining', 'rogainer' etc.) who were all members of the Surrey-Thomas Rover Crew which organized the world's first rogaine. The name was formally adopted by the Victorian Rogaining Association at its inaugural annual general meeting in August, 1976 and accepted by Scouts Australia and University bushwalking groups to give the new sport an identity in its own right.

ROGAINE is also a backronym for "Rugged Outdoor Group Activity Involving Navigation and Endurance".

World Rogaining Championships have been held every two years, with the country chosen two years in advance by the International Rogaining Federation.

- 1st World Rogaining Championship (1992): Beechworth, Australia, about 200 teams
- 2nd World Rogaining Championship (1996): Mt Singleton, Western Australia, 640 participants in 271 teams
- 3rd World Rogaining Championship (1998): Kamloops, British Columbia, Canada
- 4th World Rogaining Championship (2000): Christchurch, New Zealand
- 5th World Rogaining Championship (2002): Lesna, Czech Republic, 202 teams
- 6th World Rogaining Championship (2004): Arizona, USA, 380 participants from 15 countries and 33 U.S. states.
- 7th World Rogaining Championships (2006): New South Wales, Australia; 691 participants (311 teams), 125 from overseas
- 8th World Rogaining Championship (2008): Karula National Park, Estonia; 748 participants (339 teams) from 22 countries.
- 9th World Rogaining Championship (2010): Cheviot, New Zealand; 522 participants (251 teams)
- 10th World Rogaining Championship (2012): Pøebuz, Czech Republic
- 11th World Rogaining Championship (2013): Alol, Russian Federation
- 12th World Rogaining Championship (2014): Black Hills, South Dakota, USA
- 13th World Rogaining Championship (2015)]: Lapland, Finland
- 14th World Rogaining Championship (2016)]: Alice Springs, Australia

BASIC PLAY

Teams of two to five members visit as many checkpoints as possible in the time allowed. Shorter duration rogaines often allow solo competitors.

Checkpoints are scored differently depending on level of difficulty in reaching them; therefore teams choose a strategy (for example, to visit many low score checkpoints). Teams travel entirely on foot, navigating by map and compass between checkpoints in terrain that varies from open farmland to hilly forest. A central base camp known as a "hash house" provides hot meals throughout the event and teams may return at any time to eat, rest or sleep. Teams travel at their own pace and anyone from children to grandparents can experience the personal satisfaction that comes from cross-country navigation at their own level of competition and comfort. Team members stay within earshot of each other.

The duration of a championship Rogaine is 24 hours, but shorter variations such as 6, 8, 12 and 15 hour events are also held (sometimes concurrently with a 24 hour event). Depending on the terrain, experienced rogaining teams can cover more than one hundred kilometers over the 24 hour period. There have also been longer events (dubbed "Endurogaines") lasting 48 and 50 hours. In their native Australia, Rogaines are usually held every month during weekends near full moons, with annual state championships and an annual national championship. They require dozens of volunteers to run, including course setters and caterers and are often attended by hundreds of participants. A competitive 24-hour rogaine requires a map area of around 250 km (~ 100 mi), for relatively flat terrain; terrain with significant climbs may require far less or far more area, depending on the placement of checkpoints.

VARIANTS

Other forms of rogaining are popular, particularly in Australia during the months when normal rogaines are not held because of the weather. Popular variations include:

- Metrogaine - An event of usually around 6 hours and held in predominantly urban areas.
- Cyclogaine - Usually run for 6 hours in areas with trails suitable for mountainbiking.
- Snogaine - Held in areas that are snowbound and participants may either snowshoe or ski to reach checkpoints.
- Paddlogaine - A rogaine on a water covered area, such as a set of interconnected lakes, participants can generally use any human powered watercraft they want.

RIVER TREKKING

River climbing, river trekking or mountain stream climbing is a form of hiking or outdoor adventure activity, a traditional sport in Japan and popular in Hong Kong and Taiwan, and, in some ways, similar to canyoning or canyoneering. River trekking is a combination of trekking and climbing and sometimes swimming along the river. It involves particular techniques like rock climbing, climbing on wet surfaces, understanding the geographical features of river and valleys, knotting, dealing with sudden bad weather and finding out possible exits from the river.

RISK AND DANGER

River trekking has certain level of risk. There are occasional accidents in river trekking, including falls from steep cliffs or waterfalls, drownings, exhaustion, or getting lost. Risks that should be prepared for include the following:

First, sudden changes in weather, like rainstorms, can cause rapid rises in water levels and speed in the river. Also, the number of viable paths and climbing areas inside the river valley could be reduced suddenly in a very short period. Besides this, bad or misty weather would also cause low visibility. Low visibility may come in too quickly for trekkers to adapt to. Therefore, a torch (flashlight), preferably a head-mounted one, is a must for river trekking.

Second, steep cliffs inside river valleys require a certain level of rock-climbing skills. However, because of the humid environment inside the river valley, some rock surfaces can be very wet and some rocks can be very loose despite appearing solid. To deal with such wet climbing conditions, a pair of professional river-trekking boots are strongly advised.

RAFTING

Rafting or white water rafting is the challenging recreational outdoor activity of using an inflatable raft to navigate a river or other bodies of water. This is often done on white water or different degrees of rough water, in order to thrill and excite the raft passengers. The development of this activity as a leisure sport has become popular since the mid-1970s, evolving from individuals paddling 10 feet (3.0 m) rafts with double-bladed paddles to multi-person rafts propelled by single-bladed paddles and steered by a tour guide at the stern. It is considered an extreme sport, and can be fatal.

WHITE WATER RAFTS

The modern raft is an inflatable boat, consisting of very durable, multi-layered rubberized (hypalon) or vinyl fabrics (PVC) with several independent air chambers. Typical lengths vary from 6 m (20 ft) (with a width of 2.5 m (8 ft)) down to very portable single-person packrafts which may be as small as 1.5 metres (4.9 ft) long and weigh as little as 4 pounds (1.8 kg).

Rafts come in a few different forms. In Europe and Australasia, the most common is the symmetrical raft steered with a double-bladed paddle at the stern. Other types are the asymmetrical rudder-controlled raft, the symmetrical raft with central helm (oars), and Stern Mounts with the oar frame located at the rear of the raft. Rafts are usually propelled with ordinary paddles and or oars and typically hold 4 to 12 persons. In Russia, rafts are often hand made and are often a catamaran style with two inflatable tubes attached to a frame. Pairs of paddlers navigate on these rafts. Catamaran style rafts have become popular in the western United States as well, but are typically rowed instead of paddled.

GRADES OF WHITE WATER

Otherwise known as the International Scale of River Difficulty, below are the six grades of difficulty in white water rafting. They range from simple to very dangerous and potential death or serious injuries.

Grade 1: Very small rough areas, might require slight maneuvering. (Skill level: very basic)

Grade 2: Some rough water, maybe some rocks, might require some maneuvering. (Skill level: basic paddling skill)

Grade 3: Whitewater, small waves, maybe a small drop, but no considerable danger. May require significant maneuvering. (Skill level: experienced paddling skills)

Grade 4: Whitewater, medium waves, maybe rocks, maybe a considerable drop, sharp maneuvers may be needed. (Skill level: whitewater experience)

Grade 5: Whitewater, large waves, large volume, possibility of large rocks and hazards, possibility of a large drop, requires precise maneuvering. (Skill level: advanced whitewater experience)

Grade 6: Class 6 rapids are considered to be so dangerous that they are effectively unnavigable on a reliably safe basis. Rafters can expect to encounter substantial whitewater, huge waves, huge rocks and hazards, and/or substantial drops that will impart severe impacts beyond the structural capacities and impact ratings of almost all rafting equipment. Traversing a Class 6 rapid has a dramatically increased likelihood of ending in serious injury or death compared to lesser classes. (Skill level: successful completion of a Class 6 rapid without serious injury or death is widely considered to be a matter of great luck or extreme skill and is considered by some as a suicidal venture)

TECHNIQUES

Rafts in white water are very different vehicles than canoes or kayaks and have their own specific techniques to maneuver through whitewater obstacles.

- Punching – Rafts carry great momentum, and on rivers hydraulics that are dodged by canoes and kayaks are often punched by rafts. This involves the rafting crew paddling the raft to give it enough speed to push through the hydraulic without getting stopped.
- High siding – If a raft is caught in a hydraulic it will often quickly go sideways. In order to stop the raft flipping on its inside edge, the rafters can climb to the side of the raft furthest downstream, which will also be the side of the raft highest in the air leading to

its name. In this position the rafters may be able to use the draw stroke to pull the raft out of the head Capsizing:

- Dump truck – Rafts are inherently stable crafts because of their size and low center of mass and often they will shed gear and passengers before they actually capsize. In the industry if a raft dumps some or all of its passengers but remains upright, it is said to have dump trucked.
- Left over right or right over left – Rafts almost always flip side over side. If the left tube rises over the right tube, the raft is said to have flipped left over right and vice versa.
- Taco – If a raft is soft, or underinflated, it may taco, or reverse taco. Rafts are said to have tacoed if the middle of the raft buckles and the front of the raft touches or nearly touches the back of the raft. This often is a result of surfing in a hydraulic. A reverse taco is when the nose, or stern of the raft is pulled down under water and buckles to touch the middle or back, or nose of the raft.
- End over end – Occasionally rafts will flip end over end. This is usually after the raft has dump trucked to lighten the load, allowing the water to overcome the weight of the boat flipping it vertically before it lands upside down. Rafts will usually taco and turn sideways, making an end-over-end flip a very rare flip in most rafts.
- Down Stream Flip- A raft capsizes after encountering an obstacle i.e. rock, feature like a hydraulic or even another raft. These objects are usually stationary or possibly surfing in a hydraulic. On this occasion the raft becomes unstable and usually flips over downstream or in the direction of travel. A downstream flip may be exacerbated by the load or people in the raft. People may physically assist in the inertia of the flip by pulling the boat over on top of themselves.

Re-righting:

- Flip line – The flip line technique is the most used in commercial rafting where flips are common. The guide will take a loop of webbing that has a biner on it and attach it to the perimeter line on the raft, Standing on top of the upside down raft they will hold the line and lean to the opposite side from where the flip line is attached, re-righting the raft.
- Knee flipping – Capsized rafts that are small enough with little or no gear attached can be knee flipped. This involves the rafter holding the webbing on the underside of the raft, and pushing their knees into the outer tube, and then lifting their body out of the water, leaning back to overturn the raft.
- T rescue – Much like the kayak technique, some rafts are large enough that they need to be overturned with the assistance of another raft or land. Positioning the upturned raft or land at the

side of the raft, the rafters can then re-right the raft by lifting up on the perimeter line.

- T-grip re-flip - The T-grip on a rafting paddle may be used to re-flip light rafts by inserting the Tee into the self bailing holes around the floor perimeter and re-righting the boat in the same manner as the flip line technique.
- Alluvial - Pertaining to material carried or laid down by running water. Alluvium is the material deposited by streams. It includes gravel, sand, silt, and clay.
- Back Pivot - Turning the raft from a ferry angle to a stem-downstream position.Used in tight places to recover from an extreme ferry angle, this maneuver narrows the passing space of the boat and allows it to slide closely past obstructions.
- Back roller - A broad reversal such as that formed below a dam or ledge.
- Beam - The width of a raft at its widest point.
- Biner - Short for *Carabiner* - which means "clip" in Italian. In rafting, biners are used in rope and pulley rescue systems to secure things to a raft and as items of adornment in river rafting.

Tricks:

- Rock splats – If the rafters load the back of the raft, they can paddle the raft into a rock on the river, having it hit the bottom of the boat instead of the nose; if done correctly this can raise the raft up vertically on its stern.
- Surfing – Commercial rafts often use waves on rivers to surf.
- Nose dunks – Large rafts can enter hydraulics called holes from downstream and submerge their nose, or reverse taco. This can be a safe way to get rafters wet in a hydraulic.
- Pirouette – A move executed by either a sweep or draw stroke, sending the raft spinning with the current. Often useful for avoiding obstacles.
- Troying - This is a move done by only expert white water rafters, and is the action of popping the back of the boat for a sudden burst of speed.

Safety: White water rafting can be a dangerous sport, especially if basic safety precautions are not observed. Both commercial and private trips have seen their share of injuries and fatalities, though private travel has typically been associated with greater risk. Depending on the area, safety regulations covering raft operators may exist in legislation. These range from certification of outfitters, rafts, and raft leaders, to more stringent regulations about equipment and procedures. It is generally advisable to discuss safety measures with a rafting operator before signing on for a trip. The equipment used and the qualifications of the company and raft guides are essential information to be considered.

Like most outdoor sports, rafting in general has become safer over the years. Expertise in the sport has increased, and equipment has become more specialized and increased in quality. As a result the difficulty rating of most river runs has changed. A classic example would be the Colorado River in the Grand Canyon or Jalcomulco River in Mexico, which has swallowed whole expeditions in the past, leaving only fragments of boats. In contrast, it is now run safely by commercial outfitters hundreds of times each year with relatively untrained passengers.

Risks in white water rafting stem from both environmental dangers and from improper behavior. Certain features on rivers are inherently unsafe and have remained consistently so despite the passage of time. These would include "keeper hydraulics", "strainers" (e.g. fallen trees), dams (especially low-head dams, which tend to produce river-wide keeper hydraulics), undercut rocks, and of course dangerously high waterfalls. Rafting with experienced guides is the safest way to avoid such features. Even in safe areas, however, moving water can always present risks—such as when a swimmer attempts to stand up on a rocky riverbed in strong current, risking foot entrapment. Irresponsible behavior related to rafting while intoxicated has also contributed to many accidents.

One of the most simple ways to avoid injury while out of a raft, is to swim to an eddy to avoid being taken downstream.

To combat the illusion that rafting is akin to an amusement park ride, and to underscore the personal responsibility each rafter faces on a trip, rafting outfitters generally require customers to sign waiver forms indicating understanding and acceptance of potential serious risks. Rafting trips often begin with safety presentations to educate customers about problems that may arise.

White water rafting is often played for the adrenaline rush and this can become a problem for participants' safety. White water rafting accidents have occurred but are not common.

Due to this the overall risk level on a rafting trip with experienced guides using proper precautions is low. Thousands of people safely enjoy raft trips every year.

ENVIRONMENTAL ISSUES

Like all outdoor activities, rafting must balance its use of nature with the conservation of rivers as a natural resource and habitat. Because of these issues, some rivers now have regulations restricting the annual and daily operating times or numbers of rafters.

Conflicts have arisen when rafting operators, often in co-operation with municipalities and tourism associations, alter the riverbed by dredging and/or blasting in order to eliminate safety hazards or create more interesting whitewater features in the river. Environmentalists argue that this may have negative impacts to riparian and aquatic ecosystems, while proponents claim these measures are usually only temporary, since a riverbed is naturally subject to permanent changes during large floods and other events.

Rafting contributes to the economy of many regions which in turn may contribute to the protection of rivers from hydroelectric power generation, diversion for irrigation, and other development. Additionally, white water rafting trips can promote environmentalism. By experiencing firsthand the beauty of a river, individuals who would otherwise be indifferent to environmental issues may gain a strong desire to protect and preserve that area because of their positive outdoor experience.

PARAGLIDING

Paragliding is the recreational and competitive adventure sport of flying paragliders: lightweight, free-flying, foot-launched glider aircraft with no rigid primary structure. The pilot sits in a harness suspended below a fabric wing consisting of a large number of interconnected and baffled cells. Wing shape is maintained by its suspension lines, the pressure of air entering vents in the front of the wing and the aerodynamic forces of the air flowing over the outside.

Despite not using an engine, paraglider flights can last many hours and cover many hundreds of kilometres, though flights of 1–2 hours and covering some tens of kilometres are more the norm. By skilful exploitation of sources of lift the pilot may gain height, often climbing to altitudes of a few thousand metres.

Paragliders are unique among soaring aircraft in being easily portable. The complete equipment packs into a rucksack and can be carried easily on the pilot's back, in a car, or on public transport. In comparison with other air sports this substantially simplifies travel to a suitable takeoff spot, the selection of a landing place and return travel.

Paragliding is related to the following activities:

- Hang gliding is a close cousin, and hang glider and paraglider launches are often found in proximity. Despite the considerable difference in equipment the two activities offer similar pleasures and some pilots are involved in both sports.
- Powered paragliding is the flying of paragliders with a small engine attached.
- Speed riding or speed flying is the separate sport of flying paragliders of reduced size. These wings have increased speed, though they are not normally capable of soaring flight. The sport involves taking off on skis or on foot and swooping rapidly down in close proximity to the slope, even periodically touching it if skis are used. These smaller wings are also sometimes used where wind speeds are too high for a full-sized paraglider, although this is invariably at coastal sites where the wind is laminar and not subject to as much mechanical turbulence as inland sites.

- Paragliding can be of local importance as a commercial activity. Paid accompanied tandem flights are available in many mountainous regions, both in the winter and in the summer. In addition there are many schools offering courses, and guides who lead groups of more experienced pilots exploring an area. Finally there are the manufacturers and the associated repair and after sales services.
- Paraglider-like wings also find other uses, for example in ship propulsion and wind energy exploitation, and are related to some forms of power kite.
- Kite skiing uses equipment similar to paragliding sails.

HISTORY

In 1952, Domina Jalbert advanced governable gliding parachutes with multi-cells and controls for lateral glide. In 1954, Walter Neumark predicted (in an article in *Flight* magazine) a time when a glider pilot would be "able to launch himself by running over the edge of a cliff or down a slope ... whether on a rock-climbing holiday in Skye or ski-ing in the Alps".

In 1961, the French engineer Pierre Lemoigne produced improved parachute designs which led to the Para-Commander. The 'PC' had cutouts at the rear and sides that enabled it to be towed into the air and steered – leading to parasailing/parascending.

American Domina Jalbert invented the Parafoil which had sectioned cells in an aerofoil shape; an open leading edge and a closed trailing edge, inflated by passage through the air – the *ram-air* design. He filed US Patent 3131894 on January 10, 1963.

Meanwhile, David Barish was developing the Sail Wing (single-surface wing) for recovery of NASA space capsules – "slope soaring was a way of testing out ... the Sail Wing". After tests on Hunter Mountain, New York in September 1965, he went on to promote 'slope soaring' as a summer activity for ski resorts (apparently without great success).

Author Walter Neumark wrote *Operating Procedures for Ascending Parachutes*, and he and a group of enthusiasts with a passion for tow-launching 'PCs' and ram-air parachutes eventually broke away from the British Parachute Association to form the British Association of Parascending Clubs (BAPC) in 1973. Authors Patrick Gilligan (Canada) and Bertrand Dubuis (Switzerland) wrote the first flight manual "The Paragliding Manual" in 1985, officially coining the word Paragliding.

These threads were pulled together in June 1978 by three friends Jean-Claude Bétemps, André Bohn and Gérard Bosson from Mieussy Haute-Savoie, France. After inspiration from an article on 'slope soaring' in the *Parachute Manual* magazine by parachutist & publisher Dan Poynter, they calculated that on a suitable slope, a 'square' ram-air parachute could be inflated by running down the slope; Bétemps launched from Pointe du Pertuiset, Mieussy, and flew 100 m. Bohn followed him and glided down to the football pitch in the valley 1000 metres below. 'Parapente' (*pente* being French for slope) was born.

From the 1980s equipment has continued to improve and the number of paragliding pilots and established sites has continued to increase. The first (unofficial) Paragliding World Championship was held in Verbier, Switzerland in 1987, though the first officially sanctioned FAI World Championship was held in Kössen, Austria in 1989.

Europe has seen the greatest growth in paragliding, with France alone currently registering over 25,000 active pilots.

EQUIPMENT

Wing

The paraglider wing or canopy is usually what is known in aeronautical engineering as a "ram-air airfoil". Such wings comprise two layers of fabric which are connected to internal supporting material in such a way as to form a row of cells. By leaving most of the cells open only at the leading edge, incoming air keeps the wing inflated, thus maintaining its shape. When inflated, the wing's cross-section has the typical teardrop aerofoil shape. Modern paraglider wings are made of high-performance non-porous materials such as ripstop polyester or nylon fabric.

In some modern paragliders (from the 1990s onwards), especially higher performance wings, some of the cells of the leading edge are closed to form a cleaner aerodynamic profile. Holes in the internal ribs allow a free flow of air from the open cells to these closed cells to inflate them, and also to the wingtips which are also closed.

The pilot is supported underneath the wing by a network of suspension lines. These start with two sets of *risers* made of short (40 cm) lengths of strong webbing. Each set is attached to the harness by a carabiner, one on each side of the pilot, and each riser of a set is generally attached to lines from only one row of its side of wing. At the end of each riser of the set there is a small delta maillon with a number (2-5) of lines attached forming a fan. These are typically 4–5 metres long, with the end attached to 2-4 further lines of around 2m, which are again joined to a group of smaller, thinner lines. In some cases this is repeated for a fourth cascade.

The top of each line is attached to small fabric loops sewn into the structure of the wing, which are generally arranged in rows running span-wise (i.e., side to side). The row of lines nearest the front are known as the A lines, the next row back the B lines and so on. A typical wing will have A, B, C and D lines, but recently there is a tendency to reduce the rows of lines to three, or even two (and experimentally to one), to reduce drag.

Paraglider lines are usually made from Dyneema/Spectra or Kevlar/Aramid. Although they look rather slender, these materials are immensely strong. For example, a single 0.66mm diameter line (about the thinnest used) can have a breaking strength of 56 kg. Paraglider wings typically have an area of 20–35 square metres (220–380 sq ft) with a span of 8–12 metres (26–39 ft), and weigh 3–7 kilograms (6.6–15 lb). Combined weight of wing, harness, reserve, instruments, helmet, etc. is around 12–22 kilograms (26–49 lb).

The glide ratio of paragliders ranges from 9.3 for recreational wings, to about 11.3 for modern competition models. For comparison, a typical skydiving parachute will achieve about 3:1 glide. A hang glider ranges from 9.5 for recreational wings, to about 16.5 for modern competition models. An idling (gliding) Cessna 152 light aircraft will achieve 9:1. Some sailplanes can achieve a glide ratio of up to 72:1.

The speed range of paragliders is typically 20–75 kilometres per hour (12–47 mph), from stall speed to maximum speed. Beginner wings will be in the lower part of this range, high-performance wings in the upper part of the range.

For storage and carrying, the wing is usually folded into a stuffsack (bag), which can then be stowed in a large backpack along with the harness. For pilots who may not want the added weight or fuss of a backpack, some modern harnesses include the ability to turn the harness inside out such that it becomes a backpack.

Tandem paragliders, designed to carry the pilot and one passenger, are larger but otherwise similar. They usually fly faster with higher trim speeds, are more resistant to collapse, and have a slightly higher sink rate compared to solo paragliders.

Harness

The pilot is loosely and comfortably buckled into a harness which offers support in both the standing and sitting positions. Most harnesses have foam or airbag protectors underneath the seat and behind the back to reduce the impact on failed launches or landings. Modern harnesses are designed to be as comfortable as a lounge chair in the sitting position. Many harnesses even have an adjustable 'lumbar support'. A reserve parachute is also typically connected to a paragliding harness.

Instruments

Most pilots use variometers, radios, and, increasingly, GPS units when flying.

Variometer

The main purpose of a variometer is in helping a pilot find and stay in the "core" of a thermal to maximise height gain and, conversely, to indicate when a pilot is in sinking air and needs to find rising air. Humans can sense the acceleration when they first hit a thermal, but cannot detect the difference between constant rising air and constant sinking air. Modern variometers are capable of detecting rates of climb or sink of 1 cm per second. A variometer indicates climb-rate (or sink-rate) with short audio signals (beeps, which increase in pitch and tempo during ascent, and a droning sound, which gets deeper as the rate of descent increases) and/or a visual display. It also shows altitude: either above takeoff, above sea level, or (at higher altitudes) "flight level".

Radio

Radio communications are used in training, to communicate with other pilots, and to report where and when they intend to land. These radios normally operate on a range of frequencies in different countries—some authorised, some illegal but tolerated locally. In rare cases, pilots use radios to talk to airport control towers or air traffic controllers. Many pilots carry a cell phone so they can call for pickup should they land away from their intended point of destination.

GPS

GPS (global positioning system) is a necessary accessory when flying competitions, where it has to be demonstrated that way-points have been correctly passed. The recorded GPS track of a flight can be used to analyze flying technique or shared with other pilots. GPS is also used to determine drift due to the prevailing wind when flying at altitude, providing position information to allow restricted airspace to be avoided, and identifying one's location for retrieval teams after landing-out in unfamiliar territory. GPS is integrated with some models of variometer. This is not only more convenient, but also allows for a three dimensional record of the flight. The flight track can be used as proof for record claims, replacing the 'old' method of photo documentation.

CONTROL

- Brakes: Controls held in each of the pilot's hands connect to the trailing edge of the left and right sides of the wing. These controls are called 'brakes' and provide the primary and most general means of control in a paraglider. The brakes are used to adjust speed, to steer (in addition to weight-shift), and flare (during landing).
- Weight Shift: In addition to manipulating the brakes, a paraglider pilot must also lean in order to steer properly. Such 'weight-shifting' can also be used for more limited steering when brake use is unavailable, such as when under 'big ears'. More advanced control techniques may also involve weight-shifting.
- Speed Bar: A kind of foot control called the 'speed bar' (also 'accelerator') attaches to the paragliding harness and connects to the leading edge of the paraglider wing, usually through a system of at least two pulleys. This control is used to increase speed, and does so by decreasing the wing's angle of attack. This control is

necessary because the brakes can only slow the wing from what is called 'trim speed' (no brakes applied). The accelerator is needed to go faster than this.

More advanced means of control can be obtained by manipulating the paraglider's risers or lines directly:

- Most commonly, the lines connecting to the outermost points of the wing's leading edge can be used to induce the wingtips to fold under. The technique, known as 'big ears', is used to increase rate of descent.
- The risers connecting to the rear of the wing can also be manipulated for steering if the brakes have been severed or are otherwise unavailable.
- In a 'B-line stall'

Fast Descents

Problems with "getting down" can occur when the lift situation is very good or when the weather changes unexpectedly. There are three possibilities of rapidly reducing altitude in such situations, each of which has benefits and issues to be aware of:

- "Big ears" induces descent rates of 2 m/s or so. It is the most controllable of the techniques, and the easiest for beginners to learn.
- A B-line stall induces descent rates of 5 m/s or so. It increases loading on parts of the wing (the pilot's weight is mostly on the B-lines, instead of spread across all the lines). There is no risk of the pilot becoming disoriented as a result of using this technique.
- A spiral dive offers the fastest rate of descent, at 10–15 m/s. It places greater loads on the wing than other techniques do, and requires the highest level of skill from the pilot to execute safely.

Big Ears

Pulling on the outer A-lines folds the wing tips in drastically deteriorating the glide angle with only a small decrease in forward speed. When the lines are released the wing reinflates. As the effective wing area is reduced, the wing loading is increased and it becomes more stable. However the angle of attack is increased and the craft is closer to stall speed, but this can be ameliorated by applying the speed bar.

B-Line stall

In a 'B-line stall', the second set of risers from the leading-edge/front (the B-lines) are pulled down independently of the other risers; with the specific lines used to initiate the condition being responsible for its name. This puts a spanwise crease in the wing, thereby separating the airflow from the upper surface of the wing. This dramatically reduces the lift produced by the canopy and thus induces a higher rate of descent.

Spiral Dive

The spiral dive is the most rapid form of controlled fast descent; a sink rate of 15 m/s can be achieved.

However, spiral dives put strong G-forces on the wing and glider and must be done carefully and skilfully. The G-forces involved can induce blackouts, and the rotation can produce disorientation.

FLYING

Launching

As with all aircraft, launching and landing are done into wind.

Forward launch

In low winds, the wing is inflated with a 'forward launch', where the pilot runs forward with the wing behind so that the air pressure generated by the forward movement inflates the wing.

Reverse launch

In higher winds a 'reverse launch' is used, with the pilot facing the wing to bring it up into a flying position, then turning around under the wing and running to complete the launch.

Reverse launches have a number of advantages over a forward launch. It is more straight forward to inspect the wing and check the lines are free as it leaves the ground. In the presence of wind, the pilot can be tugged toward the wing and facing the wing makes it easier to resist this force, and safer in case the pilot slips (as opposed to being dragged backwards). These launches are normally attempted with a reasonable wind speed making the ground speed required to pressurise the wing much lower – the pilot is initially launching while walking forwards as opposed to running backward.

Towed launch

In flatter countryside pilots can also be launched with a tow. Once at full height (towing can launch pilots up to 2500 feet altitude), the pilot pulls a release cord and the towline falls away. This requires separate training, as flying on a winch has quite different characteristics from free flying. There are two major ways to tow: Pay-in and pay-out towing. Pay-in towing involves a stationary winch that winds in the towline and thereby pulls the pilot in the air.

The distance between winch and pilot at the start is around 500 meters or more. Pay-out towing involves a moving object, like a car or a boat, that pays out line slower than the speed of the object thereby pulling the pilot up in the air. In both cases it is very important to have a gauge indicating line tension to avoid pulling the pilot out of the air. There is one other form of towing; 'static' towing. This involves a moving object, like a car or a boat, attached to a paraglider or hanglider with a fixed length line. This is very dangerous because now the forces on the line have to be controlled by the moving object itself, which is almost impossible to do. With static line towing a lockout (moving to the side away from the tow direction or stalling) is very likely. Static line towing is forbidden in most countries, and should be avoided at all cost.

Landing

Landing involves lining up for an approach into wind, and just before touching down, 'flaring' the wing to minimise vertical and/or horizontal speed. This consists of gently going from 0% brake at around 2 meters to 100% brake when touching down on the ground.

In light winds, some minor running is common. In moderate to medium headwinds, the landings can be without forward speed. With strong winds even going backwards with respect to the ground, but this would usually mean that the conditions were too strong for that glider.

Additionally, at around 4 meters before touching ground, some momentary braking (50% for around 2 seconds) can be applied, then released thus using forward pendular momentum to gain speed for flaring more effectively and approach the ground with minimal vertical speed.

For strong winds during landing two techniques are common:

- 'flapping' the wing to make it lose performance and thus descend faster by alternatively braking and releasing (around once per second).
- Collapsing it immediately after touchdown to avoid being dragged by braking at maximum.

Soaring

Soaring flight is achieved by utilizing wind directed upwards by a fixed object such as a Dune or Ridge. In slope soaring, pilots fly along the length of a slope feature in the landscape, relying on the lift provided by the air which is forced up as it passes over the slope. Slope soaring is highly dependent on a steady wind within a defined range (the suitable range depends on the performance of the wing and the skill of the pilot). Too little wind, and insufficient lift is available to stay airborne (pilots end up scratching along the slope). With more wind, gliders can fly well above and forward of the slope, but too much wind, and there is a risk of being blown back over the slope.

Thermal Flying

When the sun warms the ground, it will warm some features more than others (such as rock-faces or large buildings), and these set off thermals which rise through the air. Sometimes these may be a simple rising column of air; more often, they are blown sideways in the wind, and will break off from the source, with a new thermal forming later. Once a pilot finds a thermal, he or she begins to fly in a circle, trying to center the circle on the strongest part of the thermal (the "core"), where the air is rising the fastest. Most pilots use a vario-altimeter ("vario"), which indicates climb rate with beeps and/or a visual display, to help core-in on a thermal. Often there is strong sink surrounding thermals, and there is often also strong turbulence resulting in wing collapses as a pilot tries to enter a strong thermal. Good thermal flying is a skill which takes time to learn, but a good pilot can often core a thermal all the way to cloud base.

Cross-country Flying

Once the skills of using thermals to gain altitude have been mastered, pilots can glide from one thermal to the next to go 'cross country'. Having gained altitude in a thermal, a pilot glides down to the next available thermal. Potential thermals can be identified by land features which typically generate thermals, or by cumulus clouds which mark the top of a rising column of warm, humid air as it reaches the dew point and condenses to form a cloud. In many flying areas, cross-country pilots also need an intimate familiarity with air law, flying regulations, aviation maps indicating restricted airspace, etc.

In-flight Wing Deflation (Collapse)

Since the shape of the wing (airfoil) is formed by the moving air entering and inflating the wing, in turbulent air, part or all of the wing (airfoil) can deflate (collapse). Piloting techniques referred to as "active flying" will greatly reduce the frequency and severity of deflations or collapses. On modern recreational wings, such deflations will normally recover without pilot intervention.

In the event of a severe deflation, correct pilot input will speed recovery from a deflation, but incorrect pilot input may slow the return of the glider to normal flight, so pilot training and practice in correct response to deflations is necessary. For the rare occasions when it is not possible to recover from a deflation (or from other threatening situations such as a spin), most pilots carry a reserve (rescue, emergency) parachute. Most pilots never have cause to 'throw' their reserve. Should a wing deflation occur at low altitude, i.e., shortly after takeoff or just before landing, the wing (paraglider) may not recover its correct structure rapidly enough to prevent an accident, with the pilot often not having enough altitude remaining to successfully deploy a reserve parachute (with the minimum altitude for this being approximately 60 m (200 ft), but typical deployment to stabilization periods using up 120–180 m (400 – 600 ft) of altitude).

Different packing methods of the reserve parachute affect its deploying time. It is also important to note that, should the wing collapse due to turbulence, this 'bad air' can cause the reserve parachute to take significantly longer to inflate and stabilize. In this case, it may be of greater benefit to the paraglider to purposefully lose altitude to 'clear' this turbulent air before deploying their reserve; should they have spare altitude to use on this process. Low altitude wing failure can result in serious injury or death due to the subsequent velocity of a ground impact where, paradoxically, a higher altitude failure may allow more time to regain some degree of control in the descent rate and, critically, deploy the reserve if needed. In-flight wing deflation and other hazards are minimized by flying a suitable glider and choosing appropriate weather conditions and locations for the pilot's skill and experience level.

SPORTS/COMPETITIVE FLYING

Some pilots like to stretch themselves beyond recreational flying. For such pilots, there are multiple disciplines available:

- Cross Country Competitions – races around waypoints with typical distances of 50 to 150 kilometers
- National/international records – despite continually improving gliders, these become ever more difficult to achieve; aside from longest distance and highest altitude, examples include distance to declared goal, distance over triangular course, speed over 100 km triangular course, etc.
- "Acro" – aero-acrobatic manoeuvres and stunt flying; tricks such as "helicopters", wing-overs, synchro spirals, infinity tumbles, and so on.
- Cross-country leagues – annual regional, national and worldwide leagues scored based on accumulated best distance flights
- Accuracy – spot landing competitions where pilots land on targets with a 3 cm centre spot out to a full 10 meter circle.

Competitive flying is done on high performance wings which demand far more skill to fly than their recreational counterparts, but which are far more responsive and offer greater feedback to the pilot, as well as flying faster with better glide ratios. The current FAI world champions are Klaudia Bulgakow (Poland) and Jeremie Lager (France). They won their titles in July 2013 in Sopot, Bulgaria. Their predecessors were Petra Slivova (Slovenia) and Charles Cazaux (France), who won their titles in July 2011 in Piedrahíta, Spain.

The current Paragliding World Cup (PWC) Champion is Aaron Durogati of Italy; he won the title in January 2013 in Roldanillo, Colombia.

SAFETY

Paragliding, like any extreme sport, is a potentially dangerous activity. In the United States for example, in 2010 (the last year for which details are available) one paraglider pilot died. This is an equivalent rate of 2 in 10,000 pilots. Over the years 1994 - 2010 an average of 7 in every 10,000 active paraglider pilots has been fatally injured, though with a marked improvement in recent years. In France (with over 25,000 registered fliers), 2 of every 10,000 pilots were fatally injured in 2011 (a rate that is not atypical of the years 2007 - 2011), although around 6 of every 1,000 pilots were seriously injured (more than 2 day hospital stay).

The potential for injury can be significantly reduced by training and risk management. The use of proper equipment such as a wing designed for the pilot's size and skill level, as well as a helmet, reserve parachute, and a cushioned harness also minimize risk. The pilot's safety is influenced by their understanding of the site conditions such as air turbulence (rotors), strong thermals, gusty wind, and ground obstacles such as power lines. Sufficient pilot training in wing control and emergency manoeuvres from competent instructors can minimize accidents. Many paragliding accidents are the result of a combination of pilot error, and poor flying conditions.

LEARNING TO FLY

Most popular paragliding regions have a number of schools, generally registered with and/or organized by national associations. Certification systems vary widely between countries, though around 10 days instruction to basic certification is standard.

There are several key components to a paragliding pilot certification instruction program. Initial training for beginning pilots usually begins with some amount of ground school to discuss the basics, including elementary theories of flight as well as basic structure and operation of the paraglider.

Students then learn how to control the glider on the ground, practicing take-offs and controlling the wing 'overhead'. Low, gentle hills are next where students get their first short flights, flying at very low altitudes, to get used to the handling of the wing over varied terrain. Special winches can be used to tow the glider to low altitude in areas that have no hills readily available.

As their skills progress, students move on to steeper/higher hills (or higher winch tows), making longer flights, and learning to turn the glider, control the glider's speed, then moving on to 360° turns, spot landings, 'big ears' (used to increase the rate of descent for the paraglider), and other more advanced techniques. Training instructions are often provided to the student via radio, particularly during the first flights.

A third key component to a complete paragliding instructional program provides substantial background in the key areas of meteorology, aviation law, and general flight area etiquette.

To give prospective pilots a chance to determine if they would like to proceed with a full pilot training program, most schools offer tandem flights, in which an experienced instructor pilots the paraglider with the prospective pilot as a passenger. Schools often offer pilot's families and friends the opportunity to fly tandem, and sometimes sell tandem pleasure flights at holiday resorts.

Most recognised courses lead to a national licence and an internationally recognised International Pilot Proficiency Information/Identification card. The IPPI specifies five stages of paragliding proficiency, from the entry level ParaPro 1 to the most advanced stage 5. Attaining a level of ParaPro 3 typically allows the pilot to fly solo or without instructor supervision.

WORLD RECORDS

FAI (Fédération Aéronautique Internationale) world records:

- Straight distance – 502.9 km: Nevil Hulett (South Africa); Copperton, South Africa – Lesotho; 14 December 2008. Flight record
- Previous Straight distance – 461.6 km: Frank Brown, Marcelo Prieto, Rafael Monteiro Saladini (Brazil); Quixadá – Duque, Brazil; 14 November 2007.
- Straight distance to declared goal – 411.3 km: Nevil Hulett (South Africa); Copperton, South Africa – Lesotho; 14 December 2008.
- Previous Straight distance to declared goal ◎ å¨0+å¨◎ 368.9 km: Alja• Valiè, Urban Valiè (Slovenia); Vosburg ◎ å¨0+å¨◎ Jamestown (South Africa); 7 December 2006
- Gain of height – 4526 m: Robbie Whittall (UK); Brandvlei (South Africa); 6 January 1993

OVERLANDING

Overlanding is self-reliant overland travel to remote destinations where the journey is the principal goal. Typically, but not exclusively, it is accomplished with mechanized off-road capable transport (from bicycles to trucks) where the principal form of lodging is camping, often lasting for extended lengths of time (months to years) and spanning international boundaries.

Historically, "overlanding" is an Australian term to denote the driving of livestock over very long distances to open up new country or to take livestock to market far from grazing grounds. Between 1906 and 1910 Alfred Canning opened up the Canning Stock Route. In Australia overlanding was inspired to a large degree by Len Beadell who, in the 1940s and 1950s, constructed many of the roads that opened up the Australian Outback. Those roads are still used today by Australian overlanders and still hold the names Len gave them; the Gunbarrel Highway, the Connie Sue Highway (named after his daughter), and the Anne Beadell Highway (named after his wife).

Overlanding in its most modern form with the use of mechanized transport began in the middle of the last century with the advent of commercially available four-wheel-drive trucks (Jeeps and Land Rovers). In 1949, with the Land Rover brand less than a year old, Colonel Leblanc drove his brand new 80-inch Series I Land Rover from the United Kingdom to Abyssinia.

There followed many more private journeys, with many groups setting out from Europe for remote African destinations. To aid in these endeavors the Automobile Association of South Africa published a guide titled *Trans-African Highways, A Route Book of the Main Trunk Roads in Africa*. The first edition appeared in 1949 and included sections on choice of vehicle, choice of starting time, petrol supplies, water, provisions, equipment, rules of the road, government officials and rest houses. The serious tone of this book gives some clue as to the magnitude of such a trip, and it was from these beginnings that overlanding developed in Europe and Africa. Notable early examples include Barbara Toy's solo overland journeys in a Land Rover, including one in 1951-2 from Tangier to Baghdad, and the 1955-6 Oxford and Cambridge Far Eastern Expedition, which travelled overland from London to Singapore, also in Land Rovers.

One of the most well documented overland journeys was by Horatio Nelson Jackson in 1903. In 1954, Helen and Frank Schreider drove and sailed the length of the Americas from Circle, Alaska on the Arctic Circle to Ushuaia, Tierra del Fuego in a sea-going ex-army jeep.

MODERN OVERLANDING

Overlanding has increased in the past couple of decades, and is getting ever more popular in large part influenced by the Camel Trophy event run from 1980 to 2000 with routes crossing some intensely difficult terrain. It is now quite common for groups of overlanders to organize meetings, and an annual meeting is held every Christmas at Ushuaia. Through the use of the Internet it is much easier to find the information required for extended overland trips in foreign lands and there are several internet forums where travelers can exchange information and tips as well as coordinate planning. While some commercially built overland capable vehicles are produced, many overlanders consider the preparation of their vehicle a paramount part of the experience. Both South Africa and Australia have significant industries based on making accessories for overland travel.

Commercial Overlanding

The late 1960s saw the advent of commercial overland travel. Companies started offering overland tours to groups in large, specially equipped trucks. Mostly in Africa, these journeys could last for months, and relied heavily on the participation of the paying passengers for food preparation, food purchasing and setting up camp. The ultimate of these adventures was always the 'trans', or the complete journey from Europe to Cape Town in South Africa. Commercial overlanding has since expanded to all the continents of the world save Antarctica.

MODES OF OVERLAND TRAVEL

Rail

At 9,288 km (5,771 miles), the Trans-Siberian Railway is one of the longest overland journeys in existence today, taking seven days to reach Vladivostok from Moscow, and providing an alternative to air travel for journeys between Europe and Asia.

The Indian Pacific railway, completed in 1970, links Sydney and Perth in Australia. Covering 4,343 km (2,699 miles) over four days, the railway includes the longest stretch of straight railway line in the world.

The introduction of Japan's high speed railway Tôkaidô Shinkansen in 1964 changed the face of rail travel. The railway has carried more than 4 billion passengers and its new N700 series trains are capable of 300 km/h (190 mph). France's TGV holds the record for the fastest train, with a top speed of more than 500 km/h (310 mph), making it faster than air travel for many journeys within the country.

Road

The Silk Route or Silk Road historically connects the Mediterranean with Persia and China. Today the route refers to overland journeys between Europe and China, taking either the northern route - through Russia and Kazakhstan - or the southern route - through Turkey, Iran, Pakistan and North India - to Urumqi or Xian in China. These routes are still popular today, with companies offering tours on the southern route.

OVERLAND ROUTES

Trans Africa

Some of the longest and more traditional overland routes are in Africa. The Cairo to Cape Town and v.v. route covers more than 10,000 km (6,200 miles) and currently usually follows the Nile River through Egypt and Sudan, continuing to Kenya, Tanzania, Malawi, Zimbabwe, Botswana and Namibia along the way. In 1959 the pioneering American trailer manufacturer Wally Byam and a caravan of trailers travelled the route from Cape Town to Cairo, via Rhodesia (now Zimbabwe and Zambia), Belgian Congo (now Democratic Republic of Congo), Uganda and north from Kenya.

From the mid-1980s, the non-operation of the Aswan to Wadi Halfa ferry between Egypt and Sudan as well instability in Sudan, northern Uganda and Ethiopia, made the journey impossible. In recent years however, the Cape to Cairo and Cairo to Cape Town route has again become possible and increasingly popular both with commercial overland trucks carrying groups of 20 or so paying passengers as well as independent travellers on motorcycles or with four-wheel-drive vehicles. The traditional Trans Africa route is from London to Nairobi, Kenya and Cape Town, South Africa. The route started in the 1970s and became very popular with small companies using old Bedford four wheel drive trucks carrying about 24 people each, plus lots of independents, normally run by groups of friends in 4x4 Land Rovers heading out of London from November to March every year. The usual route was from Morocco to Algeria with a Sahara desert crossing into Niger in West Africa, continuing to Nigeria. This was followed by a month long journey likened to Joseph Conrad's "Heart of Darkness" through the forests of Zaire (now Democratic Republic of Congo), surfacing into the relatively modern world in Kenya via Uganda. From Kenya the last leg was south through Tanzania to either Zimbabwe or South Africa.

This route has changed dramatically due to border closures and political instability creating no-go zones. The route has reversed itself somewhat over the last few years, with trucks now crossing from the north to the south of Africa, closely following the west coast all the way from Morocco to Cape Town with the biggest change in the route being made possible by the opening of Angola to tourism. The journey then continues through Southern and East Africa from Cape Town to Nairobi and on to Cairo.

Other Routes

In Africa, commercial overland travel began with the Trans Africa and Cape to Cairo described above. From the mid-1980s East and Southern Africa became more sought after by tourists and Nairobi to Cape Town is now the most travelled overland route in Africa. As more tourists look for adventure trips that fit into their annual holiday, shorter sections of overland routes have become available such as two- to three-week round trip from Nairobi taking in Kenya and Uganda.

Istanbul to Cairo, via Syria and Jordan, is a classic overland route. It is a route that has been travelled for centuries, particularly during the Ottoman empire. Historically it overlapped with the Hajj, with many people covering all or part of the route as part of their pilgrimage to Mecca. Backpackers discovered it in the 1970s and 1980s, with hippies searching for spiritual peace who departed to Jerusalem from Istanbul instead of going to India via Iran, Afghanistan and Pakistan. After the peace treaty between Egypt and Israel, onward travel from Jerusalem to Cairo became a possibility. It is now well travelled by backpackers and overland companies alike although the amount of travellers journeying the route can be affected by any unrest in neighbouring countries.

MOUNTAINEERING

Mountaineering or mountain climbing is the sport, hobby or profession of hiking, skiing, and climbing mountains. While mountaineering began as attempts to reach the highest point of unclimbed big mountains it has branched into specializations that address different aspects of the mountain and consists of three areas: rock-craft, snow-craft and skiing, depending on whether the route chosen is over rock, snow or ice. All require experience, athletic ability, and technical knowledge to maintain safety.

Mountaineering is often called Alpinism, especially in European languages, which implies climbing with difficulty such high mountains as the Alps. A mountaineer with such great skill is called an Alpinist. The word alpinism was born in the 19th century to refer to climbing for the purpose of enjoying climbing itself as a sport or recreation, distinct from merely climbing while hunting or as a religious pilgrimage that had been done generally at that time. The UIAA or *Union Internationale des Associations d'Alpinisme* is the world governing body in mountaineering and climbing, addressing issues like access, medical, mountain protection, safety, youth and ice climbing.

HISTORY

First Climbs

Historically, many cultures have harboured superstitions about the mountains, which they often regarded as sacred due to their proximity with heaven, such as Mount Olympus for the Ancient Greeks. During the Enlightenment, as a product of the new spirit of curiosity for the natural world, many mountain summits were surmounted for the first time. Richard Pococke and William Windham made a historic visit to Chamonix in 1741. In 1760, the Swiss scientist, Horace-Bénédict de Saussure, offered a reward for the first person to ascend Mont Blanc in France, which was claimed in 1786.

By the early 19th century many of the alpine peaks were reached; the Grossglockner in 1800, the Ortler in 1804, the Jungfrau in 1811, the Finsteraarhorn in 1812, and the Breithorn in 1813.

Emergence as a Sport

The beginning of mountaineering as a systematic sport is generally dated to the ascent of the Wetterhorn in 1854 by Sir Alfred Wills who made mountaineering fashionable, especially in Britain. This inaugurated what became known as the Golden age of alpinism, with the first mountaineering club - the Alpine Club - being founded in 1857.

Prominent figures of the period include Lord Francis Douglas, Florence Crauford Grove, Charles Hudson, E. S. Kennedy, William Mathews, A. W. Moore, Leslie Stephen, Francis Fox Tuckett, John Tyndall, Horace Walker and Edward Whymper. Well-known guides of the era include Christian Almer, Jakob Anderegg, Melchior Anderegg, J. J. Bennen, Michel Croz, Johannes Zumtaugwald.

In the early years of the "golden age", scientific pursuits were intermixed with the sport, such as by the physicist John Tyndall. In the later years of the "golden age", it shifted to a more competitive orientation as pure sportsmen came to dominate the London-based Alpine Club and alpine mountaineering overall.

One of the most dramatic events was the spectacular first ascent of the Matterhorn in 1865, by a party led by the English illustrator, Edward Whymper - four of the party members fell to their deaths. This ascent is generally regarded as marking the end of the mountaineering golden age. By this point the sport of mountaineering had largely reached it's modern form, with a body of professional guides, equipment and fixed guidelines.

Expansion Around the World

Focus shifted toward the exploration of other ranges such as the Pyrenees and the Caucasus Mountains; the latter owed much to the initiative of D. W. Freshfield who was the first man to conquer the summit of Mount Kazbek. Most of its great peaks were successfully conquered by the late 1880s.

By 1888, trained climbers had turned their attention to the mountains of The Americas; the Irish Reverend William Spotswood Green made an expedition to the Selkirk Mountains. From that time exploration went on apace with English and American climbing parties surveying most of the highest peaks; Pikes Peak (14,110 ft) having been climbed by Mr. E. James and party in 1820, and Mt. Saint Elias (18,008 ft) by the Duke of the Abruzzi and party in 1897. The exploration of the highest Andes was begun in 1879-1880, when Whymper climbed Chimborazo and explored the mountains of Ecuador. The Cordillera between Chile and Argentina was visited by Dr. Gussfeldt in 1883, who ascended Maipo (17,270 ft) and attempted Aconcagua (22,841 ft). That peak was first climbed by the Fitzgerald expedition in 1897. Aconcagua (22,831 feet), the highest peak of the Andes, was first climbed in 1897 and the Grand Teton (13,747 feet)in North America's Rocky Mountains was ascended in 1898. The Andes of Bolivia were first explored by Sir William Martin Conway in 1898. Chilean and Argentine expeditions revealed the structure of the southern Cordillera in the years 1885-1898. Conway visited the mountains of Tierra del Fuego. New Zealand's Southern Alps were first visited in 1882 by the Reverend Green and in 1894 Tom Fyfe and party climbed Aoraki / Mount Cook.

By the turn of the century, mountaineering had acquired a more international flavour; Mount Kilimanjaro in Africa was climbed in 1889 by Ludwig Purtscheller and Hans Meyer, Mt. Kenya in 1899 by Halford Mackinder, and a peak of Ruwenzori by H. J. Moore in 1900.

The last frontier: The Himalayas

The last and greatest mountain range was the Himalayas in Central Asia. They had initially been surveyed by the British Empire for military and strategic reasons. In 1892 Sir William Martin Conway explored the Karakoram Himalayas, and climbed a peak of 23,000 ft (7,000 m) In 1895 Albert F. Mummery died while attempting Nanga Parbat, while in 1899 D. W. Freshfield took an expedition to the snowy regions of Sikkim. In 1899, 1903, 1906 and 1908 Mrs Fannie Bullock Workman made ascents in the Himalayas, including one of the Nun Kun peaks (23,300 ft). A number of Gurkha sepoys were trained as expert mountaineers by Major the Hon. C. G. Bruce, and a good deal of exploration was accomplished by them.

In 1902, the Eckenstein-Crowley Expedition, led by English mountaineer Oscar Eckenstein and author and occultist Aleister Crowley, was the first to attempt to scale Chogo Ri (now known as K2 in the west). They reached 22,000 feet (6,700 m) before turning back due to weather and other mishaps. Undaunted, in 1905 Aleister Crowley led the first expedition to Kangchenjunga, the third highest mountain in the world. Four members of the party were killed in an avalanche and they failed to reach the summit.

Eckenstien was also a pioneer in developing new equipment and climbing methods. He started using shorter ice axes which could be used single handed, designed the modern crampon and improved on the nail patterns used for the climbing boots.

By the 1950s, all the eight-thousanders but two, had been climbed starting with Annapurna in 1950 by Maurice Herzog and Louis Lachenal. The last great peak was the highest of them all, Mount Everest. The British had made several attempts in the 1920s; the 1922 expedition reached 8,320 metres (27,300 ft) before being aborted on the third summit attempt after an avalanche killed seven porters. The 1924 expedition saw another height record achieved but still failed to reach the summit with confirmation when George Mallory and Andrew Irvine disappeared on the final attempt. The summit was finally reached on May 29, 1953 by Sir Edmund Hillary and Tenzing Norgay from the south side in Nepal.

Just a few months later, Hermann Buhl made the first ascent of Nanga Parbat (8,125 m), a siege-style expedition culminating in a remarkable solo push for the summit, it remains the only eight-thousander to be summited solo on the first ascent. K2 (8,611 m), the second-highest peak in the world, was first scaled in 1954 by Lino Lacedelli and Achille Compagnoni. In 1964, the final eight-thousander to be climbed was Shishapangma (8,013 m), the lowest of all the 8,000 metre peaks.

TECHNIQUE

Snow

Compacted snow conditions allow mountaineers to progress on foot. Frequently crampons are required to travel efficiently over snow and ice. Crampons have 8-14 spikes and are attached to a mountaineer's boots. They are used on hard snow (neve) and ice to provide additional traction. Using various techniques from alpine skiing and mountaineering to ascend/descend a mountain is a form of the sport by itself, called ski mountaineering. Ascending and descending a snow slope safely requires the use of an ice axe and many different footwork techniques that have been developed over the past century, mainly in Europe (e.g. French technique and German technique).

The progression of footwork from the lowest angle slopes to the steepest terrain is first to splay the feet to a rising traverse, to kicking steps, to front pointing the crampons. The progression of ice axe technique from the lowest angle slopes to the steepest terrain is to use the ice axe first as a walking stick, then a stake, then to use the front pick as a dagger below the shoulders or above, and finally to swinging the pick into the slope over the head. These various techniques may involve questions of differing ice-axe design depending on terrain, and even whether a mountaineer uses one or two ice axes. Anchors for the rope in snow are sometimes unreliable, and include the snow stakes, called pickets, deadman devices called flukes which are fashioned from aluminium, or devised from buried objects that might include an ice axe, skis, rocks or other objects. Bollards, which are simply carved out of consolidated snow or ice, also sometimes serve as anchors.

Glaciers

When travelling over glaciers, crevasses pose a grave danger. These giant cracks in the ice are not always visible as snow can be blown and freeze over the top to make a *snowbridge*. At times snowbridges can be as thin as a few inches. Climbers use a system of ropes to protect themselves from such hazards. Basic gear for glacier travel includes crampons and ice axes. Teams of two to five climbers tie into a rope equally spaced. If a climber begins to fall the other members of the team perform a self-arrest to stop the fall. The other members of the team enact a crevasse rescue to pull the fallen climber from the crevasse.

Ice

Multiple methods are used to safely travel over ice. If the terrain is steep but not vertical, then the lead climber can place ice screws in the ice and attach the rope for protection. Each climber on the team must clip past the anchor, and the last climber picks up the anchor itself. Occasionally, slinged icicles or bollards are also used. This allows for safety should the entire team be taken off their feet. This technique is known as Simul-climbing and is sometimes also used on steep snow and easy rock.

If the terrain becomes too steep, standard ice climbing techniques are used in which each climber is belayed, moving one at a time.

SHELTER

Climbers use a few different forms of shelter depending on the situation and conditions. Shelter is a very important aspect of safety for the climber as the weather in the mountains may be very unpredictable. Tall mountains may require many days of camping on the mountain.

Base Camp

The "Base Camp" of a mountain is an area used for staging an attempt at the summit. Base camps are positioned to be safe from the harsher conditions above. There are base camps on many popular or dangerous mountains. Where the summit cannot be reached from base camp in a single day, a mountain will have additional camps above base camp. For example, the southeast ridge route on Mount Everest has Base Camp plus (normally) camps I through IV.

Hut

The European alpine regions, in particular, have a network of mountain huts (called "refuges" in France, "rifugi" in Italy, "cabanes" in Switzerland, "Hütten" in Germany and Austria, "Bothies" in Scotland, "koèa" in Slovenia, "chaty" in Slovakia, "refugios" in Spain, "hytte" or "koie" in Norway, and "cabane" in Romanian). Such huts exist at many different heights, including in the high mountains themselves – in extremely remote areas, more rudimentary shelters may exist. The mountain huts are of varying size and quality, but each is typically centred on a communal dining room and have dormitories equipped with mattresses, blankets or duvets, and pillows; guests are expected to bring and to use their own sleeping bag liner.

The facilities are usually rudimentary but, given their locations, huts offer vital shelter, make routes more widely accessible (by allowing journeys to be broken and reducing the weight of equipment needing to be carried), and offer good value. In Europe, all huts are staffed during the summer (mid-June to mid-September) and some are staffed in the spring (mid-March to mid-May). Elsewhere, huts may also be open in the fall. Huts also may have a part that is always open, but unmanned, a so-called winter hut. When open and manned, the huts are generally run by full-time employees, but some are staffed on a voluntary basis by members of Alpine clubs (such as Swiss Alpine Club and Club alpin français) or in North America by Alpine Club of Canada. The manager of the hut, termed a guardian or warden in Europe, will usually also sell refreshments and meals; both to those visiting only for the day and to those staying overnight.

The offering is surprisingly wide; given that most supplies, often including fresh water, must be flown in by helicopter, and may include glucose-based snacks (such as Mars and Snickers bars) on which climbers and walkers wish to stock up, cakes and pastries made at the hut, a variety of hot and cold drinks (including beer and wine), and high carbohydrate dinners in the evenings. Not all huts offer a catered service, though, and visitors may need to provide for themselves. Some huts offer facilities for both, enabling visitors wishing to keep costs down to bring their own food and cooking equipment and to cater using the facilities provided. Booking for overnight stays at huts is deemed obligatory, and in many cases is essential as some popular huts; even with more than 100 bed spaces may be full during good weather and at weekends.

Once made, the cancellation of a reservation is advised as a matter of courtesy – and, indeed, potentially of safety, as many huts keep a record of where climbers and walkers state they planned to walk to next. Most huts may be contacted by telephone and most take credit cards as a means of payment. In the UK the term Hut is used for any cottage or cabin used as a base for walkers or climbers and these are mostly owned by mountaineering clubs for use by members or visiting clubs and generally do not have wardens or permanent staff, but have cooking and washing facilities and heating. In the Scottish Highlands small simple unmanned shelters without cooking facilities known as Bothies are maintained to break up cross country long routes and act as base camps to certain mountains.

Bivouac (bivy or bivvy)

In the mountaineering context, a bivouac or "biv(v)y" is a makeshift resting or sleeping arrangement in which the climber has less than the full complement of shelter, food and equipment that would normally be present at a conventional campsite. This may involve simply getting a sleeping bag and Bivouac sack/bivvy bag and lying down to sleep. Typically bivvy bags are made from breathable waterproof membranes, which move moisture away from the climber into the outside environment while preventing outside moisture from entering the bag. Many times small partially sheltered areas such as a bergschrund, cracks in rocks or a trench dug in the snow are used to provide additional shelter from wind. These techniques were originally used only in emergency; however some climbers steadfastly committed to alpine style climbing specifically plan for bivouacs in order to save the weight of a tent when suitable snow conditions or time is unavailable for construction of a snow cave. The principal hazard associated with bivouacs is the greater level of exposure to cold and other elements present in harsh conditions high on the mountain.

Tent

Tents are the most common form of shelter used on the mountain. These may vary from simple tarps to much heavier designs intended to withstand harsh mountain conditions. In exposed positions, windbreaks of snow or rock may be required to shelter the tent. One of the downsides to tenting is that high winds and snow loads can be dangerous and may ultimately lead to the tent's failure and collapse. In addition, the constant flapping of the tent fabric can hinder sleep and raise doubts about the security of the shelter. When choosing a tent, alpinists tend to rely on specialised mountaineering tents that are specifically designed for high winds and moderate to heavy snow loads. Tent stakes can be buried in the snow ("deadman") for extra security.

Snow Cave

Where conditions permit snow caves are another way to shelter high on the mountain. Some climbers do not use tents at high altitudes unless the snow conditions do not allow for snow caving, since snow caves are silent and much warmer than tents. They can be built relatively easily, given sufficient time, using a snow shovel. A correctly made snow cave will hover around freezing, which relative to outside temperatures can be very warm. They can be dug anywhere where there is at least four feet of snow. The addition of a good quality bivvy bag and closed cell foam sleeping mat will also increase the warmth of the snow cave. Another shelter that works well is a quinzee, which is excavated from a pile of snow that has been work hardened or sintered (typically by stomping). Igloos are used by some climbers, but are deceptively difficult to build and require specific snow conditions.

HAZARDS

Mountaineering is considered to be one of the most dangerous activities in the world. Loss of life is not uncommon on most major extreme altitude mountaineering destinations every year. Dangers in mountaineering are sometimes divided into two categories: objective hazards that exist without regard to the climber's presence, like rockfall, avalanches and inclement weather, and subjective hazards that relate only to factors introduced by the climber. Equipment failure and falls due to inattention, fatigue or inadequate technique are examples of subjective hazards. A route continually swept by avalanches and storms is said to have a high level of objective danger, whereas a technically far more difficult route that is relatively safe from these dangers may be regarded as objectively safer.

In all, mountaineers must concern themselves with dangers: falling rocks, falling ice, snow-avalanches, the climber falling, falls from ice slopes, falls down snow slopes, falls into crevasses and the dangers from altitude and weather. To select and follow a route using one's skills and experience to mitigate these dangers is to exercise the climber's craft.

Falling Rocks

Every rock mountain is slowly disintegrating due to erosion, the process being especially rapid above the snow-line. Rock faces are constantly swept by falling stones, which may be possible to dodge. Falling rocks tend to form furrows in a mountain face, and these furrows (couloirs) have to be ascended with caution, their sides often being safe when the middle is stoneswept. Rocks fall more frequently on some days than on others, according to the recent weather. Ice formed during the night may temporarily bind rocks to the face but warmth of the day or lubricating water from melting snow or rain may easily dislodge these rocks. Local experience is a valuable help on determining typical rock fall on such routes.

The direction of the dip of rock strata sometimes determines the degree of danger on a particular face; the character of the rock must also be considered. Where stones fall frequently debris will be found below, whilst on snow slopes falling stones cut furrows visible from a great distance. In planning an ascent of a new peak or an unfamiliar route, mountaineers must look for such traces. When falling stones get mixed in considerable quantity with slushy snow or water a mud avalanche is formed (common in the Himalayas). It is vital to avoid camping in their possible line of fall.

Falling Ice

The places where ice may fall can always be determined beforehand. It falls in the broken parts of glaciers (seracs) and from overhanging cornices formed on the crests of narrow ridges. Large icicles are often formed on steep rock faces, and these fall frequently in fine weather following cold and stormy days. They have to be avoided like falling stones. Seracs are slow in formation, and slow in arriving (by glacier motion) at a condition of unstable equilibrium. They generally fall in or just after the hottest part of the day. A skillful and experienced ice-man will usually devise a safe route through a most intricate ice-fall, but such places should be avoided in the afternoon of a hot day. Hanging glaciers (i.e. glaciers perched on steep slopes) often discharge themselves over steep rock-faces, the snout breaking off at intervals. They can always be detected by their debris below. Their track should be avoided.

Falls from Rocks

A rock climber's skill is shown by their choice of handhold and foothold, and their adhesion to the holds once chosen. Much depends on the ability to estimate the capability of the rock to support the weight placed on it. Many loose rocks are quite firm enough to bear a person's weight, but experience is needed to know which can be trusted, and skill is required in transferring the weight to them without jerking. On rotten rocks the rope must be handled with special care, lest it should dislodge loose stones on to those below. Similar care must be given to handholds and footholds, for the same reason. When a horizontal traverse has to be made across very difficult rocks, a dangerous situation may arise unless at both ends of the traverse there are firm positions. Mutual assistance on hard rocks takes all manner of forms: two, or even three, people climbing on one another's shoulders, or using an ice axe propped up by others for a foothold. The great principle is that of co-operation, all the members of the party climbing with reference to the others, and not as independent units; each when moving must know what the climber in front and the one behind are doing. After bad weather steep rocks are often found covered with a veneer of ice (verglas), which may even render them inaccessible. Crampons are useful on such occasions.

STYLES OF MOUNTAINEERING

There are two main styles of mountaineering: Expedition style and Alpine style.

A mountaineer who adopts Alpine style is referred to as an Alpine Mountaineer. Alpine Mountaineers are typically found climbing in *medium-sized* glaciated mountain areas such as the Alps or Rocky Mountains. Medium-sized generally refers to altitudes in the *intermediate altitude* (7,000' to 12,000') and first half of *high altitude* (12,000' to 18,000') ranges. However, alpine style ascents have been done throughout history on *extreme altitude* (18,000' to 29,000') peaks also, albeit in lower volume to expedition style ascents. Alpine style refers to a particular style of mountain climbing that involves a mixture of snow climbing, ice climbing, rock climbing, and glacier travel, where climbers generally single carry their loads between camps, in a single push for the summit. Light and fast is the mantra of the Alpine Mountaineer.

The term alpine style contrasts with expedition style (as commonly undertaken in the Himalayan region or other large ranges of the world), which could be viewed as slow and heavy, where climbers may use porters, pack animals, glacier airplanes, cooks, multiple carries between camps, usage of fixed lines etc. A mountaineer who adopts this style of climbing is referred to as an Expedition Mountaineer. Expedition mountaineers still employ the skill sets of the alpine mountaineer, except they have to deal with even higher altitudes, expanded time scale, longer routes, foreign logistics, more severe weather, and additional skills unique to expeditionary climbing. The prevalence of expedition style climbing in the Himalaya is largely a function of the nature of the mountains in the region. Because Himalayan base camps can take days or weeks to trek to, and Himalayan mountains can take weeks or perhaps even months to climb, a large number of personnel and amount of supplies are necessary.

This is why expedition style climbing is frequently used on large and isolated peaks in the Himalaya. In Europe and North America there is less of a need for expedition style climbing on most medium-sized mountains. These mountains can often be easily accessed by car or air, are at a lower altitude and can be climbed in a shorter time scale. Expedition style mountaineering can be found in the larger high altitude and extreme altitude North American ranges such as the Alaska Range and Saint Elias Mountains. These remote mountaineering destinations can require up to a 2 week trek by foot, just to make it to base camp. Most expeditions in these regions choose a glacier flight to basecamp. Route length in days from basecamp can vary in these regions, typically from 10 days to 1 month during the climbing season. Winter mountaineering on major peaks in these ranges can generally consume between 30 to 60 days depending on the route, and can generally only be tackled via expedition style mountaineering during this season.

The differences between, and advantages and disadvantages of, the two kinds of climbing are as follows:

Expedition Style

- Uses multiple trips between camps to carry supplies up to higher camps
- Group sizes are often larger than alpine style climbs because more supplies are carried between camps

- Fixed lines are often used to minimize the danger involved in continually moving between camps
- Supplemental oxygen is frequently used
- Higher margin of safety in relation to equipment, food, time, and ability to wait out storms at high camps
- Avoidance of being trapped in storms at high altitudes and being forced to descend in treacherous avalanche conditions
- Possible higher exposure to objective hazards such as avalanches or rockfall, due to slower travel times between camps
- Higher capital expenditures
- Longer time scale

Alpine Style

- Climbers only climb the route once because they do not continually climb up and down between camps with supplies
- Fewer supplies are used on the climb therefore fewer personnel are needed
- Alpine style ascents do not leave the climber exposed to objective hazards as long as an expedition style climb does; however, because of the speed of the ascent relative to an expedition style climb there is less time for acclimatization
- Supplemental oxygen is not used
- Danger of being trapped at high altitude due to storms, potentially being exposed to HAPE or HACE
- Lower capital expenditures
- Shorter time scale

3

Understanding the Adventure Tourism Management

In this course you will learn about the essential features of tourism industry, definition and meaning of various concepts, how to make travel arrangements, travel management, tourism marketing, tourism in India including emerging dimensions. In this session you will understand the different perspectives on the study of tourism, know the meaning of the term 'tourism', 'visitor tourist', 'excursionist', 'inbound' and 'outbound tourist' and the difference between travel and tourism.

CHANGING FACETS OF TOURISM

From the very inception of life, travel has fascinated man. Travel and tourism have been important social activities of human beings from time immemorial. The urge to explore new places within one's own country or outside and seek a change of environment and experience has been experienced from ancient times. Tourism is one of the world's most rapidly growing industries.

Much of its growth is due to higher disposable incomes, increased leisure time and falling costs of travel. As airports become more enjoyable places to pass through, as travel agency services become increasingly automated, and as tourists find it easier to get information on places they want to visit, tourism grows. The Internet has fuelled the growth of the travel industry by providing on line booking facilities. It has also provided people with the power to explore destinations and cultures from their home personal computers and make informed choices before finalizing travel plans. With its immense information resources, the Internet allows tourists to scrutinise hotels, check weather forecasts, read up on local food and even talk to other tourists around the world about their travel experiences for a chosen destination. This new trend has made the tourism job very challenging.

The holiday makers want a good rate of return on their investment. They are to be lured with value additions and improved customer service. This also put emphasis on the regular flow of manpower with specific skills at the appropriate levels to match and cater to global standards. The success of the hospitality industry comes from provision of quality rooms, food, service and ambience. There is no doubt that fitness has increasingly become a larger part of everyone's life. And business and leisure travellers alike look to maintain their fitness goals while away from home.

Awareness should be created about the environment and education. A collective effort and co-operation with powerful networking are the need of the hour. People should be acting as the watchdogs of the society as far as environmental issues are concerned. Eco-tourists are a growing community and tourism promotions have to adopt such eco-practices which could fit this growing community. Another growing trend in the tourism scene is the Incentive Market and the scope of the destination to attract conferences and convention traffic.

Here the prospects are better for those destinations where state of the art infrastructure has been developed along with a safe and clean image. Tourism today is much more than just developing products. It is more about quality, insightful thinking and ability to have global information about technology, partners, contacts and responding quickly to global and regional trends.

The fundamental task before tourism promotion is to facilitate integration of the various components in the tourism trade as active participants in the nation's social and cultural life. There is a long road ahead. All must work towards a society where people can work and participate as equal partners. Tourism should be a vehicle for international cooperation and understanding of the various civilizations and a harbinger of peace. From the foregoing we can see how fast the face of tourism is changing and how challenging the job of travel agencies is now. There is therefore a need for proper training of the personnel working in the industry through thorough and a detailed study of the subject A unified approach to the subject is also needed since at present people from different fields have been studying tourism from different perspectives.

DIFFERENT PERSPECTIVES ON THE STUDY OF TOURISM

GEOGRAPHICAL PERSPECTIVE

Geographical Perspective—from a geographer's perspective the main concern of tourism is to look into aspects like the geographical location of a place, the climate, the landscape, the environment, the physical planning and the changes in these emerging from provisioning of tourism facilities and amenities. A geographer feels that it is the climate, landscape or physical attributes which draw the tourist to a destination, for example; if a person from Delhi goes to Shimla in the summer he does so because of the cooler climate which he cannot get in Delhi

SOCIOLOGICAL PERSPECTIVE

From a sociologist's perspective Tourism is a social activity; it is about interaction between different communities—hosts and guests—and encounter between different cultures. This approach studies social classes, habits and customs of both hosts and guests in terms of tourism behaviour of individuals or groups of people and the impact of tourism on society.

HISTORICAL PERSPECTIVE

An historian's perspective tourism is a study of the factors instrumental in the initiation of tourism to a particular destination, the order of happenings leading to tourism development, the reasons for happening of the occurrences in that order, beneficiaries of the tourist activity and an untimely and premature identification of negative effects. For example we all know that a lot of tourists visit Taj Mahal in Agra but a historian would be interested in studying the factors that bring the tourist there, *e.g.* the architecture, the story behind the monument, or something else that draws them there.

MANAGERIAL PERSPECTIVE

The management perspective tourism is an industry, and therefore needs managerial skills in order to be properly managed. As the industry grows we see continuous changes in various organisations and services linked with the industry, the tourism products and so on so this approach concentrates on management activities such as planning, research, pricing, marketing, control etc. as vital to the operation of a tourist establishment.

ECONOMIC PERSPECTIVE

From an economist's perspective tourism is a major source of foreign exchange earnings, a generator of personal and corporate incomes, a creator of employment and a contributor to government earnings. It is a dominant global activity surpassing even trade in oil and manufactured goods. Economists study the effects of tourism industry on the economy. This is a two way process.

THE IMPORTANCE OF MANAGERIAL AND ECONOMIC PERSPECTIVES OF TOURISM

Now due to higher disposable incomes, increased leisure time and falling cost of travel, the Tourism industry has shown a very high growth and since tourism is a service industry it comprises of a number of tangible and intangible components. The tangible elements include transport systems—air, rail, road, water and now, space; hospitality services—accommodation, food and beverage, tours, souvenirs; and related services such as banking, insurance and safety and security. The intangible elements include: rest and relaxation, culture, escape, adventure, new and different experiences. As there are number of bodies involved the need arises for a management of services related to this industry and so the study of Tourism acquires a great practical necessity and usefulness. Tourism industry is very fast growing and this industry involves activities and interests of Transport Undertakings, Owners of Tourist Sites and Attractions, Various tourist Service Providers at the tourist destinations and Central and Local Government, etc.

Each of these serves both the resident population and the tourists and their management must reconcile the needs of tourists with the needs of the resident population. So it becomes important to study tourism from the perspective of Management, since the management of various bodies in this industry is invaded.

TOURISM IN INDIA—DEFINITION AND MEANING

Tourism is the largest service industry in India, with a contribution of 6.23% to the national GDP and 8.78% of the total employment in India. India witnesses more than 5 million annual foreign tourist arrivals and 562 million domestic tourism visits. The tourism industry in India generated about US$100 billion in 2008 and that is expected to increase to US$275.5 billion by 2018 at a 9.4% annual growth rate. The Ministry of Tourism is the nodal agency for the development and promotion of tourism in India and maintains the "Incredible India" campaign.

World Travel and Tourism Council, India will be a tourism hotspot from 2009–2018, having the highest 10-year growth potential. The Travel and Tourism Competitiveness Report 2007 ranked tourism in India 6th in terms of price competitiveness and 39th in terms of safety and security. Despite short- and medium-term setbacks, such as shortage of hotel rooms, tourism revenues are expected to surge by 42% from 2007 to 2017. India has a growing medical tourism sector. The 2010 Commonwealth Games in Delhi are expected to significantly boost tourism in India.

TOURISM BY STATE

Andhra Pradesh

Andhra Pradesh has a rich cultural heritage and a variety of tourist attractions. The state of Andhra Pradesh comprises scenic hills, forests, beaches and temples. Also known as The City of Nizams and The City of Pearls, Hyderabad is today one of the most developed cities in the country and a modern hub of information technology, ITES, and biotechnology. Hyderabad is known for its rich history, culture and architecture representing its unique character as a meeting point for North and South India, and also its multilingual culture. Andhra Pradesh is the home of many religious pilgrim centres. Tirupati, the abode of Lord Venkateswara, is the richest and most visited religious centre in the world. Srisailam, the abode of Sri Mallikarjuna, is one of twelve Jyothirlingalu in India, Amaravati's Siva temple is one of the Pancharamams, and Yadagirigutta, the abode of an avatara of Vishnu, Sri Lakshmi Narasimha.

The Ramappa temple and Thousand Pillars temple in Warangal are famous for some fine temple carvings. The state has numerous Buddhist centres at Amaravati, Nagarjuna Konda, Bhattiprolu, Ghantasala, Nelakondapalli, Dhulikatta, Bavikonda, Thotlakonda, Shalihundam, Pavuralakonda, Sankaram, Phanigiri and Kolanpaka.

The golden beaches at Visakhapatnam, the one-million-year old limestone caves at Borra, picturesque Araku Valley, hill resorts of Horsley Hills, river Godavari racing through a narrow gorge at Papi Kondalu, waterfalls at Ettipotala, Kuntala and rich bio-diversity at Talakona, are some of the natural attractions of the state. Visakhapatnam is home to many tourist attactions such as the INS Karasura Submarine museum, Yarada Beach, Araku Valley, VUDA Park, Indira Gandhi Zoological Gardens.

The weather in Andhra Pradesh is mostly tropical and the best time to visit is in November through to January. The monsoon season commences in June and ends in September, so travel would not be advisable during this period. Also worth visiting, the only Indian Buddhism Based Theme Park and Resorts on the Vijayawada—Guntur Highway—Agrigold Haailand.

Arunachal Pradesh

Arunachal Pradesh attracts tourists from many parts of the world. Tourist attractions include Tawang, a beautiful town famous for its Buddhist monastery, Ziro, famous for cultural festivals, the Namdapha tiger project in Changlang district and Sela lake near Bomdila with its bamboo bridges overhanging the river. Religious places of interest include Malinithan in Lekhabali, Rukhmininagar near Roing and Parshuram Kund in Lohit district. Rafting and trekking are common activities. A visitor's permit from the tourism department is required. Places like Tuting have wonderful, undiscovered scenic beauty.

Assam

Assam is the central state in the North-East Region of India and serves as the gateway to the rest of the Seven Sister States. Assam boasts of famous wildlife preserves–the Kaziranga National Park, which is home to the Great Indian One-Horned Rhinoceros and the Manas National Park, the largest river island Majuli, historic Sivasagar, famous for the ancient monuments of Ahom Kingdom, the city of eternal romance, Tezpur and tea-estates dating back to time of British Raj. The weather is mostly sub-tropical.

Assam experiences the Indian monsoon and has one of the highest forest densities in India. The winter months are the best time to visit. Assam has a rich cultural heritage going back to the Ahom Kingdom, which governed the region for many centuries before the British occupation. Other notable features include the Brahmaputra River, the mystery of the bird suicides in Jatinga, numerous temples including Kamakhya of Tantric sect. 'Gurdwara Sri Guru Tegh Bahadur also known as Damdama Sahib at Dhubri '. This famous Gurudwara is situated in the heart of the Dhubri Town on the bank of the mighty Brahmaputra river in far north-east India. Guru Nanak the first Sikh Guru visited this place in 1505 and met Srimanta Sankardeva as the Guru travelled from Dhaka to Assam, ruins of palaces, etc. Guwahati, the capital city of Assam, boasts many bazaars, temples, and wildlife sanctuaries.

Bihar

Bihar is one of the oldest continuously inhabited places in the world with history of 3000 years. The rich culture and heritage of Bihar is evident from the innumerable ancient monuments that are dotted all over this state in eastern India. This is the Place of Aryabhata, Great Ashoka, Chanakya and many more.

Attractions:

- *Patna*: The capital of Bihar, famous for its rich history and royal architecture. Golghar and Budha Smriti Park are famous lanmarks.
- *Gaya*: Known for Bodh Gaya the place at which Gautam Buddha attained enlightenment.Attraction for Buddhists across the globe.
- *Barauni*: Petrochemical work for national level
- *Muzaffarpur*: Famous for its education.
- *Kesariya*: World's largest Buddhist Stupa located here.
- *Nalanda*: World's oldest university remains here.
- *Sasaram*: Tomb of Sher Shah Suri, the great Emperor of Mughal age who defeated Humayun.
- *Sonpur*: The Sonepur Cattle Fair or Sonepur Mela,it is the biggest cattle fair of Asia and stretches on from fifteen days to one month.
- *Takht Sri Patna Sahib*: One of the famous Sikh pilgrimage known for the birth place of Sikh's Tenth Guru Sri Guru Gobind Singh Sahib.

Bihar is one of the most sacred places of various religions such as Hinduism, Buddhism, Jainism, Sikhism and Islam. Famous Attraction includes Mahabodhi Temple, a Buddhist shrine and UNESCO World Heritage Site is also situated in Bihar, Barabar Caves the oldest rockcut caves in India, Khuda Bakhsh Oriental Library the Oldest Library of India.

Delhi

Delhi is the capital city of India. A fine blend of old and new, ancient and modern, Delhi is a melting pot of cultures, religions. Delhi has been the capital of numerous empires that ruled India, making it rich in history. The rulers left behind their trademark architectural styles. Delhi currently has many renowned historic monuments and landmarks such as the Tughlaqabad fort, Qutub Minar, Purana Quila, Lodhi Gardens, Jama Masjid, Humayun's tomb, Red Fort, and Safdarjung's Tomb. Modern monuments include Jantar Mantar, India

Gate, Rashtrapati Bhavan, Laxminarayan Temple, Lotus temple and Akshardham Temple. New Delhi is famous for its British colonial architecture, wide roads, and tree-lined boulevards. Delhi is home to numerous political landmarks, national museums, Islamic shrines, Hindu temples, green parks, and trendy malls.

Goa

Goa is one of the most famous tourist destinations in India. A former colony of Portugal, Goa is famous for its excellent beaches, Portuguese churches, Hindu temples, and wildlife sanctuaries. The Basilica of Bom Jesus, Mangueshi Temple, Dudhsagar Falls, and Shantadurga are famous attractions in Goa. Recently a Wax Museum has also opened in Old Goa housing a number of wax personalities of Indian history, culture and heritage. The Goa Carnival is a world famous event, with colourful masks and floats, drums and reverberating music, and dance performances. The celebrations run three days culminating in a carnival parade on fat Tuesday.

Himachal Pradesh

Himachal Pradesh is famous for its Himalayan landscapes and popular hill-stations. Many outdoor activities such as rock climbing, mountain biking, paragliding, ice-skating, and heli-skiing are popular tourist attractions in Himachal Pradesh. Shimla, the state capital, is very popular among tourists. The Kalka-Shimla Railway is a Mountain railway which is a UNESCO World Heritage Site. Shimla is also a famous skiing attraction in India. Other popular hill stations include Manali and Kasauli. Dharamshala, home of the Dalai Lama, is known for its Tibetan monasteries and Buddhist temples. Many trekking expeditions also begin here.

Jammu and Kashmir

Jammu and Kashmir is the northernmost state of India. Jammu is noted for its scenic landscape, ancient temples, Hindu shrines, castles, gardens and forts. The Hindu holy shrines of Amarnath in kashmir attracts about.4 million Hindu devotees every year. Vaishno Devi alsoattract tens of thousands of Hindu devotees every year. Jammu's historic monuments feature a unique blend of Islamic and Hindu architecture styles.

Tourism forms an integral part of the Kashmiri economy. Often dubbed "Paradise on Earth", Kashmir's mountainous landscape has attracted tourists for centuries. Notable places are Dal Lake, Srinagar Phalagam, Gulmarg, Yeusmarg and Mughal Gardens etc. Kashmir's natural landscape has made it one of the popular destinations for adventure tourism in South Asia.Marked by four distinct seasons,Ski enthusiasts can enjoy the exotic himalayan powder during winters.

7000000 tourists arrived in kashmir in the months of April,May and June alone In recent years, Ladakh has emerged as a major hub for adventure tourism. This part of Greater Himalaya called "moon on earth" comprising of naked peaks and deep gorges was once known for the silk route to High Asia from the subcontinent. Leh is also a growing tourist spot.

Karnataka

Karnataka has been ranked as fourth most popular destination for tourism among states of India. It has the second highest number of protected monuments in India, at 507. Kannada dynasties like Kadambas, Western Gangas, Chalukyas, Rashtrakutas, Hoysalas and Vijayanagaras, ruled Karnataka particularly North Karnataka. They built great monuments to Buddhism, Jainism, Shaivism. The monuments are still present at Badami, Aihole, Pattadakal, Hampi, Lakshmeshwar, Sudi, Hooli, Mahadeva Temple, Dambal, Lakkundi, Gadag, Hangal, Halasi, Galaganatha, Chaudayya-danapura, Banavasi, Belur, Halebidu, Shravanabelagola, Sannati and many more. Notable Islamic monuments are present at Bijapur, Bidar, Gulbarga, Raichur and other part of the state.

Gol Gumbaz at Bijapur, has the second largest pre-modern dome in the world after the Byzantine Hagia Sophia. Karnataka has two World heritage sites, at Hampi and Pattadakal, both are in North Karnataka. Karnataka is famous for its waterfalls. Jog falls of Shimoga District is one of the highest waterfalls in Asia. This state has 21 wildlife sanctuaries and five National parks and is home to more than 500 species of birds. Karnataka has many beaches at Karwar, Gokarna, Murdeshwara, Surathkal. Karnataka is a rock climbers paradise. Yana in Uttara Kannada, Fort in Chitradurga, Ramnagara near Bangalore district, Shivagange in Tumkur district and tekal in Kolar district are a rock climbers heaven.

Kerala

Kerala is a state on the tropical Malabar Coast of southwestern India. Nicknamed as one of the "10 paradises of the world" by National Geographic, Kerala is famous especially for its ecotourism initiatives. Its unique culture and traditions, coupled with its varied demography, has made it one of the most popular tourist destinations in India. Growing at a rate of 13.31%, the tourism industry significantly contributes to the state's economy. Kerala is known for its tropical backwaters and pristine beaches such as Kovalam.

Madhya Pradesh

Madhya Pradesh is called the "Heart of India" because of its location in the centre of the country. It has been home to the cultural heritage of Hinduism, Islam, Buddhism, Sikhism, Jainism. Innumerable monuments, exquisitely carved temples, stupas, forts and palaces are dotted all over the State. The temples of Khajuraho are world-famous for their erotic sculptures, and are a UNESCO World Heritage Site. Gwalior is famous for its forts, the Tomb of Rani Lakshmibai, and the Palace of Tansen. Madhya Pradesh is also known as Tiger State because of the tiger population. Famous national parks like Kanha, Bandhavgadh, Shivpuri, Sanjay, Pench are located in MP. Spectacular mountain ranges, meandering rivers and miles and miles of dense forests offering a unique and exciting panorama of wildlife in sylvan surroundings.

Maharashtra

Maharashtra is the second most visited state in India by foreign tourists, with more than 2 million foreign tourists arrivals annually. Maharashtra boasts of a large number of popular and revered religious venues that are heavily frequented by locals as well as out-of-state visitors. Ajanta Caves, Ellora Caves and Chhatrapati Shivaji Terminus are the three UNESCO World Heritage sites in Maharashtra and are highly responsible for the development of Tourism in the state. Mumbai is the most cosmopolitan city in India, and a great place to experience modern India.

Mumbai famous for Bollywood, the world's largest film industry. In addition, Mumbai is famous for its clubs, shopping, and upscale gastronomy. The city is known for its architecture, from the ancient Elephanta Caves, to the Islamic Haji Ali Mosque, to the colonial architecture of Bombay High Court and Chhatrapati Shivaji Terminus. Maharashtra also has numerous adventure tourism destinations, including paragliding, rock climbing, canoeing, kayaking, snorkeling, and scuba diving in places like Kolad, Tarkarli, Koyna, Manor. aharashtra also has several pristine national parks and reserves, some of the best ones are Tadoba with excellent accommodation and safari experiences besides little known by amazing wildlife destinations like Koyna, Nagzira, Melghat, Dajipur, Radhanagari and of course the only national park within metropolic city limits in the world—Sanjay Gandhi National Park.

The Bibi Ka Maqbara at Aurangabad the Mahalakshmi temple at Kolhapur, the cities of Nashik, Trimbak famous for religious importance and the city of Pune the seat of the Maratha Empire and the fantastic Ganesh Chaturthi celebrations together contribute for the Tourism sector of Mahrashtra.

Manipur

Manipur as the name suggest is a land of jewels. Its rich culture excels in every aspects as in martial arts, dance, theater and sculpture. The charm of the place is the greenery with the moderate climate making it a tourists' heaven.

The beautiful and seasonal Shirui Lily at Ukhrul, Sangai and the floating islands at Loktak Lake are few of the rare things found in Manipur. Polo, which can be called a royal game, also originated from Manipur.

Some of the main tourist attractions are:

- Imphal
- Churachandpur
- Keibul Lamjao National Park

- War cemeteries
- Loktak Lake
- Shree Govindajee Temple
- Moreh

Meghalaya

Meghalaya has some of the thickest surviving forests in the country and therefore constitutes one of the most important ecotourism circuits in the country today. The Meghalayan subtropical forests support a vast variety of flora and fauna. Meghalaya has 2 National Parks and 3 Wildlife Sanctuaries. Meghalaya also offers many adventure tourism opportunities in the form of mountaineering, rock climbing, trekking and hiking, water sports etc.

The state offers several trekking routes some of which also afford and opportunity to encounter some rare animals such as the slow loris, assorted deer and bear. The Umiam Lake has a water sports complex with facilities such as rowboats, paddleboats, sailing boats, cruise-boats, water-scooters and speedboats. Cherrapunjee is one of the most popular tourist spots in North East of India. It lies to the south of the capital Shillong. The town is very well known and needs little publicity. A rather scenic, 50 kilometer long road, connects Cherrapunjee with Shillong. The popular waterfalls in the state are the Elephant Falls, Shadthum Falls, Weinia falls, Bishop Falls, Nohkalikai Falls, Langshiang Falls and Sweet Falls. The hot springs at Jakrem near Mawsynram are believed to have curative and medicinal properties.

Orissa

Orissa has been a preferred destination from ancient days for people who have an interest in spirituality, religion, culture, art and natural beauty. Ancient and medieval architecture, pristine sea beaches, the classical and ethnic dance forms and a variety of festivals. Orissa has kept the religion of Buddhism alive. Rock-edicts that have challenged time stand huge and over-powering by the banks of the river Daya.

The torch of Buddhism is still ablaze in the sublime triangle at Udayagiri, Lalitagiri and Ratnagiri, on the banks of river Birupa. Precious fragments of a glorious past come alive in the shape of stupas, rock-cut caves, rock-edicts, excavated monasteries, viharas, chaityas and sacred relics in caskets and the Rock-edicts of Ashoka. Orissa is also famous for its well-preserved Hindu Temples, especially the Konark Sun Temple and The Leaning Temple of Huma.

Orissa is the home for various tribal communities who have contributed uniquely to the multicultural and multilingual character of the state. Their handicrafts, different dance forms, jungle products and their unique life style blended with their healing practices have got world wide attention. The Sitalsasthi Carnival is a must see for everyone who wants to see a glimpse of the art and culture of Odisha at one place.

Puducherry

The Union Territory of Puducherry comprises four coastal regions *viz*-Puducherry, Karaikal, Mahe and Yanam. Puducherry is the Capital of this Union Territory and one of the most popular tourist destinations in South India. Puducherry has been described by National Geographic as "a glowing highlight of subcontinental sojourn". The city has many beautiful colonial buildings, churches, temples, and statues, which, combined with the systematic town planning and the well planned French style avenues, still preserve much of the colonial ambience.

Punjab

The state of Punjab is renowned for its cuisine, culture and history. Punjab has a vast public transportation and communication network. Some of the main cities in Punjab are Amritsar, Chandigarh, and Ludhiana.

Punjab also has a rich religious history incorporating Sikhism and Hinduism. Tourism in Punjab is principally suited for the tourists interested in culture, ancient civilization, spirituality and epic history.

Some of the villages in Punjab are also a must see for the person who wants to see the true Punjab, with their beautiful traditional Indian homes, farms and temples, this is a must see for any visitor that goes to Punjab. India-Pakistan border at Wagha is also a popular tourist attraction.

Rajasthan

Rajasthan, literally meaning "Land of the Kings", is one of the most attractive tourist destinations in Northern India. The vast sand dunes of the Thar Desert attract millions of tourists from around the globe every year.

Attractions:

- *Jaipur*: The capital of Rajasthan, famous for its rich history and royal architecture and motidungari lord ganesha temple.
- *Jodhpur*: Fortress-city at the edge of the Thar Desert, famous for its blue homes and architecture.
- *Udaipur*: Known as the "Venice" of India.
- *Jaisalmer*: Famous for its golden fortress.
- *Barmer*: Barmer and surrounding areas offer perfect picture of typical Rajasthani villages.
- *Bikaner*: Famous for its medieval history as a trade route outpost.
- *Mount Abu*: Is the highest peak in the Aravalli Range of Rajasthan.
- *Pushkar*: It has the first and one of the very Brahma temples in the world.
- *Keoladeo Bird Sanctuary*: A UNESCO world heritage site
- *Nathdwara*: This town near Udaipur hosts the famous temple of Shrinathji.
- *Ranthambore*: Situated near Sawai Madhopur, this town has one of the largest and most famous national parks in India.

Sikkim

Originally known as Suk-Heem, which in the local language means "peaceful home", Sikkim was an independent kingdom till the year 1974, when it became a part of the Republic of India. The capital of Sikkim is Gangtok, located approximately 105 kilometers from New Jalpaiguri, the nearest railway station to Sikkim. Although, an airport is under construction at Dekiling in East Sikkim, the nearest airport to Sikkim would be Bagdogra.

Sikkim is considered as the land of Orchids and mystic cultures and colourful traditions. Sikkim is well known among trekkers and adventure lovers, as West Sikkim has a lot to give them. Places near Sikkim include Darjeeling also known as the Queen of hills and Kalimpong. Darjeeling, other than its world famous "Darjeeling tea" is also famous for its refined "Prep schools" founded during the British Raj. Kalimpong is also famous for its flora cultivation and is home to many internationally known Nurseries.

Tamil Nadu

Tamil Nadu is the top state in attracting the maximum number of foreign tourists in India. Tamil Nadu. Marina Beach, Carnatic music, Bharata Natyam dance and country's largest Shopping locality. This city is also famous for Medical tourism and houses Asia's largest hospital. Archaeological sites with civilization dating back to 3800 years are found in Tamil Nadu. With more than 34000 temples this state also holds the credit of having maximum number of UNESCO heritage sites in India which includes Great Living Chola Temples and Mahabalipuram. Country's largest temple srirangam and Pichavaram the world's Second largest Mangrove forest are located in this state. Tamilnadu has some great temples like Madurai Meenakshi Amman Temple, Tanjore Brihadeeswarar Temple, Srirangam Ranganathaswamy Temple and all the mentioned temples has world class architecture that really mesmerize everyone. Kanyakumari is the southernmost tip of India provides sceneic view of sunset and sunshine over the Indian ocean.Hill stations like Yercaud, Kodaikanal, Ooty, Valparai, Yelagiri are widely visited. Velankanni Church and Nagoor Dharga are visited by people of all religion.Water Falls and Wildlife sanctuaries are located across the state.

Uttarakhand

Uttarakhand, the 27th state of the Republic of India, is called "the abode of the Gods". It contains glaciers, snow-clad mountains, valley of flowers, skiing slopes and dense forests, and many shrines and places of pilgrimage. Char-dhams, the four most sacred and revered Hindu temples: Badrinath, Kedarnath, Gangotri and Yamunotri are nestled in the Himalayas. Haridwar which means Gateway to God is the only place on the plains.

It holds the watershed for Gangetic River System spanning 300 km from Satluj in the west to Kali river in the east. Nanda Devi is the second highest peak in India after Kanchenjunga. Dunagiri, Neelkanth, Chaukhamba, Panchachuli, Trisul are other peaks above 23000 Ft. It is considered the abode of Devtas, Yakashyas, Kinners, Fairies and Sages. It boasts of some old hill-stations developed during British era like Mussoorie, Almora and Nainital.

Uttar Pradesh

Situated in the northern part of India, Uttar Pradesh is important with its wealth of monuments and religious fervour. Geographically, Uttar Pradesh is very diverse, with Himalayan foothills in the extreme north and the Gangetic Plain in the centre. It is also home of India's most visited site, the Taj Mahal, and Hinduism's holiest city, Varanasi. The most populous state of the Indian Union also has a rich cultural heritage, and at the heart of North India, Uttar Pradesh has much to offer. Places of interest include Varanasi, Agra, Kanpur, Lucknow, Mathura, Jhansi, Prayag, Sarnath, Ayodhya, Dudhwa National Park and Fatehpur Sikri.

West Bengal

Kolkata, one of the many cities in the state of West Bengal has been nicknamed the City of Palaces. This comes from the numerous palatial mansions built all over the city. Unlike many north Indian cities, whose construction stresses minimalism, the layout of much of the architectural variety in Kolkata owes its origins to European styles and tastes imported by the British and, to a much lesser extent, the Portuguese and French. The buildings were designed and inspired by the tastes of the English gentleman around and the aspiring Bengali Babu. Today, many of these structures are in various stages of decay. Some of the major buildings of this period are well maintained and several buildings have been declared as heritage structures.

From historical point of view, the story of West Bengal begins from Gour and Pandua situated close to the present district town of Malda. The twin medieval cities had been sacked at least once by changing powers in the 15th century. However, ruins from the period still remain, and several architectural specimens still retain the glory and shin of those times. The Hindu architecture of Bishnupur in terracotta and laterite sandstone are renowned world over. Towards the British colonial period came the architecture of Murshidabad and Coochbehar.

NATURE TOURISM

India has geographical diversity, which resulted in varieties of nature tourism.

- Water falls in Western Ghats including Jog falls.
- Western Ghats
- Hill Stations
- Wildlife reserves
- Deserts

Wildlife in India

India is home to several well known large mammals including the Asian Elephant, Bengal Tiger, Asiatic Lion, Leopard and Indian Rhinoceros, often engrained culturally and religiously often being associated with deities. Other well known large Indian mammals include ungulates such as the domestic Asian Water buffalo, wild Asian Water buffalo, Nilgai, Gaur and several species of deer and antelope. Some members of the dog family such as the Indian Wolf, Bengal Fox, Golden Jackal and the Dhole or Wild Dogs are also widely distributed. It is also home to the Striped Hyaena, Macaques, Langurs and Mongoose species. India also has a large variety of protected wildlife. The country's protected forest consists of 75 National parks of India and 421 Sanctuaries, of which 19 fall under the purview of Project Tiger.

Its climatic and geographic diversity makes it the home of over 350 mammals and 1200 bird species, many of which are unique to the subcontinent. Some well known national wildlife sanctuaries include Bharatpur, Corbett, Kanha, Kaziranga, Periyar, Ranthambore, Manas and Sariska. The world's largest mangrove forest Sundarbans is located in southern West Bengal. The Kaziranga National Park,Manas National Park, Sundarbans and Keoladeo National Park is UNESCO World Heritage Site.

Hill Stations

Several hill stations served as summer capitals of Indian provinces, princely states, or, in the case of Shimla, of British India itself. Since Indian Independence, the role of these hill stations as summer capitals has largely ended, but many hill stations remain popular summer resorts.

Most famous hill stations are:

- Mount Abu, Rajasthan
- Pachmarhi, Madhya Pradesh—It is also known as The Queen of Satpura.
- Araku, Andhra Pradesh
- Gulmarg, Srinagar and Ladakh in Jammu and Kashmir
- Darjeeling in West Bengal
- Munnar in Kerala
- Ooty, Yercaud and Kodaikanal in Tamil Nadu
- Shillong in Meghalaya
- Shimla, Kullu in Himachal Pradesh
- Nainital in Uttarakhand
- Gangtok in Sikkim
- Mussoorie in Uttarakhand
- Manali in Himachal Pradesh
- Tawang in Arunachal Pradesh
- Mahabaleshwar in Maharashtra
- Haflong in Assam

In addition to the bustling hill stations and summer capitals of yore, there are several serene and peaceful nature retreats and places of interest to visit for a nature lover. These range from the stunning moonscapes of Leh and Ladhak, to small, exclusive nature retreats such as Dunagiri, Binsar, Mukteshwar in the Himalayas, to rolling vistas of Western Ghats to numerous private retreats in the rolling hills of Kerala.

Beaches

India offers a wide range of tropical beaches with silver/golden sand to coral beaches of Lakshadweep. States like Kerala and Goa have exploited the potential of beaches to the fullest. However, there are a lot many unexploited beaches in the states of Andhra Pradesh, Gujarat, Maharastra, Tamil Nadu and Karnataka. These states have very high potential to be develop them as future destinations for prospective tourists. Some of the famous tourist beaches are:

- Beaches of Vizag, Andhra Pradesh
- Beaches of Puri, Orissa
- Beaches of Digha, West Bengal
- Beaches of Goa
- Kovalam Beach, Kerala
- Marina Beach, Chennai
- City Beach, Puducherry
- Beaches of Mahabalipuram
- Beaches in Mumbai
- Beaches of Diu
- Beaches of Midnapore, West Bengal
- Beaches of Andaman and Nicobar Islands
- Beaches of Lakshadweep Islands

Adventure Tourism

- River rafting and kayaking in Himalayas
- Mountain climbing in Himalayas
- Rock climbing in Madhya Pradesh
- Skiing in Gulmarg or Auli
- Boat racing in Bhopal
- Paragliding in Maharashtra

DIFFERENCES BETWEEN TRAVEL AND TOURISM

Though the words Travel and Tourism are synonymised and used interchangeably but Tourism is a wider concept and encompasses a lot more than travel alone. Travel implies journeys undertaken from one place to another for any purpose including journeys to work and as a part of employment, as a part of leisure and to take up residence; whereas Tourism includes the journey to a destination and also the stay at a destination outside one's usual place of residence and the activities undertaken for leisure and recreation. All tourism includes some travel, but not all travel is tourism.A person may often travel for a wide variety of purposes of which tourism is only one. However if properly handled, a part of the travel for non tourism purposes can be motivated into travel for tourism as an additional purpose. For example a person on a journey as a part of employment to a place with one or more tourist attractions –like a spot of scenic beauty or historical significance, a pilgrimage, a lake, etc. can be induced to spare some time and money for a short visit and or stay for tourism purposes alone.In this sense every traveller is a 'potential' tourist and is upto the managers of the industry to tap this 'potential' and convert the traveller into an 'actual' tourist.

Some of the characteristics that distinguish tourism:

- Temporary, to distinguish it from the permanent travel of the tramp and nomad
- Voluntary, to distinguish it from the forced travel of the exile and refugee
- Round up, to distinguish it from the one-way journey of the migrant
- Relatively long, to distinguish it from the recurrent trips of the holiday house owner

DEFINITIONS

The term Tourist is believed to have been derived from the Latin word 'TORNUS' which means a tool, a circle or a turner's wheel.

In the sense of the word of the origin, tourist is a person who undertakes a circular trip, *i.e.*, ultimately comes back to the place from where he sets about his journey.

Based on the various definitions of a Tourist here are some of the characteristics of a Tourist:

- He takes up his journey of his own free will.
- He takes up the journey primarily in search of enjoyment.
- The money spent on the visit is the money derived from home, not money earned in the places of visit.
- He finally returns to his original starting point.

We now proceed to discuss the definition of Tourist as given by WTO.But since WTO considers a tourist a type of a Visitor. As suggested, first discuss the definition of a Visitor. The WTO in a conference held in 1963 introduced the term 'Visitor'.

A Visitor is defined as 'Any person visiting a country other than that in which he has his usual place of residence for any reason other than being interested in an occupation remunerated from within the country visited.

The term includes two types of visitors:

- *Tourist*: Tourist is a temporary visitor staying for a period of at least 24 hours in the country visited and the purpose of whose journey can be classified under one of the following heads:

- Leisure
- Business, family, mission, meeting.
- *As per the WTO's definition following persons are to be regarded as tourists*:
  a. Persons travelling for pleasure, for domestic reasons, for health etc.
  b. Persons travelling for meetings or in representative capacity of any kind
  c. Persons travelling for business purposes.
  d. Persons arriving in the course of sea cruises, even when they stay for less than 24 hours in respect of this category of persons the condition of usual place of residence is waived off.
- *However persons belonging to the following categories are not considered as tourists*:
  a. Persons arriving with or without a contract to take up an occupation or engage in any business activity in that country.
  b. Residents in a frontier zone and persons domiciled in one country and working in an adjoining country.
  c. Students and young persons in boarding establishments of schools/colleges.
  d. Travellers passing through a country without stopping, even if the journey takes more than 24 hours.

• *Excursionist*: Excursionist is a temporary visitor staying for a period of less than 24hours in the country visited..

The drawback of the definition of a Visitor as per WTO is that it does not talk about the Visits made within the country. For these purposes a distinction is drawn between a Domestic and an International Visitor.

DOMESTIC VISITOR

A person who travels within the country he is residing in, outside the place of his usual environment for a period not exceeding 12 months.

INTERNATIONAL VISITOR

A person who travels to a country other than the one in which he has his usual residence for a period not exceeding 12 months. After we have discussed the definition of a visitor, tourist, and excursionist as per WTO and made a distinction between a Domestic and an International Visitor, we now come to definitions used in India for the purpose of collecting tourism statistics.

4

Adventure Tourism: Participation and Involvement

COLLECTIVE BARGAINING

In the complex area of people management paradigms, the terms Empowerment, Participation and Involvement are frequently used within the literature but often interpreted quite differently depending on the perspective of the reader and / or writer. This offer an insight into these terms and to posit them respectively within the context of unitary and pluralist people management perspectives. Firstly it is necessary to distinguish between Participation and Involvement, and then to examine where Empowerment fits within these perspectives.

Hotel Chains represent the intelligence behind the Global Councils whose representatives are specialists in the fields of Human Resources, E-Distribution, Safety and Security, Legal, Marketing, etc. Critical issues are dealt with both from a "bottom up" as well as "top down" basis. Restaurant Chains represent the intelligence behind the Global Councils whose representatives are specialists in the fields of Human Resources, Food Safety, Nutrition, Hygiene and other Foodservice issues. Employee involvement is 'a range of processes designed to engage the support, understanding and optimum contribution of all employees in an organisation and their commitment to its objectives'.

Employee participation is defined as 'a process of employee involvement designed to provide employees with the opportunity to influence and where appropriate, take part in decision making on matters which affect them'. It is clear then that there are differences between employee participation and employee involvement. The literature suggests that employee participation is a pluralist/collective approach with a continuum from 'no involvement' to 'employee control'.Employee involvement, in contrast, is more individualistic and unitarist. It aims to harness commitment to organisational objectives and relies on the maintenance of management control. Collective bargaining is a rule-making process for contract-making and contractchanging.

Having identified employee involvement, where empowerment sits within these approaches is perhaps more complex and hinges on interpretations of 'power' and how 'empowered' workers actually are where such schemes are implemented. Terms and conditions of employment are determined and regulated through the formal process of negotiation between representatives of management and employees. The outcome is a binding agreement for those employees within the bargaining unit, e.g. at national, enterprise or workplace level.

It is based on management's legitimization of employee involvement and influence over aspects of decision-making, and involves a power relationship in which employee representatives may regulate managerial authority. Acknowledgement of the right to strike is embodied within this process. Variations in the scope and coverage of collective bargaining are a reflection of different regulatory regimes across the world.

International Arrangements

The coverage of workers' and employers' organizations in the HCTS and the scope of collective bargaining vary by country and region. Trade unions may cover a number of sectors, which may include the HCTS, or cover particular occupational groups that are found in other sectors, e.g. workers in services in France. Employers' organizations are more cohesive, and largely cover hotels and restaurants.

The International Hotel and Restaurant Association is the largest employers' organization representing over 750,000 establishments in 150 countries. The largest workers' organization, the IUF, has 326 affiliated organizations representing 10 million workers in 118 countries, including the ECF.

There is only one known case of international trade union recognition between the IUF and the French Accor Group. International awareness has been facilitated through the use of websites for publicity. A dispute in a Seoul hotel came to an end in 2000 after trade unions elsewhere made representations to the Korean diplomatic mission.

There are two federations of employers' organizations in Europe: The Confederation of National Associations of Hotels, Restaurants, Cafes and Similar Establishments in the European Union and European Economic Area (HOTREC) and the European Federation of Contract Catering Organizations (FERCO).

For workers there is a special European Trade Union Liaison Committee on Tourism (ETLC). Social dialogue, launched by the ECF-IUF and HOTREC, takes place four times a year under the auspices of the European Commission (EC). Various joint declarations have been adopted including the 1999 Joint Declaration for the promotion of employment in hotels and restaurants, designed to reduce taxes and non-wage costs, and to improve training and certification.

The development of collective and social partnership is hampered by the reluctance among employers to promote partnership with trade unions. The challenges of global competition have caused employers to restructure and adopt new methods. Traditional occupational boundaries are breaking down, as jobs become more flexible. Hence issues on the collective bargaining agenda include the prevention of wage deterioration resulting from unclear definitions in new work patterns, and maintaining continuity of working and employment conditions where there is a change in ownership. The latter is more difficult where the instigating party is an MNC based outside the host country.

Variations in Global Practice

The structure and scope of collective bargaining varies according to legal and national practice. Twelve African countries have collective agreements in existence since the 1970s, and almost all explicitly mention union rights. While enterprise bargaining is more normative in North America, Asia and Africa, in Europe sectoral or sub-sectoral bargaining at national or regional level is more common. In France sub-sectoral bargaining is a function of the way employers are organized, and was for some time restricted to hotel and restaurant chains. More recently most independent firms adopted this procedure, even though workers are not unionized. Complete coverage is secured by extending the collective agreement to workers in all workplaces by government decree. In Australia trade unions have an almost exclusive right to represent HI employees and to make particular awards.

Trade union membership is not particularly high. There is no law on trade union recognition ballots as in North America and the UK, and trade unions are not especially active. Although the Shop Distributive and Allied Employees' Union (SDA) has almost exclusive rights in fast food in all states, employers are reluctant to engage in enterprise bargaining. They will negotiate with unions where a state industrial award is perceived as too costly. Agreements would incorporate conditions from other agreements that may offset the higher conditions under the award.

Hungry Jack's (a Burger King franchise) and the SDA have reached a multi-state standard agreement, which the unions regard as easier to enforce and maintain. Some successful enterprise agreements have addressed 'low road' practices, building in value-added features such as job rotation, training and performance management, and multiskilling. New Zealand used to have an employment relations system similar to the Australian system. Case study given below shows how in a more deregulated environment collectivism may be enduring on the surface, but is highly symbolic.

Case Study: Deregulation of Employment Relations in Large Hotels in New Zealand

The Employment Contracts Act 1991 replaced mandated collective bargaining and extensive trade union protection with a new regime allowing employers to engage in individualistic employment relations or innovative cooperative relations with unionized workforces. Union density within the Service Workers Union (SWU) was traditionally low in the hotel industry. The New Zealand (With Exceptions) Major Accommodation Hotel Industry Award expired in 1992.

- Collective contracts persisted but most employers abandoned traditional bargaining and moved to almost exclusively management determined 'consultation'.
- Managers espoused a more limited role for unions, including officials, although all hotels still credited union subscriptions.
- Non-union collective voice mechanisms were developed. Trade union representatives were subject to the same election procedure as their peers.
- All innovations initiated and developed by management were not consistent with high commitment strategies.

Labour-management bargaining priorities in the US have changed post-11 September, with new considerations including job security for airline employees, and employers seeking to add provisions for 'acts of war'. There is also increased video surveillance, bio-terrorism policies, employee background checks and onsite searches of employees' belongings. Current law makes virtually all changes in workplace privacy and security rules the topic of mandatory collective bargaining.

HI employees and, notably, employers, through bodies such as the BHA and BII, have traditionally not associated for collective bargaining purposes. The main trade unions representing HI workers are the TGWU, GMB, USDAW and NALHM. Historically membership levels have been very low, regardless of the regulatory framework in force. The LFS (2001) indicates that only 9 per cent of HI employees are covered by collective agreements, which drops to 6 per cent if public sector workplaces are excluded. Trade union recognition for collective bargaining is rare, and restricted mainly to the large groups, e.g. USDAW and Compass services, the GMB and Road Chef and Jarvis Hotels.

The legal framework governing the rights, actions, duties, responsibilities and behaviours of employers and trade unions in Britain was seriously weakened in the 1980s and 1990s. The proportion of employees who were members of trade unions declined from 53 per cent in 1979 to 28 per cent in 1999. Consequently similar 'hollow shell' collective agreements to those found in New Zealand have developed in Britain. The Employment Relations Act 1999 contained measures to facilitate trade union organization, including the statutory recognition procedures, although there has been no weakening of the constraints on industrial action.

Social Partnership

Social partnership is a form of collective bargaining that places more emphasis on mutual cooperation and joint problem-solving, often extending into areas such as training, skills, flexibility, career development and quality of working life, which have not been the domain of traditional collective bargaining. It is best viewed on two levels - a relationship between the summit employer and trade union bodies, and at the workplace.

Many, including the trade unions, would regard social partnership as a complementary process to collective bargaining and vehicle for union renewal, while others see it as marginalizing trade unionism as an autonomous force, undermining workplace unionism and weakening the trade union movement.

Partnership is expected to emerge from a common response to the challenges of global competition. In the Caribbean where tourism is by far the most important economic sector, active steps to improve social partnership can be observed. One major concern of trade unions is the practices of sub-contracting and franchising, which are believed to create divisions among those working in the same workplaces. At international level there is a social dialogue relationship between the partners in the HCTS, but it is at an early stage of development.

The development of trade unions as facilitators of cooperative collective relationships, often through consultative arrangements, is a key dimension of EU social policy. In 1999 agreement between the Union of Industrial and Employers' Confederations of Europe (UNICE) and the ETUC provides a forum for social dialogue leading to agreements. These provide the framework for national governments to introduce appropriate legislation, e.g. non-discrimination for workers on fixed-term contracts in respect of hours of work and holidays. Other consultative arrangements relating to redundancies, proposed business transfers, health and safety, European Works Councils (EWCs), and the forthcoming information and consultation directive, which may involve union and non-union representatives.

Reflecting the new Labour government's espousal of partnership, a Partnership at Work fund has been created to encourage employers, employees and their representatives to build trust, share information and work together to solve business problems. Since 1997 the TUC has deliberately attempted to rebuild relationships with employers by promoting a new role for trade unions based on partnership strategy, additional to collective bargaining.

Case Study: Partnership with the GMB at Gardner Merchant

This contract catering company, part of the French conglomerate Sodexho, recognizes the GMB in the UK. Previously each site negotiated their own interpretations of the standard ACAS recognition agreement, with emphasis on negative dispute resolution procedures. A new HR Director in 1994 spurred a reappraisal of Gardner Merchant's way of working in light of the positive collaborative experience gained from Sodexho's EWC. There was a shared desire to formulate a UK national agreement along the same lines.

The new agreement signed in 1998 recognized the legitimacy of each parties' role, a joint commitment to open discussion and improving trust, providing training opportunities and enhancing the company's reputation. It also contained a detailed disputes avoidance procedure, with strike action permissible only after all other avenues are exhausted. Joint policy statements have been issued on best practice in TUPE and the EU's Acquired Rights Directive.

Improved communication and consultation provides both sides with an early warning call about problems and potential areas of conflict. Training in consultation and planning for change was provided for local managers. There are twice-yearly Board level meetings and in early 2000 the company was seeking a national works council.

Nationally the trade unions believe they can play an essential role in helping to determine policy on training, jobs, investment and Europe, while at the level of the enterprise and workplace partnership agreements will help improve organizational performance and quality of working life. The joint problem-solving social partnership approach underpins the work of ACAS and the LPC, both bodies comprising equal numbers of CBI and TUC nominees plus independent members. The Information and Participation Association (IPA) shares similar ideals to the TUC on social partnership.

Case Study: Partnership in San Francisco's Hotels

San Francisco's major hotels and the Hotel Employees and Restaurant Employees International Union embarked on a new partnership oriented approach in 1994. The 'living contract' provided a mechanism for making work-rule changes by mutual agreement during the term of the contract. Joint study teams examined issues underlying problems that would otherwise have led to a dispute. Joint solutions avoided expensive, often pointless arbitration. Rules were redesigned to make the hotels' restaurants competitive with non-union hotels. The living agreement was renewed in 1999.

International Comparisons

HCT workers across the world are less likely to be organized in trade unions than workers in other sectors, and trade union density may be as little as 10 per cent or less in industrialized countries.

Even where trade unions have been afforded exclusive rights, such as in Australia and New Zealand, actual membership levels have tended to be low. Figures are difficult to come by, but selected examples of density levels in the HI are given. In many cases they indicate density levels below a level at which the 'virtuous circle between union growth and union recognition could begin'.

In her survey of the HI in New Zealand, Ryan found that two-thirds of workplaces had no union members, 18 per cent had up to 50 per cent and 4 per cent had more than half. Only 10 per cent had seen any attempt at union recognition.

National figures disguise differences within sub-sectors. In large hotels, where membership is generally highest, levels of 80 per cent have been achieved in the Canadian cities of Vancouver, Toronto and Montreal. Conversely in Auckland, New Zealand membership can vary from 5 to 20 to 32 per cent. Although density levels were never very high, they dropped in the 1990s following the deregulation of employment relations, remaining higher where trade unions maintained an active role.

In McDonald's in Germany trade union membership in the NGG becomes well established and rises rapidly to around 50 per cent or more after a works council has been created. Conversely the fast food industry in Canada and the US is almost entirely non-union.

Table: Trade Union Membership in the HI by Country

Country	*Year*	*Level (%)*
US	1993	<2
Canada	1998	9
Australia	1997	18/13.1
Finland	1995	65
Austria	1995	40
Italy	1995	25
Ireland	1995	20
Netherlands	1997	10
UK	1995	8
France	1995	5

Notes: *Where two figures are shown, they relate to full-time and part-time workers respectively. The most recent HI figure from the LFS shows 5% union density.*

Even where union density is relatively high, as in Singapore hotels, conservative and accommodative trade unions and the institutionalization of employer- employee relations mean there is little activity or conflict. As the service provided by hospitality businesses cannot be stockpiled like goods produced in a factory, industrial action is potentially more damaging and effective.

As noted, union membership in the HI in the UK is among the lowest in Europe, and may be in decline. Arguably NALHM has been the most successful union within the HI but as Case study indicates, membership has dropped by two-thirds.

Trade unions have had a chequered history in attempting to secure recognition in larger hotels. There have been isolated cases of strike action in support of recognition, including the Savoy, London and Torquay. USDAW's approach to McDonald's in the UK for 'talks about talks' was flatly rejected by the company, nor has there been any attempt by the three HI unions to make a coordinated approach to the company.

However the GMB has been actively recruiting in McDonald's and Little Chef. Recognition is pretty rare, and most likely to be found in large companies, GMB and Roadchef and GMB and Jarvis Hotels. Since the Employment Relations Act 1999 there have been no known recognition claims in the HI, although a number of recognition claims have been made in airlines and casinos.

Case Study: Neutrality Agreements and Organizing Tactics in New US Hotels

In the 1990s most hotels were organized on the basis of HERE approaching hotel companies several months before a new hotel was due to open seeking a neutrality agreement. Under this agreement employers give up their right to contest union organization and the right of employees to vote in a secret ballot election supervised by the National Labour Relations Board to determine whether they wish to be represented by HERE.

By signing the employer virtually guarantees the union will be recognized as the exclusive bargaining agent. Such agreements include a card-check provision which represents a much cheaper and more effective organizing technique than the secret ballot method, which normally goes against the unions. Labour-peace and living wage ordinances coupled with the threat of sanctions from the building-trades unions to disrupt the hotel's construction, have made it easier to union organizers to obtain employers' consent to remain neutral.

Case Study: The Decline of the National Association of Licensed House Managers

In 1997 NALHM ended 30 years of independence by joining the TGWU as an autonomous section. Membership, restricted to pubs managed by salaried managers of a brewery, as opposed to managers of free houses or tenants, peaked at 18,000 in 1982, but had declined to 6,000 by 1997.

The union's demise is attributed to a combination of local conditions specific to the sector, including the major restructuring following the Mergers and Monopolies Commission Report in 1989. The subsequent Beer Orders changed the role for many pubs and the nature of their managers who became more professional and entrepreneurial.

There have been other recent examples of strike action, for reasons other than recognition. In Norway the first strike for 11 years in 1996 forced the closure of ten leading hotels, at a daily cost of £2.4 million for three of them. A strike by bar workers in Dublin in 1994 closed 70 per cent of pubs during the World Cup.

BA sustained a number of strikes among cabin crew over the 1990s. In 1997 nearly 2000 BA staff went on sick leave rather than participating in the official strike, as they feared disciplinary action. Taking turns to go sick caused considerable disruption to flights. Recent strike action in the British HI is virtually non-existent.

Recent Experience

From WERS the state of trade membership can be ascertained in two main ways, by measuring union density and by measuring the percentage of workplaces where there are or have been trade union members in the recent past. The HI continues to sustain significantly lower trade union density in comparison with AIS and the PSS.

Although the picture is slightly more encouraging in larger workplaces, trade union incursion into the heart of the HI is, at best, highly marginal. Recent LFS figures indicate that 5 per cent of HI employees are union members (8 per cent full-time and 3 per cent part-time), and the figure drops to 4 per cent if public sector workplaces are excluded.

In three-quarters of the small caucus of HI workplaces with union members, membership is most likely to be among managers/administrative staff. Union membership is extremely rare among other occupational groups, especially white-collar groups who are most likely to be union members in AIS and the PSS.

Table: Trade Union Density in Context and by Size of Workplace (%)

	AIS	*PSS*	*HI*	*<25*	*25-49*	*50-99*	*100+*
Aggregate density	34	15	2*	2	0	0	5
Actual density No members	54	73	92*	92	94	94	73
1-59%	26	19	8*	7	6	6	27
60-100%	20	7	1*	1	0	0	0

Notes: *All weighted cases. Column percentages do not sum accurately due to rounding. *Significantly different at the 5% level from AIS and the PSS.*

Table: Trade Union Density by Sub-sector (%)

	Hotels	*Campsites*	*Restaurants*	*Bars*	*Canteens*
Aggregate density	0	9	1	1	15
Actual density No members	94	18	100	90	82
1-59%	6	82	0	10	9
60-100%	0	0	0	0	10

Notes: *All weighted cases. Column percentages do not sum accurately due to rounding.*

First, there is no de-recognition or absolute decline in union membership in the HI because none of the workplaces without unions had any members five years ago. Second, unions have been slightly more active in attempting to recruit members in the HI, but have touched only a minority of workplaces and their attempts do not appear to have proved successful.

Table: Trade Union Membership in Context and by Size of Workplace (%)

	AIS	*PSS*	*HI*	*<25*	*25-49*	*50-99*	*100+*
Any union members now	47	27	8*	8	6	6	27
Any union members 5 years ago s	5	4	0*	0	0	0	0
Any recruitment attempts in last 5 years r	5	5	12	13	20	2	5
Any recognition requests in last 5 years t	7	7	0*	0	0	0	0
Management's attitude towards unions w							
In favour	27	13	6*	6	7	3	4
Not in favour	17	22	22	18	28	25	28
Neutral	54	63	72**	76	65	67	69

Notes: *Yes responses to all weighted cases unless otherwise stated. *Significantly different at the 5% level from AIS and the PSS. **Significantly different at the 5% level from AIS. s Where no union members and establishment is five years or older. r Where no union members. t Where union members now or five years ago. w Excludes not an issue and non-codeable responses.*

Table. Trade Union Membership by Sub-sector (%)

	Hotels	*Campsites*	*Restaurants*	*Bars*	*Canteens*
Any union members now	6	82	0	10	18
Any union members 0 5 years ago s	0	0	0	0	
Any recruitment attempts in last 5 years r	2	0	14	19	0
Any recognition requests in last 5 years t	0	0	0	0	0
Management's attitude towards unions w					
In favour	2	0	0	11	10
Not in favour	23	0	20	26	7
Neutral	76	100	78	64	83

Notes: *Yes responses to all weighted cases unless otherwise stated. s Where no union members and establishment is five years or older. r Where no union members. t Where union members now or five years ago. w Excludes not an issue and non-codeable responses.*

Third, there have been no recognition requests in the last five years. Finally HI managers are significantly less likely to be in favour of trade unions. One should also caution against assuming too much from the neutral responses because Cully et al. suggested that managers who declare themselves neutral might actually hold negative views about trade unions. We can usefully consider the neutrality responses with an earlier observation that managers have an even higher level of preference for consulting directly with employees than with a union. While a majority of AIS and PSS managers do hold negative views about unions, there is a clear indication that HI managers hold even more negative views about unions than their counterparts in AIS and the PSS.

This final observation suggests that non-union representation is unlikely to be much of a force anywhere. This is borne out by the fact that fewer than 10 per cent of workplaces have present non-union representatives or representatives of non-recognized unions, affecting one in 11 workplaces in AIS, one in 12 in PSS and one in 16 the HI. These representatives are more likely to be found in unionized workplaces, and are rarely found in non-union workplaces, suggesting that they are complementary to union representation rather than substitutes for it. Thus most HI workplaces (93 per cent) have no worker representatives of any kind compared to 70 per cent in AIS and 85 per cent in the PSS.

In the HI non-union representatives are most likely to be volunteers, whereas in AIS and the PSS the most common selection method is election by employees. In most cases these representatives sit on a consultative committee covering a wide range of issues. Non-union representatives can also deal with or play a part in employment issues such as pay, recruitment, training, pay systems, grievances, staff planning, equal opportunities, health and safety, and performance appraisal. Their involvement varies from full (negotiation), partial (consultation), token (informed) or none. Although care should be taken in drawing too much from such a small number of cases, there are still some striking differences between AIS, the PSS and the HI.

The Consequences of Working without Unions

'Non-union representation can provide at best only a partial mechanism for employee involvement and participation in the absence of legal underpinnings', because they have no collective sanctions or any of the protections afforded to union representatives. Such representation has no real power base, as it is merely cooperative, and ultimately, at managerial discretion, often abandoned in times of crisis and change when managers should be at their most open if they are to convince employees of their commitment to participation and of its effectiveness.

Workers in non-union workplaces appear to be penalized in a number of other ways. Collective bargaining appears to facilitate access to and improvement on statutory rights. Unionized workplaces have more alternative voice mechanisms than non-union workplaces, where workers also lose out on family leave and gender equality. Even though trade unions have gained the right to accompany a worker in a grievance or disciplinary hearing, including where the union is not recognized, accompaniment does not imply the right to represent. Most HI employees do not actually know any trade union officials. The absence of union voice mechanisms reinforces managerial prerogative and may weaken employees' chances of resolving a dispute or grievance. In McDonald's in Australia employees raise such concerns through the Personal Action Letter (PAL), which is brought to the attention of management or head office. Few workers are aware of PAL or use it.

The individualized nature of contractual, remuneration and bargaining arrangements provides more limited provision of procedural justice and equity. Workers seek advice and representation outside the traditional labour movement and from voluntary organizations such as the Citizens' Advice Bureau (CAB). The CAB has experienced a steep rise in the number of employment problems brought to them, and is becoming increasingly active in resolving such problems, in the absence of workplace mechanisms. This may change following the introduction of new statutory minimum grievance and disciplinary procedures. On issues such as redundancy, dismissal and the unilateral variation of the terms and conditions of employment, workers also seek the help of ACAS.

Forms of Workplace Conflict

The absence of unions does not indicate an absence of conflict. Rather alternative forms of worker behaviour, other than strike action, are normally deployed. By worker behaviour we mean the ways and means used by workers to cope with or resist managerial control in the everyday conduct of their work, which arise from their lack of power as individuals. These can be individual and collective, including mass and individual absenteeism.

More days are lost from absence than from strikes. 'As with absenteeism, pilfering is arguably more costly than strikes'. Rather than raise a formal grievance about low pay that is likely to be ignored, workers enhance their pay by shortchanging customers. Employee theft may be responsible for one in three business failures, and is especially prevalent in food service, with employees' own estimates three times higher than their managers'. Ultimately workers may leave the organization voluntarily or involuntarily, and may seek resolution of the dispute outside the workplace, notably at employment tribunal.

Lucas identifies how students use their tacit skills to resist managers and customers. In customer-service work flight attendants' response to work intensification is to slow down and smile less broadly. Fuller and Smith (1991) report how the use of mystery shoppers so incensed hotel workers that they also conducted a 'smile strike'.

Law notes an interesting instance of customer protest in one of the most luxurious hotels in Hong Kong, which illustrates the effectiveness of mass action in response to the perceived inequitable treatment of a customer breast-feeding in a public area, who was asked to go somewhere more private. Eighteen women 'protested' by breast-feeding in the same area, and the hotel staff did nothing.

Three sets of circumstances are relevant to low levels of unionization:

- Do the structural characteristics of workplaces and workforces provide an environment in which it is possible to conceive effective levels of unionization?
- Do workers have an interest or motivation to join trade unions?
- What role do employers and trade unions play?

Structural Factors

The substantial presence of small workplaces and their wide geographical dispersion pose considerable challenges to trade union recruitment and organizing strategies. The ideology of a 'family culture' is a significant barrier to organizing in SMEs.

Case Study: Resisting Managers and Customers in Hospitality Work

Getting by

One student worked four eight-hour shifts per week for a 'pittance' of £3.00 an hour managing the leisure centre of a city centre hotel. She used the extensive amount of working time spent on her own to complete all her college work. Others read books or collected data for their assignments or dissertation. None claimed they were actually skiving.

Another student stated they all stuck together with difficult customers. Where the customer gave them a £20 or £50 note, they would shout out the amount to the other person in the bar to have a witness should the customer claim the note was for a different value.

Getting Back

A change in managers led to a change in management style from no procedures to enforcing the rules. Staff responded by giving customers free drinks and helping themselves.

A student serving drinks on large trays at a large arena had to step over customers and reported getting 'touched up' by men. If she reported this she knew the customer would claim it was accidental. If she had to return, she would keep the tray between her and the customer so they could not do it again. If customers were particularly horrible she would make a point of treading on their feet, of course smiling and apologizing.

Workplaces under the control of one parent company may be fragmented by sub-contracting and franchising arrangements. In the US and Canada hotel restaurants are frequently leased, becoming part of the non-union restaurant subsector. In Las Vegas where virtually all food beverage operations are leased

HERE represents 900 workers, whereas the figure would be 2,700 if they were not leased. Although trade unions are opposed to sub-contracting a priority is to negotiate protection against a deterioration of terms and conditions of employment in these circumstances. Franchised units have the legal status of an independent employer, which places them outside scope of company-wide representative bodies based on a minimum headcount. Thus agreements may only apply to a minority of a company's workplaces in a particular country, as Royle demonstrates in the case of McDonald's.

Additionally work is structured and organized around highly flexible patterns to match stochastic demand, so gaining access to a critical mass of employees is very difficult for trade union organizers to achieve. The fast food production system offers protection against trade unions through a casual and youthful labour force, which is difficult to organize, and which reduces the likelihood of union pressure for higher wages and potential interruptions through strikes.

Employees

Many, if not most, employees work in different departments or at different times on different contracts, which keeps communications and group identity low among workers, especially in larger workplaces. This, heightened by departmental rivalry and fuelled by high labour turnover, militates against the establishment any collective ethos. High turnover causes membership attrition, although this could be attenuated if check-off was available within large organizations with fluid internal mobility, e.g. breweries. Individualized contracts lead to a sense of individual identity and also sharpen competition among individuals. Individual employees doing different jobs, each with its own set of benefits, prefer to negotiate for themselves, believing strongly that they can influence their own working environment. The notion of service may instil a sense of submission, and there is little collective kudos to be gained from excellent service.

A young workforce, and to a lesser extent part-time working, is strongly correlated to lower levels of density, especially in the UK. The GMB's strategy to recruit students on a 10p a week subscription achieved only a small level of membership. Part-time workers are one of the least committed work groups and therefore less likely to be interested in trade unions, although some display strong support for the ideals and protection afforded by unions. Workers with less than two years' service, temporary and zero hours workers, and sales and customer service staff sustain substantially lower trade union density.

The issue of gender is more ambiguous, as density levels of men and women in Britain have converged towards similar levels of around 30 per cent since the early 1990s. Women with higher education qualifications have the highest density levels, and are more than twice more likely to be union members than women with no qualifications or qualifications at A-level or below. This is consistent with Lowery and Beadles' (1996) observation that industrial and craft workers are less likely to choose union representation than professional workers. Weaker affiliation to union membership among females may be attributed to their disproportionate representation in part-time and casual work, and to their irregular hours. Women often feel neglected by trade unions or are dissatisfied with their experience of them. This creates a negative perception of trade unions, as in the case of an Asian woman who found her white, male trade union official 'dismissive' and sought advice instead from the CAB.

Employers and Unions

The role of employers is also crucial. In the US employers cannot be compelled to grant union organizers access to their employees where other reasonable means are available, e.g. shopping malls and entrances to hotels.

Case Study: Anti-union Tactics in the German Fast Food Industry

Anglo-Saxon-based MNCs, including McDonald's, Pizza Hut and Burger King, are more likely to adopt anti-union policies. Employment relations in most German-owned firms appear to be less antagonistic. Maredo and Churrasco enjoyed good relations with the NGG while under German ownership, but these have become more difficult since the takeover by the UK Whitbread group. A subsidiary of the UK Compass Group 'Eurest' works cooperatively with unions.

McDonald's has sought to root out or inhibit union membership by sending 'flying squads' of senior managers to trouble spots, making 'troublemakers'' job duties more unpleasant, actual or threatened dismissal, or paying people to leave.

Where employers are unwilling to recognize trade unions, workers have less reason to join and may even fear repercussions. Positive views of trade unions are unlikely to convert into action as employees are thwarted by a sense of fatalism about the likely success of a union dealing with a hostile employer. Or it may well be the case that workers, instilled with a sense self-reliance and in the knowledge that work is temporary or readily available elsewhere, are simply not dissatisfied enough to seek trade union protection and representation.

Given the difficulties HERE has had in organizing HI workers, Lowery and Beadles (1996) suggest that unions' past patterns of organizing need to be altered, as they may be targeting the 'wrong' workers. In spite of the TUC's positive attempts to encourage the trade union movement to target women, ethnic minorities and part-time workers sex and race inequality remains institutionalized within trade unions. If unions in Britain are to stem union decline, they must overcome their traditional antipathy towards non-standard workers based on the fear that recruiting them would undercut full-time jobs. Such workers, including low-wage service workers, need to be the target of union recruitment and retention efforts. Fundamentally 'rebranding' towards non-standard workers is difficult, time-consuming and costly, even if unions change their organizing structure to facilitate their increased participation.

This is not to say that hospitality and tourism workers are 'unique'. Rather, their orientations to work and their role within the capitalist relations of production do not differentiate them from production workers. But there is a complex mix of factors that clearly contribute to an explanation of why trade unions, even where they enjoy strong institutional support, have made few incursions into large swathes of the HCTS.

Workforce Participation

Participation provides employees with the opportunity to influence and take part in organizational decision-making and is, therefore, mainly pluralist. It is based on collective representation, which may be union or union-union, and is often referred to as indirect participation. Where worker representatives are elected, trade unions are generally involved. Non-elected participation tends to be ad hoc. Effective participation is dependent upon an equitable power balance.

Participation normally extends to areas outside the focus of traditional collective bargaining, i.e. the effort-reward bargain. Hence social partnership dealing with issues such as training and skills can be regarded as a variant of participation. Initiatives for participation normally emanate from the state, trade unions or employees. Examples discussed below include transnational EWCs, the forthcoming national-level information and consultation directive, works councils and joint consultative committees.

Involvement is closely associated with 'soft' and 'best practice' HRM and is management driven. As it seeks to enhance employee support and commitment to the objectives and values of the organization, it is mainly unitarist. As any increase in employee control and decision-making is limited to the job and work operation only, involvement is sometimes called task-based or direct participation. Involvement practices addressed below include briefing groups, suggestion schemes, problem-solving groups, teamworking and empowerment.

Worker representation at employers' initiative rarely addresses fundamental issues of pay and working time. Rather, it has more to do with improving management and workforce communications, and with improving day-to-day business issues and training. In one Accor hotel, while two-thirds of the staff attended meetings, only half of them participated actively. The remaining third did not bother to attend. Employee support and enthusiasm for meetings may be patchy, particularly where management determines the 'consultation' agenda.

Since the 1980s successive WIRS/WERS have shown an increase in direct participation and a decline in indirect participation and collective bargaining in Britain. Hence involvement 'may be desirable to enhance the status, opportunity and work satisfaction of the individual it may reduce the capacity of employees to challenge and influence managerial decisions by undermining collectivism and the representational role and power of trade unions'. Involvement and participation are not discrete or mutually exclusive practices and can be depicted on a continuum. Ultimately participation hinges upon the extent to which managers control workers and the degree of control afforded to workers within the organization or in their work.

IndirectPparticipation

EWCs came into being as a result of the EWC Directive (1994), and are crossborder meetings between worker representatives and managers of companies with businesses in more than one country. Every enterprise with at least 150 employees in each of at least two countries and a total of at least 1,000 employees in the European Economic Area (EEA) is required to have an EWC. The procedure for consultation is if at least 150 employees from at least two countries require it. The meetings are for information and consultation purposes, not collective bargaining, as employee representatives have no powers to block management decisions.

A number of MNCs operating in the EU established EWCs by 'voluntary agreement' ahead of the legally required implementation date of 1996. This enabled companies to appoint employee representatives instead of those determined by national law or practice. By August 2000 there were 14 EWCs, only two of which were set up after the deadline for voluntary agreements.

Case Study: Positive Outcomes from European Works Councils

- Club Mediterranee consulted and came to an agreement on closing operations and restructuring processes.
- Accor concluded an agreement with the IUF on trade union rights.
- Compass extended equal opportunities policies to all subsidiaries and promised training for all employees. Compass committed itself to becoming the 'Preferred Employer', linking customer satisfaction to employee satisfaction.

Case Study: Pizza Express Forum

A structure for feedback and consultation for more than 250 British restaurants was established in 2000. This was developed by a working party of volunteers, with a former waiter recruited to act as full-time coordinator. Each restaurant has its own staff representative, who feeds into one of 27 Area Forums (each covers around nine restaurants). Each Area Forum elects a representative for one of three Regional Forums.

Issues raised by representatives have included a new menu and a service charge. At the National Forum representatives have brought up questions about training, pay slips and recycling. Most of Pizza Express's 6,000 staff are in the UK, and the aim is to ensure that the Forum complies with rules on EWCs. Although some staff are union members, the initiative will have failed if staff see joining unions as an alternative to the Forum. Examples of those agreements signed jointly with trade unions are European and include Accor (French), Bass plc and Compass (UK) and Scandic Hotels (Swedish). By contrast agreements affecting EWCs in American MNCs, such as McDonald's, Tricon Global Restaurants and the tour operator American Express, were not signed by trade unions. McDonald's was able to negotiate the kind of EWC it wanted, which applies only to one-third of their workers because franchised stores are excluded.

Britain was excluded from coverage of the Directive until the new Labour government opted into the Social in 1998. Transition arrangements meant that British-based MNCs had until 1999 to make voluntary agreements, as the UK regulations to comply with the Directive did not come into force until 2000.

Other Driven Consultation

Other EU directives have required the UK to legislate for consultation with representatives in circumstances of collective redundancies, transfers of undertakings and health and safety. In keeping with EWCs, representatives do not have to be union representatives, and in health and safety employers may consult directly with employees or their representatives. However a number of factors limit their practical effect in the HI. Redundancy consultation with workers' representatives is required only when 20 or more employees at an establishment are to be made redundant within 90 days.

Many workplaces will not qualify because they are too small, and the use of atypical labour, high labour turnover and dismissal to regulate headcount means the HI sustains relatively few redundancies. Because redundancies and transfers are sporadic, often situation-specific events, standing structures for such purposes are rare anywhere in Britain. There may be little real consultation as employers may use such procedures to legitimize their decisions or to reassure workers.

As James (1994) has observed, the ongoing nature of health and safety may assure some continuity of management-employee dialogue. Health and safety is the one domain where there is some form of representative structure in non-union workplaces. Workers in non-union workplaces face difficulties in gaining access to health and safety representation.

Our WERS analysis shows, in the absence of any consultative committee or a committee that deals with health and safety matters, HI workplaces are significantly less likely to have joint committee to deal with health and safety matters. Such committees are most likely to deal with health and safety matters only. HI representatives are most likely to have been volunteers, whereas slightly more democratic methods are used in AIS and the PSS.

Adding the number of workplaces with health and safety committees to the number of workplaces with a JCC that discusses health and safety conveys a more complete picture of health and safety consultation. Even on this measure only one- fifth of HI workplaces consult formally on health and safety issues, significantly below AIS (48 per cent) and the PSS (37 per cent).

Table: Health and Safety Arrangements in Context, by Size of Workplace and Sub-sector (%)

	AIS	*PSS*	*HI*	*<25*	*25-49*	*50-99*	*100+*
Joint committee	27	21	10*	0	13	33	61
Any representatives where no committee	37	29	14*	4	45	15	33

	Hotels	*Campsites*	*Restaurants*	*Bars*	*Canteens*
Joint committee	23	24	13	0	13
Any representatives where no committee	23	0	12	11	4

Notes: *All weighted cases. *Significantly different at the 5% level from AIS and PSS.*

Where there is no consultative committee that deals with health and safety issues, HI workplaces are significantly less likely to have representatives that deal with management over health and safety matters. The Directive on information and consultation adopted in 2002 is to be phased in from 2005, following consultation arising from the discussion paper High Performance Workplaces: The Role of Employee Involvement in a Modern Economy.

It will also apply a size of firm threshold. Initially it may apply only to companies with 150 or more employees, and by 2008 it will still only affect businesses with more than 50 employees. The Directive will extend consultation beyond the issues discussed above. Employees have the right to be:

- Informed about the business's economic situation;
- Informed and consulted about employment prospects;
- Informed and consulted about decisions likely to lead to substantial changes in work organization or contractual relations, including redundancies and transfers.

Information must be given in time to allow employee representatives to examine and prepare for consultation. The government is likely to encourage voluntary agreements within social partnership, imposing a statutory minimum framework where this is not possible. As with EWCs, there will be some impact among larger, but not most, HI businesses.

Works Councils

Many European countries have highly formal institutional arrangements providing for works councils with written constitutions covering inter alia the election of representatives, frequency of meetings, and terms of reference. The German system of co-determination is often heralded as the 'best practice' model. Two-level worker participation comprises a works council in the workplace, and worker representatives on the supervisory board of the enterprise. While McDonald's theoretically has a works council in every store, very few have been established because of company interference to delay and discourage any attempts to elect one.

Tactics have included transferring the store into different ownership, buying out the instigators of a works council and nominating management candidates to provide a management-based agenda.

Employee acquiescence and inadequate legislation have enabled McDonald's to stick to its American-style approach to participation, which is more in keeping with employee involvement, and to circumvent requirements for works councils in many other European countries. Similar avoidance strategies are deployed by other Anglo-Saxon-based MNCs in the German fast food industry.

JointCconsultative Committees

One covers similar terrain to works councils (integrative participation), another allows employees to influence decisions before they are taken (classical consultation), while a third is largely symbolic, entailing downward communication only (pseudo participation). JCCs may be upgraded to marginalize collective bargaining and downgraded to deal with trivia.

Table: Consultation and Communication in Context and by Size of Workplace (%)

	AIS	*PSS*	*HI*	*<25*	*25-49*	*50-99*	*100+*
System of briefings	83	82	84	79	91	96	91
Consultative committee	23	18	11***	0	25	21	53
Problem solving or quality groups	33	28	16*	9	17	35	48
Formal opinion survey p	39	36	43	36	46	56	58
Other dd Entire workforce meetings	42	42	47	55	40	27	36
Management chain/ cascade	54	47	37***	28	47	54	71
Suggestion schemes	24	25	25	21	36	24	29
Newsletter	43	39	42	41	48	42	39
Disclosure of information bb Internal investment plans	50	46	55	52	56	64	70
Financial position of establishment	63	58	69	69	68	67	73
Financial position of organization m	66	67	78	92	67	44	57
Staffing plans	63	59	53	50	59	55	55

Notes: *Yes responses to all weighted cases unless otherwise stated. p In last five years for establishments five years or older. dd Four most frequently mentioned other ways in which management consults or communicates with employees (multi-response). bb Regularly given by management to employees or their representatives. m Where part of a larger organization or sole UK establishment. *Significantly different at the 5% level from AIS and PSS. ***Significantly different at the 5% level from AIS.*

WERS tells us that management committees for consultation, rather than negotiation, are significantly rarer in the HI, although they are only present in around one-quarter of AIS workplaces. While the likelihood of such a committee increases with workplace size they are rarely present in some sub-sectors.

Committees are very rare in very small HI workplace and most common in large workplaces. None of the smaller HI workplaces without committees had had one during the previous five years. However, one-quarter of the large workplaces no longer had a committee (all hotels), although the reasons for its disappearance are unknown.

Where committees function in the HI, health and safety is most likely to be discussed, followed by training, working practices and welfare services and facilities. Pay and government regulations are the least frequently discussed issues. HI committees are significantly less likely to discuss employment and pay issues. There is a different emphasis on the range of issues discussed in AIS and the PSS, making for a fuller, more rounded agenda. Even so the vast majority of committees discuss a range of issues rather than a single topic, with the exception of restaurants where most discuss a single topic.

Table: Consultation and Communication by Sub-sector (%)

	Hotels	*Campsites*	*Restaurants*	*Bars*	*Canteens*
System of briefings	97	94	91	73	81
Consultative committee	22	28	5	9	3
Problem-solving or quality groups	25	0	17	4	49
Formal opinion survey p	36	78	50	39	62
Other dd					
Entire workforce meetings	22	6	59	61	18
Management chain/ cascade	52	100	37	30	20
Suggestion schemes	20	24	39	22	12
Newsletter	29	24	36	51	66
Disclosure of information bb					

Internal investment plans	71	100	34	55	77
Financial position of establishment	76	96	49	74	88
Financial position of organization m	64	72	76	89	71
Staffing plans	65	78	68	34	62

Notes: *Yes responses to all weighted cases unless otherwise stated. p In last five years for establishments five years or older. dd Four most frequently mentioned other ways in which management consults or communicates with employees (multi-response). bb Regularly given by management to employees or their representatives. m Where part of a larger organization or sole UK establishment.*

In the very few HI workplaces where a consultative committee deals with a range of issues (N = 13, all of which employ 50 or more workers), employee representatives are significantly more likely to be elected and not to be appointed by management than in AIS and the PSS. In AIS there are proportionately more workplaces where committees deal with a range of issues (N = 441), but representatives are less likely to be elected, and appointment by management features in one-quarter of workplaces. These committee meetings occur slightly more frequently in AIS and the PSS. HI managers were significantly more likely than their AIS and PSS counterparts to consider these committees as fairly influential or not very influential.

Direct Participation

Marchington and Wilkinson identify a fourfold schema of involvement, all of which embrace empowerment to differing degrees. Whether involvement schemes benefit all or are wholly exploitative, benefiting only employers depends on the context and the processes, and employees can simultaneously experience greater job discretion and increased satisfaction and increased work demands. Workers will always resist so it is 'unrealistic to expect these sorts of schemes to remove problems from work, given that the employment relationship in any organization is built upon both conflict and co-operation'.

The use of employee involvement practices to foster an open, supportive and participatory employment relations climate will be positively linked to improving SQ. Communication systems, based on the 'involvement' model of indirect participation are an important prerequisite to culture change. Guest and Conway see a parallel between managing organizational culture and the psychological contract, as both embody people-building and high trust relationships. The process is complex and, if left to chance, will lead to poor relations with employees.

Communication is most effective at entry and on-job, while communicating down the organization is the most difficult aspect. The problem for managers in attempting to communicate full and accurate information is that simple explanations may distort reality. Most of the literature on employee involvement in the HI is concerned with empowerment and team working. After discussing these we focus on other involvement mechanisms drawn mainly from WERS.

Empowerment

Empowerment is a central component of SQ management and, like team working, is managerially led. It is wider than delegation, as power and authority are devolved, giving employees greater responsibility to solve problems, akin to Friedman's (1977) 'responsible autonomy'. Rather than providing greater autonomy or self-

A four-fold schema of Involvement

Downward communication is the most diluted, and includes written documentation, face-to-face meetings, house journals and team briefing. Its purpose is to convey information, reinforce managerial prerogative and shape employee expectations. Upward problem solving taps into employees' knowledge and ideas, and includes suggestion schemes and ad hoc problem-solving groups or quality circles, where small groups meet voluntarily on a regular basis to identify, analyse and solve quality-related work problems. These practices are part of 'best practice' HRM. Like downward communication it is essentially unitarist and 'bolted' onto the work process.

Task-based participation is integral to the job and part of everyday working life, and includes quality of working life programmes. It may entail performing more tasks at the same level or at a higher level, or some managerial/supervisory responsibility. Teamworking and self-management (one of Pfeffer's (1998) seven key HRM practices) allows employees to take responsibility for the task, work without direct supervision, to have discretion over work methods and time, to multi-skill and to recruit team members. Managerial control is at its most subversive and effective when employees take on responsibility for peer surveillance management, empowerment may lead to greater work intensification and increased stress, and may represent a form of control. Lashley (1997) identifies four meanings of empowerment through:

- Participation (autonomous work groups, job enrichment);
- Involvement (quality circles, team briefings);
- Commitment (share ownership, profit-sharing);
- Delayering (job redesign, job enrichment).

Claims for empowerment need to take account of the way managers use these different definitions and meanings, as different forms of empowerment lead to different working arrangements and boundaries for what employees can and cannot do. Empowerment as participation is observed in Marriott Hotels where employees have to identify and satisfy customer needs. In Harvester Restaurants where delayering requires staff to make decisions about

work organization or scheduling, the culture is still largely control-oriented. Empowerment as involvement is practised in Hilton Hotels (team briefing), McDonald's (suggestion schemes) and Accor (quality circles).

The challenge for international companies is how to balance the consistency and certainty demanded by customers with elements of employee discretion necessary to add the nebulous quality factor to social interactions in variety of cultural contexts. Jones et al. (1997) report how one American hotel company encourages employees to 'share' and 'celebrate' employment stories, including access to a worldwide empowerment hotline. This helps reinforce a level of commitment perceived as necessary to go 'beyond contract'.

Managers find themselves caught between the contradictory impulses of standardization and customization, and cannot abandon either. Legge (1995a) identifies a similar contradiction within quality management, which seems to argue for delegation and control simultaneously.

Marriott Corporation and Harvester Restaurants use empowerment to produce greater efficiency, improve employee commitment, and ultimately increase customer satisfaction. At Harvester Restaurants the removal of a layer of management and the formation of employees into self-managing teams succeeded because of low turnover, the commitment of the team manager and the active support of senior managers. The greater autonomy and discretion afforded by team working may be accompanied by work intensification and increased surveillance, e.g. management, peers, customer feedback and 'mystery shoppers'. 'Quick fix' empowerment will rarely succeed.

Case Study: From Empowerment to Control in a Canadian Nightclub

Employees had developed an articulate and sophisticated culture with an elaborate customer-service hierarchy and system of reward and punishment, based on high-tipping customers. The main product was status not alcohol. There was low staff turnover and high flexibility, and core values were instilled in informal after-work gatherings, where employees shared stories, thereby training each other. There was high group cohesion although staff developed their own highly personalized styles of service to suit their particular customers.

The change was designed to generalize service to as wide a market as possible, with a new manager exercising control from the top. Job training was to manipulate employees' perception of their role. All intermediate supervisory posts were removed, so grievances had to be taken to the top. Employees' behaviour was monitored by 'spotters'. Superficial agreeability, a form of industrial sabotage, replaced authoritative emotional exchange. Employees were deskilled because they engaged in more limited social interaction and lost income because they had to serve different customers.

After-work gatherings reduced and workers became stressed. Customers went elsewhere, sales fell, morale declined and employees lost any respect they had had for the manager.

The key to success is communication that builds a shared understanding of what empowerment means, surrounded by commitment, ownership, skills and competencies, leadership and sustainability.

Hales and Kildas claim that 'The notion of empowerment is beset by conceptual ambiguities, contradictions and a lack of compelling supporting evidence.' Their study of five-star hotels in Amsterdam found little evidence of empowerment in spite of management rhetoric. What there was amounted to increased employee responsibility rather than greater choice over how work is done or more voice in organizational decisions. Support systems of recruitment, training and remuneration were mostly absent.

The critical issue of how to balance control and autonomy in securing both compliance and cooperation is also addressed by others. As Lashley points out, 'Employers are concerned with both employee control and commitment. Employers are merely shifting the locus of control from one imposed externally on employees, to one which generates increased self-control in each employee.' At best worker power in enhanced but in highly controlled circumstances.

Sosteric's ethnographic account of a nightclub provides a case of empowerment in reverse, as a management sought to impose direct control in a workplace where work organization was based on responsible autonomy.

Teamworking

Service industry characteristics and customer orientation are conducive to teamworking, which is one of the three key principles of SQ management. Claims that teamworking is used in two-thirds of British workplaces are rather hollow as only 5 per cent actually had autonomous work groups.

Rees examined the nature and extent of employee involvement through teamworking in hotels, including the methods used and the levels of responsibility and autonomy afforded to teams. Two approaches were used. Task-based teams were created to make workers functionally flexible, e.g. within food and beverage operations across the bar, restaurant and room service.

Problem-solving teams met to discuss improving customer service when management signalled a problem. Actual levels of discretion and responsibility were low because managers deployed various mechanisms to limit empowerment. Although the employees reported a strong sense of teamwork, they felt it should allow them to have more input into problem-solving and decision-making. Rees defines constrained responsible autonomy as 'reorganized control', as the increased level of employee involvement is within increasingly defined and measured limits.

WERS shows that HI workplaces are significantly less likely to have most of the LOG working in formally designated teams. Higher levels of teamworking occur in large HI workplaces, where three-quarters of workplaces have half or more workers so involved. The HI is also significantly more likely to have just a few or no workplaces using teamworking, especially in very small workplaces. The lack of teamworking is interesting given that it is one of Redman and Mathews' eight key HRM practices necessary to make a positive contribution to SQ.

Workforce Briefing

WERS tells us that a large majority of workplaces in AIS, the PSS and the HI operate a system of briefings for one or more sections of the workforce. Nine in ten HI workplaces employing 25 or more workers operate a system of briefings.

An all-inclusive approach involving the whole workforce is especially marked in very small workplaces. A more selective or tiered approach of departmental or work group/section/team briefing occurs as workplace size increases, and is most common in hotels.

Briefing occurs less frequently in the HI than in AIS and the PSS, with six in ten HI workplaces briefing on a monthly or less frequent basis compared to half in AIS. Infrequency of briefing is particularly marked in very small HI workplaces and bars, with more frequent briefing occurring in large workplaces and hotels. HI workplaces give slightly less time at meetings to questions from employees or for employees' views, and the amount of time available decreases with HI workplace size.

Thus nearly two-thirds of large workplaces allocate less than a quarter of time at meetings for this purpose, while six in ten very small workplaces allow one-quarter or more of the meeting for employee feedback. This suggests that employees in very small workplaces do have more opportunity to participate in such meetings although the opportunity for them to do this is less frequent. Conversely briefing in large workplaces is less 'consultative' although it occurs more frequently.

The vast majority of HI workplaces in New Zealand communicate directly with individuals, usually on an 'as and when' basis, although more formal methods such as JCCs are found in larger workplaces. Workplaces are less likely to seek employees' input than to supply information. Newsletters, suggestion schemes and notice boards were common only in hotels and fast food.

Problem-solving Groups

The HI is significantly less likely to have problem-solving groups for specific problems or to discuss aspects of performance or quality than AIS and the PSS. In the HI the probability of a group operating increases with workplace size. Where there is no group and the establishment is five or more years old, groups have been used during the last five years in only a tiny minority of workplaces.

Although such groups are more likely to be permanent in the HI than in AIS and the PSS, the HI is significantly more likely to have groups with a finite life than AIS. In the HI a group's contribution is significantly more likely to be recognized by non-financial reward and is significantly less likely to get nothing at all. Financial rewards are given in around one-third of cases.

Whether or not such groups exist, employees in most workplaces in AIS, the PSS and the HI can make suggestions for improving working methods through other channels, most commonly through their managers.

Opinion Surveys

A significant minority of workplaces in AIS, the PSS and the HI has used formal surveys to elicit employees' views or opinion during the last five years. In the HI this is more likely to happen in workplaces employing 50 or more workers than in workplaces employing fewer than 50 employees. The results are most likely to be made available in written form to all employees than not made fully available.

However, full disclosure is more likely not to take place at all in very small HI workplaces. Chung (1997) suggests that opinion surveys enable employees to provide valuable information about guests' characteristics, appropriate people to hire and the training they need, and how best to reward employees. The results may be used to adjust HR practices in support of SQ.

Communication and Consultation

The HI is most likely to communicate or consult using regular meetings with the whole workforce, while the management chain and cascading information are most likely to be used in AIS and the PSS. In addition to these two methods, regular newsletters distributed to all employees and suggestion schemes constitute the four most often used methods in AIS and the HI. Even, so one-fifth of HI workplaces (16 per cent in AIS) offers no other forms of communication and consultation.

Disclosure of information relating to plans about organizational and establishment financial performance and internal investment and staff plans is a majority practice in AIS, PSS and HI workplaces. Regular information about the financial position of the whole organization (where part of larger organization or sole UK establishment) is the issue most likely to be disclosed to employees or their representatives. Looking at all HI workplaces, financial information about the establishment is more likely to be disclosed than information about internal investment plans and staffing plans.

It appears through pluralist, democratic processes i.e. an employee participation paradigm with collectivized relations that share decision making and power; 'empowerment' as currently applied within many organizations inside and outside of the hospitality and tourism industries, appears largely to be of the unitarist / HRM variety which seeks to gain commitment through an employee involvement paradigm.

These sources investigate in depth, the complex concept of empowerment as it is applied across a number of hospitality organisations. It recognises a broad spectrum of interpretations of 'empowerment' including 'participatory' approaches, however the main foci are on forms of empowerment centred on 'employee involvement'.

5

Reflections on the Adventure Tourism Significance

INTEGRATING PERSPECTIVES

A hotel is an establishment that provides paid lodging, usually on a short-term basis. Hotels often provide a number of additional guest services such as a restaurant, a swimming pool or childcare. Some hotels have conference services and meeting rooms and encourage groups to hold conventions and meetings at their location.

Hotels differ from motels in that most motels have drive-up, exterior entrances to the rooms, while hotels tend to have interior entrances to the rooms, which may increase guests' safety and present a more upmarket image. A comfortable room, good food, and a helpful staff can make being away from home an enjoyable experience for both vacationing families and business travellers. While most lodging managers work in traditional hotels and motels, some work in other lodging establishments, such as camps, inns, boardinghouses, dude ranches, and recreational resorts.

In full-service hotels, lodging managers help their guests have a pleasant stay by providing many of the comforts of home, including cable television, fitness equipment, and voice mail, as well as specialized services such as health spas. For business travellers, lodging managers often schedule available meeting rooms and electronic equipment, including slide projectors and fax machines.

Lodging managers are responsible for keeping their establishments efficient and profitable. In a small establishment with a limited staff, the manager may oversee all aspects of operations. However, large hotels may employ hundreds of workers, and the general manager usually is aided by a number of assistant managers assigned to the various departments of the operation. In hotels of every size, managerial duties vary significantly by job title.

It is an honour to provide a commentary to the JIBS 2005 Decade Award-winning article 'Revisiting Multinational Firms' Tolerance for Joint Ventures: A Trust-Based Approach' by Anoop Madhok, a truly international scholar by background, training, spirit and vocation, and a prolific author who has enriched the field of international business (IB).

Madhok's trust-based approach shifted the attention from ownership as a means for multinational companies to control their international ventures to trust as a source of long-term resilience of the partnership. By building a bridge between Stopford and Wells (1972) and Franko's (1971) mainstream IB theories of ownership and the literature on trust, including earlier work on international joint ventures (IJVs) by Beamish (1985) and Parkhe (1993) among other insights, Madhok changed the discourse in the field of IB.

Furthermore, his award-winning article is a manifestation of a fruitful cross-disciplinary exchange: on the one hand, it brought into IB insights from disciplines such as sociology and anthropology, and on the other hand, it successfully exported IB contributions to other domains, through the universal appeal of the proposed framework. A decade after the article's publication, both the questions it poses and its integrative approach appear remarkably contemporary. The issue of what makes alliances persistently popular despite the challenges in achieving resilience and success continues to draw attention and re-kindle vigorous debates in the field.

This provides some reflections on the significance and implications of Madhok's (1995) article. It is structured as follows. First, I review a number of aspects of the original paper, high-lighting their contribution to the field of IB. Second, I trace the diffusion of some of the article's core ideas in subsequent scholarly publications in IB and other related domains. Lastly, revisiting Madhok's claim that trust matters, I pose some questions for further research.

Albeit Madhok's award-wining article is full of insights, I have chosen to focus on two main contributions: first, the shift in perspective from ownership to relationship, suggesting that trust matters in making IJVs resilient and successful; and, second, the integration rather than substitution of perspectives, using the relationship-centred approach in conjunction with the ownership-based approach in order to better understand the tolerance of multinational firms for IJVs with local partners.

The gist of Madhok's (1995) article is that trust is critical for cooperation. That trust-centred perspective focused attention on those aspects of the relationship that have been overlooked in the mainstream structural concern with control through ownership. In elaborating the framework for a trust-based approach, Madhok distinguished two mutually reinforcing components of trust, a 'yin and yang' of a kind, which he labelled 'structural' and 'social' trust.

The so-called structural component captured the synergic complementarities of the partners' resources and capabilities and, hence, their potential to create more value together than separately. The social component of trust, which Madhok himself has labelled 'social glue', kept the parties together, allowing the value-creating potential of their collaboration to be realised. In that sense, Madhok's trust-based approach appears to me to be concerned not so much with the multinational firm's tolerance for JVs but, rather, with its ability to create and capture value by paying attention to the social aspects of its partnerships.

This distinction between value-attainment potential and value realisation has been further elaborated by Madhok and Tallman (1998), who defined the inter-firm relationship as a productive resource in need of specific expenditures.

In addition to value, another essential element of Madhok's trust-based approach is the notion of trust-building expenses, which the parties of the IJV incur over time. Drawing on extant studies, Madhok posited that the building of a trusting relationship is a lengthy process demanding relational investment and 'various forms of hard and soft commitments'. In his framework, he argued that this investment was more likely to be made by partners in a relationship characterised by both strong structural and social components of trust — that is, a relationship that counts with strategically complementary resource bundles and with willingness to operate jointly in an efficient and flexible manner.

In addition, Madhok arteculated that investment requirements for trust-building depended on the life cycle of the relationship, with larger investment expected in the beginning, so that shared commitment can be established. Once there is a sound shared foundation, he hypothesised, maintaining the relationship usually becomes less investment-intensive. In the application of his trust-based framework to the case of multinational firms engaged in collaboration with local partners, Madhok argued that the investment in trust-building would differ depending on the strategy and structure chosen by the multinational firms. Madhok sustained that above-normal return would give a multinational firm the slack resources necessary for making what he called 'trust-building gestures' to its local partners. In my interpretation, this view of trust-building investment is rather instrumental and associates trust with payoff.

A related contribution is Madhok's attempt to elaborate on and clarify the dynamic nature of trust. Trust needs time to emerge. In addition, it requires repeated successful interactions as well as ongoing perception of equity. The nature and pattern of these interactions, Madhok posited, are influenced by the combination of structural and social trust. The stickiness of the relationship through the investment in trust allows for conflicts to be addressed and transitory states of inequity endured.

This dynamic assumes that the increased flexibility of the relationship resulting from its relational quality will in turn enable greater adaptability to changes in the environment, and will ultimately lead to improved performance of the alliance. Yet, this is but an assumption, and a recent study by Carson et al. (2003) reveals that the performance of trust-based governance is contingent on the ability of partners to read each other's behaviour in the process.

Madhok did not position his trust-based view as an alternative to the ownership-centred perspective. Rather, he argued that the two approaches were compatible and complementary, and demanded an integration of insights that could advance the understanding of IJVs' success and resilience. Such integration was possible because the two approaches had a common objective of achieving flexibility and efficiency in the way a relationship operates. In addition, they had different orientations, which allowed different aspects of the joint venture to be revealed.

For the ownership-centred perspective, flexibility and efficiency are achieved through hierarchical relations, that is, through control based on ownership. For the trust- or relationship-centred approach, they are attained through the management of the social relationship. By investigating cooperative phenomena, such as JVs, within a structural framework, the ownership-centred approach is outcome-oriented and relatively static. It fails to address the critical role of social context in inter-organisational relationships.

The so-called relationship- or trust-based approach is dynamic, process-oriented and concerned with issues such as reciprocity, commitment and forbearance, rather than control. Another distinction is that the ownership-centred perspective is a macro-approach, which connects strategy-structure-ownership levels of the MNCs with JV's tolerance. The relationship-centred approach is a micro-approach in that it pays attention to the dynamic processes underlying a relationship. Taken together, the two approaches overcome their respective limitations and provide a more balanced and refined understanding of what makes IJVs tick.

One final distinction is that, in addition to flexibility and efficiency, a trust-based approach is attentive to the coordination aspects of the partnership and the need for resolution of conflicts triggered by differential contribution and/or learning by the partners, temporary inequity, as well as exogenous events that can change the partners' strategic priorities.

Beyond its direct contribution to a field, a published piece of scholarly work gains a life of its own in those studies that build on its ideas and the articles that cite it in their theoretical and empirical developments. In this, seek to identify some of the influences of Madhok's article upon studies of IB and the related domain of interorganisational relationships. Also, I trace the article's diffusion to other fields and scholarly discourses.

A decade since its coming into print, Madhok's (1995) article in JIBS is alive and oft-cited. It has served as a building block or inspiration for studies on international JVs and cross-cultural collaboration, as well on strategic alliances in general. Moreover, its ideas have travelled to fields such as marketing, supply chain management, engineering, psychology and law, thus proving their universal appeal and usefulness.

There are two main areas in which Madhok's ideas have been most visible and have exercised the most significant impact — international JVs and strategic alliances. In the first theme — IJVs — scholars who have delved into the issues of control and collaboration with particular interest in trust have found Madhok's framework relevant. Their work has centred on the effectiveness of the JVs, the processes of trust-building, the multi-levelled nature and meaning of trust or the partnering skills needed for success.

The second theme, that of strategic alliances, represents a phenomenon much broader than the original scope of Madhok's framework, centred on IJVs of multinational companies with local partners. Beyond that, Madhok's trust-based framework has become part of a fruitful stream of research into alliances. Scholars dealing with issues of inter-firm relationships have taken on Madhok's ideas when examining formation of strategic alliances or their co-evolution, establishment of commitment through bonding and trust, sources of alliance success or failure, or the link between trust and risk.

Understandably, the biggest diffusion and impact of Madhok's (1995) article has taken place on the pages of JIBS, with numerous scholars drawing inspiration from it. However, the seeds of Madhok's (1995) framework have been planted in a wealth of other journals in the field of strategy, management and organisation, which place the issues of alliances, relational advantage and inter-organisational relationships at the heart of their editorial agendas.

Thus, the article has been referenced in publications in the following journals (listed alphabetically) including: Academy of Management Review; Accounting, Organization, and Society; Group and Organization Management; International Journal of Management Reviews; Journal of Business Research; Journal of Management; Journal of Management Studies; Journal of Organizational Change Management; Journal of World Business; Long Range Planning; Organizational Science; Organizational Studies; Research Policy; Strategic Management Society.

Furthermore, scholars from various fields and domains have built upon Madhok's ideas. Some examples of diffusion, infrequent in academic circles that tend to operate as silos, include Batt's (2003) article on supply chain performance, Farrelly and Quester's (2005) work on relationship quality in sponsorship exchanges, Robson and Dunk's (1999) article on co-marketing alliances, Salbu's (1997) contribution to business law with work on contracts as device for flexible coordination and control, and Tjosvold's (1998) work in psychology, with focus on cooperative and competitive approach to conflict.

Hence, it is not surprising that journals from other disciplinary domains have also published articles that acknowledged Madhok's (1995) original ideas, including: American Business Law Journal; Applied Psychology — An International Review; Industrial Marketing Management; International Marketing Review; Journal of Engineering and Technology Management; Journal of International Marketing; Journal of the Academy of Marketing

Science; and Supply Chain Management — An International Journal. This diffusion of IB ideas to fields of strategy, management and organisation, as well as to other, not necessarily adjacent, areas and disciplines, signals with optimism that IB research is capable of inspiring and informing scholarly conversations in other domains.

Future Research

Madhok (1995) suggested broadening the scope of his trust-based approach beyond the particular case of a multinational firm and its local partners. Madhok proposed a potential extension in the direction of partnerships between two multinational companies, in which the geographical, product and activity scope of the partnership is much broader and the dynamics much more complex. In my view, another fruitful avenue for further exploration, for which the JIBS 2004 Decade Award-winning article by Oviatt and McDougall (1994) has paved the way, is the perspective of the entrepreneurial firms forming the alliance and the dynamics of the partnerships these international new ventures form.

They are distinctive types of player in the IB arena and lack the resources that multinational companies possess to invest in trust-building gestures. In addition, as a variety of new alliance forms have come into being in the decade following the publication of Madhok's award-winning article, the nature of their dynamics is also worthy of further investigation. In that sense, thinking in network rather than dyadic terms can be insightful and informative.

Madhok (1995) employed trust, relationship and cooperation as interchangeable descriptors of his trust-based perspective. Upon reviewing the developments in the trust literature and the cumulative contribution to the field of alliances in the last decade, in my interpretation these three terms are not interchangeable, as they evoke different emphases in understanding the stability of interfirm partnerships. For example, cooperation is not necessarily sustained by trust, and a relationship can be glued by shared social norms and sanctions instead of trust as a 'social lubricant'.

Hence, there is a risk of trust becoming 'a residual term for the complex socio-psychological processes necessary for social action to occur'. Special issues of the Academy of Management Journal (1998), Organization Studies (2000) and Organization Science (2003) have furthered knowledge of the levels, types and effects of trust. Despite their collective contributions, however, trust continues to be an unresolved concern and a rather fragmented and diverse theme.

Doubts continue to be raised 'about the universality of the effect of trust on business transactions'. In this sense, the focus and, in some cases, over-reliance on trust in the alliance literature has obscured a more general treatment of the nature and role of enforcement mechanisms. It may have also confounded the most interesting sources of variation in safeguarding inter-firm relationships and their stability.

Concluding his 1995 JIBS article, Madhok admitted that '[i]t would be naive to overemphasize trust'. In subsequent articles, he continuously and vigorously sought to clarify or deepen understanding of certain aspects and terminology of his trust-based framework. For example, he and Tallman proposed 'a nontrust explanation of why firms might knowingly forgo opportunities to take advantage of their partners'. Recently, Carson et al. (forth-coming) raised doubts on whether social sanctions suffice in stopping opportunism in situations of high ambiguity.

They sought to clarify the contingency nature of formal and relational contracting in conditions of volatility and uncertainty. Furthermore, they went beyond merely assuming opportunism to directly testing its relationship with uncertainty. All these efforts enriched and expanded the scholarly conversation on alliances. Yet, they also signalled the need to consider approaches that provide alternative, integrative and more nuanced explanations of why inter-firm relationships continue experiencing high rates of both foundings and failures, and how their stability can be enhanced.

Svejenova et al. (2005) argue that, in order to improve understanding of the issue of stability in international alliances, attention should be paid to enforcement. Enforcement ensures that behaviours are enacted or that individuals would act in a particular way. Enforcement mechanisms differ from deterrence mechanisms in that the latter rely on avoidance and preclusion of particular types of behaviour, whereas the former enable collaboration and ensure partners' actions are consistent with expectations. They are also likely to evolve with the strategic intent of partners. The sources and certainty of enforcement remain a relatively little explored theme. There is a lack of agreement in the literature on when trust is the enforcement mechanism and when other mechanisms create an enforcement environment that results in trust-like outcomes.

Svejenova et al. (2005) proposed a framework of enforcement. (1) With it they seek to clarify the role of trust in safeguarding inter-firm collaboration and identify other mechanisms that could generate trust-like outcomes of the kind of reliability or predictability of partners' cooperative behaviour. In elaborating their enforcement perspective, they do not allege that trust is unwarranted or unlikely to emerge in a process of productive cooperation; only that its many roles may have been overstated.

The theoretical perspective advanced by Svejenova et al. (2005) defines an enforcement space that takes shape along ownership, legal and social dimensions. Legal enforcement is manifested in the existence of a reliable legal system, with its codification and transparency of laws (e.g., property, contract and commercial law), and a realistic expectation for fair and relatively speedy legal adjudication in the courts. The agreement can be formal, informal, written, oral or just plain 'taken-for-granted'.

The creative complexity and variety of alliance forms has outpaced the legal arena and the analytical tools used by antitrust enforcement agencies to assess their legality. Hence, mechanisms other than contracts have been used as complements to or substitutes for legal enforcement. Social embeddedness has been considered another source of enforcement of cooperation through mechanisms such as friendship (enforcement by the strength of the interpersonal relationship), reputation (enforcement by an open network of third parties) and social norms and sanctions (enforcement by a closed, cohesive network such as kinship relations).

A third source of enforcement is the ownership dimension. To its traditional depiction, understood and conceptualised in terms of financial equity, Svejenova et al. (2005) added two other ownership-related mechanisms: revenue-sharing and brand equity. Revenue-sharing agreements do not involve equity participation of the partners in their respective companies or in their joint venture.

Brand equity is another enforcement mechanism, particularly relevant in franchising and licensing relationships and especially in those cases in which the intellectual property of technology included as the basis of the alliance is proprietary and difficult to imitate. For example, Contractor and Kundu (1998) found that, in the hotel business, registered brand names are a potent source of control, and the threat of withdrawing permission to use the brand moderates the opportunistic behaviour of the firm's international partners.

Taking into account mechanisms with different nature, the framework advanced by Svejenova et al. (2005) seeks to identify when trust is a requisite for the alliance and when it may not be essential. This is especially useful in the cases of cross-border alliances, when local partners can occupy enforcement spaces different from those of the multinational company that seeks to partner with them. While each of the three dimensions — legal, social and ownership enforcement — has important individual implications for the enforcement of a partnership, they may act as complements rather than substitutes.

There is a range of intermediary cases shaped by different combinations of the three enforcement mechanisms. For example, within this framework, trust is a requisite enforcement mechanism in the case of friends who cooperate on the basis of a handshake or an oral agreement and share revenues. Trust is dispensable when there is some kind of assurance, that is,

> *"expectations of benign behaviour from an exchange partner based on knowledge of an incentive structure that encourages such behaviour rather than exploitation. Mechanisms that provide assurance include legal or normative authorities that impose sanctions for violations of agreements or failure to fulfil one's obligations, guarantees such as collateral that protect against loss, warranties that assure certain standards of quality, and so forth."*

For example, assurance rather than trust can enforce cooperation in the case of a partnership embedded in a closed, cohesive network, based on a detailed contract and exchange of financial equity.

Further understanding of, and empirical work on when trust matters remains to be done. Future research should consider a broader range of dimensions for the enforcement of stability in a partnership. It should seek to identify what factors may influence the parties in an alliance to seek certain types of enforcement. In his analysis of the smaller economies of Pacific Asia and their business systems, Redding (2005) described how their social and legal embeddedness differs owing to differences in culture, religion, legacies of the former colonial powers (the English, Dutch or the French), etc. Using the enforcement framework, Svejenova et al. (2005) hypothesise that firms that have been historically and spatially embedded in cultures where institutions are weak or underdeveloped will tend to favour relations, as opposed to contracts, in safeguarding the exchange.

In the case of China, for example, 'Personal networks are ... particularly significant modes of economic transacting in China because of the weak institutional sanctions against reneging on commitments'. However, those personal networks can be of little use to a foreign company without access to these networks or previous history of collaboration, when considering a partnership with a Chinese firm.

In that sense, a focus on the dynamics of nation-institutional configurations rather than on culture may be more meaningful in capturing differences along the enforcement dimensions. Importing and integrating insights from political-institutional approaches to sociology into the field of IB could contribute to a more comprehensive view of inter-firm collaborations. How do adjustments in nation-state institutional arrangements affect inter-firm relationships and choices of alliance partners?

How are differences in institutional contexts imprinted on management decisions about initiating and maintaining international alliances? There is a need for studies into alliances being established in developing countries, not only from the perspective of the foreign organisation but also from the point of view of the local partners, which has been largely unaccounted for.

A better understanding is needed of the role played by interlocked business and state elites in purporting their impact on alliances not only as a source of reputation but also as matchmakers. A range of well-known Italian, French and Asian cases illustrate the importance of powerful, well-connected individuals in the business and political elite in triggering and guaranteeing inter-organisational collaboration. Bank managers are in a position to identify from among the portfolio of their clients potential partners whose interests could match theirs. Further attention is needed to the strategies that firms pursue not only to safeguard a partnership by securing partners who behave according to expectations but also to convey an image of a reliable partner. This is especially true for entrepreneurial firms in need of a partner with incumbents to enhance their legitimacy and reputation.

In addition, given that alliances usually have proponents and detractors in the partnering organisations, more studies on the role of organisational politics in developing or detracting from the realisation of the value potential of a partnership over time could enhance understanding and better management of the alliance dynamics. Expected contribution of comparative sociology to understanding alliance differences across nation-states, along with the accentuated role of political behaviour, individual cognition and attachments in maintaining inter-organisational relationships, raise the issue of the need for multi-level studies and co-evolutionary perspectives. They also suggest that IB literature can benefit from insights coming from other domains, which in turn would allow it to advance knowledge that can be inspirational for scholars from those domains.

Another element in an agenda on inter-firm relationships may encompass their dysfunctional consequences and negative effects. Here, a critical issue that future studies could clarify is the concept of failure in a strategic alliance. Furthermore, research on the dysfunctional outcomes of alliances and networks could help in understanding how and why firms get locked into and sustain unproductive partnerships that could hinder opportunities to collaborate with other viable firms.

International alliances continue to be a vast and vibrant scholarly domain in IB studies in need of further clarification and integration of disparate contributions. In order for future research to result in a better understanding of the enforcement of stability in alliances, studies must incorporate approaches from comparative sociology and economic geography, which can provide a broader and better foundation than merely the culture-based one for understanding alliance differences. In addition, researchers must strive to separate trust from trust-like mechanisms for initiating and maintaining a partnership, which would afford an explanation of how firms who are 'strangers' can initiate a potentially profitable relationship in the absence of a common relational history.

Since its publication, Madhok's award-winning article has enriched and expanded the IB discourse and opened up numerous avenues for theoretical and empirical work on inter-firm relationships. With the extent of its diffusion and influence, it has also revealed that the IB literature could successfully integrate insights from other domains and, in turn, serve as a source of inspiration to scholarship in other disciplines.

By considering the benefits from change in assumptions from opportunism to trust 'till proven otherwise', Madhok (2006) poses yet another challenge to researchers in IB and inter-firm relationships. I am convinced that he will continue planting the seeds of his ideas in numerous forthcoming publications and igniting the imagination of scholars to come.

Staffing Policies and Strategic Control

While the effective management of human resources is increasingly being recognized as a major determinant of success or failure in international business, in practice many organizations are still coming to terms with the human resources issues associated with international operations.

In the international arena, the quality of management seems to be even more critical than in domestic operations. This is primarily because the nature of international business operations involves the complexities of operating in different countries and employing different national categories of workers. Yet, while it is recognized that HRM problems become more complex in the international arena, there is evidence to suggest that many companies underestimate the complexities involved in international operations. The field of international human resource management, however, is only slowly developing as a field of academic study and has been described by one authority as being in the infancy stage. Moreover, there is relatively little empirical research that documents the international HRM strategies and practices of international firm - particularly firms that have their headquarters outside North America.

This reports some of the findings from a recent study of international human resource management in Britain- and Ireland-based international firms. One particular feature of the study was the exclusive focus on "managing managers." Particular attention is given to three key issues in the area of international human resource management: international staffing, international recruitment, and the variety of issues surrounding the problem of shortages of international managers. I will also briefly consider the nature of the human resource management challenges facing companies in the light of the Single European Market.

A study of how companies deal with the international human resource management issues outlined above is particularly appropriate for the reasons enumerated below.

First, the international staffing process is of considerable importance to an international firm: "Virtually any type of international problem, in the final analysis, is either created by people or must be solved by people. Hence, having the right people in the right place at the right time emerges as the key to a company's international growth. If we are successful in solving this problem, I am confident we can cope with all others".

The staffing problems facing international firms are more complex than in domestic firms, and inappropriate staffing policies may lead to difficulties in managing overseas operations. The international literature indicates that expatriate failure is a persistent and recurring problem, particularly for U.S. multinationals. Frequently, the human and financial costs of failure in the international business arena are more severe than in domestic business. In particular, indirect costs such as loss of market share and damage to overseas customer relationships may be considerable.

Second, the shortage of international managers is becoming an increasing problem for international firms. A survey of 440 executives in European firms claimed that a shortage of international managers was the single most important factor constraining corporate efforts to expand abroad. Almost one-third of the executives surveyed had experienced difficulties in finding managers with the necessary international experience and orientation. The findings of the survey suggest that the successful implementation of global strategies depends, to a large extent, on the existence of an adequate supply of internationally experienced managers.

Third, there is little empirical research on the international human resource management issues associated with the management of managers in British and Irish international firms, especially in comparison to the considerable literature on international human resource management in U.S. firms.

Fourth, the advent of the Single European Market and the rapid growth of British direct investment abroad since the early 1980s mean that issues of international staffing, recruitment, and development are increasingly important concerns in a far wider range of organizations than the traditional giant multinationals. International HRM problems are becoming increasingly important for a growing number of smaller and medium-sized companies that have significantly internationalized their operations in recent years.

Research Methodology and Sample

The principal research method was structured interviews with each company's corporate personnel or human resources director, or with a senior corporate HR executive. The majority of interviews were conducted in 1990, the remainder in 1991. The duration of interviews varied from two hours to three and a half hours. During each interview, information was sought on company structure and international operations. The interviewer also asked questions concerning international staffing, expatriate performance, international HRM policies, and international management development.

These questions were adapted from a study by Tung (1981) and through consultation with a number of international HRM practitioners. The purpose of the questions was to provide a structured basis for each interview, and responses to questions were noted by the interviewer since interviewees were not asked to fill in a questionnaire. Additional information was obtained from company reports, company documents such as international personnel policies, and newspaper articles.

Forty-five international companies participated in the study. Forty companies were British-owned and five were Irish-owned international firms. The sample was specifically chosen to include companies from both the manufacturing and the service sectors. Twenty-six companies in the study were primarily manufacturing firms and sixteen were service sector firms. Two oil companies and one mining company also participated.

The size of the companies in this international firm sample ranges from medium to very large, with the total number of employees worldwide ranging from 9,500 to 240,000. The smaller size of the Irish international firms and their relatively recent internationalization were two principal reasons for their inclusion in the study. For the sample as a whole, there was a wide range in the number of countries the companies operated in, and in the length of experience in international operations.

International Staffing Policies and Practices

International firms face three alternatives with respect to the staffing of management positions abroad - namely, the employment of parent-country nationals, host-country nationals, or third-country nationals. Much of the existing research focuses on the advantages and disadvantages of using expatriates as opposed to local managers and it identifies a range of host-country, company, and individual factors as important considerations in international staffing decisions. Most studies are, however, largely inconclusive on the question of when parent-country nationals should be sent abroad.

The findings of the present study on staffing practices in British and Irish international firms reveal that a majority of the companies continued to rely heavily on parent country nationals to run their foreign operations. The research findings showed that, while almost 50 per cent of companies had formal policies favouring the use of host-country managers to run their foreign operations, in practice just over one-third operated with host-country nationals in senior management positions in their foreign operations.

In other words, two-thirds of the companies relied primarily on expatriates to run their foreign operations. Furthermore, the trend has moved in the direction of greater use of expatriates. Half of the companies in the sample (22 out of 45) reported an increase in the use of expatriates over the previous decade and only 20 per cent indicated that they had reduced their use of expatriates. The remainder reported no significant change.

These findings raise serious questions about the ability and commitment of some British multinationals to identify and develop host-country managers effectively in their foreign operations. Therefore, the recruitment, selection, and development of host-country managers emerges as a vital issue for British and Irish multinationals, given the need to develop global teams with a variety of different perspectives and competences.

The findings of the present study on staffing practices in British and Irish firms reveal sharp differences with U.S. experience. Indeed, recent work by Kobrin suggested that the tendency of U.S. multinationals to reduce the numbers of expatriates had gone too far. He argued that U.S. firms have tended to substitute host-country nationals to replace expatriates primarily in response to the difficulties U.S. managers have experienced in adjusting to other cultural environments.

Kobrin recognized that the increased use of host country managers may in part reflect the cost of maintaining expatriates abroad, the greater sensitivity of local managers to local culture, and local market needs and the growing international maturity of some multinationals. It is suggested, however, that expatriate reduction may result in U.S. multinationals facing reduced identification with the worldwide organization and its objectives, difficulties in exercising control, and a lack of opportunities for U.S. managers to gain international experience abroad. The principal concern is that U.S. multinationals could face major strategic management control problems where managers identify with local units rather than with global corporate objectives.

The present study identified a number of principal reasons for employing expatriates. The first was the lack of availability of management and technical skills in some countries. There was a greater tendency for companies to use expatriates in less developed countries due to the weak pool of available local management talent. This was also true for those companies that used host-country managers to run their foreign operations in advanced countries.

The second major reason cited for using expatriates was the objective of control of local operations. Thirty-three out of forty-five firms in the present study identified control as a key reason for their use of expatriates. Expatriates were felt to be more familiar with the corporate culture and the control system of headquarters, and this was felt to result in more effective communication and coordination. Indeed, a key role for senior expatriates was to train local managers to understand corporate financial and control systems.

This point is illustrated by a comment by the human resource director of a financial services company: "The main advantage of using expatriates is that they understand our [corporate] culture and reporting systems and they teach the locals how to relate to the centre. This is vital when you are establishing a new foreign business."

This finding on the importance of control is consistent with previous research on European multinationals which shows control to be an important reason for expatriate transfers. Yet, in previous research, only rarely has control been identified as an important aim of expatriate assignments. This probably reflects the North American origin of much previous research and the tendency of some managers and researchers to view control as a rather disreputable rationale for using expatriates.

A further key reason for using senior expatriates was to maintain trust in key foreign businesses, following large international acquisitions. This finding is particularly interesting because previous research has suggested that the employment of expatriates will be lower in acquisitions by comparison with greenfield sites. The emergence of trust as a major factor is related to the rapid growth in the number and scale of foreign acquisitions by British companies in the 1980s.

For example, in the late 1980s, a U.K. brewing and leisure company emerged as one of the world's leading hotel groups, following a massive [pounds]2 billion acquisition of a global hotel chain. In this example, a major reason given for using expatriates to run the acquisition was "the need to have the peace of mind which comes from having our people running such a large and strategically important investment." There was often an unwillingness to allow newly acquired foreign businesses to be run by the existing host-country national management, primarily because they were not known well enough and their loyalty to the business was not proven.

The research also found that using expatriates for management development purposes was important and was increasing in significance for British multinationals. Thirty-four out of forty-five companies reported that expatriates were used for development purposes, and twenty-five of these firms claimed that use of expatriates for this purpose was becoming more important. This reflects the tendency of British companies to see expatriation as part of the career-development process. In this context, it is interesting to note that, in most cases, the management of expatriates was the responsibility of the corporate human resource function. This was the case even in some highly decentralized organizations (e.g., engineering companies) where the corporate human resource role was rather limited.

One very recent trend identified by the research was the tendency for companies to give younger managers international experience much earlier in their career than previously. Over half of the companies in the sample (26 out of 45 companies) reported significant changes in this respect. This was linked to the growing problems of mobility (spouse's job, children's education, etc.) for older managers. This also reflects the strategy of some companies to broaden the opportunities for international development, and the growing recognition in some quarters that the payback on the investment of a developmental assignment may well be greater with a younger manager.

The performance of foreign subsidiaries also emerged as a significant factor influencing the use of expatriates. There was a greater tendency for the companies in the sample to use senior expatriates where the acquired business had been underperforming before the foreign acquisition. Similarly, poor performance by host-country managers in the post acquisition phase was cited as an important reason for replacing them with expatriates. This finding is well supported in the literature, which has frequently reported that crisis accentuates headquarters control.

This is well illustrated by the case of a major British food and drinks company that made two very large acquisitions in the United States in the late 1980s. The first acquisition was a global drinks business with its headquarters in the United States, and the second was a large U.S. food business. The staffing policy differed sharply in the two acquisitions. In the former case, the existing management team (composed entirely of host-country managers) continued to run the business. "In this case," said a corporate HR executive, "we inherited an excellent management team who were achieving first-class results. Why change a winning team and upset morale by introducing expatriates?" In the second case, by contrast, the entire U.S. management team was replaced by expatriates, "mainly due to poor financial results and weak managerial performance."

Another factor influencing the approach adopted by companies was a strong expectation on the part of major foreign customers (and sometimes foreign governments) that the top managers in their country should be parent-country nationals. Thirteen of the sixteen international firms in the service sector and a minority of manufacturing firms (6 out of 26) said they had taken this into account in deciding their policy. Public relations and marketing were usually the key roles in this context. Previous research has largely ignored this factor because it has concentrated on the very largest multinationals and tended to neglect the service sector.

For example, two Irish banks operating in the United States felt that there were considerable marketing and public relations advantages in using expatriates, given their marketing strategy of targeting the ethnic Irish population. In the banking, insurance, and finance areas, British companies reported that, in many countries, major foreign customers frequently had a strong preference for their senior executives to be British expatriates.

There is also strong evidence from the present research that expatriates are more likely to be used in the early stages of new foreign operations. This is consistent with previous research that shows this practice is common in the early stages of internationalization where a company is setting up a new business, process, or product in another country, and prior experience is considered essential. A majority of firms indicated that control and trust were particularly important in the early stages of internationalization. In the present study, this factor had become more significant due to the rapid growth of international business in the last decade.

Nearly half of the companies (21 out of 45) also cited weaknesses in their training and development of host-country national and third-country national managers to explain their continued use of expatriates, despite a formal policy to replace expatriates with host-country managers after the startup phase. A typical comment in this respect came from a pharmaceutical company: "The training and development of host-country nationals and third-country nationals is a major weakness in achieving our objective of localising management in our operating companies."

Shortages of International Managers

It was argued above that the successful implementation of global strategies depends, to a large extent, on the existence of an adequate supply of internationally experienced mangers. In the present study, two-thirds of the companies (30 out of 45) said that they had experienced shortages of international managers and over 70 per cent indicated that future shortages were anticipated.

While the faster pace of internationalization was cited as the primary reason for shortages by thirty-four of forty-five firms in the sample, the findings suggest that over half the firms (24 out of 45) reported that failures to recruit, retain, and develop host-country managers effectively were another key reason why shortages exist. A number of factors make the recruitment of host-country managers more difficult and costly compared with recruiting in the home country. These include: lack of knowledge of local labour markets; ignorance of the local education system and the status of qualifications; language and cultural problems at interviews and trying to transfer recruitment methods that work well in the United Kingdom to foreign countries.

Many international firms have tended to neglect the training and development needs of their host-country managers and focus virtually all of their managerial development efforts on their parent-country nationals' managers. Twenty-six of the forty-five firms in the sample reported that weaknesses in their training and development in respect of host-country managers had contributed to shortages of international managers. The failure to develop local managers effectively was frequently given by British multinationals as a reason for continuing to use U.K. expatriates in similar management positions rather than using local managers. Alternatively, this could be interpreted as something of an excuse for their preference to use expatriates beyond the development phase of international operations.

The present research highlighted three important lessons for those international firms that are seriously attempting to provide management training and development for host-country nationals and third-country nationals. First is the need to avoid the mistake of simply exporting parent-country training and development programmes to other countries. This point is illustrated by the following comment from the personnel director of a large chemical firm: "We have learned from some tough experiences that training and development programmes for local managers must be culturally adapted to local conditions."

Second, the management development programmes for host-country and third-country nationals need to be linked to the strategic situation in each country, as well as to the overall strategy of the firm. This need to take into account a variety of foreign product-market situations superimposed upon the overall strategic thrust of the firm adds considerably to the complexity of devising appropriate management development programmes.

The third lesson is the need to utilize much further the practice of developing host-country managers through developmental transfers to corporate headquarters. It has been argued that this type of international transfer exposes host-country nationals and third-country nationals to the headquarters' corporate culture and facilitates their developing a corporate perspective, rather than simply reflecting their own local interests.

It has also been argued that this approach to development can be very effective in helping to develop global management teams and is a necessary part of successfully operating a truly global firm. The present research indicated, however, that a majority of British companies still failed to recognize the need to develop high-potential host-country national managers to senior positions that exist outside their own countries, and this exacerbates the problem of attracting and retaining high-potential young managers in the host countries.

The Shortages of International Managers

Nineteen of the forty-five companies had responded to the shortage of international managers by attempting to identify parent-country managers of high potential at an earlier stage in their career, and by giving them international experience at a much younger age. Over one-third of the companies reported that they were sending young managers of high potential on international assignments partly for developmental purposes.

This was in sharp contrast to the previous practice when many MNCs relied on developing a cadre of career expatriates who moved from one international position to the next. The trend towards giving younger managers from the parent country the opportunity for international experience earlier in their careers was often part of a more general trend to give international experience to a wider range of managers, and not just to a relatively small group of expatriates. Increasing numbers of international firms were also using short-term developmental assignments in order to develop larger pools of employees with international experience.

Another significant response to the shortage of international managers was the rapid growth in importance of external recruitment to fill management positions abroad. Until a few years ago, the majority of firms had relied almost exclusively on internal recruitment for foreign management positions. British MNCs traditionally had a strong preference for well-known internal managers for expatriate management positions, as they had established track records and their loyalty to the company was proven. Over one-quarter of the firms in the study had, in the past five years, introduced external recruitment to fill management positions abroad, and several others were planning to do so. Financial services companies were a good example of this: some of these companies had rapidly internationalized relatively recently and felt they had to recruit externally at the senior level to establish their foreign operations.

A third response to the shortages of international managers by fourteen of the forty-five companies was to attempt to sell themselves more effectively to graduates through various types of marketing designed to highlight the international nature of their activities (e.g., in graduate recruitment brochures and in national press advertising). This type of marketing highlighted the prospects of early international experience to attract graduates seeking an international career. This can be illustrated by the example of the two textile companies that had a policy of sending young graduates on international assignments within three or six months of joining the firm.

This policy was very effective and was designed specifically to recruit high-potential young graduates who were particularly interested in an international career. The corporate human resources director of one of the textile companies commented: "Textiles is not a particularly fashionable industry. We are competing for the best graduates with companies that enjoy a more glamorous image. The fact that we can offer the opportunity of very early international experience is the main reason we can attract some high potential graduates when the big guns, such as Shell, BP, and ICI, are fishing in the same pool."

A minority of companies were also broadening their sources of graduate recruitment to include some continental European countries, and this reflected their anticipation of a growth in the competition for high-potential graduates following the advent of the Single European Market. Two computer companies had recently introduced Euro-graduate management development programmes.

A feature of these programmes was that graduates were recruited from several European countries for a two-year period of training and development in the United Kingdom. On completion of their training, graduates were transferred to a management position in a third country. The need to develop more flexible succession planning systems to support the development of Euro-graduates was identified as an important issue by both firms operating this type of programme.

There was also growing recognition of the importance of developing effective international management development programmes to help secure an adequate supply of international managers. The majority of firms reported that they were spending more money and more time on international management education, particularly for top and senior management. These firms were using a combination of internal and external international management development programmes. One interesting feature of these programmes was that teachers frequently came from prestigious foreign business schools in Europe and the United States, as well as from internal sources. However, only three of the forty-five firms claimed they had effective systems for evaluating their international management development programmes.

The introduction of language training for top, senior, and middle levels of management by the majority of companies in the study was seen as an important development in light of the acute shortages of international managers with language skills. This suggests that the importance of language training is increasingly being recognized by British multinationals. This finding is in sharp contrast with studies of U.S. MNCs, which found that only a minority of U.S. MNCs felt that knowledge of foreign languages was necessary for conducting business abroad.

Increasingly, it was recognized that language training increased the effectiveness of staff working abroad and helped them relate more easily to a foreign culture. There was also a growing awareness that language training promoted a better image of the MNC in the host country.

There were two areas, however, where the companies were clearly failing to take effective action to ease the acute shortage of international managers. First, there was no evidence that British multinationals were taking serious steps to increase the proportion of women in international management. International management has long been a masculine preserve in Europe and the United States. Adler's study estimates that under 3 per cent of North American expatriates are female.

In the present study, no company claimed to have more than 3 per cent of female expatriates. Indeed, the evidence suggests that women in British multinationals are not making as much progress in international management as women in U.S. multinationals. For example, in the U.S. banking and financial sector, there has been a significant increase in female expatriates.

The under representation of women in international management is illustrated by a quote from a woman HR executive of a U.K. pharmaceutical company: "In the UK, the majority of marketing staff are women. By contrast, in our foreign operations, the vast majority of marketing staff are male. Companies still tend to shy away from using female expatriates because of fears that women will not be accepted in some countries and the major problem of disrupting the career of their partner." The lack of willingness to recruit and develop women as international managers is worrying as recent research suggests that, in many ways, women are well suited to international management.

The second area that impacts on the supply of internationalists is the failure by many companies to adequately address repatriation problems. The repatriation of managers has been identified as a major problem for multinational companies in the United Kingdom and North America. Over 70 per cent of the firms (33 of 45) in the present study said they faced significant problems regarding reentry. Further, it was generally recognized that this may lead to low morale and a higher turnover of expatriates.

For example, only three of the firms claimed that repatriates had no difficulty reintegrating into the U.K. organization. A key problem for the majority of companies was finding suitable posts for repatriates of similar status and responsibility to those they held abroad. For many British MNCs, this problem had become more acute in recent years because, for many of the companies, expansion of overseas operations had taken place at the same time as the rationalization of U.K. operations, thereby reducing the number of senior posts in the United Kingdom.

Other problems associated with reintegrating into the United Kingdom are loss of status, loss of autonomy, loss of career direction, and a feeling that international experience is undervalued by the company. Further, there was growing recognition that where companies are seen to deal unsympathetically with the problems faced by expatriates on reentry, managers will be more reluctant to accept the offer of international assignments.

Research in North America indicates that 20 per cent of all managers who complete foreign assignments wish to leave their company on return. This was a growing problem for British multinationals, particularly when many companies are willing to pay a premium to attract the experienced international manager. Yet, while it is widely accepted that the costs of expatriate turnover are considerable, very few firms had introduced formal repatriation programmes to assist managers and their families with repatriation difficulties.

Similarly, very few companies had introduced mentor systems to check the career progression of the international manager. Many expatriate managers were concerned about losing out on opportunities at home, and, in some companies, this was a constraint on their willingness to go abroad. Clearly, British companies need to give a higher priority to the issue of repatriation in order to encourage international mobility and to help secure an adequate future supply of international managers.

Barriers to International Mobility

This briefly considers the reasons why shortages of international managers are expected to continue. In particular, it examines the growing restrictions on international mobility and their significance for the international capability of the firm.

Over 70 per cent of the firms (34 out of 45) reported that they anticipated shortages of international managers over the next five years. There was a growing concern on the part of many firms that the pace of internationalization would further outstrip the supply of international managers. The growing internationalization of European firms and the advent of the Single European Market in 1993 led firms to expect a more international and competitive market for managers and graduates.

For example, one financial services corporate HR executive expressed the problem like this: "Attracting and retaining high potential graduates and managers with international experience is vital if we are going to implement our corporate objective of achieving a much stronger presence in Europe. The problem is that the pool of available talent is not growing fast enough to meet demand." The same executive commented: "In the short run, we have to ensure that our reward package becomes internationally competitive, but this will not be enough. We need to look at new sources of labour supply such as women, host-country managers, third-country nationals and reduce our dependency on expatriates."

The problem of ensuring an adequate supply of international managers is further exacerbated by growing resistance to international mobility. Indeed, it was suggested by twenty-six of the forty-five firms in the sample that individuals were becoming less internationally mobile just when there was a growing need for international managers because of expansion abroad. The reduction in international mobility was attributed to several factors, including continued rationalization in the United Kingdom, which created uncertainties regarding reentry; the growing unwillingness to disrupt the education of children; the growing importance of quality of life considerations; and finally, continued uncertainty regarding international terrorism and political unrest.

Concerns about dual-career problems and disruption to children's education were seen as major barriers to future international mobility by many companies. In the past, working spouses were less common, generally female, and were prepared to follow their partners' career transfers. More frequently now, however, spouses must also leave a job or career in order to follow their partner to the foreign country. The growing significance of the dual-career problem is well illustrated by a quote from the HR corporate executive of a large oil company: "Nowadays families are less willing to disrupt personal and social lives even where they accept that international experience will enhance the manager's career prospects."

And a banking HR executive described the problem in these words: "More and more women have careers and not just jobs. For many it would be impossible to continue their careers in a foreign country. Increasingly international mobility is limited by the dual-career factor. Also we need to recognise that dual-career problems can seriously affect career development plans for our international managers."

Two further restrictions on international mobility are illustrated by the following quote from an HR executive in a chemical firm: "It's becoming more common for offers of foreign assignments to be rejected because the location does not appeal to the family, and when managers are willing to go abroad, they are much more demanding about all aspects of the remuneration package."

The above discussion would suggest that restrictions on international mobility appear to be growing just at the time when the need for international mobility is becoming vital for the internationalization of U.K. business. Indeed, the problem of international mobility could emerge as a key factor in determining the international capability of a firm.

In the present study, companies were asked to identify the main HRM challenges they faced arising from the advent of the Single European Market. Eighty per cent (36 out of 45) of firms felt that the main challenge was to secure an adequate supply of international managers. A majority of firms said they needed to upgrade management skills and competences in order to compete effectively in Europe, and many companies were concerned about the poaching of graduates and managers by firms based in continental Europe.

Over 70 per cent of companies identified recruitment as a priority area. It was felt that the Single European Market would intensify competition for labour, increase the mobility of labour, and augment pressure on U.K. salaries. While some companies identified a number of positive opportunities presented by 1992 - namely, an increase in opportunity to recruit labour and management from other European countries - the majority of firms felt there would be a net loss of staff to continental Europe.

A small minority of companies were seeking to develop a pan-European approach to recruitment, but they were facing many practical problems such as which journals to advertise in and which qualifications to seek. In addition, there is a problem of the profile of a company abroad, because a company that is well known in the United Kingdom may be much less well known in other countries.

The need to develop a more international top management team to reflect the growing international nature of the business was increasingly recognized as a major challenge because, at the present time, very few British companies can claim to have a truly international top management team. Similarly, a growing concern was the need to assess what new knowledge, skills, and competencies are required to operate effectively in the internal European market.

There was also growing anxiety about the managerial skills and competencies needed to deal with the complex HRM issues and problems associated with the growth of international joint ventures (e.g., the evaluation and promotion of managers and the problem of conflict of loyalty of managers to the joint venture or to the parent companies.

There was also a growing recognition by the companies of the need to understand the importance of cultural differences within Europe. This is particularly interesting in the light of the finding that only a very small minority (3 out of 45) of companies currently use cross-cultural training to help prepare managers for international transfer within Europe. By contrast, it was much more common for firms to provide cultural training for transfers to countries in the Far and Middle East, where the culture gap was seen to be greater. Specialist external courses were often used but not for international transfers within Europe.

The above discussion suggests that the most formidable task facing British companies wishing to operate across Europe is the recruitment and development of a cadre of managers and executives who understand and can operate effectively in the international environment. In practice, the impact of the Single European Market on human resource management strategy varied according to the stage of internationalization and the overall strategy of the firm. Most multinational firms traditionally pass through various stages of internationalization between the evolution from a domestic to a truly global organization.

For some well-established international firms, the Single European Market intensifies and sharpens the focus of problems associated with internationalization, rather than creating new problems. A small number of highly internationalized businesses that regarded themselves as transnationals (companies with the ability to manage across national boundaries, retaining local flexibility while achieving global integration) felt the nature of the HR challenge of 1992 would be marginal rather than central. Such companies (e.g., the oil companies) tended to see pan-European recruitment and language training initiatives as a response to the single market, but they stressed that fundamental issues such as the supply of managers and management development should be related to the broader international strategy of the business rather than to the Single European Market alone.

The single market did, however, represent a major HR challenge for "new" international firms that had internationalized in the recent past, and for firms that were significantly shifting the focus of their international activities towards Europe. International human resource management strategy, like human resource management strategy generally, must be linked to the strategic evolution of the firm.

This has highlighted some of the HRM issues and challenges that such firms will face as they undergo the internationalization process. It also suggests that, for British international firms, the recruitment and development of international managers will be the key challenge of the 1990s.

Competitive Advantage

An impressive body of literature on the management of service companies has emerged since 1977' that services "break free". The unique characteristics of services have received acceptance, while related issues of service design and production, services marketing, and services management have been given an impressive amount of attention in books and leading journals.

Despite this progress, a number of issues mandate continued scrutiny. There is the growing recognition that the boundaries between goods and services have become increasingly blurred and that the majorities of goods contain significant service components and vice versa. For example, some commentators have noted the potential for competitive advantage that is inherent in correctly leveraging the service components of products. This fluidity is perhaps best captured in Shostack's (1977) molecular model, which views all market entities as containing some tangible and intangible elements with services being defined as intangible-dominant entities.

The outcome of this dialogue has been an increase in the number of services management perspectives that are applicable in what were traditionally considered manufacturing domains and, conversely, an increase in the level of attention given to the strategic management of service firms. Central to this debate is the issue of how service companies can attain a sustainable competitive advantage."

Service businesses generally are noted for their high level of mimetic or imitative behaviour. Innovations, such as new types of bank accounts or investment vehicles, are invariably quickly imitated by competitors. Innovative airlines, which sought to use frequent flyer programmes to build switching costs for customers, found that, very quickly, many other major airlines were offering similar incentives. This level of imitation has focused attention on what kinds of resources and capabilities a service firm might leverage in order to gain a competitive advantage.

Gaining positions of competitive strength has become more important in an environment that has become increasingly global and competitive. Competition in industries such as air travel and transportation is inherently more global than in many manufacturing businesses. Deregulation in the likes of financial services has ushered in a new era of global competition and quick competitive reactions. The size and importance of the service sector has grown considerably. This sector accounted for 74 per cent of gross domestic product and about 79 per cent of national employment in the United States in 1992. In addition. almost 60 per cent of total value added in the U.S. economy in 1992 came from private (nongovernment) services.

This responds to these developments by proposing a model of competitive advantage in the international services sector, which is designed to help managers evaluate the potential sources of such advantage. It draws heavily on an existing foundation of literature spanning the disparate fields of services marketing, strategic management, international business, and industrial organization economics. At the intersection of these strands of thought is the resource-based view (RBV), which is the conceptual premise of this chapter.

The next outlines the perspectives provided by the RBV for international services firms. Subsequently, a conceptual model is presented, and selected sources of international competitive advantage are outlined. Finally, conclusions are drawn and implications discussed.

Competition in international business: Insights from the resource-based view.

Organizational strategy has long been viewed as the challenge of matching internal resources and strengths with the opportunities existing in the environment. This is perhaps best summarized in the seminal framework of Learned, Christensen, Andrews, and Guth. Thus, the task of strategic management is viewed in terms of the interplay of the personal values of management with the firms' skills and resources, and of how these are matched to environmental opportunities/threats and broader societal expectations.

Throughout the early 1980s, the broad thrust of strategy research focused on the second quadrant. This research is best demonstrated by the work of Porter (1980, 1981). It posited that a firm's performance was largely a function of the structure of the industry and the firm's position in the industry. However, empirical research toward the end of the decade increasingly began to show greater performance differences among firms in the same industry than across industry boundaries.

Allied to this was a conceptual swing toward the end of the decade back to a forgotten portion of the LCAG framework, namely quadrant 1. Building on earlier work by Penrose (1959) and Nelson and Winter (1982), what has become known as the resource-based view is illustrated by the work of Barney

(1986, 1991), Conner (1991), Dierickx and Cool (1989), Grant (1991), Mahoney and Pandian (1992), and Peteraf (1993), to name but a few.

The resource-based view focuses on heterogeneity among firms in the same industry. It views firms in terms of unique bundles of resources and capabilities that provide the basis upon which a competitive advantage can be pursued. The normative implication of this view is that the firm should base its strategy on its own resources and capabilities. Irrespective of the markets or combination of markets served, firms should seek to leverage the resources best suited to those markets.

This may even lead to a situation where the firm will choose to compete in inherently less structurally attractive markets if it possesses resources that are valuable in serving those markets. Of course, in an international context, there may be other motives for competing in structurally unattractive markets, most notably defensive foreign direct investment or cross-subsidization, where firms try to preempt the strategic moves of international rivals.

Conditions Necessary for Competitive Advantage

The potential to confer a competitive advantage is not inherent in all resources but, rather, in only those that meet a rigorous set of conditions. The first condition is that the resource must be valuable — it must provide the opportunity to exploit some environmental opportunity or neutralize some threat. Resources are considered valuable when they enable a firm to conceive of or implement strategies that improve the firm's efficiency or effectiveness. Some authors construe value in terms of meeting a key buyer need.

In addition, resources must have the characteristic of rareness. If valuable resources are possessed by a large number of competitors or potential competitors, they no longer represent a source of competitive advantage.

This is the key issue of heterogeneity underlying the resource-based view — firms possessing unique bundles of skills and resources can attain a sustainable competitive advantage. Third, there must be the condition of imperfect mobility of resources. Where resources are easily traded between competitors, no competitive advantage can be maintained.

Imperfectly mobile resources include those that are idiosyncratic to the firm, those for which property rights arc not well defined, or those that are co-specialized assets.(2) The imperfect mobility of assets is a critical factor in service businesses as people are the key assets in many cases, and their high mobility frequently results in the loss of accounts and the emergence of new competitive threats as in the case, for example, with personnel employed by advertising agencies and moving to other ones.

Finally, for an advantage to be sustained, resources must be imperfectly imitable or provide some ex-post limits to competition: That is, subsequent to a firm gaining a superior position and earning rents, forces must exist that limit competition for those rents. It was noted above that innovations such as the development of a new type of account by a retail bank or a new advertising style by a creative department frequently results in a host of imitations from competitors.

For a firm to be in a position to exploit a valuable and rare resource, there must be a resource position barrier preventing imitation by other firms. Sustaining a competitive advantage over a period of time requires the presence of isolating mechanisms that prevent imitation. Several such barriers that have been cited in the literature include causal ambiguity and uncertain imitability, where the drivers of success are difficult to identify. Imitation may also be prevented by the process of asset stock accumulation within the firm.

Where these stocks possess the characteristics of time compression diseconomies (accumulation has taken place over a long period of time), asset mass efficiencies (a critical mass of stocks has been developed), and interconnectedness (stocks are interrelated), then imitation is difficult. Indeed, the significance of asset stock accumulation in the services sector has been demonstrated elsewhere, when the "reservoir of organizational and managerial expertise that has been built up over the years can provide branch offices with information at a cost very much lower than a de novo indigenous firm would have to incur" — in other words, an ownership advantage in international competition.

Thus, service firms must seek to identify the skills and resources they possess and that meet the above criteria, and to leverage such resources to attain a competitive advantage. For service firms trading internationally, there is the added dimension of the location of such resources, which may be in the home or host country, or both.

The traditional international-business literature and the more recent global strategic management literature have identified that the success of a multinational firm is likely to be based on some combination of three sets of advantages, namely, firm-specific advantages, country-specific advantages, and internalization advantages. In resource terms, this effectively amounts to the combination of country-specific and firm-specific resources since internalization or coordination can be viewed as a managerial capability and hence a firm-specific resource.

The conceptual lens of the RBV demonstrates important differences between these two sets of resources. Country-specific resources derive from the resource endowments of countries or, in neoclassical economics terms, its comparative advantages. Country-specific resources are available on equal terms to all firms competing in an industry. Therefore, there are no barriers to prevent competing firms from imitating a given firm's portfolio of country-specific advantages. It is recognized, however, that a given firm's ability to gain access to these resources or to preempt their usage may be dependent on firm-specific political competences.

In addition, some authors suggest that country-specific advantages are dynamic and change over time — for example, Japan's move from a low-labour-cost country to a high-labour-cost country. However, firm-specific resources are considered unique to the firm, and, therefore, are likely to possess greater barriers to imitation, which suggests that they will be a more important source of competitive advantage.

Resources Versus Capabilities

Authors have recently sought to distinguish between the potential rent-generating assets of an organization. A variety of distinctions have been suggested, including assets and core competences, resources and capabilities, intellectual assets and nonintellectual assets, tangible and intangible resources, and assets and skills. Despite the range of nomenclature, the issue being addressed by the various authors is similar, namely, that the rent-generating assets of an organization can be broadly classified in terms of two basic types.

On the one hand, there are the organization's resources, which are tangible, can be either inputs or outputs, and possess two key attributes: ownership and value. Ownership can be legal in terms of title deeds to land, property, or equipment, or in intellectual property such as patents, trademarks, licenses, or trade secrets. In addition, the firm may own assets that are not legal in nature, such as reputation with customers, organizational or personal networks, and databases. The most acceptable measure of value from an accounting perspective is exchange value. Thus, resources in the main are viewed as relatively easy to trade between firms.

On the other hand, organizations also possess capabilities or competences — that is, the capacity to deploy resources, usually in combination, in order to effect a desired end. The key characteristics of capabilities are that they are firm-specific and developed over time, but, unlike resources, they are not easily tradable between firms. In general, capabilities are information-based or intellectual assets.

In addition, they tend to be cross-functional or arise from the integration of individual functional capabilities and thus are sometimes referred to as "intermediate goods" in the production process. Therefore, by definition, capabilities meet the requirements of rareness and inimitability and are a strong basis for competitive advantage. The normative implication of this logic is that service-firm capabilities are likely to be the most sustainable source of competitive advantage.

The issue of potential synergies between home- and host-country firm-specific advantages has been a central issue in the vast body of work that broadly falls within the gambit of globalization. The globalization debate began in the early 1980s and has continued with intensity ever since. One of the primary hypotheses of globalization was that markets were converging. Reaching back to the marketing-standardization literature of the 1960s, this meant that companies could be successful by selling standardized products throughout a global market at low prices due to the resulting economies of scale, in effect utilizing only home-country firm-specific advantages.

This was in sharp contrast to the earlier view of the multinational corporation as a collection of autonomous subsidiaries tailoring resource use and strategy to particular local market needs. However, even some of the early proponents of globalization conceded that this hypothesis might be a little simplistic, and began to suggest that standardization was a matter of degree.

From this recognition of complexity emerged the view that, to be successful in the global marketplace. the firm must organize itself to achieve the benefits of global integration, national responsiveness, and learning. In resource terms, this meant that the firm should not rely solely on the resources of the parent company (global integration) or the subsidiary (national responsiveness), but must seek to emphasize both and successfully transfer learning in both directions (i.e., from the home-country headquarters to the subsidiary and vice versa). So, while several authors contend that a company should pursue a global strategy on the basis of the globalization potential of the industry, there is a contrasting view that firms need to combine both global and local dimensions, sometimes known crudely as ""localization".

Stated in resource terms, this "transnational solution" suggests that superior performers in international business will combine both home- and host-country firm-specific resources and capabilities. This suggests that service firms must consider extensive foreign direct investment and create an opportunity for the successful combination of home- and host-country firm-specific resources and capabilities.

However, other "nonequity" forms of organization, with origins largely in the services sector, such as licensing, franchising, and management contracts, equally present an opportunity for the successful integration of home-and host-country resources. Their effectiveness in achieving such integration seems to be greater in consumer services than in industrial or business services.

Firm-specific Resources

Porter (1990) highlighted that many firm-specific resources were rooted in the firm's country of origin. This is illustrated by the strength of German companies in engineering, of U.S. companies in consumer goods and services, and of Italian companies in craft-based industries. Kogut (1991) extended this analysis to show that long cycles of country leadership in international competition can be explained by differences in country capabilities embodied in the firms in these countries.

In addition, many of these capabilities are sticky and diffuse slowly across borders due to four factors: technological opportunities, selection forces, identifiability, and institutional lock-in. In terms of technology, many firms have established relationships with country-specific research centres, trade associations, educational institutions, and skilled individuals. These relationships are built up over a long time and are not easy to replicate in other countries. In many cases, these are the clusters of organizations identified in Porter's "diamond" framework.

Equally, selection pressures are analogous to Porter's concept of domestic rivalry, an essential requirement to the development of globally competitive firms. Identifiability refers to domestic firms having a better understanding of the sources of success of domestic competitors than do international competitors.

This understanding can have numerous reasons and results in a greater propensity to imitate domestic competitors that leads to greater national rather than international diffusion of management capabilities. Institutional lock-in is analagous to the notions of administrative heritage or strategic commitment at a national level where the change and adoption of new techniques are impeded by previous investment, past practices, and perceived wisdom. The immediate implication of this analysis is that the firm-specific advantages underlying service-firm strategy are likely to vary from country to country, reflecting the fact that such advantages derive largely from the country of origin and diffuse slowly across borders.

Kogut (1991), however, noted that long cycles of country leadership are driven not only by technological investments (resources) but also by the efficiency of the dominant organizing principles (capabilities).

Foreign direct investment is the extension of the organizing principles of domestic firms to foreign markets. Organizational types, such as the global firm, provide a vehicle for the diffusion of capabilities across borders due to the high level of integration or coordination of its activities. Close interaction between parents and subsidiaries is also a central aspect of the transnational firm, which has been advocated as the organizational type most suitable, given the current complexity of international business. though not necessarily in every industry.

Most major multinational firms have at various times experimented with increasing the integration of their operations. The learning that has accrued from these integration efforts suggests that the firm-specific advantages underlying the strategy of leading international competitors will not vary from one host country to another, thereby reflecting the diffusion of management capability.

Toward a resource-based model of competitive advantage in international business. The process by which resources and capabilities are translated into a competitive advantage for the multinational firm is outlined, which demonstrates that superior performance is likely to be attained through the adoption of strategies based on a combination of home- and host-country firm-specific resources with host-country location-specific resources.

It highlights that management plays an essential role in leveraging this resource pool in ways that enable the firm to gain advantage. Management must make choices regarding which product markets to compete in, whether to try to attain a position of low-cost leadership or differentiation, or both, and which resources and capabilities to use in order to attain these positions of competitive leadership. Superior performance, which can be measured in the conventional terms of market share leadership or return on investment, accrues to firms achieving a competitive advantage. Sustaining the advantage over time requires reinvestment on the basis of competitive strength.

This model is an extension of the model of competitive advantage that can be found in the strategic-management literature, but it clearly sits very comfortably with the extant international business literature, as well as the "transnational solution" proposed by Bartlett and Ghoshal (1989) to help managers deal with the complexity of international business.

The model presented is designed to assist managers of service firms in building a sustainable competitive advantage on the foundation of the resources and capabilities inherent in the company. It also helps managers identify which skills and resources are most likely to be an important source of advantage and to realize the importance of being able to combine potential advantages from both home- and host-country locations. In specific cases, the actual skills and resources underlying competitive advantage are likely to be contingent on the characteristics of the service itself, the service firm, and the service industry as well as of the country of origin of the firm.

However, sources of advantage in service industries identified elsewhere can be seen to meet the requirements outlined in the model. For example, Stalk, Evans, and Schulman (1992) contend that the growth and subsequent market dominance of WalMart resides in the company's unique logistics capability, which confirms the importance of capabilities as a potential source of competitive advantage. The logistics system known as "cross-docking" ensures that goods are simply moved from one loading dock to another in forty-eight hours or less, resulting in minimal inventories and shaving between 2 per cent and 3 per cent off the cost of sales.

The system is a source of competitive advantage because it meets all of the criteria outlined earlier. It is used in a value-generating way — creating cost savings in a business where tight margins are critical and low costs are a key success factor. It is a rare system, and, because it combines people, delivery vehicles, and communication systems, it is clearly immobile. But it is its inherent barriers to imitation that help to confer a competitive advantage on WalMart. It is extremely difficult to duplicate the required constant communication between suppliers, distribution centres, and sales outlets achieved through the company's investment in a private satellite communications system.

Similarly, Pleval, Nellis, Lane, and Schuler (1994) attribute the success of AT&T's Global Business Communication Systems (GBCS) division to its unique human resource capability. Its human resource strategy is linked to overall business strategy, and review and reward mechanisms are designed to increase personal motivation while simultaneously achieving company goals. The company views its employees as "its only sustainable competitive advantage." Again, this division of AT&T has been successful because it utilizes a set of resources/capabilities that meet the criteria necessary for competitive advantage. GBCS uses people in a value-generating way by explicitly connecting their efforts with key company goals. such as using a total quality management approach, being a leader in customer-led applications of technology, and being the best value supplier.

People can always leave an organization, so why do many firms contend that their people are their only sustainable advantage? In the ease of GCBS, mobility of personnel is not a major concern, as its success resides not in individuals but rather in a complex set of relationships among individuals reflected in performance management, recognition, compensation practices, and communication programmes. Furthermore, even though individuals who are hired away by competitors are able to describe them, these systems prove difficult to imitate because of the levels of reaming that occur while these "asset stocks" are being accumulated.

The key role of people, as a source of competitive advantage in internationally traded services, is demonstrated by the high level of foreign direct investment by firms in industries like financial and management services in order to maintain control over this resource.

This chapter contends that competitive advantage for service firms lies in the unique resources and capabilities possessed by the firm. Not all resources or capabilities are a source of competitive advantage-only those that meet the stringent conditions of value, rareness. The actual sources of competitive advantage are likely to vary depending on the nature of the service, the particular traits of the firm, the nature of the industry, and the country of origin.

The normative implication of this analysis is that service managers conduct a rigorous analysis of internal resources and capabilities. What eve resources and capabilities does the firm have, and which of any of these strengths are unique? What scope is there for making investments to develop unique resources and capabilities that would yield competitive advantages in the future? The analysis also raises the question of control of key sources of competitive advantage.

Foreign direct investment arguably creates the greatest potential not only for control but also for the effective integration of resources across national boundaries. More traditional forms of organization in the services sector, such as licensing, franchising, and management contracts, have been shown to be effective control mechanisms in consumer, though not in business, services. Their effectiveness as a means for integrating resources may represent a fruitful area for further research.

6

Risk Management in Adventure Tourism

The owner of a fast food franchise in East Los Angeles panicked when his drive-through cashier was robbed at gunpoint. While the criminals escaped with all the day's receipts, an even greater loss was the owner's peace of mind. Since his wife and daughter both worked at the restaurant, he stood to lose a lot more than money if the robbers returned. What could the owner have done to make his business and his family safe?

In this case, a simple bulletproof one-way drive-through window would have made the robbery impossible. More importantly, such a deterrent might make criminals think twice about their chosen target.

American businesses lose billions of dollars each year as a result of crime. Small operations are especially likely to be victims, losing at least 20 times more money than do large corporations. In fact, shoplifting, robbery and burglary put such a disproportionate strain on small firms that many disintegrate as a result. Business owners can even be held liable for crimes against people that are committed on their property, meaning their livelihood can be threatened by random acts of violence as well.

Employees of a sportswear manufacturing facility in Los Angeles were devastated when a man came in during working hours and murdered two of their coworkers before killing himself. The company's owner was shocked to learn that he could be held financially responsible for the trauma his staff experienced because access to the work area was not controlled effectively.

However, if the sportswear manufacturer had been able to prove to a judge that he had taken precautions — even minimal ones — to safeguard his building and his employees, he would have been absolved of liability.

No matter what kind of venture you own, you have assets and employees that require protection. Many entrepreneurs fail to realize the amount of damage crime can cause. They are also unaware that the most important security measures are inexpensive and simple to implement. As a business owner, you need to step back occasionally and conduct a security review, keeping in mind the three Ds of crime prevention: deter, delay and detect.

Deterring criminals is the key to making sure your business is not an easy target. Simple and inexpensive measures such as replacing old locks, hiding expensive equipment from passers-by, and putting bars on windows can cause would-be criminals to seek more vulnerable prey. Anything that tells potential thieves you have paid attention to the security of your building can be an effective deterrent.

Delaying a crime, or preventing quick access to valuable merchandise or equipment, is the second crucial step in protecting your business. The owner of a California office supply store learned the importance of delaying criminals after experiencing repeated burglaries, each of which resulted in losses of almost $10,000 in merchandise. Although the store had a locked accordion gate behind glass entrance doors, the gate was secured with a cheap lock. A sturdier, slightly more expensive lock could have occupied the burglars long enough for the police to reach the scene after the alarm was activated.

The last of the three Ds, detection, is accomplished by more complex technology like alarms or surveillance equipment. However, these products — such as window glass bugs or motion detectors — can actually give a false sense of security. For experienced criminals know that alarm companies and police communications centers must go through a number of steps before reaching the location of a break-in. This gives them ample opportunity to escape with valuable equipment or merchandise. For this reason, law enforcement officials maintain that alarms and surveillance should only be used as back-up security devices.

Although detection is generally not effective at preventing a crime, it can decrease the amount of time a burglar has inside the building and is therefore an important component of building security. However, don't spend disproportionate amounts of money on high-tech equipment. Focus instead on inexpensive, low-tech tools for deterring or delaying criminals.

After you install new security precautions, the job is not finished until you have also made adjustments to your daily operations and employee training. "Not enough people are looking at the big picture," asserts Michael Harding, a Southern California law enforcement officer. "Your physical security will not be effective without operational security and good employee training. The three are tied together."

In the case of the Los Angeles fast-food franchise that was robbed at gunpoint, Harding found simple solutions to the many security problems existing there. The restaurant's back door and a storage room door were left unlocked during business hours, for example, and employees tended to leave them wide open for the sake of fast movement between areas of the building. "All I had to do was tell them to close and lock their doors," says Harding. "It sounds obvious, but it could really save a lot of worry."

With careful thought, you can probably identify most of your own security weaknesses. First, determine exactly what requires protection in your office, store or factory. Use common sense. For instance, don't spend a lot of money on alarms and access control for a storage area that only houses basic supplies such as boxes or business forms. For areas such as this, good locks should be sufficient. In addition, step back and look realistically at your neighborhood and personnel. Don't go overboard by surrounding your building with Dobermans, or conversely, take unnecessary risks with valuable resources by depending only on trust for security.

Also evaluate how well your existing security arrangements address likely threats to your business. Be sure to go over every detail from the types of locks you install and your system of key distribution to employee identification and after-hours use of the facility. Even simple things like lighting can be extremely important.

If you are uncertain about the vulnerable points in your building and how to protect them, consider calling in a security professional to conduct a comprehensive evaluation of your premises and daily operations.

The best analysis will only be possible after the consultant observes typical personnel activity and thoroughly examines the various access points at all sides of the building and on the roof. Ask for a complete report of the evaluations and recommendations after the professional has explained them to you in a face-to-face consultation.

Keep in mind as you look for a consultant that the person you hire may have a product to sell other than knowledge about security. Although the professional often provides excellent advice, use common sense about any product recommendations the consultant makes.

Officer Harding recommends consultants who are currently in law enforcement because they have the greatest expertise in crime prevention and nothing to sell but the most up-to-date information. Just as fashion and food trends change with the times, so do crimes. "We get to interview the bad guys when we arrest them for a break-in," Harding says, "so we know all their latest secrets."

Aside from carefully controlling traffic through your premises, access control keypads and card readers provide many benefits that will save you money and worry in the long run.

To keep track of who goes in and out of the various doors in their four buildings, Insignia Commercial Group in Austin, Texas has used access control keypads for years. Michael Osborne, chief engineer, says he utilizes the system for much more than security purposes, however. "We've got the access system tied into energy control too," he says. "That way, only designated people can turn on the air conditioning and lights after hours by using their codes."

The system, designed by Hirsch Electronics in Irvine, California, has appeared in films like "Jurassic Park." "The keypads have a high-tech look that many business owners really like. Employees feel safer, and visitors know they're dealing with the latest in security," reports Rob Zivney of Hirsch Electronics. Osborne agrees that appearance is one of the added benefits of electronic access control. Just as with other building security measures, access control systems require thorough user training to work well. Osborne says all the companies located in Insignia's buildings have a tenant manual that describes exactly how to operate the system. As he explains, "The manual reminds people not to let anyone in behind them as they enter, for example, and never to punch in a code while someone is watching."

When looking around the inside of your building, do you see valuable equipment or merchandise that a thief could collect in five minutes or less? Then maybe your alarm system just isn't enough. Consider the steps and time involved between the alarm being triggered and the arrival of a police officer at your site.

1. The alarm goes off when someone breaks in or trespasses.
2. The security company must identify the location of the alarm.
3. The security company calls the location to make sure the alarm was not set off accidentally by someone authorized with a special code.
4. The security company contacts the local sheriff or other police communication center.
5. The police enter the location into a computer and look for an on-duty officer in the area.
6. The police communication center sends an officer to the location.
7. The officer arrives on the scene of the break-in, often five minutes or more after the alarm originally sounded.

Whether a business operates out of a factory, garage, store or office suite, good key control can protect the people, property and information inside.

The little words "Do Not Duplicate" on all of your office keys sound like good insurance against unauthorized entry. Unfortunately, they mean almost nothing in most cases, says Alan Stelzer of Antrim's Security Co. in Pasadena, California. Stelzer strongly recommends keys that can only be duplicated by the manufacturers or their agents when you present a registration card and positive identification. All of the copies should then be listed by their consecutive serial numbers and the employees who use them.

One of the best features of the latest locks is that they can be installed into existing door hardware. A locksmith inserts or removes a columnar unit rather than installing expensive new materials. "This system, including a master key which only you use to unlock all of the doors, is a must for security, especially since it requires little time and investment," says Stelzer.

In today's high-tech world, a decidedly low-tech solution can still be effective. For many types of businesses like automobile dealerships, construction sites or warehouses, guard dogs can be an excellent crime deterrent.

Unlike security systems or alarms, guard dogs can cover large outdoor areas, and they continue to work during a power outage. Unlike a human guard, a well-trained dog stays alert throughout the night, and a dog's heightened senses of smell and hearing can detect intruders long before humans can. Dogs are also the least expensive guards, costing about $500 a month for full service.

At the minimum, a good guard dog service should provide nightly delivery and pick-up, in which case you and your employees do not have to come into actual contact with the animal. Your guard dog service must also must carry liability insurance, which protects you from responsibility for injuries the dog might inflict on passers-by or trespassers.

If you are thinking about using a guard dog to protect your premises, consider several issues. First, a good guard dog is an effective deterrent, but should only be used for that purpose. "If people want to steal, they're going to steal," claims J.R. Ewing of Century Dogs in Los Angeles, California. The second thing to remember is that a determined criminal can find ways around almost any defense, including guard dogs. For example, mace, sedatives or other weapons can effectively disable even the most vigilant of animals. However, the presence of a guard dog does make your business far less appealing to would-be thieves who might decide to move on to more poorly protected premises.

To thoroughly safeguard your business, combine guard dog service — if appropriate — with other measures like good fences, locks and an alarm system.

The following is a simplified list of building features a security consultant would examine. Assess whether your security provisions are good, satisfactory, unsatisfactory or nonexistent.

Fixing a few simple problems can go a long way in preventing crime.

Perimeter

Lighting: Do you have lights at all entrances? Are they protected from vandals and thieves?

Fences / Walls: Is it possible to get over or under them? What are they made of? Are they in good condition?

Gates: Are any left unsecured? Are they in good condition?

Storage Yard: Do you have materials next to the fence or entrance? Are the materials hidden from passers-by?

Parking Lots: Is employee parking separate from parking for the general public? How close to the building is it? Is there enough lighting?

Address Numbers: Are they legible and visible from the street?

Pedestrian / Vehicle Access: How well is it monitored? Is it in front of the building?

Doors

Can they be pried open? Are they solid in construction? Do they have reliable dead bolts? What kind of strike plates do they have? Are your closing procedures listed and uniform?

Windows

Are they secured with screw locks, pins or sturdy cranks? Are louvers glued shut or otherwise secured? Are there drapes or blinds that prevent would-be thieves from seeing inside your property?

Roof

Are all skylights, vents and hatchways secured or covered? Do trees, drain pipes or walls allow easy access to the roof?

Interior

Lighting: Do you have lights on after hours? Is there an emergency back-up system?

Valuables: Are they out of view of any passers-by?

Storage / Offices / Saferoom: Are they secured with high-quality locks? Are there phones in each room to allow emergency calls?

Special Areas

Loading Docks: Are they well-marked and secure?

Employee Training: Have your employees been trained in crime awareness and prevention?

Key Control: Do you have a foolproof system to keep track of key distribution? Do you know many copies have been made? Trash Areas: Are your trash bins enclosed and locked?

Security Systems

Alarm System: Is it monitored? Does it include a panic device? Do you have prominent signs announcing its presence?

Closed-Circuit TV: How is it monitored? Is there a time delay?

Guards: What kind of training do they have? Are they bonded? How thorough a background check have you conducted on them?

Guard Dogs: How many do you have? During what hours are they present? Have you posted warnings prominently? Are you aware of your liability in case of attack?

If you are unable to answer many of these questions, a professional security consultation is in order. Remember that by investing a few hundred dollars now, you may be saving thousands of dollars in the long term.

Excerpted with permission from "Small Business Success" magazine, Volume X, produced by Pacific Bell Directory in partnership with the U.S. Small Business Administration and the Partners for Small Business Excellence.

RISK MANAGEMENT FUNDAMENTALS

Risk management is attempting to identify and then manage threats that could severely impact or bring down the organization. Generally, this involves reviewing operations of the organization, identifying potential threats to the organization and the likelihood of their occurrence, and then taking appropriate actions to address the most likely threats.

Traditionally, risk management was thought of as mostly a matter of getting the right insurance. Insurance coverage usually came in rather standard packages, so people tended to not take risk management seriously. However, this impression of risk management has changed dramatically. With the recent increase in rules and regulations, employee-related lawsuits and reliance on key resources, risk management is becoming a management practice that is every bit as important as financial or facilities management.

There are several basic activities which a nonprofit organization can conduct to dramatically reduce its chances of experiencing a catastrophic event that ruins or severely impairs the organization.

Organizations should regularly undertake comprehensive, focused assessment of potential risks to the organization. This focused assessment should occur at least twice a year by a team of staff members representing all the major functions of the organization. The assessment should be carefully planned, documented and methodically carried out.

Comprehensive checklists help a great deal to quickly review a wide range of organizational aspects. Other aspects require more careful review.

Checklists in the following sections cover almost 140 considerations to ensure a well run and highly protected organization.

GOOD MANAGEMENT

Efforts undertaken to manage an organization well also contributes to sound risk management. For example, a fully attentive board with a wide range of skills may be the most important guard against major threats to an organization.

Careful strategic planning and effective supervision helps ensure organizational resources are closely aligned to accomplishing the organization's mission, and that staff and volunteers are treated fairly and comply with rules and regulations.

Every organization must have up-to-date policies which guide the relationships between staff and management. There has been a noticeable increase in lawsuits regarding wrongful termination, harassment and discrimination, disagreements about promotions or salary actions, etc. Parties to lawsuits include the organization, management and/or board members. Therefore, personnel policies must be reviewed at least once a year by an outside advisor who is an expert about all of the employee-related laws and regulations.

Be sure that management is well versed about the policies. Typically, courts will interpret actions by organizational personnel as representative of the organization's preferred course of action and superseding related, documented policies.

You might first review this information and then invite an insurance agent (or better yet, an insurance broker) to visit your organization to provide you an overview of the types of insurance typically sold to nonprofits. Note that many insurance professionals might not understand the nature of nonprofits. Therefore, you might first ask a few people from fellow nonprofits for references.

As dreadful as it may sound, you must schedule two hours sometime during the year to close your door and study your insurance policies. Note any questions and pose them to your insurance professional. Ask him or her to provide you a written, clear description regarding any ambiguities and to do so on company letterhead with his or her signature.

Note that Directors and Officers Insurance (D & O, and covered in the above "Insurance Against Liabilities" section) is increasingly considered because of the increasing number of lawsuits. In addition, D & O insurance helps attract highly experienced board members. Be sure your D & O insurance covers "insured vs. insured" which covers employee-related lawsuits and also covers ongoing costs to address a lawsuit (rather than paying only when the outcome of a lawsuit has been decided).

RESOURCE MANAGEMENT

People

This aspect of risk management is often overlooked. Each key role in an organization should have some type of resource to back up performance of that role. For example, another person in the organization should have general understanding of another person's role in case that other person for some reason is not able to perform the role. The use of up-to-date job descriptions, todo lists and receiving regular status reports both help to ensure understanding of how others carry out their roles. Have a staff member back up another member who is on vacation. During staff meetings, have a staff member give a presentation about their role and how they carry it out. Ensure that each critical role has at least one backup person who can step in to conduct the role. The backup assignment should be part of the person's job description to help the person take the assignment seriously.

General Facilities:

1. Always lock your doors. This seems obvious, but too many organizations fail to do so.
2. Ensure your fire protection systems are fully functional by scheduing to test fire alarms twice a year or demanding that your facility's owner test alarms twice a year. Note that certain electrical equipment can be severely damaged from water sprinklers. Arrange adequate covering or arrangement to minimize water seepage if overhead sprinklers open up.
3. Conduct inspections twice a year, including to:
   (a) Inspect floors for ripped carpets

(b) Look for cables or wires laying on the floor (tape over them if you have to)
(c) Notice any electical outlets with black soot hear outlets (this indicates electrical shortages)
(d) Ask all staff if their office accommodations are sufficient, e.g., their chairs are entirely comfortable (tilted correctly for their backs and at the right heights), is lighting sufficient for desk and computer work, etc.
(e) Notice any heavy items on or near the floor which staff must continually stoop to lift, e.g., boxes of paper for the copier or printers; open boxes before they're set on the floor or stack heavy items in a storage room on a shelf
(f) Ensure all doors have fully functional door knobs (it's amazing how long people can tolerate something as small as a knob that continually jams so the door is difficult to open)
(g) Ensure there is a well-stocked first-aid kit available to all staff
(h) Post emergency numbers on the wall near the central phone
(i) During the winter, ensure adequate ice removal, e.g., spread sand over ice or use salt to melt ice
(j) Schedule ten minutes in a staff meeting once a year for the entire staff to reflect on the quality of the facilities

Organizations should regularly undertake comprehensive, focused assessment of potential risks to the organization. This focused assessment should occur at least twice a year by a team of staff members representing all the major functions of the organization. The assessment should be carefully planned, documented and methodically carried out.

Comprehensive checklists help a great deal to quickly review a wide range of organizational aspects. Other aspects require more careful review.

Checklists in the following sections cover almost 140 considerations to ensure a well run and highly protected organization.

PREVENTING EMPLOYEE THEFT

Many people consider accounting a tedious job, but not John Lewis. Throughout his three-year tenure with Unified Trucking he had ostensibly been a model employee, missing only a few days of work and conquering the Herculean task of bookkeeping single-handedly. The companyOs continued growth and profitability were the only indications management had ever needed to determine that John performed his job well. His professionalism and dedication made supervision unnecessary. John insisted on handling any problems or discrepancies personally, and made it clear that the buck stopped with him.

In fact, many bucks did stop with him, followed him home and neatly deposited themselves into his bank account. In three short years John managed to use his authority and exclusive bookkeeping access to bilk the company of nearly $100,000. As often happens, Johnos illicit activities were only revealed by accident. If janitorial workers had not discovered a suspicious amount of discarded receipts, the theft would have continued undetected.

Specialists say the cost of employee theft and embezzlement adds up to billions of dollars annually. For most companies, employee theft is a much more serious concern than burglars or shoplifters. In the retail industry, where theft of all types is a recurring problem, businesses recover an average of $1,350 from each employee apprehended for stealing, compared to $196 recovered from shoplifters. With dramatic figures like these, taking steps to eliminate theft and graft within a firm are sure to yield returns.

Should you consider your business immune to employee theft, think again. Security experts estimate that as many as 30 percent of all employees do steal, and that another 60 percent will steal if given sufficient motive and opportunity. The current economic hard times only add to the temptation of personnel to take what does not belong to them.

Yet protecting yourself from pilfering may be easier than you think. A comprehensive programme to eliminate employee theft can be simple and inexpensive, while at the same time increasing productivity and providing avenues for improved management-worker relations.

Know the Frequently Used Schemes having an elementary understanding of the more common forms of employee theft will help you formulate a strategy for subverting them. Here are just a few:

- Forging Receipts: Salespersons can charge a customer one sum, ring up a receipt for less, and pocket the difference.
- Hiding Receipts: When bookkeeping is sloppy and little supervision exists, employees can keep cash and receipts without raising an eyebrow.
- Pocketing Loose Change: Small sums of money, such as fees or petty cash, may not be missed at all.
- Pilfering Merchandise: Goods your firm purchases may never even make it to the shelves.
- Fictitious Payroll: Occasionally personnel managers will authorize salary for fictitious workers, then keep it for themselves.
- Overbilling Expenses: Managers with expense accounts may submit receipts twice and be reimbursed twice, or inflate actual expenses incurred.
- Purchasing Fraud: Employees sometimes declare themselves suppliers of nonexistent goods, and subsequently reimburse themselves handsomely.

Watch for the tell-tale signs of internal theft. One subtle but noticeable indication of dishonest employees may be an unexplained rise in their living standards. Be careful, however, as newfound wealth or sudden success may occur for a number of reasons of which you might not be aware. Be absolutely certain about a staff memberOs misconduct before making accusations that can strain worker relations, or even elicit a lawsuit.

Pay close attention to management-level personnel who insist on handling routine clerical tasks themselves. And be on guard for clients complaining about overcharging or inconsistencies in shipping and billing practices. Following up on customer grievances often reveals clandestine theft.

Some employees have theft in mind from the start. You should be able to weed out these people by performing thorough background checks on all new hire prospects, particularly for sensitive positions involving the flow of money. Call previous employers to verify resume and application information. Invest sufficient time to make sure applicants do not have a history of stealing from previous employers, and that all credentials and references are valid. Do not be overly zealous, however. Some good workers have made mistakes they genuinely regret and have never repeated them.

Many businesses conduct honesty testing in their hiring procedures and evaluations of current staff members. Honesty tests are standardized, commercially available written examinations that provide psychological evaluations of a candidateOs ethical dispositions and attitudes toward work. These tests can purportedly identify problem employees who have either stolen in the past or who will be unproductive workers. Honesty testing has been hailed by some for helping to eliminate pilfering, reduce employee turnover and increase productivity. It has also been criticized and challenged by those who feel the tests are either inaccurate or a violation of rights to privacy and other civil rights.

While the majority of workers will not go out of their way to steal, the best defense is careful supervision that removes any easy opportunities. Even though delegation of tasks is unavoidable, try to have a management-level supervisor oversee inventory and bookkeeping. If this is not possible, consider dividing these tasks among several staff members so no single employee has too much authority. Shifting responsibilities from one person to another allows them to check each otherOs work for accuracy and suspicious activities. It also makes collusion between employees, or between an employee and an outside source, such as a distributor, considerably less likely.

Occasional inspections or audits of inventory and bookkeeping help in preventing fraud and theft. Have an outside auditor or top manager perform the inspection on a periodic but unscheduled basis, thereby keeping records current and reducing theft opportunities. Requiring accounting employees to take vacations can also help the monitoring of bookkeeping records. Those who cover during vacation absences serve as an additional check on accounting discrepancies.

Most successful embezzlement schemes would have failed if inventory and accounting records were organized and up to date. If records are always behind and the work is sloppy, theft will be much harder to detect. You should regularly reconcile invoices and payments, as well as shipping and receiving bills. At least one software package is available that automatically examines your records and checks them for suspicious activities. Even without the sophistication of specialized software, your current accounting system may be able to give you useful information, such as revealing accounts that consistently show discrepancies. It is possible to install physical obstacles to theft, such as alarm systems and secured, restricted areas. However, be aware that such obvious measures can have a negative effect on morale. While overt tactics to deter theft help prevent losses, they also convey very clearly to employees that they are not trusted.

Workers will be less likely to steal if you create an environment in which they think there is a good chance of being caught. Training and "employee awareness" programs can inform workers about stealing problems and keep them on the lookout for theft of any kind. A good programme can be motivational and enjoyable — highlighted, for example, by group rewards for departments that show decreased rates of theft. When management and labour work together to solve the problem, an additional result can be improved relations and higher morale.

To make a security programme such as this effective, it is crucial employees know they can turn over incriminating information on anyone in the firm without fearing job loss or other repercussions. Stress that management and supervisors are not above suspicion and that employee complaints will be taken seriously. Some programs feature special phone numbers or other means for workers to leave anonymous tips. Others offer rewards for informants while still guaranteeing their anonymity. A more positive approach may be to institute a profit-sharing plan which fosters loyalty, encourages personnel to monitor one another, and brings each employeeOs interests closer in line with those of the company.

The most troubling cases of employee theft occur when workers are in desperate financial straits. Common problems, such as heavy medical expenses, can temporarily put people into situations where stealing seems necessary for survival.

Let employees know in advance that they can come to management for assistance rather than resorting to theft. Although no company is a charitable organization, consider helping distressed staff members find financial counseling. Some businesses even go so far as to provide short-term loans for reliable personnel.

Intimately linked with financial problems and theft is employee substance abuse. If your firm does not already have a procedure for screening workers for drugs or alcohol, it may benefit from one. Even if the company doesnOt actually test, the mere threat has an effect and may weed out some people who might otherwise steal to support their drug or alcohol habit. A programme that assists with counseling for personnel who admit to problems could help ameliorate the stranglehold these substances put on employees lives, including their finances.

To reinforce these other measures, a company should distribute clear, written policies on ethical behaviour to be signed by each employee — including the owner. It should be emphasized that there is no such thing as an "acceptable amount" of employee crime, and that, in fact, none at all will be tolerated. There should also be no double standard at work: all infractions should be punished regardless of how important the person or how small the infraction.

When formulating policies for theft and graft, some difficult decisions are involved. For example, should every employee found stealing be dismissed, or worse yet prosecuted? Or should the punishment fit the nature of the crime and be sensitive to extenuating circumstances, such as financial troubles? Be aware that severe punishments can sometimes do more harm than good, straining relations with employees and causing those who do steal to be extra careful in covering their tracks.

Employees need to know that one uniform ethical standard applies to everyone in the firm. Executives and managers should be positive role models for workers. If management is found dipping into petty cash, fudging on expense accounts or taking home equipment, personnel will feel justified in doing the same. As is always ideally the case, leadership and direction begin at the highest level.

When an envelope containing an entire dayOs worth of transactions disappeared, Dianne Oliver — owner of an eight-employee Merle Norman cosmetic franchise in Concord, California — immediately decided to institute a more formal system of storing money. "It's now put into a locked cash drawer under the computer after each transaction, with the employee entering the stock number if a product was sold, the method of payment, and how much was paid. The computer indicates the amount of change to be given. Each night, We tabulate to see that everything matches up." Oliver, who finds this method also helps her "keep control of inventory," does frequent checks on popular items to ensure no stock is missing. "And employees can buy all beauty products at wholesale, which helps eliminate temptation." "High ticket" items are placed at the back of the 1,000-foot store, with only a few display products kept up front near the door. In addition to a wide range of beauty supplies, Oliver also sells watches and jewelry, which are kept in locked cases. "The watch case is even chained to the countertop," she explains. "And whenever an employee permanently departs, every lock is changed."

PROJECT MANAGEMENT

Project management is a carefully planned and organized effort to accomplish a specific (and usually) one-time effort, for example, construct a building or implement a new computer system. Project management includes developing a project plan, which includes defining project goals and objectives, specifying tasks or how goals will be achieved, what resources are need, and associating budgets and timelines for completion. It also includes implementing the project plan, along with careful controls to stay on the "critical path", that is, to ensure the plan is being managed according to plan. Project management usually follows major phases (with various titles for these phases), including feasibility study, project planning, implementation, evaluation and support/maintenance. (Programme planning is usually of a broader scope than project planning, but not always.)

Almost any human activity that involves carrying out a non-repetitive task can be a project. So we are all project managers! We all practise project management (PM).

But there is a big difference between carrying out a very simple project involving one or two people and one involving a complex mix of people, organisations and tasks.

This has been true for millennia, but large-scale projects like the Pyramids often used rather simple control and resource techniques including brute force to 'motivate' the workforce!

The art of planning for the future has always been a human trait. In essence a project can be captured on paper with a few simple elements: a start date, an end date, the tasks that have to be carried out and when they should be finished, and some idea of the resources (people, machines etc) that will be needed during the course of the project.

When the plan starts to involve different things happening at different times, some of which are dependent on each other, plus resources required at different times and in different quantities and perhaps working at different rates, the paper plan could start to cover a vast area and be unreadable.

This was a problem facing the US Navy in the development of the Polaris missile system. There were so many aspects to the project that a new technique had to be invented to cope with it: the PERT technique. This and later developments led to mathematical techniques that can be used to find the critical path through a series of planned tasks that interconnect during the life of a project.

You could begin the story of modern project management from this time. But that would be unfair as project management is not only about planning but also about human attributes like leadership and motivation.

Nevertheless, the idea that complex plans could be analysed by a computer to allow someone to control a project is the basis of much of the development in technology that now allow projects of any size and complexity not only to be planned but also modelled to answer 'what if?' questions.

The original programs and computers tended to produce answers long after an event had taken place. Now, there are many project planning and scheduling programs that can provide real time information, as well as linking to risk analysis, time recording, costing, estimating and other aspects of project control. But computer programs are not project management: they are tools for project managers to use. Project management is all that mix of components of control, leadership, teamwork, resource management etc, that goes into a successful project.

Project managers can be found in all industries. Their numbers have grown rapidly as industry and commerce has realised that much of what it does is project work. And as project-based organisations have started to emerge, project management is becoming established as both a professional career path and a way of controlling business.

So opportunities in project management now exist not only in being a project manager, but also as part of the support team in a project or programme office or as a team leader for part of a project. There are also qualifications that can be attained through the professional associations.

One reason for the rapid growth is the need to understand how to look after complex projects, often in high tech areas, which are critical to business success but also have to use scarce resources efficiently.

Most people still want their projects to be on time, meet quality objectives, and not cost more than the budget. These form the classic time, quality, cost triangle.

In fact if you have an unlimited budget and unlimited time, project management becomes rather easy. For most people, however, time and money are critical and that is what makes project management so important today.

PLANNING A PROJECT

Before describing the role and creation of a specification, we need to introduce and explain a fairly technical term: a numbty is a person whose brain is totally numb. In this context, numb means "deprived of feeling or the power of unassisted activity"; in general, a numbty needs the stimulation of an electric cattle prod to even get to the right office in the morning. Communication with numbties is severely hampered by the fact that although they think they know what they mean (which they do not), they seldom actually say it, and they never write it down. And the main employment of numbties world-wide is in creating project specifications. You must know this - and protect your team accordingly.

A specification is the definition of your project: a statement of the problem, not the solution. Normally, the specification contains errors, ambiguities, misunderstandings and enough rope to hang you and your entire team. Thus before you embark upon the the next six months of activity working on the wrong project, you must assume that a numbty was the chief author of the specification you received and you must read, worry, revise and ensure that everyone concerned with the project (from originator, through the workers, to the end-customer) is working with the same understanding. The outcome of this deliberation should be a written definition of what is required, by when; and this must be agreed by all involved. There are no short-cuts to this; if you fail to spend the time initially, it will cost you far more later on.

The agreement upon a written specification has several benefits:

- The clarity will reveal misunderstandings
- The completeness will remove contradictory assumptions
- The rigour of the analysis will expose technical and practical details which numbties normally gloss over through ignorance or fear
- The agreement forces all concerned to actually read and think about the details

The work on the specification can seen as the first stage of Quality Assurance since you are looking for and countering problems in the very foundation of the project - from this perspective the creation of the specification clearly merits a large investment of time.

From a purely defensive point of view, the agreed specification also affords you protection against the numbties who have second thoughts, or new ideas, half way through the project. Once the project is underway, changes cost time (and money). The existence of a demonstrably-agreed specification enables you to resist or to charge for (possibly in terms of extra time) such changes. Further, people tend to forget what they originally thought; you may need proof that you have been working as instructed.

The places to look for errors in a specification are:

- The global context: numbties often focus too narrowly on the work of one team and fail to consider how it fits into the larger picture. Some of the work given to you may actually be undone or duplicated by others. Some of the proposed work may be incompatible with that of others; it might be just plain barmy in the larger context.
- The interfaces: between your team and both its customers and suppliers, there are interfaces. At these points something gets transferred. Exactly what, how and when should be discussed and agreed from the very beginning. Never assume a common understanding, because you will be wrong. All it takes for your habitual understandings to evaporate is the arrival of one new member, in either of the teams. Define and agree your interfaces and maintain a friendly contact throughout the project.
- Time-scales: numbties always underestimate the time involved for work. If there are no time-scales in the specification, you can assume that one will be imposed upon you (which will be impossible). You must add realistic dates. The detail should include a precise understanding of the extent of any intermediate stages of the task, particularly those which have to be delivered.
- External dependencies: your work may depend upon that of others. Make this very clear so that these people too will receive warning of your needs. Highlight the effect that problems with these would have upon your project so that everyone is quite clear about their importance. To be sure, contact these people yourself and ask if they are able to fulfil the assumptions in your specification.

- Resources: the numbty tends to ignore resources. The specification should identify the materials, equipment and manpower which are needed for the project. The agreement should include a commitment by your managers to allocate or to fund them. You should check that the actual numbers are practical and/or correct. If they are omitted, add them - there is bound to be differences in their assumed values.

This seems to make the specification sound like a long document. It should not be. Each of the above could be a simple sub-heading followed by either bullet points or a table - you are not writing a brochure, you are stating the definition of the project in clear, concise and unambiguous glory.

Of course, the specification may change. If circumstances, or simply your knowledge, change then the specification will be out of date. You should not regard it as cast in stone but rather as a display board where everyone involved can see the current, common understanding of the project. If you change the content everyone must know, but do not hesitate to change it as necessary.

Having decide what the specification intends, your next problem is to decide what you and your team actually need to do, and how to do it. As a manager, you have to provide some form of framework both to plan and to communicate what needs doing. Without a structure, the work is a series of unrelated tasks which provides little sense of achievement and no feeling of advancement. If the team has no grasp of how individual tasks fit together towards an understood goal, then the work will seem pointless and they will feel only frustration.

To take the planning forward, therefore, you need to turn the specification into a complete set of tasks with a linking structure. Fortunately, these two requirements are met at the same time since the derivation of such a structure is the simplest method of arriving at a list of tasks.

WORK BREAKDOWN STRUCTURE

Once you have a clear understanding of the project, and have eliminated the vagaries of the numbties, you then describe it as a set of simpler separate activities. If any of these are still too complex for you to easily organise, you break them down also into another level of simpler descriptions, and so on until you can manage everything. Thus your one complex project is organised as a set of simple tasks which together achieve the desired result.

The reasoning behind this is that the human brain (even yours) can only take in and process so much information at one time. To get a real grasp of the project, you have to think about it in pieces rather than trying to process the complexity of its entire details all at once. Thus each level of the project can be understood as the amalgamation of a few simply described smaller units.

In planning any project, you follow the same simple steps: if an item is too complicated to manage, it becomes a list of simpler items. People call this producing a work breakdown structure to make it sound more formal and impressive. Without following this formal approach you are unlikely to remember all the niggling little details; with this procedure, the details are simply displayed on the final lists. One common fault is to produce too much detail at the initial planning stage. You should be stop when you have a sufficient description of the activity to provide a clear instruction for the person who will actually do the work, and to have a reasonable estimate for the total time/effort involved. You need the former to allocate (or delegate) the task; you need the latter to finish the planning.

TASK ALLOCATION

The next stage is a little complicated. You now have to allocate the tasks to different people in the team and, at the same time, order these tasks so that they are performed in a sensible sequence.

Task allocation is not simply a case of handing out the various tasks on your final lists to the people you have available; it is far more subtle (and powerful) than that. As a manager you have to look far beyond the single project; indeed any individual project can be seen as merely a single step in your team's development. The allocation of tasks should thus be seen as a means of increasing the skills and experience of your team - when the project is done, the team should have gained. In simple terms, consider what each member of your team is capable of and allocate sufficient complexity of tasks to match that (and to slightly stretch).

The tasks you allocate are not the ones on your finals lists, they are adapted to better suit the needs of your team's development; tasks are moulded to fit people, which is far more effective than the other way around. For example, if Arthur is to learn something new, the task may be simplified with responsibility given to another to guide and check the work; if Brenda is to develop, sufficient tasks are combined so that her responsibility increases beyond what she has held before; if Colin lacks confidence, the tasks are broken into smaller units which can be completed (and commended) frequently.

Sometimes tasks can be grouped and allocated together. For instance, some tasks which are seemingly independent may benefit from being done together since they use common ideas, information, talents. One person doing them both removes the start-up time for one of them; two people (one on each) will be able to help each other.

The ordering of the tasks is really quite simple, although you may find that sketching a sequence diagram helps you to think it through (and to communicate the result). Pert charts are the accepted outcome, but sketches will suffice. Getting the details exactly right, however, can be a long and painful process, and often it can be futile. The degree to which you can predict the future is limited, so too should be the detail of your planning. You must have the broad outlines by which to monitor progress, and sufficient detail to assign each task when it needs to be started, but beyond that - stop and do something useful instead.

At the initial planning stage the main objective is to get a realistic estimate of the time involved in the project. You must establish this not only to assist higher management with their planning, but also to protect your team from being expected to do the impossible. The most important technique for achieving this is known as: guesstimation.

Guesstimating schedules is notoriously difficult but it is helped by two approaches:

- Make your guesstimates of the simple tasks at the bottom of the work break down structure and look for the longest path through the sequence diagram
- Use the experience from previous projects to improve your guesstimating skills

The corollary to this is that you should keep records in an easily accessible form of all projects as you do them. Part of your final project review should be to update your personal data base of how long various activities take. Managing this planning phase is vital to your success as a manager.

Some people find guesstimating a difficult concept in that if you have no experience of an activity, how can you make a worthwhile estimate? Let us consider such a problem: how long would it take you to walk all the way to the top of the Eiffel Tower or the Statue of Liberty? Presuming you have never actually tried this (most people take the elevator part of the way), you really have very little to go on. Indeed if you have actually seen one (and only one) of these buildings, think about the other. Your job depends upon this, so think carefully. One idea is to start with the number of steps - guess that if you can. Notice, you do not have to be right, merely reasonable. Next, consider the sort of pace you could maintain while climbing a flight of steps for a long time. Now imagine yourself at the base of a flight of steps you do know, and estimate a) how many steps there are, and b) how long it takes you to climb them (at that steady pace). To complete, apply a little mathematics.

Now examine how confident you are with this estimate. If you won a free flight to Paris or New York and tried it, you would probably (need your head examined) be mildly surprised if you climbed to the top in less than half the estimated time and if it took you more than double you would be mildly annoyed.

If it took you less than a tenth the time, or ten times as long, you would extremely surprised/annoyed. In fact, you do not currently believe that that would happen (no really, do you?). The point is that from very little experience of the given problem, you can actually come up with a working estimate - and one which is far better than no estimate at all when it comes to deriving a schedule. Guesstimating does take a little practice, but it is a very useful skill to develop.

There are two practical problems in guesstimation. First, you are simply too optimistic. It is human nature at the beginning of a new project to ignore the difficulties and assume best case scenarii - in producing your estimates (and using those of others) you must inject a little realism. In practice, you should also build-in a little slack to allow yourself some tolerance against mistakes. This is known as defensive scheduling. Also, if you eventually deliver ahead of the agreed schedule, you will be loved. Second, you will be under pressure from senior management to deliver quickly, especially if the project is being sold competitively. Resist the temptation to rely upon speed as the only selling point. You might, for instance, suggest the criteria of: fewer errors, history of adherence to initial schedules, previous customer satisfaction, "this is how long it takes, so how can you trust the other quotes".

ESTABLISHING CONTROLS

When the planning phase is over (and agreed), the "doing" phase begins. Once it is in motion, a project acquires a direction and momentum which is totally independent of anything you predicted. If you come to terms with that from the start, you can then enjoy the roller-coaster which follows. To gain some hope, however, you need to establish at the start (within the plan) the means to monitor and to influence the project's progress.

There are two key elements to the control of a project

- Milestones (clear, unambiguous targets of what, by when)
- Established means of communication

For you, the milestones are a mechanism to monitor progress; for your team, they are short-term goals which are far more tangible than the foggy, distant completion of the entire project. The milestones maintain the momentum and encourage effort; they allow the team to judge their own progress and to celebrate achievement throughout the project rather than just at its end. The simplest way to construct milestones is to take the timing information from the work breakdown structure and sequence diagram. When you have guesstimated how long each sub-task will take and have strung them together, you can identify by when each of these tasks will actually be completed. This is simple and effective; however, it lacks creativity.

A second method is to construct more significant milestones. These can be found by identify stages in the development of a project which are recognisable as steps towards the final product. Sometimes these are simply the higher levels of your structure; for instance, the completion of a market-evaluation phase. Sometimes, they cut across many parallel activities; for instance, a prototype of the eventual product or a mock-up of the new brochure format.

If you are running parallel activities, this type of milestone is particularly useful since it provides a means of pulling together the people on disparate activities, and so:

- They all have a shared goal (the common milestone)

- Their responsibility to (and dependence upon) each other is emphasised
- Each can provide a new (but informed) viewpoint on the others' work
- The problems to do with combining the different activities are highlighted and discussed early in the implementation phase
- You have something tangible which senior management (and numbties) can recognise as progress
- You have something tangible which your team can celebrate and which constitutes a short-term goal in a possibly long-term project
- It provides an excellent opportunity for quality checking and for review

Of course, there are milestones and there are mill-stones. You will have to be sensitive to any belief that working for some specific milestone is hindering rather than helping the work forward. If this arises then either you have chosen the wrong milestone, or you have failed to communicate how it fits into the broader structure.

Communication is your everything. To monitor progress, to receive early warning of danger, to promote cooperation, to motivate through team involvement, all of these rely upon communication. Regular reports are invaluable - if you clearly define what information is needed and if teach your team how to provided it in a rapidly accessible form. Often these reports merely say "progressing according to schedule". These you send back, for while the message is desired the evidence is missing: you need to insist that your team monitor their own progress with concrete, tangible, measurements and if this is done, the figures should be included in the report. However, the real value of this practice comes when progress is not according to schedule - then your communication system is worth all the effort you invested in its planning.

At the planning stage, you can deal with far more than the mere project at hand. You can also shape the overall pattern of your team's working using the division and type of activities you assign.

Ask your team. They too must be involved in the planning of projects, especially in the lower levels of the work breakdown structure. Not only will they provide information and ideas, but also they will feel ownership in the final plan.

This does not mean that your projects should be planned by committee - rather that you, as manager, plan the project based upon all the available experience and creative ideas. As an initial approach, you could attempt the first level(s) of the work breakdown structure to help you communicate the project to the team and then ask for comments. Then, using these, the final levels could be refined by the people to whom the tasks will be allocated. However, since the specification is so vital, all the team should vet the penultimate draft.

There are two pitfalls to avoid in project reviews:

- They can be too frequent
- They can be too drastic

The constant trickle of new information can lead to a vicious cycle of planning and revising which shakes the team's confidence in any particular version of the plan and which destroys the very stability which the structure was designed to provide. You must decide the balance. Pick a point on the horizon and walk confidently towards it. Decide objectively, and explain beforehand, when the review phases will occur and make this a scheduled milestone in itself.

Even though the situation may have changed since the last review, it is important to recognise the work which has been accomplished during the interim. Firstly, you do not want to abandon it since the team will be demotivated feeling that they have achieved nothing. Secondly, this work itself is part of the new situation: it has been done, it should provide a foundation for the next step or at least the basis of a lesson well learnt. Always try to build upon the existing achievements of your team.

No plan is complete without explicit provision for testing and quality. As a wise manager, you will know that this should be part of each individual phase of the project. This means that no activity is completed until it has passed the (objectively) defined criteria which establishes its quality, and these are best defined (objectively) at the beginning as part of the planning.

When devising the schedule therefore you must include allocated time for this part of each activity. Thus your question is not only: "how long will it take", but also: "how long will the testing take". By asking both questions together you raise the issue of "how do we know we have done it right" at the very beginning and so the testing is more likely to be done in parallel with the implementation. You establish this philosophy for your team by include testing as a justified (required) cost.

Another reason for stating the testing criteria at the beginning is that you can avoid futile quests for perfection. If you have motivated your team well, they will each take pride in their work and want to do the best job possible. Often this means polishing their work until is shines; often this wastes time. If it clear at the onset exactly what is needed, then they are more likely to stop when that has been achieved. You need to avoid generalities and to stipulate boundaries; not easy, but essential.

The same is also true when choosing the tools or building-blocks of your project. While it might be nice to have use of the most modern versions, or to develop an exact match to your needs; often there is an old/existing version which will serve almost as well (sufficient for the purpose), and the difference is not worth the time you would need to invest in obtaining or developing the new one. Use what is available whenever possible unless the difference in the new version is worth the time, money and the initial, teething pains. A related idea is that you should discourage too much effort on aspects of the project which are idiosyncratic to that one job. In the specification phase, you might try to eliminate these through negotiation with the customer; in the implementation phase you might leave these parts until last. The reason for this advice is that a general piece of work can be tailored to many specific instances; thus, if the work is in a general form, you will be able to rapidly re-use it for other projects. On the other hand, if you produce something which is cut to fit exactly one specific case, you may have to repeat the work entirely even though the next project is fairly similar. At the planning phase, a manager should bare in mind the future and the long-term development of the team as well as the requirements of the current project.

As a manager, you have to regulate the pressure and work load which is imposed upon your team; you must protect them from the unreasonable demands of the rest of the company. Once you have arrived at what you consider to be a realistic schedule, fight for it. Never let the outside world deflect you from what you know to be practical. If they impose a deadline upon you which is impossible, clearly state this and give your reasons. You will need to give some room for compromise, however, since a flat NO will be seen as obstructive. Since you want to help the company, you should look for alternative positions.

You could offer a prototype service or product at an earlier date. This might, in some cases, be sufficient for the customer to start the next stage of his/her own project on the understanding that your project would be completed at a later date and the final version would then replace the prototype.

The complexity of the product, or the total number of units, might be reduced. This might, in some cases, be sufficient for the customer's immediate needs. Future enhancements or more units would then be the subject of a subsequent negotiation which, you feel, would be likely to succeed since you will have already demonstrate your ability to deliver on time.

You can show on an alternative schedule that the project could be delivered by the deadline if certain (specified) resources are given to you or if other projects are rescheduled. Thus, you provide a clear picture of the situation and a possible solution; it is up to your manager then how he/she proceeds.

The most common error in planning is to assume that there will be no errors in the implementation: in effect, the schedule is derived on the basis of "if nothing goes wrong, this will take...". Of course, recognising that errors will occur is the reason for implementing a monitoring strategy on the project. Thus when the inevitable does happen, you can react and adapt the plan to compensate. However, by carefully considering errors in advance you can make changes to the original plan to enhance its tolerance. Quite simply, your planning should include time where you stand back from the design and ask: "what can go wrong?"; indeed, this is an excellent way of asking your team for their analysis of your plan.

You can try to predict where the errors will occur. By examining the activities' list you can usually pinpoint some activities which are risky (for instance, those involving new equipment) and those which are quite secure (for instance, those your team has done often before). The risky areas might then be given a less stringent time-scale - actually planning-in time for the mistakes.

Another possibility is to apply a different strategy, or more resources, to such activities to minimise the disruption. For instance, you could include training or consultancy for new equipment, or you might parallel the work with the foundation of a fall-back position.

At the end of any project, you should allocate time to reviewing the lessons and information on both the work itself and the management of that work: an open meeting, with open discussion, with the whole team and all customers and suppliers. If you think that this might be thought a waste of time by your own manager, think of the effect it will have on future communications with your customers and suppliers.

VARIOUS MODELS FOR CHANGE MANAGEMENT

There are numerous well-organized approaches (or models) from which to manage a change effort. Some of the approaches have been around for many years — we just haven't thought of them as such. For example, many organizations undertake strategic planning. The implementation of strategic planning, when done in a systematic, cyclical and explicit approach, is strategic management. Strategic management is also one model for ensuring the success of a change effort. Many people would agree that traditional models of organizational performance management are also models for managing change.

A typical planned, systemic (and systematic) organizational development process often follows an overall action research approach. There are many variations of the action research approach, including by combining its various phases and/or splitting some into more phases. This section provides resources that are organized into one variation of the action research approach. Note that the more collaborative you are in working with members of the organization during the following process, the more likely the success of your overall change effort.

Phase 1

This phase is sometimes called the "Contracting" and/or "Entry" phase. This phase is usually where the relationship between you (the initial change agent) and your client starts, whether you are an external or internal consultant. Experts assert that this phase is one of the most - if not the most - important phases in the organizational change process. Activities during this stage form the foundation for successful organizational change. The quality of how this phase is carried out usually is a strong indicator of how the project will go.

Phase 2

The more collaborative the change agent is in working with members of the client's organization, the more likely that the change effort will be successful. Your client might not have the resources to fully participate in all aspects of this discovery activity — the more participation they can muster, the better off your project will be.

Whether you are an external or internal change agent in this project, you and your client will work together during this phase to understand more about the overall priority of the change effort and how you all can effectively address it. It might be a major problem in the organization or an exciting vision to achieve. Together, you will collect information, analyze it to identify findings and conclusions, and then make recommendations from that information. Sometimes the data-collection effort is very quick, for example, facilitating a large planning meeting. Other times, the effort is more extensive, for example, evaluating an entire organization and developing a complete plan for change. The nature of discovery also depends on the philosophy of the change agent and client. For example, subscribers to the philosophy of Appreciative Inquiry (referenced above) might conduct discovery, not by digging into the number and causes of problems in the organization, but by conducting interviews to disover the visions and wishes of people in the organization.

Sometimes, people minimize the importance of - or altogether skip - this critical discovery phase, and start change management by articulating an ambitious and comprehensive vision for change. Many would argue that it is unethical to initiate a project for organizational change without fully examining (or discovering) the current situation in the client's organization. Focusing most of the change efforts on achieving a robust vision, without at least some careful discovery, often can be harmful to your client's organization because your project can end up dealing with symptoms of any current issues, rather than the root causes. Also, the project could end up pushing an exciting vision that, while initially inspiring and motivating to many, could be completely unrealistic to achieve — especially if the organization already has many current, major issues to address. Therefore, when working to guide change in an organization that already is facing several significant issues, you are usually better off to start from where your client is at — that usually means conducting an effective discovery to identify priorities for change.

One of the most powerful means to cultivate collaboration is by working with a project team. Besides, no change agent sees all aspects of the situation in the organization — team members help to see more of those various aspects.

Phase 3

In the previous phase about discovery, you and your client conducted research, discovered various priorities that needed attention, generated recommendations to address those priorities, and shared your information with others, for example, in a feedback meeting. Part of that meeting included discussions - and, hopefully, decisions - about the overall mutual recommendations that your client should follow to in order address the priorities that were identified by you and your client during your discovery. This phase is focused on further clarifying those recommendations, along with developing them into various action plans. The various plans are sometimes integrated into an overall change management plan. Thus, the early activities in this phase often overlap with, and are a continuation of, the activities near the end of the earlier discovery phase. This is true whether you are an external or internal consultant. Action plans together can now provide a clear and realistic vision for change. They provide the "roadmap" for managing the transition from the present state to the desired future state.

Development of the various action plans is often an enlightening experience for your client as members of their organization begin to realize a more systematic approach to their planning and day-to-day activities. As with other activities during change management, plans can vary widely in how they are developed. Some plans are very comprehensive and systematic (often the best form used for successful change). Others are comprised of diverse sections that are expected to somehow integrate with each other. Subscribers to the philosophy of Appreciative Inquiry (referenced above) might do planning by building on past positive outcomes and on the strengths of members of the organization.

Phase 4

During this phase, emphasis is on sustaining and evaluating the change effort, including by addressing resistance that arises from members of the organization — and sometimes in the change agent, as well.

Evaluation occurs both to the quality of implementation of plans so far during the project and also regarding the extent of achievement of desired results from the project. Results might be whether certain indicators of success have been achieved, all issues have been addressed, a vision of success has been achieved, action plans have been implemented and/or leaders in the organization agree the project has been successful.

As part of the final evaluation, you might redo some of the assessments that you used during the discovery phase in order to measure the difference made by the project.

If the Project Gets Stuck

During this phase, if the implementation of the plans gets stalled for a long time, for example, many months, then you might cycle back to an earlier phase in the process in order to update and restart the change management project. Projects can get stuck for a variety of reasons, e.g., if the overall situation changes (there suddenly are new and other priorities in the client's organization), people succumb to burnout, key people leave the organization, the relationship between the consultant and client changes, or people refuse to implement action plans.

Project Termination

These activities are very important to address, even if all participants agree that the project has been successful and no further activities are needed. Project termination activities recognize key learnings from the project, acknowledge the client's development, and identify next steps for you and your client. They also help to avoid "project creep" where the project never ends because the requirements for success keep expanding.

The field of Organization Development uses a variety of processes, approaches, methods, techniques, applications, etc., (these are often termed "interventions") to address organizational issues and goals in order to increase performance. The following partial list of interventions is organized generally in the order presented by Cummings and Worley in their "Organization Development and Change". The following types of interventions are often highly integrated with each other during a project for change.

There are no standard activities that always successfully address certain types of issues in organizations. Many times, the success of a project lies not with having selected the perfect choice of activities, but rather with how honest and participative people were during the project, how much they learned and how open they were to changing their plans for change.

However, there are some basic considerations that most people make when selecting from among the many choices for organizational development, or capacity building, activities. Considerations include:

1. First, does the change-management method (if one was used) suggest what organizational development activities to use now, for example, the method of strategic management might suggest that a SWOT analysis be done, strategic goals be established along with action plans for each goal, and then implementation of the action plans be closely monitored.
2. Is the activity most likely to address the findings from the discovery, that is, to solve the problems or achieve the goals? To find out, review any research about use of the activity, discuss the potential outcomes with experts and also with members of the organization. Consider posing your questions in online groups of experts about change.
3. Does the nature of the activity match the culture of the organization? The best way to find out is to discuss the activity with members of the organization.
4. Does the change agent and key members of the organization have the ability to conduct the activity? For example, technostructural

and strategic interventions sometimes require technical skills that are not common to many people.

5. Does the activity require more time to conduct than the time available in which to address the problem or goal? For example, a cash crisis requires immediate attention, so while a comprehensive strategic planning process might ultimately be useful, the four to five months to do that planning is impractical.
6. Does the client's organization have the resources that are necessary to conduct the activity, considering resources such as funding, attention and time from people and facilities.

Before you and your client select types of interventions for the project, be aware of your strong biases about how you view organizations. Without recognizing those biases, you might favor certain types of interventions primarily because those are the only ones you can readily see and understand, even if other types of interventions might be much more effective in your project.

With today's strong emphasis on humanistic values, the following interventions are getting a great deal of attention and emphasis during efforts for change. They focus on helping members of the organization to enhance themselves, each other and the ways in which they work together in order to enhance their overall organization. Although the types of interventions selected for a project depend on a variety of considerations and the interventions in a project often are highly integrated with each other, the following human process interventions might be particularly helpful during change projects in organizations where there is some combination of the following: many new employees, different cultures working together, many complaints among organizational members, many conflicts, low morale, high turnover, ineffective teams, etc.

HUMAN RESOURCE MANAGEMENT INTERVENTIONS

Performance is in regard to setting goals, monitoring progress to the goals, sharing feedback, reinforcing activities to achieve goals and dissuading those that don't. Performance also is in regard to developing employees, including by enhancing their overall sense of well-being. Although the types of interventions selected for a project depend on a variety of considerations and the interventions in a project often are highly integrated, the following human resource interventions might be particularly helpful in the following kinds of situations: new organizational goals have been established, a major new system or technology must be implemented in a timely fashion, many new employees, plans don't seem to get implemented, productivity is low, ineffective teams, etc.

The following activities focus especially on the organization and its interactions with its external environment, and often involve changes to many aspects of the organization, including employees, groups, technologies, products and services, etc. Although the types of interventions selected for a project depend on a variety of considerations and the interventions in a project often are highly integrated, the following strategic interventions might be particularly helpful in the following kinds of situations: rapid changes in the external environment, rapid or stagnant sales, significantly increased competition, rapid expansion of markets, mergers and acquisitions, the need for quick and comprehensive change throughout the organization, etc.

Significant organizational change occurs, for example, when an organization changes its overall strategy for success, adds or removes a major section or practice, and/or wants to change the very nature by which it operates. It also occurs when an organization evolves through various life cycles, just like people must successfully evolve through life cycles. For organizations to develop, they often must undergo significant change at various points in their development. That's why the topic of organizational change and development has become widespread in communications about business, organizations, leadership and management.

Leaders and managers continually make efforts to accomplish successful and significant change — it's inherent in their jobs. Some are very good at this effort (probably more than we realize), while others continually struggle and fail. That's often the difference between people who thrive in their roles and those that get shuttled around from job to job, ultimately settling into a role where they're frustrated and ineffective. There are many schools with educational programs about organizations, business, leadership and management. Unfortunately, there still are not enough schools with programs about how to analyze organizations, identify critically important priorities to address (such as systemic problems or exciting visions for change) and then undertake successful and significant change to address those priorities. This Library topic aims to improve that situation.

Successful organizational change can be quite difficult to accomplish — it can be like trying to change a person's habits. Fortunately, there is an increasing body of research, practice and tools from which we all can learn. A major goal of this Library topic is to make this body of information much more accessible to many — to give the reader more clear perspective on overall organizational change and development, along with sufficient understanding to begin applying principles and practices for successful change in their roles and organizations. The following resources are not sufficient to guide a large, comprehensive and detailed organizational change effort — that amount of resources comprises a significantly sized book — and besides, there is no standard procedure for guiding change. However, the following resources might be sufficient to provide the reader at least a framework that takes him or her from which to begin guiding change in smaller efforts for organizational change — and then to begin to learn more.

There are many approaches to guiding change — some planned, structured and explicit, while others are more organic, unfolding and implicit. Some approaches work from the future to the present, for example, involving visioning and then action planning about how to achieve that vision. Other approaches work from the present to the future, for example, identifying current priorities (issues and/or goals) and then action planning about to address those priorities (the action research approach is one example). Different people often have very different — and strong — opinions about how change should be conducted. Thus, it is likely that some will disagree with some of the content in this topic. That's what makes this topic so diverse, robust and vital for us all.

7

Action Research in Hotel Management

Interactive social science research may be regarded as a pragmatic, utilitarian, or user-oriented approach to research and incorporates a value-base that is committed to promoting change through research. It is democratic and participatory by nature and is in sharp contrast to the positivistic 'top-down' approach which has been accused of 'lifting decisions from the village square' and placing them with 'experts or outside agencies' (Bryant, 2001). The practice goes by many names: community-based research, participatory research, collaborative research, and others, but rests on two main principles: democratization of the knowledge process, and social change.

Action research forms part of this genre, and is associated with attempts to bring about emancipation and social justice based on the desires and direct involvement of ordinary people. Its roots may be traced to writers such as Marx, Engels, Gramsci and Freire, and has been used to promote the empowerment of disadvantaged and oppressed groups through the development of common knowledge and critical awareness which are suppressed by the dominant knowledge in a society. Action research is now used within a range of settings and has developed by drawing from pragmatic philosophy, critical thinking, and humanistic and transpersonal psychology, constructionist theory, systems thinking and complexity theory.

An important element of action research is participation by 'informants' who engage in 'collective, self-reflective enquiry...in social situations in order improve the rationality and justice of their own social practices'. A key feature is empowerment through participation. This may, for example, involve the researcher identifying the user group, working in close collaboration with the users, and getting them involved in identifying their needs, setting up research questions, and using the research findings. The practice involves people reflecting on issues and processes during the research, participants as co-researchers, and entails an element of risk given that the process and outcomes are in a state of on-going change. It is transformed by emergent findings, which, in turn, impact upon the process itself, and subsequent outcomes. As the focus becomes redirected, outcomes may not be readily predicted and, for this reason alone, power holders may not be fully at ease with what they are not in control of: the 'knowledge' it produces, the thinking it stimulates, or the action it promotes.

Action research has now found its way into a diverse range of areas, including the experiential learning movement, community development, action learning, humanistic psychology, popular education, organization development, and feminist thinking. Each field has shaped and redefined 'action research' according to its particular requirements. For example, interactive research has been closely associated with the environmental movement, democratic evaluation has links with education, and empowerment evaluation aims to 'help others to help themselves' in areas that include substance abuse prevention, HIV/AIDS prevention, and adult probation.

When commissioning research, an organisation may perceive that subsequent outcomes will take place within specified parameters that will help to further its overall aims, including the need to develop or maintain working relations with other bodies (eg Tackling Drugs to Build a Better Britain, 1998). What they may not realise, however, is that action research has the potential to instigate certain forms of action which undermine the 'collaborative' framework that they seek. Unlike more professionally-directed models of research, action research can be difficult to 'manage' once underway.

In the area of drugs prevention, action research has been used in tandem with an approach that stresses the role of community development and community involvement. As a philosophy, 'community drugs prevention' entails residents gaining access to a range of social, political and economic resources. In this respect, drugs prevention is concerned with wider quality of life issues that residents define as important and will serve to reduce the demand for drug use. Action research has been used to mobilise communities in order to achieve these objectives.

The research used as a case study for the purpose of this chapter took place in a locality exhibiting the usual indices of long-term social and economic decline, including widescale drugs-related difficulties. Initially, the commissioning agency (administered by the Home Office) was committed to devising a community-led drugs prevention strategy. Its original intention was that through operationalising action research, community concerns about drug misuse would be elicited alongside residents' perceptions of what 'drugs prevention' should involve, and residents would be encouraged to get involved in setting up projects and lobbying policy makers for relevant change. The commissioning agency perceived that the local urban regeneration agency would be a key funder for any future projects that may result from the research.

Initially, in-depth individual and group interviews became central to the research process. Later, a series of small-scale public meetings occurred, and community newsletters were produced. At the meetings the earlier findings were fed back to residents who, in turn, commented on them and suggested future directions that the project should take. Residents' participation took various forms. Apart from acting as 'informants' during the interviews, they produced articles that appeared in the newsletters, were actively involved in developing and conducting interviews with other residents, initiated and developed an on-going community forum which discussed the issues emerging from the research, and began lobbying local agencies to take part in various working groups in order that their concerns may be addressed. Although the initial research agenda had been more or less professionally-led, as time progressed, residents were changing the agenda and were leading the process through their actions.

The research had stimulated community awareness around 'drugs prevention' issues, had succeeded in producing an action plan for prevention, and a community forum had emerged comprising of local residents and representatives from local agencies. The regeneration agency (which had not become directly involved in the research process) became critical of the agency that had commissioned the research, the researcher, and the 'biased' outlook of residents that was being put forward in the newsletters published by the forum, and through the emerging research findings published in a working paper which was widely distributed within the locality.

According to its view, the research was merely serving to stir-up and magnify unjustified hostility toward its role in the area. The consequence was that other key agencies in the area (and involved with the forum) became reluctant to continue to support the activities of the local residents for fear of producing tensions between themselves and the powerful regeneration agency. Consequently, as the forum lacked backing from certain key voluntary and statutory sector agencies, the regeneration agency felt justified in not providing funding for projects outlined in the action plan. Funding for the action research and for the researcher expired after a six month period and residents were either unable or unwilling to continue their activities through the forum.

In some ways the action research ignited a powder keg that had been waiting to go off. Simmering tensions between sections of the community and the regeneration agency had frequently boiled over during a long period of time prior to the research. The locality traditionally had a strong and vocal community sector, and was predominantly staunchly left-wing in political outlook. They possessed little faith in the overall aims and objectives of the regeneration agency from not long after its inception - perceiving it to be an imposition from central government whose outlook was regarded as having changed little from those of previous Conservative administrations. The action research became part of the local political process and arguably politicized those residents who were previously not very vocal within the area.

At the outset, the commissioning body expressed a commitment toward 'community involvement' in drugs prevention, but it is doubtful whether it fully appreciated the potential implications of the action research. Based on a model used elsewhere, the agency perceived that the research would primarily involve a consultation exercise culminating in greater levels of community representation in existing and potential new projects. The agency perceived that the research would contribute toward an integrated approach for prevention, bringing organisations and residents together.

Residents expressed a strong commitment to the action research, given the emancipatory and participatory background of the paradigm, and viewed it as a welcome change from previous professionally controlled research that they had regarded as having been an end in itself: a mechanism for integrating residents and community groups into government and prevailing structures thereby giving programmes a degree of credibility and legitimacy, but not bringing about the changes for communities and residents that they desire (Todhunter, 2001). However, action research may appear to offer a potential for change, but just how much change may be expected given the wider interests of agencies and organisations that may be juxtaposed to proposed change?

Agencies may (unconsciously) seek to define residents' needs according to their specific remit, and attempt to set a research agenda accordingly - even though they may label it as 'action' research. In the case outlined here, the commissioning body appeared to put into operation their own limited notion of 'action research'. However, through the research residents emphasised a desire for exerting more direct power in order to facilitate their identity and rights as citizens. They were calling for equal participation on the partnership board of the regeneration agency which they felt was slanted against the interests of local people in favour of statutory sector and business interests. In effect, they were challenging the prevailing power structures by questioning the legitimacy of key agencies. Subsequently, the agency that commissioned the research was not able to respond fully to the needs or views of residents once unpacked.

In the shorter term, action research may produce a 'feel good' factor among participants - consciousness raising, 'participation' and mobilisation may instill a self-belief in ordinary people's capacity to bring about change. In the longer term, real and radical change may indeed come about. To do this however, commitment to change must be forthcoming among all local agencies and interest groups. Otherwise, action research may leave a bitter taste in the mouths of residents, whose expectations are raised, and subsequent programmes for change may have to cope with the damage done by previous projects that failed to deliver. Any good faith which may have been present among residents may have drained away leaving an embittered community that is hostile or cynical toward future programmes which come along.

In many respects the pitfalls that emerged in the case study presented here have been somewhat reminiscent of those surrounding the Community

Development Projects of the 1970s. Workers in many of the projects came to reject the analysis and strategies of the original project proposals. They sought to organise and research around larger questions of inequality and deindustrialisation Workers who entered the field in the late 1960s and early 1970s exhibited a readiness to take up oppositional positions. By 1974 the Home Office had largely given up on the projects and they were wound up in 1976.

Commissioning bodies need to be fully aware of the potential pitfalls of undertaking action research. They must understand what 'action research' implies, and that it does not sit easily with conventional and easily manageable 'consultation' exercises - thus making it a high risk strategy. By committing to a process of action research, agencies are legitimizing residents' voices and actions, and their participation in social policy. In some respects they will embarking upon a programme that bucks a wider cultural and social trend encouraging 'involvement' which seeks to guarantee consensus and integration rather than change, and may find themselves in uncomfortable situations.

Action research is a tool that research commissioners must not take lightly, and not undertake impulsively. The groundwork has to be prepared thoroughly, given the potential impact. Agencies must give due thought about imposing a standard model of action research applied elsewhere to a different area, as in the study outlined here. They have to decide how feasible action research and change may be, given wider trends and local political situations, and must also prepare the groundwork effectively prior to committing to the research, bringing on board key players who may find themselves bearing the brunt of residents' frustrations and providing them with a chance to negotiate the shifting research agenda in tandem with residents.

For at least seventy years, some researchers around the world have been identifying what they do using terms like 'action research', or 'participatory research', or a combination of these. Some have stressed the action component,1 while others have focused more on the participatory process. Still others have come from the field of social science and have identified it as a means of inquiry or research per se.

This chapter came about in response to requests to speak about some of the collective wisdom that has been generated over many decades by people who have identified what they do using the term 'participatory action research'. It is the way I tell the story.

Throughout this account participatory action research is contrasted with formulations of conventional research science. For me, participatory action research is not a different and separate matter from science at all, but constitutes a formulation of how I understand all science in the wake of the wave of thinking that is popularly being called the 'new physics'. This 'new physics' or 'new paradigm science' in the natural physical world seems to me to match a 'new paradigm science' in the social world. I identify 'participatory action research' not as an optional variant or specialist technique, but as one of the more inclusive descriptions of this new understanding of social science.

This short paper sets out to identify some of the main characteristics of participatory action research for me, and to try and show why I have come to the following two conclusions:

- 'Participatory action research' is a description of social research per se (albeit social research which is more conscious of its underlying assumptions, and collectivist nature, its action consequences and its driving values).
- It faces numerous barriers to its practice which mean that, even when we think we might be doing 'it', we often have our doubts! I have come to conclude that pretty much all of the research we are involved in, is more or less an approximation in the direction of 'it'. That is, every piece of research is more or less participatory. It more or less enables action as part of the process. And it all involves more or less critical reflexive, skeptical and imaginative inquiry.

What do we typically do when we 'do a piece of research'? Let's take a couple of everyday examples.

We are going about our business and a piece of equipment fails to work. We are pulled up in our tracks as we experience a discrepancy between our practice and our expectations. Out of our need for it to 'work', a question arises: 'Why is it so?'. We have a look at the piece of equipment: perhaps involving a little piece of hands-on 'participant observation' fieldwork! Perhaps we employ also some 'secondary analysis' as we consult the maker's manual for their theories and advice! We may develop a hunch (hypothesis) and draw some conclusions.

Then we try it out in a form of a naturalistic experiment and we 'give it a go'. Again we go about our business. The equipment works and we carry on. Or, it fails to work again and we again stop in our tracks and raise our question again, and try further fieldwork to develop yet another theory and try yet another tack, and so on.

We are looking for our daughter's shoes in the early morning scramble. We review previous 'historical data' (memories of earlier experiences!) as part of planning our 'research design'. We generate several hypotheses and move quickly into the 'field' to involve other participants and gather new data to test them! We use some observational anthropology.

Two brief interviews with daughter and sibling result in reports of failed hunches! (they weren't in their cupboards or on the back verandah!); we engage in further open-ended interviews with the entire household population.

Then secondary analysis of the previous day's timetable generates a further hunch (Sports Day!: shoes replaced with runners) and an additional round of observation reveals: shoes in school bag!

These trivial microcosms contain a structure which reliably:

- commences - ironically - with stopping. That is, we do not begin to inquire until we actually suspend our current action because of the:
- Raising of a question; which then provokes us to go about:
- Planning ways to get answers - ways which will involve identifying and involving 'questioners', 'the questioned' and an idea of for who or for what we desire answers;
- Engaging in fieldwork about new, current or past action in order to get answers and improve our experiential understanding of the problematic situation;
- Generating from the 'answers' an imaginative idea of what to do to change and improve our actions;
- The putting into practice of the new actions (followed by further stopping, reflecting and possible 'problematisation').

This is precisely the cycle of action, reflection, raising of questions, planning of 'fieldwork' to review current (and past) actions - its conduct, analysis of experiences encountered, the drawing of conclusions, and the planning of new and transformed actions - that characterizes all research endeavor. If we are to distinguish this cycle in any ways from what we 'do all the time', we find the important distinctions are in degree rather than kind. That is, in participatory action research we are:

- More conscious of 'problematising' an existing action or practice and more conscious of who is problematising it and why we are problematising it;
- More explicit about 'naming' the problem, and more self-conscious about raising an unanswered question and focusing an effort to answer it;
- More planned and deliberate about commencing a process of inquiry and involving others who could or should be involved in that inquiry;
- More systematic and rigorous in our efforts to get answers;
- More carefully documenting and recording action and what people think about it and in more detail and in ways which are accessible to other relevant parties;
- More intensive and comprehensive in our study, waiting much longer before we 'jump' to a conclusion;
- More self-sceptical in checking our hunches;
- Attempting to develop deeper understandings and more useful and more powerful theory about the matters we are researching, in order to produce new knowledge which can inform improved action or practice; 6 and
- Changing our actions as part of the research process, and then further researching these changed actions.

One of the ways this understanding of research differs from conceptions of conventional research or 'old paradigm science' is revealed in the diagrams below. Conventional research often sees itself as proceeding from point A to point B along a straight line - commencing with a hypothesis and proceeding to a conclusion which may then be published in a journal. However new paradigm social science (or participatory action research) considers it critical to the success of the inquiry that the hypothesis is relevant and useful and thus asks: Where did the hunches or hypotheses come from? Are they just any old hypotheses? Or have they been carefully constructed and well-grounded, over time, from deep and engaged involvement in the field being studied? Are they plausible? Are they relevant? Are they already well-evidenced and thus already substantiate new action? (rather than having to spend time re-discovering or re-confirming the already-established).

Furthermore, new paradigm science asks: Have they been checked in practice? Findings, 'discoveries' or new ideas are not accepted until tested in action - otherwise they remain merely 'interesting ideas' or 'just academic'.

Instead of a linear model, participatory action research thus proceeds through cycles, 'starting' with reflection on action, and proceeding round to new action which is then further researched. The new actions differ from the old actions - they are literally in different places.

Interestingly, all science seems to me to follow this logic. However many 'old paradigm' scientists are unaware of their implication in this. There is always new action resulting - even if it is just the same as the old (which we might describe as reproducing the 'status quo'). Inquiry inevitably leads somewhere - even if it isn't far from where it started, or only a small number of people are consciously aware of it. Once inquirers are aware of the implications of inquiring, they are faced with a choice. They can ignore it (or treat it as peripheral or of nuisance value), or they can resolve to work with it as a positive feature of their research environment. Action researchers, it seems to me, are really just researchers who have come to understand the practical and ethical implications of the inevitability of the value-driven and action-effects of their inquiry, that is:

- The effects of raising some questions and not others,
- The effects of involving some people in the process (or even apparently only one) and not others,
- The effects of observing some phenomena and not others,
- The effects of making this sense of it and not alternative senses, and
- The effects of deciding to take this action (or 'no' action) as a result of it rather than any other action and so on.

All research involves these kinds of decisions. Participatory action research attempts to make these decisions more consciously and in relation to more clearly-worked out purposes, and using more appropriate designs and techniques for exploring them.

The Action Element

All research seems to me to be implicated in action. Not only is research itself an action in and on existing situations, but it also always has consequences. Things inevitably change as a result of research - the mere act of asking questions is an intervention in a situation, and giving and hearing answers and making sense of them inevitably brings about changes in those involved. Whether people then choose to continue as before or to change course means that the new situation will either be different from that before, or it will be the same. To 'not change' is nevertheless action: some might call it inaction!

Participatory action research is aware of its inevitable intervention in the social situations within which it operates and seeks to turn these to consciously-applied effect. Most participatory action research sets out to explicitly study something in order to change and improve it. It most often arises from an unsatisfactory situation that those most affected wish to alter for the better (although it can also arise from the experience of something which works well, which provokes the desire to reproduce or expand it).

The moving to new and improved action involves a creative 'moment' of transformation. 7 This involves an imaginative leap from a world of 'as it is' to a glimpse of a world 'as it could be'. Where existing situations benefit or promote some but disadvantage or subordinate others, then creative change may be construed as 'political'. As well, participatory action research does not conceptualise this as the development of predictive cause-effect theory ('if this, then that'). Instead, as in the slogan: 'the future is made, not predicted', it is more like 'what if we..., then maybe'. Possibility theory rather than predictive theory. That is, human actors are both wilful and capable of thwarting research prediction, and wilful and capable of selecting and implementing theories or probabilities they want to see manifested! Conventional science sees this as undesirable 'contamination' and 'bias'. Participatory action research sees this as a goal, and the stuff of which 'real life' is made or enacted.

Action research, like the discovery phase of any science, knows it is coming from somewhere and going to somewhere, even though it does not know in advance where precisely it is going to end up or what the new state will look like. Participatory action research, unlike conventional science, does not consider this to be an embarrassment! However it can be difficult for researchers (and research funders) accustomed primarily to a formal experimental approach (the verificationist phase of science), since all that can be stated at the outset is that certain parties have noticed certain problematic matters and have planned certain participatory processes in order to try and 'crack it' for a new way to approach the matter. It may be that funders need to fund iterative or emergent research in connecting stages of 'seeding', 'sapling' and 'tree' phases (and not with up to a year's time lapse in between, as at present). As there is an infinity of 'could be' worlds, then the action phase is crucially guided by the depth and quality of theorising achieved by the research participants. Superficial or trivial research will result in superficial and trivial ideas for practice.

The major challenge for all participatory action researchers (and indeed all researchers) is to design a process which can result in maximum creativity and imagination. Some of the most spectacular ideas have come about because researchers (or self-researchers) were able to draw on unusual sources for ideas, and then submit them to their critical reference group 10 to see if they 'resonated'. If such creative and imaginative efforts have been well-driven by a critical reference group perspective and well-grounded in an understanding of the critical reference group and their context or environment (including the effects of others and of 'structural' matters or opportunities impinging), then they stand a much better chance of 'getting it right' and ideas 'taking off'. Pretty much every initiative we now see around us as A Good Thing happened in this way: as a product of people who 'knew their turf', knew who they were doing it for, and had the imagination to collectively envision a desirable new state and attract others who shared that vision.

In participatory action research, while there is a conceptual difference between the 'participation' 'action' and 'research' elements, in its most developed state these differences begin to dissolve in practice. That is, there is not participation followed by research and then hopefully action. Instead there are countless tiny cycles of participatory reflection on action, learning about action and then new informed action which is in turn the subject of further reflection.

Every minute of every hour may see participants absorbing new ways of seeing or thinking in the light of their experience, leading to new related actions being taken on the spot. Often these will pass unnoticed and unrecorded, but with practice these too become the subject of further reflection and group self-understanding. Change does not happen at 'the end' - it happens throughout. A hallmark of a genuine participatory action research process is that it may change shape and focus over time (and sometimes quite unexpectedly) as participants focus and refocus their understandings about what is 'really' happening and what is really important to them.

It is not possible to do any social research without the participation of other human beings. In typical research there might be one or more 'researchers', there might be people who are 'researched', and there might be people who are 'researched for' - such as those who are to be informed or influenced by findings, or, at a more fundamental level, those who have a problem on which the research is to cast light. However even the research that seems to involve 'no-one', such as the most lone and unobtrusive academic researcher, examining written historical records of people long dead, who seems to be isolated from 'real world practice', and is relatively unknown to peers, still exists in a social world peopled by family, friends, fellow academics, academic administrators, tax-payers and politicians, funding bodies, editors of journals or thesis-examiners, as well as by the written representations of the researched (and there may also be some living representatives) which nevertheless must 'speak' and be 'heard' and understood by the researcher. These all impinge on, and 'construct' the research environment and it's findings, regardless of their apparent invisibility.

More usually there are known groups of researchers, people who commission the research, and live populations of 'researched' and 'researched for', many of whom may know of the research and want to have a say about its conduct or contribute a view about its subject-matter.

Various parties to research 'participate', but the questions become 'Who is treated as participants?', 'How much do they participate?', 'In what ways do they participate?', and 'How is their participation taken into account or not taken into account?'.

Indeed the reason why many of us have felt compelled to add the "p" for participation to the "ar" for action research has been because we have noticed that many have taken existing levels of conventional 'participation' for granted. More importantly there may have been a complacency about the adequacy of current input. Here is a chicken and egg. How do existing participants know the limits of their own perceptions without new participants being there to illuminate the relativism of the existing participants' perceptions - and how would the new participants get to be involved, invited (or tolerated) if their value is not known?

It is worth drawing out the differences between the parties to research in more detail to examine the new possibilities for participation.

In a conventional piece of research there may be less apparent participation. For example, management (group iv), is puzzled or uneasy about some existing matter, or under pressure from another group (iii) or (iv) to Do Something. They might typically employ an independent researcher, (i), to go and study some of the people-with-a-problem, (iii) and perhaps also have some informal discussions with staff, (iv). They may limit their involvement to an initial briefing, the receipt of progress reports, attendance at a steering committee, and receipt of a final report. The researcher may be an academic or a private consultant with some other interests in the matter themselves, (i) and (iv). They are constrained to appear to be neutral or perhaps mildly on everyone's side. They may also be on a short term, highly paid contract with high performance expectations. They expect to get into the field, get the data, get out cleanly, write it up, add some recommendations that seem feasible and then move on to the next demanding job.

The people-with-a-problem: 'clients', 'patients', 'students', or other group of disadvantaged people, (iii), may be directly hurt or disadvantaged by the existing problematic matter, and may or may not have questioned whether there might be a reason for it, and/or a better way. This group is frequently part of 'the researched', although sometimes they may not know it. If they do, they may typically find themselves on the receiving end of a questionnaire or an interview. One of their number may be invited to sit on an Advisory Committee.

Some other 'stakeholders': staff, carers, providers, (iv), may be indirectly involved. In conventional research, they may also be questionnaire or interviewed about the group-with-the-problem, or about their service to them or care of them, and perhaps even asked what they think should be changed; and they might also be on the Committee. All then await the researchers' announcement of their 'findings'.

What can typically plague the whole process of such conventional research are the consequences of non participation:

- In the first place there can be confusion or lack of agreement regarding the direction and purpose of the inquiry (for whom and for what).
- There is subsequent disagreement about the form the study should take (how, where, when, who should be involved).
- Alternatively the wrong direction is taken and dissent suppressed or ignored. The wrong questions are asked. The data is then irrelevant. And the conclusions useless.
- There can be misunderstandings about participants' perceptions (about the situation being studied).
- There can be conflict over interpretations and analyses (the 'why' and 'how').
- And there can be disagreement about what these imply for change in action (what next).
- And there can be shooting of the messenger! Or of the manager. Or mutinous troops. And critical reference groups' situations left unchanged.

There is an important point to be made here. Over many years I have observed that where the parties (i), (ii), (iii) and (iv) are more distant from each other and from involvement in the process of inquiry, trouble ensues.

Once in the past a place might have been seen for participation by the various parties at the outset on a committee, or at the end as recipients of a report. Increasingly instead they might become contributors to all stages of the research cycle - as designers, selectors of methods, contributors of 'data', 'analysers' and 'concluders', and then 'takers (or monitors) of new actions', and so on. All parties begin to operate much more as both co-researchers and co-subjects.

In participatory action research, the four conceptual categories of participants may thus in practice become much more overlapping depending on the purposes of the research, and who is 'driving' it. For example, there may be more participation, where a self help group (iii), self-researches (i) its own experiences (ii) and those of others (iv), for itself or for others (i or iv).

The arguments for there being more rather than less participation by all four parties are as follows:

- Those commissioning or carrying out the research These usually already participate the most since they choose the questions, decide how they will be answered, interpret the answers and decide what has been 'discovered'. Yet frequently even they feel constrained to disguise, restrict or eliminate their ideas and values, or refrain from putting in their experiences or their views or opinions, on the grounds the research should be 'objective' and 'unbiased', and 'value-free'. In this way, other participants may never be properly informed about the nature and purposes of the research, and the research design may begin way back 'behind the eight ball' instead of where there is a genuine unanswered question. This may truly bias or distort the research. Feminist 13 and other critical theory 14 research as well as so-called fourth generation evaluation 15 has begun to show a way for researchers (and those commissioning the research) to be more genuine and honest participants in and contributors to their own research.

These approaches have shown also how there can be more of a dissolution of the distinction between researcher/s and 'researched for' (the critical reference group).

- Thus, for example, a more participating researcher would be more clear about why they are interested in the research - perhaps describing their own personal experiences that have led to the questions they are wanting to ask. This clarifies the purposes for other participants, and helps each participant know where the other is 'coming from'. Further, the participating researcher/s, having identified the interests they wish to pursue, can see (and be seen in) their relationship to the critical reference group, and pursue more consciously and sceptically, alternative formulations of the situation.
- The critical reference group: This group conventionally participates least since professional and academic research largely researches on and about and speaks for the disadvantaged, or groups with unmet needs the research is meant to benefit. Laura Nader has called this approach 'studying down' (1972). The identification and involvement of the critical reference group, or even broad relevant critical reference 'arenas' or critical reference 'publics' however, I have noticed leads to:
  - Improved relevance of the inquiry to those who share in the problem;
  - Sharper focusing of the research questions;
  - Enhanced relevance of the inquiry to those whose jobs are to

do something about the problem (whether as a service provider, a carer, an administrator, a funder, etc.);

— Increased effectiveness of the research design (what is asked, by whom, of whom, when, where and how);
— Improved meaningfulness of the information thus gained (the researched especially have a say in whether any inquiry 'got it right' in regard to the meaning of what they said or did);
— The power and accuracy of the theory developed to understand the problem;
— The relevance, creativity and effectiveness of the new actions decided-on;
— And the commitment to observing the new actions and acting on and researching of them further.

The difficulties in involving critical reference groups and them remaining involved are numerous. The discussion of how to achieve these conditions of mutual involvement, participation and collaboration are very similar to the discussions about how to achieve 'community development'. For example, the more disempowered you are, the less hope you may have about either the value of participating or even the chances of something good coming out of it. If you are radically disempowered you may not even be able to envisage something better, when even a vague or indistinct vision is a prerequisite for pursuing one at all.

Nevertheless, members of critical reference groups who have problematised a situation are in the most strategic position to work on its improvement. Participatory action research, in its most-developed form, works to assist critical reference groups - and those who share their perspective - pursue their inquiries, by themselves and for themselves, as a community-of-interest. The role of 'outsiders' or those who are not members of critical reference groups changes radically. Rather than operating as the independent expert determiner of the truth-of-the-situation (with critical reference groups assisting the researcher in their pursuit of The Truth), the 'researcher' becomes a facilitator of or an assistant to the critical reference group's own pursuit of their truth (or truths).

- Stakeholders other than the researcher/s and the critical reference group (and whether interested or hostile)

  These typically participate only at the outset: perhaps to convene a Committee or allocate a research brief or contribute funds, or just at the end: to receive a research report or hear of its findings. The pitfalls and wastage that can be associated with this level of participation are numerous. A few possible results include:

  — Manipulation of the research process 'off stage' (by powerful parties who never participated in a democratic process around a table with all other parties), and possible ultimate resistance by other parties when their participation proves to be pointless;

- Rejection of a report by some or all because they simply never went through the same learning process as did the researcher/s and the critical reference group and never reached the same conclusions;
- Frustration with a process that does not reflect their realities;
- Inability to see what are the practical consequences of a set of findings or recommendations.

Service providers can specially benefit from full participation so that the link between their 'theory' (why they do what they do) is in closer connection with their 'practice' (what they actually do). Indeed, in much action research in Western countries, the primary participants are service-providers who work in small circles, examining their practice and trying out alternative ways of working. For the value of this to be maximised, participation needs to be organised around the interests of the critical reference group or driven by a critical reference group perspective, or else the research can risk becoming sidetracked.

- The researched: This may typically be the critical reference group, along with some service-providers or their representatives. However, again I have found that the more there is active participation the greater the chances of maximising both the accuracy and meaningfulness of all contributions, and also the sharing of perceptions and of emerging understandings about the value of what new actions should next be taken.

Research which involves the collaboration of people, rarely is sustained without a shared purpose, and this 'shared purpose' stems from what understandings people have together developed about what is of value. If understanding is not for 'its own sake', but directed towards understanding something 'in order to...', then the point of purposeful inquiry is action. As pointed out before, where the categories 'the researched' and 'the researchers' and 'the researched for' begin to become less distinct, this collaboration can become more cohesive.

What kind of action is for the parties to decide - focused by the perspective of the critical reference group. As pointed out earlier, that new action might be the reproduction of the same old action as was taken previously if it involves researchers who believe they neither are contributing (nor want to contribute) to change. This is research which may carefully reproduce the status quo. Other research, which is self-conscious about why it asked the questions it does, wishes instead to head towards a different and improved state of affairs.

Participatory action research is a term that brings together a set of assumptions underlying 'new paradigm' science and in contrast to those of traditional or 'old paradigm' science. These new assumptions underline the importance of social and collective processes in reaching conclusions about 'what is the case', and what the implications are for change which is deemed useful by those whose problematic situation led to the research in the first place.

In 'real life', actual researchers often straddle (more or less uncomfortably) the two paradigms, but the paradigms themselves are coherent bodies of thought that are not theoretically commensurable. But a paradigm addresses the unsolved problems of the previous paradigm. So while positivism arose to bring certainty and verifiability to a world construed as 'irrational', post positivism addresses the inability to handle enormous complexity in large, cybernetic, self-changing human systems. If conventional science wanted to give a group of people the power to determine 'truth' for and on behalf of others, the new science arose from a world of multiple and competing versions of truth and reality as a way of assisting people both come to the truth of their own reality, and also to embrace that of others.

The urgency of such mutual understanding is to be found in the topics selected by PAR practitioners - mostly concerned with difficult situations of social change, the loss of ways to meet human needs, the rise of anxieties and fears as we become strangers to each other, and the threat of dissolution into violence and alienation.

On such big fronts, participatory action research proceeds modestly, but it does proceed! For all these reasons participatory action research is not just research which we hope will be followed by action! It is action which is researched, changed and re-researched, within the research process by participants. Nor is it simply an exotic variant of consultation. Instead, it aims to be active co-research, by and for those to be helped. Nor can it be used by one group of people to get another group of people to do what is thought best for them - whether that is to implement a central policy or an organisational or service change. Instead it tries to be a genuinely democratic or non-coercive process whereby those to be helped, determine the purposes and outcomes of their own inquiry. Paradoxically it is quite close to a common-sense way of 'learning by doing'. But at the same time it is very hard to achieve the ideal conditions for putting it fully into practice.

Essentially participatory action research is research which involves all relevant parties in actively examining together current action (which they experience as problematic) in order to change and improve it. They do this by critically reflecting on the historical, political, cultural, economic, geographic and other contexts which make sense of it.

'Current problematic action' may range from the trivial to the life-threatening. Much participatory action research lies between these ends of the scale, and typically involves yourself; those who share your concerns, experiences and interests; others suffering from the problematic situation; others trying to assist it to change; and those who oversee the material resources needed to underpin the change effort (such as funds, people, salaries, services, office resources, etc.). Bringing these parties together, and absorbing new ones as the action research effort proceeds to unfold and implicate parties further afield, is not merely a side issue of 'entry to the field' but a central focus for achieving understanding and change. As well, action research is not research which sees these as 'contaminating' processes which 'bias' the scientific effort, nor does it have a problem with the 'researcher/s' identifying with 'the researched' and the 'researched for', - seeing this rather as essential to the gaining of engaged understanding.

What 'drives' participatory action research, like any research, is our 'need to know' in order to bring about desired change. We often shorthand term this our 'values' - which are our precious images of valued states or ways of being. Rather than seeing this holding-of-values as subjective and potentially a source of bias, the strength of the values we hold will determine the power and direction of our research efforts. Two key additional factors which will shape what we do is the strength of our imaginations (to theorise more creatively, deeply and imaginatively) and our scepticism (to keep our theory closely in relationship to the practices we are observing). Like any other research, the critical moment is that of 'discovery' or rather: 'invention' of a different and better way of seeing and understanding our realities. The old adage about science being 5% inspiration and 95% perspiration may hold true enough! The hard sweat and toil comprises the long hours of talking and thinking and sharing the results of our 'fieldwork' with one another. The moment of inspired thinking is when collective values are expressed in a new way of connecting ideas or a new way of 'naming' the world, that advances the collective situation of participants.

The field of action research deriving from education (particularly school room practice) and third world development more often have stressed the necessity of moving relatively quickly towards new action.

The post-war British field of action research, drawing on theory about group psychology or group dynamics, stressed the area of process, sometimes involving very diverse interests from the outset.

They include the classical social anthropology-trained sociologist William Foote Whyte who has moved to action research from what he now calls 'participatory research' (eg. his classic 1943 ethnographic study of an inner city immigrant American-Italian community). Another prominent American sociologist Shulamit Reinharz tells her story of moving from disembodied researching 'on' people to humanistic, qualitative and experiential researching 'with' people (1979). I, myself (Yoland Wadsworth), a Monash-trained sociologist have told of a similar trajectory (1985), moving from using standard large-scale random sample surveys analysed by the obligatory SPSS, to embracing interpretivist phhenomonology to working increasingly with and for critical reference groups using a critical constructivist methodology.

Old paradigm social science is often popularly termed 'positivist'. This refers to a school of philosophical thought which saw the world as having a single 'reality' which existed independently of the observer, and which could only be discovered by an objective and uninvolved scientist through acts of pure perception, ideally in a laboratory setting where all variables could be controlled and manipulated, and exact causation determined. This account has been difficult to sustain in practice - as with Newtonian science - given the limitations of such an uninvolved science. Far more engaged research - literally 'going native' - yields far better understanding. As well, when the social world is encountered, it takes as many forms as there are people. That is, understanding the social world depends on the exchange and communication of interpretations about what is going on. These are multiple and may be conflicting. As with post-Einsteinian physics, the 'observed' is importantly constructed by 'the observer' - and in the social world, is then further reconstructed by the observed (sometimes in the light of the observer's observations!).

For old paradigm science this is all so much unwanted 'bias' and 'contamination'. For new paradigm science it is the nature of the 'beast', and all so much more material for illuminating inquiry. New paradigm science also grasps the value-driven nature of inquiry and is in a position to focus its research in the interests of those who might problematise their existing undesirable situations. This offers a better chance of 'driving' theory towards better contributing to practice, and also avoiding the unethical and totalitarian consequences of a science which sees itself as 'value free'.

More formal language which is used to describe 'participatory action research' as a particular philosophy of knowledge (theory of how we know, or the grounds for knowledge, i.e. epistemology) also includes 'critical constructivist', 'post positivist' or 'critical interpretive' methodology.

Ironically, conventional experimental science can have its own problems and 'fail' when an ungrounded (irrelevant and wide of the mark) hypothesis is elaborately and expensively tested, only to discover that it was a poor proposition in the first place. Alternatively, in social science, such poor propositions can survive in the literature and even make their researchers famous (and lead to high status positions!) in the absence of participatory processes or testing in practice which would supply the necessary feedback about their faulty or narrow character. The spectacular failure of European sociologists to predict the bringing down of the Berlin Wall testifies in the same way as the failure of meteorologists to predict the weather accurately. Mostly both sociologists and meteorologists (as well as ordinary people who are observant and shrewd, and who can tap their barometers and feel the aches in their bones) pretty much get it right. Newtonian science mainly works. The break downs occur when matters are enormously complex and defy 'control of variables'. Unfortunately these may be precisely the critical times in messy complex changing human societies.

As well, some academic researchers claim with pride that there are no known beneficiaries of research (and not even an arena of potential beneficiaries). This is what they might call 'pure' research, or 'curiosity-driven' research 'for its own sake'. It is very important that there be time and space for curiosity and speculative forays out into unknown waters and apparently 'irrelevant' matters. However even 'idle' curiosity is always historically and socially located (eg. Fleming's noticing of the penicillin mould) and thus shaped by the social world in which the 'idle curious' have grown up, learned language, learned values, and learned to notice some things and not others. 80% of all scientists, 'pure' and 'applied' alike, just happen to be curious in ways helpful to defence establishments all around the world. On the other hand even the most apparently esoteric inquirer frequently has quite well-formed views about the relevance of their line of inquiry (for example the relationship between Jacobin clothing styles and early capitalist modes of economy, and its relevance to late twentieth century post modernity). Where researchers themselves have no insight, someone else might well be able to carry out a little 'archaeology' and suggest something. For most research in the human services area, the critical reference group is very much more readily identified as service users.

Feminist research utilises (more or less sucessfully) a participatory action research methodology and additionally works in a topic area determined by a particular critical reference group: that of women. The kind of feminist theory used will reflect and in turn determine what kind of use is made of the research, and by whom.

Critical theory is a school of social science which developed firstly in Frankfurt and then in the United States of America after its members went into exile before and during the second world war. It has attempted to bring together the insights of Freudian (and now post Freudian) psychology and Marxian economics, in order to understand how the personal and the structural come together into ideological forms from which some benefit at the expense of others. Its better-known theorists include Adorno, Horkheimer, Habermas and Marcuse. It is now used as a term to describe a range of approaches which raise critical questions about the conditions which sustain existing forms of social life that are experienced as problematic by particular groups of people.

Fourth generation evaluation is a term coined by the Americans Egon Guba and Yvonna Lincoln to describe the application of constructivist methodology to evaluation (in the wake of three previous generations of evaluation which they have criticised on the grounds of over-adherence to a positivist epistemology and to managerialist dominance). They argued for the admission of all relevant parties to the process, and re-cast the evaluator as a facilitator of an essentially self-evaluation process.

For example school-based action research where parents and students may be involved, however the primary questions identified are those of the teachers. See also hospital projects which similarly stem from nurses' concerns in the absence of patients. Or welfare research about youth suicide or single mothers without any representation of these groups in the research team or committee. Where the questions are not necessarily those of the critical reference group, the research relies on disembodied critical theory to illuminate the assumptions behind things and thus reveal new choices of more relevant topics.

For example, say psychiatric nurses want to research how to protect themselves from patient violence. They could recommend regular time off for themselves to recover from their stress. The asking of critical question, such as 'what would be also good for patients?' might lead to this particular solution being problematised however, and set in train a further search for a different solution which does not meet the needs of one group at the expense of another. If patients participate in the research, they might give their perceptions of why the violence arises, leading to a different solution which also might not compound patients' existing problems of loss of staff continuity.

CONSENSUS DECISION-MAKING

Consensus decision-making is a decision-making process that not only seeks the agreement of most participants, but also to resolve or mitigate the objections of the minority to achieve the most agreeable decision. Consensus is usually defined as meaning both: a) general agreement, and b) the process of getting to such agreement. Consensus decision-making is thus concerned primarily with that process.

Decision making is the cognitive process leading to the selection of a course of action among alternatives. Every decision making process produces a final choice. It can be an action or an opinion. It begins when we need to do something but we do not know what. Therefore, decision making is a reasoning process which can be rational or irrational, and can be based on explicit assumptions or tacit assumptions.

Common examples include shopping, deciding what to eat, when to sleep, and deciding whom or what to vote for in an election or referendum.

Decision making is said to be a psychological construct. This means that although we can never "see" a decision, we can infer from observable behaviour that a decision has been made. Therefore, we conclude that a psychological event that we call "decision making" has occurred. It is a construction that imputes commitment to action. That is, based on observable actions, we assume that people have made a commitment to affect the action.

Structured rational decision making is an important part of all science-based professions, where specialists apply their knowledge in a given area to making informed decisions. For example, medical decision making often involves making a diagnosis and selecting an appropriate treatment. Some research using naturalistic methods shows, however, that in situations with higher time pressure, higher stakes, or increased ambiguities, experts use intuitive decision making rather than structured approaches, following a recognition primed decision approach to fit a set of indicators into the expert's experience and immediately arrive at a satisfactory course of action without weighing alternatives.

Due to the large number of considerations involved in many decisions, computer-based decision support systems have been developed to assist decision makers in considering the implications of various courses of thinking. They can help reduce the risk of human errors. The systems which try to realize some human/cognitive decision making functions are called Intelligent Decision Support Systems (IDSS).

According to behaviouralist Isabel Briggs Myers, a person's decision making process depends to a significant degree on their cognitive style. Starting from the work of Carl Jung, Myers developed a set of four bi-polar dimensions, called the Myers-Briggs Type Indicator (MBTI). The terminal points on these dimensions are: thinking and feeling; extroversion and introversion; judgement and perception; and sensing and intuition. She claimed that a person's decision making style is based largely on how they score on these four dimensions. For example, someone that scored near the thinking, extroversion, sensing, and judgement ends of the dimensions would tend to have a logical, analytical, objective, critical, and empirical decision making style.

COGNITIVE AND PERSONAL BIASES IN DECISION MAKING

It is generally agreed that biases can creep into our decision making processes, calling into question the correctness of a decision. It is not generally agreed, however, which normative models are to be used to evaluate what constitutes an erroneous decision. Nor is the scientific evidence for all of the biases agreed upon. So, while it is agreed that decision making can be biased, how to tell when it is, and specific cases of biases, are often challenged. The issue in general can be quite controverial among scholars in the field. Below is a list of some of the more commonly debated cognitive biases.

- Selective search for evidence - We tend to be willing to gather facts that support certain conclusions but disregard other facts that support different conclusions.
- Premature termination of search for evidence - We tend to accept the first alternative that looks like it might work.
- Inertia - Unwillingness to change thought patterns that we have used in the past in the face of new circumstances.
- Contrariness or rebelliousness - Unwillingness to share a view with a perceived oppressive authority.
- Experiential limitations - Unwillingness or inability to look beyond the scope of our past experiences; rejection of the unfamiliar.
- Selective perception - We actively screen-out information that we do not think is salient.

- Wishful thinking or optimism - We tend to want to see things in a positive light and this can distort our perception and thinking.
- Choice-supportive bias occurs when we distort our memories of chosen and rejected options to make the chosen options seem relatively more attractive.
- Recency - We tend to place more attention on more recent information and either ignore or forget more distant information.
- Repetition bias - A willingness to believe what we have been told most often and by the greatest number of different of sources.
- Anchoring and adjustment - Decisions are unduly influenced by initial information that shapes our view of subsequent information.
- Group think - Peer pressure to conform to the opinions held by the group.
- Source credibility bias - We reject something if we have a bias against the person, organization, or group to which the person belongs: We are inclined to accept a statement by someone we like.
- Incremental decision making and escalating commitment - We look at a decision as a small step in a process and this tends to perpetuate a series of similar decisions. This can be contrasted with zero-based decision making.
- Inconsistency - The unwillingness to apply the same decision criteria in similar situations.
- Attribution asymmetry - We tend to attribute our success to our abilities and talents, but we attribute our failures to bad luck and external factors. We attribute other's success to good luck, and their failures to their mistakes.
- Role fulfillment - We conform to the decision making expectations that others have of someone in our position.
- Underestimating uncertainty and the illusion of control - We tend to underestimate future uncertainty because we tend to believe we have more control over events than we really do. We believe we have control to minimize potential problems in our decisions.
- Faulty generalizations - In order to simplify an extremely complex world, we tend to group things and people. These simplifying generalizations can bias decision making processes.
- Ascription of causality - We tend to ascribe causation even when the evidence only suggests correlation. Just because birds fly to the equatorial regions when the trees lose their leaves, does not mean that the birds migrate because the trees lose their leaves.

COGNITIVE NEUROSCIENCE OF DECISION MAKING

The anterior cingulate cortex (ACC) and orbitofrontal cortex are brain regions involved in decision making processes. A recent neuroimaging study, Interactions between decision making and performance monitoring within prefrontal cortex, found distinctive patterns of neural activation in these regions depending on whether decisions were made on the basis of personal volition or following directions from someone else.

Another recent study by Kennerly, et al. (2006) found that lesions to the ACC in the macaque resulted in impaired decision making in the long run of reinforcement guided tasks suggesting that the ACC is responsible for evaluating past reinforcement information and guiding future action. Decision making in groups is sometimes examined separately as process and outcome. Process refers to the interactions group. Some relevant ideas include coalitions among participants as well as influence and persuasion. The use of politics is often judged negatively, but it is a useful way to approach problems when preferences among actors are in conflict, when dependencies exist that cannot be avoided, when there are no super-ordinate authorities, and when the technical or scientific merit of the options is ambiguous.

In addition to the different processes involved in making decisions, group decision support systems (GDSS) may have different decision rules. A decision rule is the GDSS protocol a group uses to choose among scenario planning alternatives.

- Unanimity is commonly used by juries in criminal trials in the United States. Unanimity requires everyone to agree on a given course of action, and thus imposes a high bar for action.
- Majority requires support from more than 50% of the members of the group. Thus, the bar for action is lower than with unanimity and a group of "losers" is implicit to this rule.
- Consensus decision-making tries to avoid "winners" and "losers". Consensus requires that a majority approve a given course of action, but that the minority agree to go along with the course of action. In other words, if the minority opposes the course of action, consensus requires that the course of action be modified to remove objectionable features.
- Gathering involves all participants acknowledging each other's needs and opinions and tends towards a problem solving approach in which as many needs and opinions as possible can be satisfied. It allows for multiple outcomes and does not require agreement from some for others to act.
- Sub-committee involves assigning responsibility for evaluation of a decision to a sub-set of a larger group, which then comes back to the larger group with recommendations for action. Using a sub-committee is more common in larger governance groups, such as a legislature. Sometimes a sub-committee includes those individuals most affected by a decision, although at other times it is useful for the larger group to have a sub-committee that involves more neutral participants.

Less desirable group decision rules are:

- Plurality, where the largest block in a group decides, even if it falls short of a majority.
- Dictatorship, where one individual determines the course of action.

Plurality and dictatorship are less desirable as decision rules because they do not require the involvement of the broader group to determine a choice. Thus, they do not engender commitment to the course of action chosen. An absence of commitment from individuals in the group can be problematic during the implementation phase of a decision.

There are no perfect decision making rules. Depending on how the rules are implemented in practice and the situation, all of these can lead to situations where either no decision is made, or to situations where decisions made are inconsistent with one another over time.

The ethical principles of decision making vary considerably. Some common choices of principles and the methods which seem to match them include:

- The most powerful person/group decides
  — Method: dictatorship or oligarchy
- Everyone participates in a certain class of meta-decisions
  — Method: parliamentary democracy
- Everyone participates in every decision
  — Direct democracy, consensus decision making

There are many decision making levels having a participation element. A common example is that of institutions making decisions that affect those for whom they provide. In such cases an understanding of what participation level is involved becomes crucial to understand the process and power structures dynamics.

Some of the decision making techniques that we use in everyday life include:

- Listing the advantages and disadvantages of each option, popularized by Benjamin Franklin
- Flipping a coin, cutting a deck of playing cards, and other random or coincidence methods
- Accepting the first option that seems like it might achieve the desired result
- Tarot cards, astrology, augurs, revelation, or other forms of divination
- Acquiesce to a person in authority or an "expert"
- Calculating the expected value for each option. For example, a person is considering two jobs. At the first job option the person has a 60% chance of getting a 30% percent raise in the first year. And at the second job option the person has a 80% chance of getting a 10% raise in the first year. The decision maker would calculate the expected value of each option, calculating the probability multiplied

by the increase of value. (0.60*0.30=0.18 [option a] 0.80*0.10=0.08 [option b]) The person deciding on the job would chose the option with the highest expected value, in this example option a.

An alternative may be to apply one of the processes described below, in particular in the Business and Management section.

In the health care field, the steps of making a decision may be remembered with the mnemonic BRAND, which includes

- Benefits of the action
- Risks in the action
- Alternatives to the prospective action
- Nothing: that is, doing nothing at all
- Decision

DECISION MAKING MODELS

- Economic men and women is a mathematical model used for human behaviour. This model is used to describe three things:
- Decision makers are informed on all possible options for their decisions and know of all possible outcomes
- Decision makers are infinitely sensitive to the small distinctions among their different options. They are capable of knowing all the differences between their options, regardless of how small they are.
- Decision makers are rational in their choices. They are capable of making a choice to maximize or increase value.
- Subjective expected theory. This is the goal of human action to seek happiness and avoid pain.
- Subjective utility – the prospects based on individual's value than on objective criteria.
- Subjective probability – prospects based on individual's estimates of likelihood rather than mathematical equations.

Using the example in Decisions for One's Personal life, a person would use the subjective expected theory to take into account comfort of the job, how the long hours can affect personal time with family and friends, as well as possible job relocation. This theory also people to take into account the many subjective variables.

PATH DEPENDENCY

It is perhaps pertinent to note that the cost of making no decision at all itself is a factor, and that the benefit of making some decision, even a random choice, can be beneficial in the longer term.

Thus the reversibility of an action may be a good way to judge whether or not an action or process is beneficial. A resource can also be viewed as something expendable, or bearing a cost, rather than the implication of selecting something irrevocably.

DECISION MAKING IN BUSINESS AND MANAGEMENT

In general, business and management systems should be set up to allow decision making at the lowest possible level.

Several decision making models for business include:

- SWOT Analysis - Evaluation by the decision making individual or organization of Strengths, Weaknesses, Opportunities and Threats with respect to desired end state or objective.
- Analytic Hierarchy Process - procedure for multi-level goal hierarchy
- Buyer decision processes - transaction before, during, and after a purchase
- Complex systems - common behavioural and structural features that can be modelled
- Corporate finance:
  - The investment decision
  - The financing decision
  - The dividend decision
  - working capital management decisions
- Cost-benefit analysis - process of weighing the total expected costs vs. the total expected benefits
- Decision trees
  - Programme Evaluation and Review Technique (PERT)
  - critical path analysis
  - critical chain analysis
- Force field analysis - analizing forces that either drive or hinder movement toward a goal
- Grid Analysis - analysis done by compairing the weighted averages of ranked criteria to options. A way of comparing both objective and subjective data.
- Kepner tregoe - A Management Consultancy firm specialising in rational Problem Solving and Decision Making processes
- Linear programming - optimization problems in which the objective function and the constraints are all linear
- Min-max criterion
- Model (economics)- theoretical construct of economic processes of variables and their relationships
- Monte Carlo method - class of computational algorithms for simulating systems
- Morphological analysis - all possible solutions to a multi-dimensional problem complex
- optimization
  - Constrained optimization

- Paired Comparison Analysis - paired choice analysis
- Pareto Analysis - selection of a limited of number of tasks that produce significant overall effect
- Scenario analysis - process of analyzing possible future events
- Six Thinking Hats - symbolic process for parallel thinking
- Strategic planning process - applying the objectives, SWOTs, strategies, programmes process
- Ubiquitous command and control is a concept for dynamic decision making based on "agreement between an individual and the world", and "agreements between individuals"

Decision-makers and Influencers

In the context of industrial goods marketing, there is much theory, and even more opinion, expressed about how the various 'decision-makers' and 'influencers' (those who can only influence, not decide, the final decision) interact. Decisions are frequently taken by groups, rather than individuals, and the official buyer often does not have authority to take the decision.

Miller & Heiman, for example, offered a more complex view of industrial buying decisions (particularly in the area of 'complex sales' of capital equipment). They see three levels of decision making:

'Economic buying influence' - the decision-maker who can authorize the necessary funds for purchase

'User buying influences' - the people in the buying company who will use the product and will specify what they want to purchase

'Technical buying influence' - the `experts' (including, typically, the buying department) who can veto the purchase on technical grounds

Webster and Wind, in a similar vein, identify six roles within the 'buying centre':

'Users' - who will actually use the product or service

'Influencers' - particularly technical personnel

'Deciders' - the actual decision-makers

'Approvers' - who formally authorize the decision

'Buyers' - the department with formal authority

'Gatekeepers' - those who have the power to stop the sellers reaching other members of the `buying centre'

Some have said that true consensus involves "meeting everyone's needs." Consensus decision-making is intended to deemphasize the role of factions or parties and promote the expression of individual voices. The method also increases the likelihood of unforeseen or creative solutions by juxtaposing dissimilar ideas. Because it seeks to minimize objection, it is popular with voluntary organizations, wherein decisions are more likely to be carried out when they are most widely approved. Consensus methods are desirable when enforcement of the decision is unfeasible, such that every participant will be required to act on the decision independently.

Consensus decision-making is also found in groups where participants have different areas of expertise but are working toward a common goal. Examples of this include high technology project design teams which must integrate the opinions of people with different areas of expertise.

Minority views must be considered to a greater degree than in circumstances where a majority can take the action and enforce the decision without any further consultation with the minority voters. It is often thought that consensus can require more time and effort to achieve. Thus some groups may reserve consensus decision methods for particularly complex, risky or important decisions. However, there are many examples of groups who employ consensus decision-making in ways that enable them to both consider minority views and make decisions in a timely and efficient manner. Consensus decision making could result in group polarization, where team members make more extreme decisions compared to their prior individual positions. This could potentially have beneficial effects on team decisions (enhance commitment and conviction), or detrimental effects (escalate towards greater risk or greater conservative behaviours). Use of computer-mediated communication could further heighten the effects of group polarization.

Rather than simply list known alternatives, debate for a short time, vote, and then accept or reject by some percentage of majority (ex. over 50%, over 2/3), a consensus decision-making process involves identifying and addressing concerns, generating new alternatives, combining elements of multiple alternatives and checking that people understand a proposal or an argument.

This empowers minorities, those with objections that are hard to state quickly, and those who are less skilled in debate. Therefore, consensus decision-making can be seen as a form of grassroots democracy.

Egalitarian groups that seek to reduce the amount of power delegated to leaders, chairpersons or agenda setters often use consensus methods. Such methods can reduce the amount of harm or loss imposed on minorities (or individuals) by a majority. Consensus methods may be appropriate when personal (or emotional) risk to members is high, trust is low, and time is available for a prolonged discussion. Consensus may be used to remedy patterns of decision-making based on habit, subservience or carelessness.

Alternatively, it can be argued that in a situation of abundant trust - in which each party assumes that any objections or reservations regarding a proposal are meaningful - consensus methods may not only be appropriate, but necessary.

Like any group decision-making, consensus decision-making can disempower those not present in the debating forum, as they cannot expect to have input on the new measures that are proposed (whereas they might have had the opportunity for input into the known alternatives prior to the debate). Accordingly, most systems of consensus decision-making place a premium on participation.

Three key issues tend to define a particular type of consensus decision-making:

1. Degree of agreement or unanimity required;
2. Timing of presentation including division of time among urgent versus important matters;
3. Follow-up to action including the monitoring that arises from dissent, and from claims of majority proponents whose preferred course of action is being taken over minority objections.

There is also the question of facilitation or process leadership, which is handled

A healthy consensus decision-making process usually encourages and outs dissent early, maximizing the chance of accommodating the views of all minorities. It also often assigns a role to the dissenter, e.g. the Vatican used to assign the role of Promotor Fidei to a specific priest who argued against beatification of a saint, to ensure the case 'against' remains well represented. After the decision, the dissenting minority may have some role to play in monitoring the decision. In the Supreme Court of the United States, both the majority opinion and minority opinion are equally well documented, as the legal grounds for agreeing with either may exist in some court in the future.

Many groups consider unanimous decisions a sign of agreement, solidarity, and unity. However, there is evidence that unanimous decisions may be a sign of coercion, fear, undue persuasive power or eloquence, inability to comprehend alternatives, or plain impatience with the process of debate. (For example, elections in which 99% or 100% of the voters support the candidate are generally discredited.) When there are concerns about these aspects of unanimity, various alternatives can be pursued. These include the following:

- Unanimity minus one (or U-1), requires all delegates but one to support the decision. The individual dissenter cannot block the decision although they may be able to prolong debate (e.g. via a filibuster). The dissenter may be the ongoing monitor of the implications of the decision, and their opinion of the outcome of the decision may be solicited at some future time. Betting markets in particular rely on the input of such lone dissenters. A lone bettor against the odds profits when his or her prediction of the outcomes proves to be better than that of the majority. This disciplines the market's odds.
- Unanimity minus two (or U-2), does not permit two individual delegates to block a decision, but tends to curtail debate with a lone dissenter more quickly. Dissenting pairs can present alternate views of what is wrong with the decision under consideration. By focusing on a pair of dissenters, and allocating less time to lone wolves or 'consensus thugs', a U-2 system tends to form stronger bonds among

those who find themselves "alone on an island" with each other. Pairs of delegates can be empowered to find the common ground that will enable them to convince a third, decision-blocking, voter to join them. If the pair are unable to convince a third party to join them within a set time, their arguments are deemed to be unconvincing, immature or self-interested. If two people dissent against some common measure, it is more likely that the discussion between them can be extended to third parties easily, since it is already verbalized and illustrated. Western European court systems recognize this by strongly encouraging criminal defendants or civil plaintiffs to get an attorney's aid, so that their case can be fully heard out long before the decision.

- Unanimity minus three, (or U-3), and other such systems recognize the ability of three or more delegates to actively block a decision. However, there is controversy over whether a small group of dissenters, (e.g., militants or terrorists), is morally different from a large minority, (e.g., an opposition party with support of double-digit percentages of the population). Accordingly U-3 and lesser degrees of unanimity are usually lumped in with statistical measures of agreement, such as: 80%, mean plus one sigma, two-thirds, or greater than half (majority) levels of agreement. Such measures do not fit within the definition of consensus given at the beginning of this article.
- The IETF working group process has a tradition of "rough consensus", where there is no specific rule for "how much is enough", but it is left to the judgment of the working group chair. This makes it harder for a small number of disruptors to block a decision, but puts a lot of responsibility on the chair, and has frequently led to angry debates about whether rough consensus has in fact been correctly identified.

The quality of alternatives considered is, all else being equal, proportional to the amount of time spent gathering and comparing and combining them. The term deliberative democracy reflects the deliberation that underlies all good consensus decision-making. Ralph Nader and others have advocated deliberative measures to extend the time for "sober second thought."

A fictional example of deliberative democracy is the Entmoot from J. R. R. Tolkien's novel The Lord of the Rings. The Ents, who are large ancient living intelligent trees, spend days discussing the issue of whether to go to war, in their verbose and many-syllabled language. This is an example of a decision for which the stakes were high, the individual risk also high, and coercive force difficult or lacking; therefore suited to consensus methods.

Timeliness of decisions is an important issue. In some cases, a wrong decision taken in time can be better than a good decision taken later. Key responsibilities of facilitators of any decision making process, but particularly in consensus decision-making, include:

- Establishing measures to place items on the agenda, or deny them time on the agenda.
- Setting deadlines for changes to the agenda (e.g. can the agenda itself be changed during the meeting?).
- Agenda forming and presentation of issues at the right time, when there is sufficient time for their debate.
- Ensuring that less urgent issues are excluded from the debate, but dealt with at another time.

To achieve a balance between urgency and importance, it is common to reserve enough time for matters that are not urgent, but are nevertheless important, (for e.g., the decision process itself, which takes care to maintain). Consensus decision processes tend to accelerate as rising trust over the course of the meeting, combined with fatigue, increase individual tolerance and the cost of dissent. Placing difficult agenda items first tends to speed a meeting, with the risk that important, but less complex decisions will not be achieved before adjournment.

Decisions about when to split up into working groups, how to handle agendas, how to deal with changes to agendas or working groups from the floor, etc., are affected by the allocation of the group's time to urgent versus important matters.

These procedural matters are held to be crucial to the survival of a consensus decision process, along with issues of safety, fairness, and closure which arise from their application in practice.

Action, Monitoring and Follow-up

Action is the point of decision; without action, the decision is just talk. Military leaders from Alexander the Great to the present have emphasized that orders simply do not get carried out unless they are personally followed up by the commander. The same applies to group decisions, perhaps even more so.

One would not expect the opposing minority to do a good job of ensuring that a measure is carried out, but they can ensure that problems resulting from it are well-documented, and that inconveniences of its implementation are contained. However, they can also take steps to ensure that the inconvenience of implementation is maximized, so as to make the point that the measure was impractical and ill-advised from the beginning. A major issue in consensus decisions is whose view of the actual outcome to trust, and who to permit time to present their view.

Consensus decisions are especially vulnerable to sabotage of all kinds, so the assignment of action roles, monitoring (from the original majority and minority opinion to some future time when the results of both sets of predictions can be debated), and other follow up (e.g. assessing support of the public for a party after it has taken and publicized a particular measure), is a key responsibility of consensus decision leaders.

QUAKER-BASED CONSENSUS

The model used by the Quakers is effective because it puts in place a simple, time-tested structure that moves a group towards consensus. The Quaker model has been well-received when employed in secular settings because it gives everyone a chance to speak while limiting potential disruptors (e.g., people who want unlimited airtime, or who have a particular axe to grind).

The following aspects of the Quaker model can be effectively applied in any consensus decision-making process:

- Multiple concerns and information are shared until the sense of the group is clear.
- Discussion involves active listening and sharing of information.
- Norms limit number of times one asks to speak to ensure that each speaker is fully heard.
- Norms limit repetition and long speeches.
- Norms include a short silence after every comment so deliberations are truly thoughtful.
- Ideas and solutions belong to the group; no names are recorded.
- Differences are resolved by discussion. The facilitator ("clerk" or "convenor" in the Quaker model) identifies areas of agreement and names disagreements to push discussion deeper.
- The facilitator articulates the sense of the discussion, asks if there are other concerns, and proposes a minute of the decision.
- The group as a whole is responsible for the decision, and the decision belongs to the group.
- The facilitator can discern if one who is not uniting with the decision is acting without concern for the group or in selfish interest.
- Dissenters' perspectives are embraced.

Key components of Quaker-based consensus are: 1) that the guidance of Spirit is available to each participant who honestly seeks the truth, 2) belief in a common humanity, and, 3) the ability to decide together. The goal is "unity, not unanimity."

Ensuring that group members speak only once until others are heard encourages a diversity of thought. The facilitator is understood as serving the group rather than acting as person-in-charge. By articulating the emerging consensus, members can be clear on the decision, and, as their views have been taken into account, will be likely to support it.

Many intentional communities use consensus decision-making. In many cases, with cohousing groups, business must be transacted within time constraints. Thus efficiency is important. If the group genuinely wants to make decisions by consensus, a method is needed that is both efficient and effective.

An open discussion needs to be animated by a process that moves towards a timely, and sound, decision that is supported by all. Various techniques have been developed whereby this can be achieved.

In some groups, the cards are used in two ways; one for discussion and another for decisions:

A group member who wishes to speak, holds up a card:

- A green card means "I have something to say" or "I have a question." When several group members hold up a green card, they are noted and placed in a "stack" of people waiting to speak. Each person speaks in turn, in a way that is similar to Quaker-based consensus.
- A yellow card means "I can clarify" or "I need clarification (on what was just said)."
- The red card is the process card. A red card, when raised, asks members to look at the process. For example, an individual who displays a red card might say: "Are we getting off track, here?" or "What is our objective in doing this?" or even "How about we take a break?" It gives all members an equal chance to be facilitator.

Following discussion, the facilitator articulates the proposal and calls for a show of cards:

- The green card means: "I agree."
- The yellow card means: "I can live with it." This is often referred to as "standing aside"
- The red card means: "I don't agree, but am willing to work to find a better way, taking into account what has been said by all group members." Thus holding up a red card does not block progress, it signifies that the person who displayed it will work with others on the matter in question and bring it back to a subsequent meeting. This tends to ensure that red cards are not used lightly.

In the Uniting Church of Australia, orange and blue cards are used to mean "I am warm toward this" or "I am cool toward this." The use of orange and blue allows people who are colourblind, and cannot distinguish red and green, to participate in the discussion.

If groups agree to apply methods such as these, and all group members are willing to work at it, consensus decision-making can be both effective in meeting a group's goals, and time-efficient.

A similar method has come to be used in other forums, such as W3C and other computer standards bodies. There, is it known as the Quaker poll.

In lieu of coloured cards, some consensus-based groups use a system of simple hand signals. While the nature, meaning and popularity of such signals changes from group to group, there is a common 'vocabulary':

- Twinkle: Wiggling of the fingers of one or both hands, with palms facing downward. Used by non-speakers to indicate agreement with the speaker. Also often used as a replacement of a raised hand to indicate a 'yea' vote to a proposal.

- Triangle: Forming of a triangle with the thumbs and index fingers of both hands. Used to indicate a point of order or procedure to the facilitator.
- Crossed arms: Forearms crossed with hands in fists. Used to indicate a strong disagreement with the speaker or to cast a 'block' vote to a proposal.

In the Internet Engineering Task Force (IETF), decisions are assumed to be taken by "rough consensus." The IETF has studiously refrained from defining a mechanical method for verifying such consensus, apparently in the belief that any such codification will lead to attempts to "game the system." Instead, a working group (WG) chair or BoF chair is supposed to "recognize it when I see it."

One tradition in support of rough consensus is the tradition of humming rather than (countable) hand-raising; this allows a WG to quickly tell the difference between "one or two objectors" or a "sharply divided community", without making it easy to slip into "majority rule". However, hand-raising is also used, especially in larger meetings, but actual counting is frowned upon.

Much of the business of the IETF is carried out on mailing lists, where all parties can speak their view at all times; the social dynamics of mailing lists is worthy of a study in itself.

8

Effective Marketing, Planning, Communication and Promotion for Adventure Tourism

DEFINITION OF MARKETING

The concept of marketing can be viewed from social and managerial perspectives. At its simplest, marketing can be defined as exchange transactions that take place between the buyer and the seller. Marketing is the management function, which organizes and directs all those business activities involved in assessing and converting customer purchasing power into effective demand. Philip Kotler defines marketing as "a social process by which individuals and groups obtain what they need and want through creating, offering and freely exchanging products and services of value with others".

ASPECTS OF MARKETING CONCEPT

The important aspects of marketing concept are:

- *Creation of demand*: Marketing tries to create demand through various means. The producers first ascertain what the customers want and then produce goods just as to the needs of the customers. There is a systematic effort to sell goods and services just as to the needs of the customers.
- *Customer Orientation*: Marketing involves undertaking a range of business activities directed at the creation of customer satisfying products and services.
- *Integrated Marketing*: The customer orientation alone is not enough on the part of management. To be effective must be backed by an appropriate set up within the country. The responsibility of marketing department is to ensure coordination of the various departments of the company *i.e.*, finance, purchase, research and development.

- *Profitable sales volume through customer satisfaction*: Marketing tries to realise long-term goals of profitability, growth and stability through satisfying customers' wants. All the basic activities of a company are planned to meet the wants of customers and still making reasonable profits. Modern marketing thus begins with the customer and ends with the customer.

MARKETING MIX

Marketing concepts had been originally developed in the context of tangible consumer goods. Marketing mix refers to the ingredients or the tools, which the marketer mixes in order to interact with a particular market. Kotler defines marketing mix as "set of marketing tools that the firm uses to pursue its marketing objectives in the target market". Each of the elements in the marketing mix is important and has an influence on the customer.

4 P'S OF MARKETING MIX

McCarthy has classified the main elements of a marketing programme in terms of 4 Ps-Product, Price, Promotion and Place.

- Product includes design, features, quality, range, size, models, appearance, packaging, and warranties. It also includes pre-sales and post-sale services like training for use, repairs, maintenance or replacements.
- Price includes concessions on basic price, discounts, rebates, credits, installation facilities and delivery terms.
- Promotion includes advertising, publicity media choices, messages, and frequency of exposure, campaigns, sales promotion, point-of-purchase, displays and merchandising.
- Place or channels of distribution includes retail outlets, wholesalers, transportation, warehousing, inventory levels, order processing procedures, etc.

Consumers generally form their perceptions of products and services based on prices. Pricing products and services is a complex process. It is based on the uniqueness of product attributes and the perceived value, which the consumer is willing to pay. Pricing strategies are planned just as to consumers' cultural norms and the political, legal and social environment of the place where the tourist product is located.

Example of Price: Indian Airlines has offered Super Saver tickets in January 2006, a multicoupon ticket is being offered with each coupon valid for travel between any two domestic destinations connected by a direct flight. The offer gives two options, one is about four-ticket option priced at ₹20000 in Economy class and the other is ₹28000 in Executive class. This is an example of good Bargain. There is also the option of buying additional ticket at incredibly low prices. Such convenience of booking provides the comforts of flying with wide choice of travel. Distribution systems or channels serve as the intermediary between consumers and suppliers and are an essential part of the travel and hospitality marketing strategy.

Many companies such as hotels or airlines use their central reservation systems to facilitate sales directly to customers. Example of Channels of Distribution: It is estimated that in the year 2004, out of a total 730 million Internet users, only 35.8 per cent use English language websites. Therefore, local language should be part of the distribution strategy and many hospitality companies also provide localized websites with several languages.

Let us understand how a marketer uses the tools of marketing mix by taking the example of a product like 'Tanishq' watches by Titan Industries. The watch is packed in plastic box, has a design, features, quality and company ensures warranty.

It has list price but at times the dealer permits discount or rebate. The company distributes the watch through exclusive retail outlets. The company promotes it by using advertising and sales force. All the activities of Titan are the ingredients that have gone into the making of 'Tanishq' for the purpose of creating exchanges with the potential customers.

TARGET MARKET

The term 'market' refers to the collective of existing and prospective customers for the product. People who need to stay outside their usual residence use a hotel. A person may not have such a need but if such a need arises later, he is a prospective customer.

The marketing effort is aimed at such prospective customers who would choose to buy the marketer's hotel services. However, all persons who need to stay outside are not prospective customers for the 5-star hotels. They may stay at budget hotels.

Hence, the market for the five star hotels is only part of the total market of total hotel users. Such parts are called segments of the market. The customers of the hotel are those who come to stay as well as users of other facilities.

They are different groups and each group constitutes different segments since the needs and expectations of each one of these groups are different. For example, segmentation is possible on the basis of usage of swimming pool. The segments using the pools for training are different from regular guests in terms of age, behaviour, attention required, hours spent in the pool or cleanliness demanded and so on.

MARKET SEGMENTATION

Market segmentation is the process of identifying groups of buyers of the total market with different desires. Most markets are too large for an organization to provide all the products and services needed by all buyers in that market. This leads organizations selecting target markets necessitating market segmentation.

Market segmentation has certain obvious advantages in that the organization is:

- Better placed to spot and compare marketing opportunities,
- Cater to the specific needs of the buyers,
- Develop marketing programmes for specific market segments.

In tourism, market segmentation is very important. The strategy of market segmentation in tourism is to divide the present and the potential market on the basis of some characteristic and then concentrate marketing efforts like pricing, supply and promotion efforts to the target markets.

BASES FOR MARKET SEGMENTATION

Segmentation is usually done on the basis of one or more of the following characteristics:

- *Buying behaviour*: Volumes of purchase, delivery requirements.
- *Demographic*: Family size, religion, gender, income, occupation, language, education.
- *Geographic*: Region, district, density of population, climate, urbanrural.
- *Psychographics*: Value system, lifestyles, and personality types.

Usually the tourist market is segmented in terms of demographic, geographic, psychographic, social and economic criteria. For example the market for a particular area might be the businessmen in the age group of 40-60 years who have an income of over $100,000 per year and who live in southern parts of Germany.

The tourist market may be segmented on the basis of:

- Destinations.
- Economic status and spending tendencies.
- Place or origin of tourists.
- Preferences of staying, like camping, luxury hotels, caravans, etc.
- Preferences of travel, like air, sea, road, or rail.
- Purpose of tour like holidays, pilgrimage, sightseeing, shopping, etc.

Each segment of the market differs in terms of needs and expectations. No one organization can cater to the needs of all segments. Each organization has to decide on the particular segment or segments it would cater to. The segment so identified is called the target segment. Having identified the market, all activities will have to be planned keeping this target market in mind.

The services being offered, the messages in communication, the media used for communication, the pricing policies, the arrangements have to be consistent with the preferences and behaviour patterns of the target market. For example, if the hotel is targeting on the domestic tourists at religious places, then providing foreign food or advertising in business magazines would be the waste of resources. Instead, provide vegetarian thali food and advertise in religious magazines and on channels like Aastha and Sanskar.

TOURISM MARKETING

It is a well known fact that as long as the inherent sense of curiosity and adventure dwells in the hearts of human beings, the desire to travel in order to see new sights and experience new things, to live under different environments will always grows.

The marketing in tourism industry has evolved as part of the process initiated by the desire for travel in people. Without exception, all human beings will always nurture a desire to travel in order to see places.

The question arises that if the desire is ever present in people to travel and experience new things, why then would the tourism industry need marketing efforts at all? The marketing problems in tourism is quite different from marketing problems in other industries, and this justifies making marketing in tourism, a subject for separate and specialized enquiry.

The concepts and principles, the techniques and methods of marketing can be equally applied to tourism. The concept of tourism marketing can be better understood by identifying and considering the differences between markets for physical, tangible goods on the one hand and the market for tourism on the other. Tourism marketing could be defined as the systematic and coordinated efforts exerted by tourist enterprises at international, national and local levels to optimize the satisfaction of tourists, groups and individuals, in view of a sustained tourism growth. Krippendorf, "Marketing in tourism is to be understood as the systematic and coordinated execution of business policy by tourist undertakings, whether private or state owned, at local, regional, national or international levels to achieve the optimal satisfaction of the needs of identifiable consumer groups, and in doing so to achieve an appropriate return."

Tourism is a very complex industry because of its multifaceted activities, which together produce the tourist products otherwise considered as independent industry. Besides, its complexity lies mostly in the fact that tourists are located in different places, have different socio-economic structures, different needs, tastes, attitudes, expectations, and behaviour patterns.

The marketing concept helps the tourist organization to establish a consistent and effective communication system with actual and potential tourists in the selected markets. It also helps them to know their customers' wishes, needs, motivations, likes and dislikes.

SPECIAL FEATURES OF TOURISM MARKETING

From ancient times when travel was a prerogative of a select few who travelled in search of adventure to the present day jet travel, there have been many changes. Travel in ancient times was a simple affair. The type of facilities that were required by the people to travel was provided by a handful of suppliers of such services. In the present scenario of travel expansion, markets necessitated the application of marketing techniques. Marketing of tourist products has certain peculiarities.

The difference arises due to peculiar nature of tourist products:

- *A tourist product is assembled by many producers*: The tourist product cannot be provided by a single enterprise. In tourism, airline provides 'seat' to travel, hotels provide 'accommodation', a travel agent 'bookings' while a museum provides 'place of experience'. So, the tourist product is an amalga-mation of many components, which together make a complete product.
- Intermediaries play a dominant role: In tourism, sales intermediaries like tour operators, travel agents, reservation services and hotel brokers play a dominant role. They determine to a large extent which services will be sold and to whom.
- *Production and consumption of tourist services are closely Interrelated*: The travel agent who sells his product cannot store it since there is a close link between production and consumption of tourist services. Production can only take place or can only be completed if the customer is actually present.
- *Tourism demand is highly unstable*: Tourism demand is influenced by seasonal, economic, political and other such factors. For example, political unrest affects inflow of tourist to a particular destination.
- *Tourism is an intangible, non-material product*: Unlike a tangible product, no transfer of ownership of goods is involved in tourism. Instead certain facilities are made available for a specified time and for a specified use like a seat in an aeroplane or room in a hotel.
- *Travel motivations are diverse in nature*: The reasons, expectations, and desires, which influence tourists' choice for certain holiday destinations, types of accommodation and vacation activities are varied. Very often people make exactly the same choice for entirely different reasons.

To a considerable extent, tourism marketing depends on various market factors. Therefore, marketing of tourism as compared to other industries needs a somewhat different approach.

PRODUCT IN TOURISM

The needs of the tourist relate to comfort and pleasure in travel, stay, food arrangements and visiting spots of interest and attraction.

Hence, the tourist expectations are:

- Able to experience the new places–their life-styles, food, culture, heritage, etc. as per one's own choice.
- Be able to visit places of interest, spend adequate time at such places.
- Facility of transportation available.
- Facing no risk to one's person or belongings, etc.

- Getting suitable food to one's tastes and health.
- Not to be hurried or hustled against the preferred place.
- To be looked after and cared for.

The three basic components of a tourist product are:

- Attractions,
- Facilities, and
- Accessibility.

Attractions constitute an important feature of the product. Attractions are those elements in the tourist product, which determine the choice of the particular tourist product, to visit one particular destination rather than another. These are things to see and enjoy like cultural sites, historical buildings, beaches, mountains, national parks, or events like trade fairs, exhibitions, music festivals, etc. Facilities are those elements in the tourist product, which are a necessary aid to the tourist centre. The facilities complement the attractions. These include accommodation, food, communications, guides and so on.

Accessibility is a means by which a tourist can reach the areas where attractions are located. Tourists' attractions are of little importance if their locations are inaccessible by the normal means of transport. It also relates to the formalities in reaching the places like visas, customs, bookings etc.

In Tourism, the products are varied. A travel agent may arrange for itineraries and airline bookings and may also help in getting passport, visas, foreign exchange clearances, embarkation facilities at airport and so on. Similarly attractions are added to a destination. For example, 18 rooms of Buckingham Palace have been opened to visitors, which are a major tourist attraction to visitors. Apart from the Throne Room, Drawing Room and the Picture Gallery, the Souvenir shop selling white china mugs with Buckingham Palace written on it or Crystal Balls with details from the State Dining Room is also a part of the attraction. A product in tourism is the place of destination and what one may experience while proceedings to and staying at that destination.

For example,

- Sentose islands of Singapore, is packaged as a place where there are no shops, no skyscrapers, no offices-a place of quiet and tranquility, to relax and be with nature, so different from Singapore. Travelling by cable car to the island is also a part of the package.
- Places in Rajasthan like Jaisalmer are being offered as tourism products to experience the life-style of Maharajas, living in real palaces with kingly comforts, travelling on ' Palace on Wheels', the luxuriously fitted railway train, going hunting on elephant back and so on. The product is not merely the city of Jaisalmer and what it may offer as historical and cultural importance. The product is the total experience of travel and other attractions, all related to the royalty of Jaisalmer.

The tourism product may be developed with emphasis on art, architecture, culture, religion, history, sports, leisure, temples, life-styles, etc.

- Himalayas are a product not only for sports and adventure tourism, but also for nature lovers and spirituality.
- Varanasi is a product based on religion, the Ganges capturing the essence of Oldest Hindu heritage.
- The accommodation provided, is as much a part of the safari in the African forests as the prospect of seeing wild-life. Many prefer and pay more to live in the open country 'with nature' instead of in five-star comfort.

CHARACTERISTICS OF TOURISM PRODUCTS

A product is something that a producer makes and offers to consumers to provide satisfaction of needs. Like all products, tourism also needs marketing and it is different from marketing of manufactured goods since tourism product has different characteristics.

INTANGIBLE

Manufactured goods are tangible in the sense that they have physical dimensions and attributes and can be seen, felt, or tasted. The tourism product is an intangible product. Take for example, an aviation industry. One can see the airplane, the facilities provided within, etc. But none of these would determine the nature and quality of services imparted by the airline. One cannot see, feel, smell, touch or measure a service performed. It can only be experienced from the effects produced during the journey.

INSEPARABILITY

A physical product is produced in the factory, bought in the shop and consumed in the customer's premises at his convenience. But when the customer buys a service like travelling in an airline, the production and consumption of the services takes place at the same time. The experience of the tourist product exists when it is produced as well as consumed. The service in the airline is the promptness of delivery of baggage or courtesy of the airhostess or safety of travel.

PERISHABILITY

A manufacturer of a physical product can anticipate the demand in advance and store the goods in warehouse and deliver them to the customers at the time of need. But the supply of the tourism product cannot be stored because tourism products are highly perishable. A seat in the plane or a room in the hotel not used today is a total waste. If an advertisement placed in the media channel is not seen or read, it is a waste. If the supply is not used, it perishes. So, the seats in an aircraft, the rooms in the hotels, the space in the ship, the services of a tourist guide, the time of the travel agency, etc. all perish if not utilized when available. What is not sold cannot be carried forward like stocks to be sold the next day or at any other time.

OWNERSHIP

No ownership passes from seller to buyer in a service. The buyer only acquires the right to certain benefits of what the seller offers. One may have the right to use a hotel room or a railway berth for a period of time, but the ownership of the room or berth remains with the hotel or the railways.

MARKETING MIX IN TOURISM MARKETING

Tourist marketing mix is largely a complex group of factors to achieve the 'end products', which helps the marketing manager to understand the demand in relation to supply and marketing investments. A balanced mix is necessary to reach this targeted result.

The tourist marketing mix can include the following elements:

- *The Product*:
  - Image, reputation, positioning
  - Size and facilities offered
  - Staff members and their attitudes
  - The characteristics of the product
- *The Price*:
  - Corporate
  - Discounted
  - Normal
  - Promotional
  - Seasonal
  - Wholesaler rates
- *The Promotion*:
  - Advertising
  - Direct mail
  - Public relations
  - Sales promotion
- *The Distribution*:
  - Airlines
  - Channels of distribution
  - Clubs/Associations
  - Intermediaries
  - Reservation systems

'Marketing mix' has both short-term as well as long-term aspects. Long-term plans are based on study of natural, economic, social and technological aspects of the markets and customers. The short-term aspects relate to price reduction, aggressive promotion, or introduction of a new product in the market.

TOURISM MARKETING STRATEGY

One of the basic considerations for successful marketing strategy is the need for research. It provides the information base for effective marketing. It relates to providing answers to various questions pertaining to the marketing activities. Market research can be defined as the "systematic collection of information relating to supply and demand for the product in such a way that the information may be used to make decisions about its policies and objectives". In order to formulate any marketing strategy, it is essential for a tourist organization and others engaged in marketing of tourist products to know the answer of following questions:

- Who are the persons engaged in tourism and where do they live?
- Who are the potential customers and where do they come from?
- What are their likes and dislikes?
- What are their travel preferences and interests?
- What do they buy and where do they stay?
- What mode of transport do they use?
- What are their entertainment preferences?
- What are the trends in competition?
- What type of marketing programmes would be needed?

Market research provides answers to all the above questions. To make the overall marketing efforts effective and successful, as in the case of manufactured products, the tourist organization has to be totally aware of the trends in travel habits, vacation habits and complete knowledge about potential customers. It is very important to have detailed information on all aspects of a market. Results of such research will work as a guideline for designing and launching a successful marketing programme. A lot of data can be collected through publications, commercial analysis, trade information, press cuttings, previous studies etc.

Other ways to obtain data are:

- Tourism Departments,
- Discussion with tourists,
- Observation of customers at premises,
- Observations and discussions with visitors in exhibitions and trade shows,
- Attitudes, image perceptions and awareness studies,
- Advertisement and other media response studies,
- Studies of usage pattern.

UNDERSTANDING TOURISM PLANNING

Tourism is one of many activities in a community or region that requires planning and coordination. Here we provide a simple structure and basic guidelines for comprehensive tourism planning at a community or regional level. Planning is the process of identifying objectives and defining and evaluating methods of achieving them. By comprehensive planning we mean planning which considers all of the tourism resources, organizations, markets, and programmes within a region. Comprehensive planning also considers economic, environmental, social, and institutional aspects of tourism development.

TWO SIDES OF TOURISM PLANNING

Tourism planning has evolved from two related but distinct sets of planning philosophies and methods. On the one hand, tourism is one of many activities in an area that must be considered as part of physical, environmental, social, and economic planning. Therefore, it is common to find tourism addressed, at least partially, in a regional land use, transportation, recreation, economic development, or comprehensive plan.

The degree to which tourism is addressed in such plans depends upon the relative importance of tourism to the community or region and how sensitive the planning authority is to tourism activities. Tourism may also be viewed as a business in which a community or region chooses to engage. Individual tourism businesses conduct a variety of planning activities including feasibility, marketing, product development, promotion, forecasting, and strategic planning. If tourism is a significant component of an area's economy or development plans, regional or community-wide marketing plans are needed to coordinate the development and marketing activities of different tourism interests in the community. A comprehensive approach integrates a strategic marketing plan with more traditional public planning activities. This ensures a balance between serving the needs and wants of the tourists versus the needs and wants of local residents. A formal tourism plan provides a vehicle for the various interests within a community to coordinate their activities and work towards common goals. It also is a means of coordinating tourism with other community activities.

STEPS IN THE PLANNING PROCESS

Like any planning, tourism planning is goal-oriented, striving to achieve certain objectives by matching available resources and programmes with the needs and wants of people. Comprehensive planning requires a systematic approach, usually involving a series of steps. The process is best viewed as an iterative and on-going one, with each step subject to modification and refinement at any stage of the planning process.

There are six steps in the planning process:

- Define goals and objectives.
- Identify the tourism system.
  - Resources
  - Organizations
  - Markets
  - Generate alternatives.

- Evaluate alternatives.
- Select and implement.
- Monitor and evaluate.

STEP ONE

Obtaining clear statements of goals and objectives is difficult, but important. Ideally, tourism development goals should flow from more general community goals and objectives. It is important to understand how a tourism plan serves these broader purposes. Is the community seeking a broader tax base, increased employment opportunities, expanded recreation facilities, better educational programmes, a higher quality of life? How can tourism contribute to these objectives? If tourism is identified as a means of serving broader community goals, it makes sense to develop plans with more specific tourism development objectives.

These are generally defined through a continuing process in which various groups and organizations in a community work together towards common goals. A local planning authority, chamber of commerce, visitors bureau, or similar group should assume a leadership role to develop an initial plan and obtain broad involvement of tourism interests in the community. Public support for the planning process and plan is also important. Having a good understanding of tourism and the tourism system in your community is the first step towards defining goals and objectives for tourism development.

The types of goals that are appropriate and the precision with which you are able to define them will depend upon how long your community has been involved in tourism and tourism planning. In the early stages of tourism development, goals may involve establishing organizational structures and collecting information to better identify the tourism system in the community. Later, more precise objectives can be formulated and more specific development and marketing strategies evaluated.

STEP TWO

Identifying Your Tourism System When planning for any type of activity, it is important to first define its scope and characteristics. Be clear about exactly what your plan encompasses. A good initial question is, "What do you mean by tourism?" Tourism is defined in many ways. Generally, tourism involves people traveling outside of their community for pleasure. Definitions differ on the specifics of how far people must travel, whether or not they must stay overnight, for how long, and what exactly is included under traveling for "pleasure".

Do you want your tourism plan to include day visitors, conventioneers, business travellers, people visiting friends and relatives, people passing through, or seasonal residents? Which community resources and organizations serve tourists or could serve tourists? Generally, tourists share community resources with local residents and businesses.

Many organizations serve both tourists and locals. This complicates tourism planning and argues for a clear idea of what your tourism plan entails.

You can begin to clarify the tourism system by breaking it down into three subsystems:

- Tourism resources,
- Tourism organizations, and
- Tourism markets.

An initial task in developing a tourism plan is to identify, inventory, and classify the objects within each of these subsystems.

Tourism Resources are any:

- Natural,
- Cultural,
- Human, or
- Capital resources that either are used or can be used to attract or serve tourists.

A tourism resource inventory identifies and classifies the resources available that provide opportunities for tourism development. Conduct an objective and realistic assessment of the quality and quantity of resources you have to work with. Some data suggested classification to help obtain a broad and organized picture of your tourism resources. Tourism Organizations combine resources in various proportions to provide products and services for the tourist.

A partial list and classification of organizations that manage or coordinate tourism-related activities. It is important to recognize the diverse array of public and private organizations involved with tourism. The most difficult part of tourism planning is to get these groups to work towards common goals. You should develop a list of these organizations within your own community and obtain their input and cooperation in your tourism planning efforts.

Setting up appropriate communication systems and institutional arrangements is a key part of community tourism planning.

TOURISM RESOURCES

- *Natural Resources*:
  - Climate-seasons
  - Fauna-fish and wildlife
  - Flora-forests, flowers, shrubs, wild edibles
  - Geological resources-topography, soils, sand dunes, beaches, caves, rocks and minerals, fossils
  - Scenery-combinations of all of the above
  - Water resources-lakes, streams, waterfalls
- *Cultural Resources*:
  - Anthropological resources
  - Cuisine

  - Ethnic cultures
  - Historic buildings, sites
  - Industry, government, religion, etc.
  - Local celebrities
  - Monuments, shrines
- *Human Resources*:
  - Craftsman and artisans
  - Hospitality skills
  - Local populations
  - Management skills
  - Other labour skills from chefs to lawyers to researchers
  - Performing artists-music, drama, art, storytellers, etc.
  - Seasonal labour force
- *Capital*:
  - Availability of capital, financing
  - Infrastructure-transportation roads, airports, railroads, harbors and marinas, trails and walkways
  - Infrastructure: utilities water, power, waste treatment, communications.

Tourism Management Organizations and Services

Off-Site

Coordination, planning, technical assistance, research, regulation:

- Educational organizations and consultants, *e.g.*, Travel and Tourism Research Association; U.S. Travel Data Centre; Travel Reference Centre, Univ. of Colorado, Boulder; Travel, Tourism, and Recreation Resource Centre, Michigan State University.
- Federal and state departments of commerce, transportation, and natural resources
- Federal, state, regional, and local tourism associations
- Travel information and reservation services

On-Site

Development, promotion and management, of tourism resources:

- Federal agencies, NB. departments of commerce, transportation, and land management agencies.
- Local government organizations, *e.g.*, visitor information, chamber of commerce, convention and visitor's bureaus, parks.
- State agencies, NB. departments of commerce, transportation, and land/facility management agencies

Businesses:

- *Accommodations*: Hotels, motels, Lodges, resorts, bed and breakfast cabins and cottages, Condominiums, second homes, Campgrounds

- *Food and Beverage*: Restaurants, Grocery, Bars, nightclubs, Fast food, Catering services
- *Information*: Travel agencies, Information and reservation services, Automobile clubs
- Transportation: Air, rail, bus; Local transportation: taxi, limo, Auto, bicycle, boat rental; Local tour services

Recreation Facilities and Services

Winter sports: Ski, skating, snowmobile areas; Golf courses, miniature golf; Swimming pools, water slides, beaches; tennis, handball, racquetball courts, bowling alleys; Athletic clubs, health spas; Marinas, boat rentals and charters; hunting and fishing guides; Horseback enterprises; Sporting goods sales and rentals:

- *Entertainment*: Nightclubs, amusement parks, spectator sport facilities; Gambling facilities: casinos, horse racing, bingo; video arcades; art galleries and studios, craft shops, studios, demonstrations; performing arts: theater, dance, music, film; historic and prehistoric sites; museums: art, history, science, technology; arboreta, zoos, nature centres,
- *Support services*: Auto repair, gasoline service stations; boat and recreation vehicle dealers and service; retail shops: sporting goods, specialties, souvenirs, clothing; health services: hospitals, clinics, pharmacies; laundry and dry cleaning; beauty and barber shops; babysitting services; pet care; communications: newspaper, telephone; banking and financial services

Tourism Markets

Tourists makeup the third, and perhaps most important subsystem. Successful tourism programmes require a strong market orientation. The needs and wants of the tourists you choose to attract and serve must be the focus of much of your marketing and development activity. Therefore, it is important to clearly understand which tourism market segments you wish to attract and serve. Tourists fall into a very diverse set of categories with quite distinct needs and wants. You should identify the different types of tourists, or market segments that you presently serve or would like to serve. This may involve one or more tourism market surveys.

A visitor survey identifies the size and nature of the existing market and asks the following questions:

- How did they find out about your community?
- How satisfied are they with your offerings?
- What are the primary market segments you presently attract?
- What attracted them to the community?
- What local businesses and facilities do they use?

- Where do they come from?

A market survey (usually a telephone survey) also can be conducted among households in regions from which you wish to attract tourists. This type of study helps identify potential markets, and means of attracting tourists to your area.

Tourism Market Segments

In a general tourism plan, some clear target tourism market segments should be identified. You might begin by defining the market area from which you will draw most of your visitors.

The size of your market area depends upon the uniqueness and quality of your "product", transportation systems, tastes and preferences of surrounding populations, and your competition. Identifying the market area will help target information and promotion and define transportation routes and modes, competition, and characteristics of your market.

Next, divide your travel market into the following trip length categories:

- Day trips from 50 to 200 miles away,
- Day trips from a 50 mile radius,
- Extended overnight vacation trips.
- Overnight trips of 1 or 2 nights (most likely weekends), and
- Pass-through travellers,

After you have an idea of your market area and kinds of trips you will be serving, begin defining more specific market segments like vehicle campers, downhill skiers, sightseers, family vacationers, single weekenders, and the like.

These segments can be more clearly tied to particular resources, businesses, and facilities in your community. What kinds of products and services are likely to attract each of these groups? Tourist needs as well as their impact on the local community are quite different for day tourists versus overnight tourists.

Areas catering primarily to weekend traffic will experience large fluctuations in use. In deciding the relative importance of these different segments, communities need to assess both their ability to provide required services (do you have enough rooms?), as well as the demand for different types of trips relative to the supply and your competition.

THE ENVIRONMENT

A tourism plan is significantly affected by many factors in the broader environment. Indeed, one of the complexities of tourism planning is the number of variables that are outside of the control of an individual tourism business or community. These include such things as tourism offerings and prices at competing destinations, federal and state policy and legislation, currency exchange rates, the state of the economy, and weather. These factors are discussed more fully in Extension bulletin E-1959 as part of the market environment analysis. Local populations also must be considered in tourism planning. As they compete with tourists for resources, they can be significantly affected by tourism activity, and they are an important source of support in getting tourism plans implemented.

A survey of local residents can be conducted to assess community attitudes towards tourism development, identify impacts of tourism on the community, and obtain local input into tourism plans. Public hearings, workshops, and advisory boards are other ways to obtain public involvement in tourism planning. Local support and cooperation is important to the success of tourism programmes and should not be overlooked.

STEP THREE

Generating alternative development and marketing options to meet your goals requires some creative thinking and brainstorming. The errors made at this stage are usually thinking too narrowly or screening out alternatives prematurely. It is wise to solicit a wide range of options from a diverse group of people. If tourism expertise is lacking in your community, seek help and advice outside the community. Tourism planning involves a wide range of interrelated development and marketing decisions.

The following development questions will get you started:

- How much importance should be assigned to tourism within a community or region?
- What are the relative roles of public and private sectors?
- Which general community goals is tourism development designed to serve?
- Which organization(s) will provide the leadership and coordination necessary for community tourism planning?

Tourism marketing decision questions include:

- *Place*: Where should tourism facilities be located?
- *Price*: What prices should be charged for which products and services. Who should capture the revenue?
- *Product*: What kinds of tourism products and services should be provided? Who should provide what?
- *Promotion*: What kinds of promotion should be used, by whom, in which media, how much, when? What community tourism theme or image should be established?
- *Segments*: Which market segments should be pursued; geographic markets, trip types, activity or demographic subgroups?

STEP FOUR

Tourism development and marketing options are evaluated by assessing the degree to which each option will be able to meet the stated goals and objectives. There are usually two parts to a systematic evaluation of tourism development and marketing alternatives:

- Feasibility analysis, and
- Impact assessment.

These two tasks are interrelated, but think of them as trying to answer two basic questions:

- Can it be done?, and
- What are the consequences?

A decision to take a specific action must be based both on feasibility and desirability. Feasibility Analysis: First, screen alternatives and eliminate those that are not feasible due to economic, environmental, political, legal, or other factors. Evaluate the remaining set of alternatives in more paying particular attention to the market potential and financial plan. Make a realistic assessment of your community's ability to attract and serve a market segment or segments. This requires a clear understanding of the tourism market in your area and how this market is changing. Also carefully identify your competition and evaluate your advantages and disadvantages compared to the competition. Plan towards the future because it takes time to implement decisions and for your actions to take effect. Therefore, look at the likely market and competition for several years to come. Review forecasts for the travel market in your area, if available. Careful tracking of tourism trends in your own community can help identify changes in the market that you will have to adapt to.

Impact Assessment

When evaluating alternative development and marketing strategies it is important to understand the impacts, both positive and negative, of proposed actions. A classification of economic, environmental, and social impacts associated with tourism development. The types of impacts and their importance vary across different communities and proposed actions.

Generally, the size, extent, and nature of tourism impacts depend upon:

- Degree of concentration/dispersal of tourist activity in the area
- How well tourism is planned, controlled, and managed.
- Length and nature of tourist contacts with the community
- Similarities or differences between local populations and tourists
- Stability/sensitivity of local economy, environment, and social structure
- Volume of tourist activity relative to local activity

Look at both the benefits and costs of any proposed actions. While tourism development can increase income, revenues, and employment, it also involves costs. Evaluate benefits and costs of tourism development from the perspectives of local government, businesses, and residents.

IMPACTS OF TOURISM

- *Economic Impacts*:
  - Economic base and structure

  - Employment
  - Fiscal impact-taxes, infrastructure costs
  - Prices
  - Sales, revenue, and income
- *Environmental Impacts*:
  - Air
  - Flora and fauna
  - Infrastructure
  - Lands
  - Waters
- *Social Impacts*:
  - Community spirit and cohesion
  - Congestion and crowding
  - Education
  - Occupations
  - Population structure and distribution
  - Quality of life
  - Safety and security
  - Values and attitudes

Impacts on Local Government

Local government provides most of the infrastructure and many of the services essential to tourism development, including highways, public parks, law enforcement, water and sewer, garbage collection and disposal. Evaluate tourism decisions with a clear understanding of the capacity of the local infrastructure and services relative to anticipated needs, and take into account both the needs of local populations and tourists.

A fiscal impact analysis evaluates the impact of tourism on the community's tax base and local government costs. It entails predicting the additional infrastructure and service requirements of tourism development, estimating their costs, deciding who will pay for/provide them, and how. Will tourism generate increased local government revenue through fees and charges, local sales or use taxes, increased property values or property tax rates, or larger local shares of federal and state tax revenues?

Impacts on Business and Industry

Businesses that are directly serving tourists benefit from sales to tourists. Through secondary impacts, tourism activity also benefits a wide range of businesses in a community. For example, a local textile industry may sell to a linen supply firm that serves hotels and motels catering primarily to tourists. A local forest products industry sells to a lumberyard where local woodcarvers or furniture makers buy their supplies.

They in turn sell to tourists through various retail outlets. All of these businesses benefit from tourism. If most products and services for tourists are bought outside of the local area, much of the tourist spending "leaks" out of the local economy. The more a community is "self-sufficient" in serving tourists, the larger the local impact.

Impacts on Residents

Local residents may experience a broad range of both positive and negative impacts from tourism development. Tourism development may provide increased employment and income for the community. Although tourism jobs are primarily in the service sectors and are often seasonal, part time, and low-paying, these characteristics, are neither universal nor always undesirable.

Residents may value opportunities for part time and seasonal work. In particular, employment opportunities and work experiences for students or retirees may be desired. Residents may also benefit from local services that otherwise would not be available.

Tourism development may mean a wider variety of retailers and restaurants, or a better community library. It may also mean more traffic, higher prices, and increases in property values and local taxes. The general quality of the environment and life in the community may go up or down due to tourism development. This depends on the nature of tourism development, the preferences and desires of local residents, and how well tourism is planned and managed.

STEPS FIVE AND SIX

As suggested, not attempt a complete discussion of decision making, plan implementation, and monitoring, but these are critical steps in the success of a tourism plan. A set of specific actions should be prescribed with clearly defined responsibilities and timetables.

Monitor progress in implementing the plan and evaluate the success of the plan in meeting its goals and objectives on a regular basis. Plans generally need to be adjusted over time due to changing goals, changing market conditions, and unanticipated impacts. It is a good idea to build monitoring and evaluation systems into your planning efforts.

CONCLUDING REMARKS

Successful tourism planning and development means serving both tourists and local residents. The bulletins in this series stress the importance of a market orientation for attracting and serving tourists. This market orientation must be balanced with a clear view of how tourism serves the broader community interest and an understanding of the positive and negative impacts of tourism development. Remember, tourism should serve the community first and the tourist second.

Tourism development must be compatible with other activities in the area and be supported by the local population. Therefore, the tourism plan should be closely coordinated with other local and regional planning efforts, if not an integral part of them.

NATIONAL AND REGIONAL TOURISM PLANNING

The importance of effective tourism planning in ensuring economic benefit and sustainability is now widely recognized. Here we introduce concepts of national and regional tourism planning and look at the basic approaches, techniques and principles applied at this level. It is now recognized that tourism must be developed and managed in a controlled, integrated and sustainable manner, based on sound planning. With this approach, tourism can generate substantial economic benefits to an area, without creating any serious environmental or social problems. Tourism's resources will be conserved for continuous use in the future.

There are numerous examples in the world where tourism has not been well planned and managed. These uncontrolled developments may have brought some short-term economic benefits. Over the longer term, however, they have resulted in environmental and social problems and poor quality tourist destinations. This has been detrimental to the area's residents, and tourist markets have been lost to better planned destinations elsewhere. Many of these places are now undergoing redevelopment. It is obviously better to plan for controlled development initially, and prevent problems from arising in the first place.

Tourism planning is carried out at all levels of development-international, national, regional and for specific areas and sites. National and regional planning lays the foundation for tourism development of a country and its regions. It establishes the policies, physical and institutional structures and standards for development to proceed in a logical manner. It also provides the basis for the continuous and effective management of tourism which is so essential for the long-term success of tourism. This publication is divided into two parts.

The first part briefly explains planning concepts and describes planning and marketing methodologies. Emphasis is placed on the integrated approach, balancing economic, environmental and socio-cultural factors, and achieving sustainable development. Importance is also given to techniques that need to be used in implementing plans. Without adopting and applying these techniques, tourism plans cannot be realised.

The second part presents case studies of tourism policies and plans which have actually been prepared and, for the most part, are being implemented. The case studies have been selected to represent the several different elements of plans that must be considered in integrated development. Most of the case studies are ones that have been prepared by the WTO for several countries and regions during the past decade. One of the important functions of the WTO is its technical cooperation activities. The organization has assisted many countries throughout the world in preparing planning, marketing, economic and other types of tourism studies, advising on all aspects of tourism development, and training local tourism-related personnel.

Both Parts I and II of this publication reflect the WTO's basic approach to planning for the integrated and sustainable development of tourism in its global technical cooperation activities. The WTO hopes that this publication will provide tourism officials, planners and others involved in tourism with an understanding of national and regional tourism planning. Their application of sound planning practice can then provide the basis for their countries to achieve successful tourism development.

THE IMPORTANCE OF PLANNING TOURISM

Planning tourism at all levels is essential for achieving successful tourism development and management. The experience of many tourism areas in the world has demonstrated that, on a long-term basis, the planned approach to developing tourism can bring benefits without significant problems, and maintain satisfied tourist markets. Places that have allowed tourism to develop without the benefit of planning are often suffering from environmental and social problems. These are detrimental to residents and unpleasant for many tourists, resulting in marketing difficulties and decreasing economic benefits. These uncontrolled tourism areas cannot effectively compete with planned tourist destinations elsewhere. They usually can be redeveloped, based on a planned approach, but that requires much time and financial investment. Tourism is a rather complicated activity that overlaps several different sectors of the society and economy. Without planning, it may create unexpected and unwanted impacts. Tourism is also still a relatively new type of activity in many countries. Some governments and often the private sector have little or no experience in how to develop tourism properly.

For countries that do not yet have much tourism, planning can provide the necessary guidance for its development. For those places that already have some tourism, planning is often needed to revitalize this sector and maintain its future viability. First, tourism should be planned at the national and regional levels. At these levels, planning is concerned with tourism development policies, structure plans, facility standards, institutional factors and all the other elements necessary to develop and manage tourism. Then, within the framework of national and regional planning, more detailed plans for tourist attractions, resorts, urban, rural and other forms of tourism development can be prepared. There are several important specific benefits of undertaking national and regional tourism planning.

These advantages include:

- Developing tourism so that its natural and cultural resources are indefinitely maintained and conserved for future, as well as present, use.
- Establishing the guidelines and standards for preparing detailed plans of specific tourism development areas that are consistent with,

and reinforce, one another, and for the appropriate design of tourist facilities.

- Establishing the overall tourism development objectives and policies-what is tourism aiming to accomplish and how can these aims be achieved.
- Integrating tourism into the overall development policies and patterns of the country or region, and establishing dose linkages between tourism and other economic sectors.
- Laying the foundation for effective implementation of the tourism development policy and plan and continuous management of the tourism sector, by providing the necessary organizational and other institutional framework.
- Making possible the coordinated development of all the many elements of the tourism sector. This includes inter-relating the tourist attractions, activities, facilities and services and the various and increasingly fragmented tourist markets.
- Offering a baseline for the continuous monitoring of the progress of tourism development and keeping it on track.
- Optimizing and balancing the economic, environmental and social benefits of tourism, with equitable distribution of these benefits to the society, while minimizing possible problems of tourism.
- Providing a physical structure which guides the location, types and extent of tourism development of attractions, facilities, services and infrastructure.
- Providing a rational basis for decision-making by both the public and private sectors on tourism development.
- Providing the framework for effective coordination of the public and private sector efforts and investment in developing tourism.

The planned approach to developing tourism at the national and regional levels is now widely adopted as a principle, although implementation of the policies and plans is still weak in some places. Many countries and regions of countries have had tourism plans prepared. Other places do not yet have plans, but should consider undertaking planning in the near future.

In some countries, plans had previously been prepared but these are now outdated. They need to be revised based on present day circumstances and likely future trends. Founded on accumulated experience, the approaches and techniques of tourism planning are now reasonably well understood. There is considerable assurance that, if implemented, planning will bring substantial benefits to an area.

APPROACHES TO TOURISM PLANNING

It is important to understand the basic approaches to planning and managing tourism development.

PLANNING TOURISM AS AN INTEGRATED SYSTEM

An underlying concept in planning tourism is that tourism should be viewed as an inter-related system of demand and supply factors. The demand factors are international and domestic tourist markets and local 'residents who use the tourist attractions, facilities and services. The supply factors comprise tourist attractions and activities, accommodation and other tourist facilities and services. Attractions include natural, cultural and special types of features-such as theme parks, zoos, botanic gardens and aquariums-and the activities related to these attractions. Accommodation includes hotels, motels, guest houses and other types of places where tourists stay overnight.

The category of other tourist facilities and services includes tour and travel operations, restaurants, shopping, banking and money exchange, and medical and postal facilities and services. These supply factors are called the tourism product.

Other elements also relate to supply factors. In order to make the facilities and services usable, infrastructure is required. Tourism infrastructure particularly includes transportation (air, road, rail, water, etc.), water supply, electric power, sewage and solid waste disposal, and telecommuni-cations.

- *Demand Factors*:
  - Domestic tourist markets
  - International tourist markets
  - Residents' use of tourist attractions, facilities and services
- *Supply Factors*:
  - Attractions and activities Ïper cent Accommodation
  - Institutional elements
  - Other infrastructure
  - Other tourist facilities and services Ïper cent Transportation

Provision of adequate infrastructure is also important to protect the environment. It helps maintain a high level of environmental quality that is so necessary for successful tourism and desirable for residents. The effective development, operation and management of tourism requires certain institutional elements.

These elements include:

- Availability of financial capital to develop tourist attractions, facilities, services and infrastructure, and mechanisms to attract capital investment.
- Education and training programmes, and training institutions to prepare persons to work effectively in tourism.
- Marketing strategies and promotion programmes to inform tourists about the country or region, and induce them to visit it, and tourist information facilities and services in the destination areas.
- Organizational structures, especially government tourism offices and private sector tourism associations such as hotel associations.

- Tourism-related legislation and regulations, such as standards and licensing requirements for hotels and tour and travel agencies.
- Travel facilitation of immigration (including visa arrangements), customs and other facilities and services at the entry and exit points of tourists.

The institutional elements also include consideration of how to enhance and distribute the economic benefits of tourism, environmental protection measures, reducing adverse social impacts, and conservation of the cultural heritage of people living in the tourism areas. As an inter-related system, it is important that tourism planning aim for integrated development of all these parts of the system, both the demand and supply factors and the physical and institutional elements. The system will function much more effectively and bring the desired benefits if it is planned in an integrated manner, with coordinated development of all the components of the system. Sometimes, this integrated system approach is also called the comprehensive approach to tourism planning because all the elements of tourism are considered in the planning and development process. Just as important as planning for integration within the tourism system is planning for integration of tourism into the overall development policies, plans and patterns of a country or region. Planning for this overall integration will, for example, resolve any potential conflicts over use of certain resources or locations for various types of development. It also provides for the multi-use of expensive infrastructure to serve general community needs as well as tourism. Emphasis is given to formulating and adopting tourism development policies and plans for an area in order to guide decision-making on development actions.

The planning of tourism, however, should also be recognized as a continuous and flexible process. Within the framework of the policy and plan recommendations, there must be flexibility to allow for adapting to changing circumstances. Planning that is too rigid may not allow development to be responsive to changes. There may be advancements in transportation technology, evolution of new forms of tourism and changes in market trends.

Even though allowed to be flexible, the basic objectives of the plan should not be abrogated although the specific development patterns may be changed. Sustainable development must still be maintained. Planning for tourism development should make recommendations that are imaginative and innovative, but they must also be feasible to implement. The various techniques of implementation should be considered throughout the planning process.

This approach ensures that the recommendations can be accomplished, and provides the basis for specifying the implementation techniques that should be applied. Implementation techniques can also be imaginative and not only rely on established approaches. It is common practice for a tourism plan to include specification of implementation techniques, and sometimes a separate manual on how to achieve the plan recommendations.

PLANNING FOR SUSTAINABLE DEVELOPMENT

The underlying approach now applied to tourism planning, as well as to other types of development, is that of achieving sustainable development. The sustainable development approach implies that the natural, cultural and other resources of tourism are conserved for continuous use in the future, while still bringing benefits to the present society The concept of sustainable development has received much emphasis internationally since the early 1980s, although tourism plans prepared even before that period often were concerned with conservation of tourism resources.

The sustainable development approach to planning tourism is acutely important because most tourism development depends on attractions and activities related to the natural environment, historic heritage and cultural patterns of areas. If these resources are degraded or destroyed, then the tourism areas cannot attract tourists and tourism will not be successful. More generally, most tourists seek destinations that have a high level of environmental quality-they like to visit places that are attractive, clean and neither polluted nor congested.

It is also essential that residents of the tourism area should not have to suffer from a deteriorated environment and social problems. One of the important benefits of tourism is that, if it is properly developed based on the concept of sustainability, tourism can greatly help justify and pay for conservation of an area's natural and cultural resources. Thus, tourism can be an important means of achieving conservation in areas that otherwise have limited capability to accomplish environmental protection and conservation objectives. A basic technique in achieving sustainable development is the environmental planning approach.

Environmental planning requires that all elements of the environment be carefully surveyed, analysed and considered in determining the most appropriate type and location of development. This approach would not allow, for example, intensive development in flood plain and steep hillside areas. An important aspect of sustainable development is emphasizing community-based tourism. This approach to tourism focuses on community involvement in the planning and development process, and developing the types of tourism which generate benefits to local communities. It applies techniques to ensure that most of the benefits of tourism development accrue to local residents and not to outsiders.

Maximizing benefits to local residents typically results in tourism being better accepted by them and their actively supporting conservation of local tourism resources. The communitybased tourism approach is applied at the local or more detailed levels of planning, but it can be set forth as a policy approach at the national and regional levels. The benefits accruing to local communities are also beneficial to the country, through the income and foreign exchange earned, employment generated and support that local communities give to national tourism development and conservation policies. Also related to sustainable development is the concept of quality tourism.

This approach is being increasingly adopted for two fundamental reasons-it can achieve successful tourism from the marketing standpoint and it brings benefits to local residents and their environment. Quality tourism does not necessarily mean expensive tourism. Rather, it refers to tourist attractions, facilities and services that offer 'good value for money', protect tourism resources, and attract the kinds of tourists who will respect the local environment and society. Quality tourism development can compete more effectively in attracting discriminating tourists. It is also more environmentally and socially self-sustaining. Achieving quality tourism is the responsibility of both the public and private sectors. This concept should be built into the tourism planning, development and management process.

LONG-RANGE AND STRATEGIC PLANNING

Long-range comprehensive planning is concerned with specifying goals and objectives and determining preferred future development patterns. Tourism development policies and plans should be prepared for relatively long-term periods-usually for 10 to 15 and sometimes 20 years-depending on the predictability of future events in the country or region. These may seem to be long planning periods, but it commonly requires this length of time to implement basic policy and structure plans. Even development of specific projects, such as major resorts or national park-based tourism, can require a long time.

A planning approach which has received considerable attention in recent years, and is applicable to some tourism areas, is strategic planning. While the outcomes of strategic and long-range comprehensive planning may be very similar, strategic planning is somewhat different. It focuses more on identification and resolution of immediate issues. Strategic planning typically is more oriented to rapidly changing future situations and how to cope with changes organizationally. It is more action oriented and concerned with handling unexpected events.

Applied only by itself, strategic planning can be less comprehensive in its approach. By focusing on immediate issues, it may deviate from achieving such long-term objectives as sustainable development. But if used within the framework of integrated long-range policy and planning, the strategic planning approach can be very appropriate.

PUBLIC INVOLVEMENT IN PLANNING

Planning is for the benefit of people, and they should be involved in the planning and development of tourism in their areas. Through this involvement, tourism development will reflect a consensus of what the people want. Also, if residents are involved in planning and development decisions-and if they understand the benefits the tourism can bring-they will more likely support it. At the national and regional levels of preparing tourism plans, the common approach to obtaining public involvement is to appoint a steering committee.

This committee offers guidance to the planning team and reviews its work, especially the draft reports and policy and planning recommendations that are made. A planning study steering committee is typically composed of representatives of the relevant government agencies involved in tourism, the private sector, and community, religious and other relevant organizations. Also, open public hearings can be held on the plan. These hearings provide the opportunity for anybody to learn about the plan and express their opinions. Another common approach, when the plan is completed, is to organize a national or regional tourism seminar.

This meeting informs participants and the general public about the importance of controlled tourism development and the recommendations of the plan. Such seminars often receive wide publicity in the communications media. In a large country or region, the usual procedure is for the tourism plan to be prepared by the central authority with public involvement. This can be termed the 'top-down' approach. Another procedure sometimes used is the 'bottom-up' approach. This involves holding meetings with local districts or communities to determine what type of development they would like to have. These local objectives and ideas are then fitted together into a national or regional plan.

This approach achieves greater local public involvement in the planning process. But it is more time consuming and may lead to conflicting objectives, policies and development recommendations among the local areas. These conflicts need to be reconciled at the national and regional levels in order to form a consistent plan.

It is important that the development patterns of the local areas complement and reinforce one another, but also reflect the needs and desires of local communities. Often a combination of the 'top-down' and 'bottom-up' approaches achieves the best results.

THE TOURISM PLANNING PROCESS

The first step in the planning process is careful preparation of the study so that it provides the type of development guidance that is needed. Study preparation involves formulating the project terms of reference, selecting the technical team to carry out the study, appointing a steering committee, and organizing the study activities. The terms of reference (TOR) for the planning study should be carefully formulated so that the study achieves its desired results and outputs.

The TOR for a national or regional plan indicates the outputs and activities that are necessary to prepare the development policy and plan. The special considerations to be made in planning-such as economic, environmental or social issues and the critical institutional elements-should be specified in the

TOR. Identification of implementation techniques are also specified. The TOR format typically follows the planning process explained here, but it is tailored to the specific characteristics and needs of the planning area. Many places already have some limited tourism development, and these existing patterns must be considered in formulating the TOR. Other countries or regions will have considerable existing tourism development, but it may be declining or not be in a form that generates optimum benefits.

The TOR will therefore emphasize how to rejuvenate and improve existing development, along with how to provide guidance on the future expansion of tourism. It is common for a single study include various levels of tourism planning, such as national and regional plans along with detailed planning for priority development areas and projects. The planning for all these levels will need to be specified in the TOR.

BUDDHIST CIRCUIT

India is the birthplace of one of the most widely accepted religions in the world-Buddhism. The four holy places associated with Gautam Buddha in India are-Lumbini, his birthplace, which now lies in Nepal; Bodhgaya, where he attained enlightenment; Sarnath, near Varanasi, where he preached his first sermon; Kushinagar, near Gorakhpur, where he achieved Mahanirvana. The other important tourist places associated with Buddhism are: Sanchi, Vaishali, Nalanda, Amravati and Nagargunakonda.

All these places together are known as the famous Buddhist circuit in India. Bodhgaya is the most important Buddhist pilgrimage amongst all these places in India. Apart from being a significant archaeological site, it is renowned for the Mahabodhi Temple, which houses a 50 metre high pyramidal spire and an image of the Buddha. Sarnath near Varanasi is a vital centre of the Buddhist world where he delivered his first sermon and set in motion the wheel of law, the Dharmachakra. Buddhism germinated in Sarnath amidst the deer park. Nalanda is the famous education centre of Buddhism where the Chinese scholar and traveller Hiuen Tsang stayed in the 7th century to explore the roots of Buddhism.

Vaishali is significant to Buddhists as Lord Buddha announced his impending Nirvana here. One of the famous pillars erected by Ashoka to propagate Buddhism also stands here in Nalanda. Sanchi in Madhya Pradesh is known for its numerous stupas, monasteries, temples and pillars dating from the 3rd century B.C. to the 12th century A.D. Amaravati on the bank of river Krishna in the South India, is famous for its temple, dedicated to Lord Amarewara. The temple is the dilapidated 2000-year-old Buddhist stupa that draws millions of archaeologists and pilgrims every year. Named after the great scholar of Buddhism, Nagarjunakonda, located on the banks of river Krishna retains its status as the greatest centre of Buddhist learning in the South of Vindhyas. Earlier known as Vijayapuri, Nagarjunakonda was the venue of the massive congregation of monks and scholars during the bygone era. The Buddhist circuit in India thus introduces you with the major townships in India that mark the evolution, development and propagation of Buddhism. After Gautam Buddha, it was Emperor Ashoka followed by his daughter and son Sanghmitra and Mahindra, who took the charge of propagating Buddhism in India as well as the South Asian countries like Burma, Nepal, China, Japan, Malaysia, Sri Lanka etc.

INFORMATION AND COMMUNICATION TECHNOLOGIES

"Atithi Devo Bhava"—Lets welcome tourists as guests and send them back as friends." The new advertisement by the Ministry of Tourism has been seen by all of us. Using Information Technology, this message, is being sent out for Tourists, Tour operators, Travel agents, public at large for the following two basic purposes.

- To create a sense of security amongst Tourists.
- To change the attitude towards Tourists in India.

ICT Information Communication Technologies have been transforming tourism globally. The ICT driven re-engineering has gradually generated a new paradigm-shift completely changing the Industry structure and developing a whole range of opportunities and threats. The new technologies enable the customers to customise, purchase and select the tourism products with pace and ease.

In fact the information technologies are undergoing a revolution world over. They are a key determinant for maximizing the gains. However the success of ICT deployment requires constant improvement and innovative management. The customer's decision risk has increased manifold because he has only information to rely on as he neither sees or inspects or tries out tourist services before deciding to use them. He can rely on the Internet, which is the latest product of Information Technology. It is possible once the customer has access to Internet site; he gets various opportunities out of which E-mail is one.

The latest one to be used is video-conferencing, which is fast being identified as a powerful means of communication between the service providers of Tourism and the users of such services. In fact the communication technologies have completely revolutionized the Tourism Industry. Role of Communication Technologies is vital to any business and particularly to the tourism business. They are important for cost savings and improved communications that arise from an internal network. They help in reaching out and connecting with customers, suppliers and collaborators, which, in the case of Tourism Industry are:

- Airways, Railways and Roadways
- Hotels and all the other types of accommodation
- Tour operators and Travel agents
- Tourists and Travellers

To be precise, following benefits are offered by telecommunication to Tourism as well as other businesses:

- Enables sharing and dissemination of information of all tourism partners.
- Helps geographically separate persons to come together.
- Promotes new ways of tourism partnership.
- Restructure relationship with partners.

However the communication technologies are also prone to following limitations:

- High initial set-up cost
- Practical difficulties
- Security Risks

Inspite of the limitations, Information Communication Technologies are being used in a big way by the Tourism Industry. In fact, it will not be wrong to say that no successful Tour operator or Travel Agent can function without using information technologies. It is, therefore, extremely significant to the Tourism Industry. It will be appropriate here to extend the following quote. "A Journey of a thousand miles must begin with a single step" Lao Tzu. "No single step by a tourist can be taken without using Information Technologies".

OBJECTIVES

So far you have learnt about the concept of marketing and understood that Tourism marketing stands apart from marketing of other products and their advertising techniques and Public relations are also unique. After having this basic knowledge, with respect to tourism marketing, this session will deal with the basic concepts of information technologies in tourism marketing.

After having gone through this session, you should be able to:

- Define and explain different information technologies.
- Know various sectors of Tourism that require information technologies.
- Realise the benefits of information technologies for the user as well as Tour and Travel agents.
- Understand how the use of information technology has led to the growth of Tourism world over.
- Understand the role of Information Technologies in Information Centres.
- Understand Tourism with respect to changing communication technologies.

COMMUNICATION TECHNOLOGY: SIGNIFICANCE

The communication technology is significant in tourism industry in following ways:

- Allows organizations to use their resources more wisely and profitably.
- Creates a sense of security amongst tourists and also provides a friendly environment.

- Develops new avenues and new tourist spots.
- Enables central control and outsourcing of non-core functions.
- Helps in development of extensive growth between partner organizations and between employees, consumers and organizations.
- Helps in sustaining and promoting the existing ones.
- Information technology devices help in linking and sharing data and processes electronically, to build complementary services, expand, reach and enhance collaboration.
- Most devices result in information power storage and profitability.
- Possibility of handling complex details with increase in speed.
- Results in enhancement of processing capabilities.

Davis and Meyer state "Almost instantaneous communication and computation, for example, are shrinking time and focusing us on speed. Connectivity is putting everybody and everything on line in one way or the other and has led to the "the death of distance", a shrinking of space. Intangible value of all kinds, like services and information is growing explosively reducing the importance of tangible mass". The opinion clearly highlights the importance and impact of emerging communication technologies in this highly dynamic industry.

The concept of "Global Village" would be very appropriate in this scenario because it is growing communication technologies, which have opened doors for tourists and travellers and have made availability of information only with the press of a button, with the help of several new Information Technologies.

NEW INFORMATION TECHNOLOGIES

- Cable Television Technology
- Computer Technology
- Internet and Travel and Tourism
- Satellite Television
- Sky Track Technology
- Telecopy Technology
- Telefax Technology
- Teletex Technology
- Videotex Technology
- Websites

COMPUTER TECHNOLOGY

Computer is a tool, which is capable of processing a very large amount of data rapidly, or it is any device capable of processing information to produce a desired result. No matter how large or small they are, computers typically perform their work in three well-defined steps:

- Accepting input
- Processing the input just as to predefined rules

- Producing output

Computer is a multi-function electronic device that can execute instructions to perform a task. Therefore an electronic device that performs pre-defined or programmed computations at a high speed and with great accuracy; a machine that is used to store, transfer, and transform information is known as "Computer" to us. It has made its entry in the field of tourism in a big way. In fact, computers are in use in some way or the other in various branches of tourism since the early sixties.

Be it travel agencies, hotels, Airlines or recently even in the Railways, Computers have played a key role in making the task of providers of travel services an easy affair. Not only this, through home terminals, computers are undertaking, among other jobs, the planning of vacations for an individual and his family.

Computer applications are used in:

- Airlines
- Cargo
- Hotels
- Terminals
- Travel Agency
- Railways

In the year 1983–Thompson Holidays first used computers using online programmes and introduced reservations via Prestel. Several other big tour operators, since then used similar to sell their various programmes.

SATELLITE TELEVISION

Satellite television is television operated by means of orbiting communication satellites located 37,000 km above the earth's surface. The first satellite television signal was relayed from Europe to the Telstar satellite over North America in 1962. The first domestic North American satellite to carry television was Canada's Anik 1, which was launched in 1973. Satellite can also be described as a television system in which the signal is transmitted to an orbiting satellite that receives the signal and amplifies it and transmits it back to earth.

Therefore, it refers to courses that are broadcast, usually live, by an electronic signal sent to a satellite orbiting the earth and then retrieved by a satellite dish. The satellite dish broadcasting the programme is called an "uplink", and the receiving dish is called a "downlink". For Tour operators, as well as Travel agents it serves as a linking device for making available the information of one corner of world to the other corner and Tourists are also, accordingly, benefitted by this linking device.

CABLE TELEVISION TECHNOLOGY

Cable television or Community Antenna Television is a system of providing television, FM radio programming and other services to consumers via radio waves transmitted directly to people's televisions through fixed coaxial cables as opposed to the over-the-air method used in traditional television broadcasting in which a television antenna is required. Cable system covering defined areas, such as the UK's franchise to install and operate a cable system granted by the Cable Authority and Department of Trade and Industry, offering TV channel output and, increasingly, local loop digital telephony services. The Cable Television Association is the CATV industry's representative organization.

Therefore it is a transmission system that distributes and broadcasts television signals and other services by means of a coaxial cable. Cable Television Technology has also greatly helped in information transfer and information sharing. Therefore, it has brought the tourists, the tour operators and the destinations close. It immensely helps in advertising and marketing of Tourism products.

VIDEOTEX TECHNOLOGY

Videotex is a system for sending of pages of text to a user in computer form, typically to be displayed on a television. It is computer technology of the 1980s that uses ordinary television sets, or similar low-cost monitors, to display computer information.

Videotex systems, such as Canada's Telidon, were a complete commercial failure in North America, but achieved a modicum of success in Europe–*e.g.* France's Teletel and, to a much lesser degree, the UK's Prestel. Therefore, it is a form of electronic publishing consisting of computer-generated text distributed through telecommunications and received and viewed on home television.

It occupies a special position among the 'new media'. It plays a key role in the link between telecommunication and the computer sciences. Its advantage lies in the possibility it provides for linking computers and also in its interactive dialogue capabilities. Using Videotex, information and communication systems can be converted into interactive systems capable of communicating with one another. In fact, Videotex is a multipurpose instrument with multiplicity of uses.

It serves as:

- An instrument for data processing
- An information medium
- An organizational aid
- A communication system
- A marketing instrument

This relatively new service connects various forms of use of the facilities and at the same time offers some other possibilities. To operate this service, a television set with a decoder and telephone is necessary, without which the service cannot operate. In Europe, nearly all the households have television sets and a telephone and with the help of Vedeotex, separate households can be reached in large areas. Members of German BTX service as well as Members of France Telecom services can now obtain all kinds of information from external computers or use data bank all through their television sets. In many other European countries and USA, similar systems are in use.

It is being used in a big way in Tourism, also in India because:

- It allows rapid message transmission
- Fast and inexpensive data collection
- Keeps up-to-date information, which is crucial for advertising

It has been found that Videotex is the most advantageous means of Communication, taking into account its low cost and wider range of applications. This technology enables the tour operators and travel agents or hoteliers to send complete pages of information text to the tourist to assist him in deciding and finalizing his tour plans. Satellite, Cable and Videotex technologies are very important because of their wider coverage and their technical methods of transmission, however, they have one shortcoming that none can be directed to one specific person. In addition, the person receiving information is only partially informed. The receiver of information cannot also start a dialogue or communicate. However, the following gives possibility of direct transmission of information to a single consumer:

TELETEX TECHNOLOGY

Teletex is a text and document communications service that could be provided over telephone lines. Teletex allows for the transmission and outing of Group 4 facsimile documents. It is neither like Telex nor like Teletex. Although it may not be as versatile a technology as some others that have been mentioned earlier in this session, but helps in transmitting information which is required by a tourist from a tour operator, Travel agent or a Hotel. Computer information and even copies of documents can be transferred to the tourist with efficiency. It is an improvement over telex and has in fact developed from it.

The receiver for Teletex is an electronic 'typewriter', which can send electronically enriched 'letters' to owners of ordinary telex equipment. The transmission of message time is usually shorter in comparison with time taken with telex. Besides, it is also possible to transmit more office typewriters, symbols. A normal electronic typewriter can also be used as a receiver for telefax.

TELEFAX TECHNOLOGY

It is an electronic post office box system. Each member of the system has his or her 'post office box' in the computer, where other members can leave their message. The owner of each box can electronically contact the others. All the means discussed permit the exchange of information electronically through a data 'network'. The exchange of information between the members with the assistance of electronic transmission is very fast. The data is also available in written form in printouts. 'Network' is a system of transmission linking facilities for automatic data processing. In this way, different computers are connected, permitting data exchange and processing over long distances. Telecommunication is possible only when there is such a network available.

Telephone is the simplest and best communication network. In addition there is also separate clear data network for the exchange of data, which works digitally. In this way, a high transmission speed is achieved and there is a very low ratio of errors during transmission. There are different types of networks, which can be used for telecommunication purposes either separately or combined. In Tourism, in addition to travel agents, tour operators, hoteliers, airlines, travel journalist's etc. use this technology.

TELECOPY

It provides the possibility of exchanging photocopies through a data network. Information, in the form of either written document or technical drawing, is remote copied. This means that two facilities for copying are connected.

One at the sender's end and the other at the receiver's end. Transmission time is only a few minutes. Usually the details of packages, booking details or list of itineraries are sent to this tourist by the Tour operator, Travel agent or the Hotel.

INTERNET AND TRAVEL AND TOURISM

So far the information technology dealt with has been of the kind where intermediaries, travel agents, tour operators etc. are an indispensable part in the distribution and marketing of travel and tourism products, and as an important point of sale or product outlets. This is an information technology where the producer and the consumer are directly communicating, by putting the indispensability of travel intermediaries in question.

As has been discussed earlier, the intangibility of the product where risk and uncertainty for the customer is higher, his need for reliable prepurchase information is stronger. Through Internet, which is the latest product of information technology, this need is fulfilled.

This interactive information-supplying medium is user friendly and gives enormous information of all kinds related to travel. Apart from supplying information about the world's leading and emerging tourist destination of all kinds, it is now possible to book and buy holidays through Internet using plastic money. It gives information on all Airlines, Hotels and Car hire companies, which are in its database. Microsoft is a travel agent. Its Internet site branded Expedia is one of the most important examples of the new generation of travel intermediaries.

Distribution of travel and tourism products using the Internet has a substantial cost reduction advantage for providers of tourism services. The cost incurred by suppliers in receiving a customer booking is the one, which is costly. So, Internet gives a practical aid both in supplying information and receiving bookings or selling tourism products on the principal's behalf. Marketing tourism products on the Internet is also possible. This is done through the page of the company's Internet site.

Once the company gets access to the Internet, it gets various opportunities. Of these, Electronicmail is one. As a tourism product supplier, especially with business travel as a selected target market, it can communicate with the person through his/her e-mail address wherever the client is. Unlike telephone communication, there is no need for the presence of the receiver of the message during message transmission. It also gives a typed copy of the message. E-mail communication medium is very cheap yet efficient and effective. On the other hand, marketing on the Internet has an advantage of being used by all company's of all sizes as long as they can establish their Web Site on the Internet.

WEBSITES

A website is a collection of all pages under one domain. Sometimes, the subdirectories of large ISP(s) are also referred to as websites as they have been designed by different users and with different interests in mind.

Benefits of Websites

No matter how small or large a business is, one can profit enormously from a website in following ways.

- Reduces advertising costs.
- Information remains on line and always up-to-date.
- Pictures, product description, newly won awards, customer questions and instruction videos are possible on the web-site.
- Announcement of a package, deal, and sale can be promptly updated on the website.
- Customers find it simpler to surf the net and log-on to the websites for desired information.
- Websites almost eliminate waste of time in travelling for the desired information centre.

The tourist can make use of the websites, sitting back at home for making tour plans. Accordingly enormous websites are there by tour operators, travel agents, Hotels etc, some of which are given below.

- Luxury Resortsindia.com
- Destinations India.com
- Jaipur JodhpurUdaipur.com
- India Tours and Travels.com
- Asia Tours and Travel.com
- TravelinIndia.com

SKY TRACK

It is an automated airline reservation system, which enables travel agents to make bookings on hundreds of world's airlines using standard Prestel Television set and a keyboard. Possibility of direct transmission between tourists, tour operators and travel agents. This system invented by British Telecom is a way of providing computerized information terminal. The only requirement is a Telephone line and a standard colour Television set with an Adapter to link it to a decoder and keyboard. The information is transmitted quickly and accurately via ordinary telephone lines. The required information is rapidly transmitted through this technology and is very helpful in providing desired information to tourists.

INFORMATION TECHNOLOGY IN THE TRANSPORT SECTOR

Transport provides the essential link between tourism origin and destination areas and facilitates the movement of holidaymakers, business travellers, people visiting friends and relatives and those undertaking educational and health tourism. Before setting out on a journey of any kind, every traveller makes sure which Transport Company has a good safety record. To this effect, airplane coaches and even taxis are equipped with good communication equipment. An Airplane flies with the help of modern information technology equipment, which provides information ranging from weather, altitude and other information to the pilot, to communication made during emergency by the pilot with other airplanes and air traffic control stations.

In-flight entertainment is also a product of information technology, video games, video films are examples. In the case of buses/coaches and taxis, in many countries with developed tourism business, they are equipped with radio communication systems for various uses. For example, the driver or the tour guide updates the Tour Company headquarters about the progress of the tour throughout the touring period. This communication ensures the safety of tourists. Fast and easy information flow is of paramount importance to build confidence in the travelling public. In recent years, the confidence built due to the use of modern IT has been demonstrated by a tremendous increase in the number of travellers worldwide.

INFORMATION TECHNOLOGY IN THE ACCOMMODATION SECTOR

In the accommodation sector also the contribution of information technology is prominent. Any individual or group wishing to travel to any part of the world now has an easy access to the accommodation service providers. A visitor can access information about the kind of hotels at the destination, their ranges of product, the price and other relevant information without leaving his/her office or home. What one has to do is to ring up a travel agency and get the expert advice. This will help any visitor greatly as to where to stay during any kind of trip away from home.

Here the information can be obtained aided by still or moving pictures in order to give an exact feature of an accommodation, facilities and services of one's choice. At a destination also visitors are at ease during their stay in every respect, in getting information about their business, family or other information back home. They are also at ease to relaxing with the videos and television entertainment programmes, which nowadays are part and parcel of many accommodation units.

INFORMATION TECHNOLOGY IN THE ATTRACTION SECTOR

In the case of attractions, both man-made and natural the owners need to communicate or inform their customers and potential customers about their product. Information about the kind of attraction, where it is located and how to get there is of vital importance. The attraction owners, particularly the national tourist offices, discharge their duty of promoting their country's tourist attractions using the information technology products.

Information through promotional videos, Internet web Sites, television advertisements and travel documentaries are the main information dissemination tools. There is, in fact, competition amongst tour operation to create better and better sites for the user to enable the tourist to decide in their favour. More and more people around the Globe are getting computer literate or so to say computer savvy, due to which, they have increasingly become information seekers. Before deciding on the desired destination, they not only rely on the sites of tour operators or travel agents, they even take feedback from other travellers to find out about their experiences. In the Attraction Sector communication technologies are thus very significant.

INFORMATION CENTRES AND COMMUNICATION TECHNOLOGIES

Several information centres and tourist offices of Government of India are currently located at India and abroad. Overseas offices are located in Australia, Canada, France, Germany, Italy, Japan, Netherlands, Singapore, Spain, Sweden, UAE, U.K., U.S.A., New York, Israel, the Russian Federation and South Africa.

INFORMATION TECHNOLOGY AND GROWTH OF TOURISM WORLD OVER

It was in 1908 that the first move was made for promoting tourism by only three countries namely Spain, France and Portugal who founded the France Hispano Portuguese. Federation of Tourist Association is considered the first international tourist organization. After first the World War, several other countries realised the need as well, but due to lack of communication technologies, the endeavour could not take off inspite of setting up the International Union of National Tourist Propaganda Organization in 1925.

After the Second World War, this endeavour was revived from the year 1963. With the revolution in the Information Communication Technologies the world Tourism, as a joint effort gained momentum. It was in the 1980s that the Tourist did not feel lost or insecure due to lack of information. Interestingly, during the same period, India was perceived as a country, which was backward and inhabited with wildlife and natives because India lagged far behind in growth of communication technologies.

It was only the late 1980s due to the advent of computer technology in a big way and satellite network that India could change that perception among foreigners. India also saw tourism increasing due to changed perceptions, advertising, marketing and attracting the tourists using information technologies. Currently, tourist arrivals are predicted to grow by an average 4.3% a year over the next two decades, while receipts from international tourism will climb by 6.7% a year.

Tourism: Mega Trends for the 21st century:

- Globalization versus localization
- Electronic technology will become all-powerful in influencing destination choice and distribution
- Fast track travel–emphasis will be placed on facilitation and the speeding up of the travel process
- Customers 'call the shots' through technology such as CDROM atlases, internet, internet inspection of hotels and other facilities, brokers offering discounted rooms on websites, last minute e-mails, low fares etc.
- The tourist world shrinking by the day, due to technology, the tourist is nearly reaching 'space tourism'
- Growing impact of technologies, helping aggressive campaign is kindling the urge for travel consumption.

However, growth and related benefits of tourism cannot be taken for granted. The competition among countries, tour operators, destinations, etc. is becoming so fierce, that, in order to be a winner the following imperatives will have to be kept in mind by every country,

- Development focused on quality and responsibility
- Value for money
- Full utilization of information technology to identify and communicate effectively with market segments and niches.

TOURISM PROMOTION

Promotion means activities that communicate the merits of the product and persuade target customers to buy it. Ford spends about $2.3 billion each year on advertising to tell consumers about the company and its many products. The franchised dealers and salespeople assist potential buyers to buy a Ford car. Ford and its dealers offer promotions-sales, cash rebates and low financing rates as purchase incentives.

The promotion activities of marketing are concerned with communication with the customers that the product is available at the right price and at the right place. The promotional communication aims at informing and persuading the actual and potential customers into actual purchase of the product. An effective marketing programme moulds all the marketing mix elements–product, price, place and promotion to achieve the marketing objectives.

PROMOTIONAL OBJECTIVES

Effective promotion starts from an analysis and formulation of clear-cut objectives.

These include:

- Identification of the target audience to be reached;
- Identification of the purpose of the communication;
- Formulation of message to achieve the goal;
- Choice of media for delivering the message to the target audience;
- Allocation of the budget to achieve the desired purpose;
- Evaluation in terms of sales and feedback obtained from the customers.

The more carefully objectives are set the better promotion works.

Promotional planning can be done with a view:

- To create new ideas and attitudes: The purpose could be to create awareness of completely new tourism products such as Spa and Spirituality in Himalayas.
- To change the image: The purpose could be to change the unfavourable image of an existing tourism product in the minds of customers. For example New York, in late seventies changed the image of the city to promote tourism.
- To reinforce the image: Larger firms try to reinforce the attitude of customers to retain their existing market like visit to Disneyland and destinations like Goa, Uttaranchal and Singapore.

INTEGRATING COMMUNICATION PROCESS WITH PROMOTION PROGRAMMES

Every consumer goes through various stages of the decision-making process to arrive at a satisfactory decision.

The process of decision-making is a sequence of various steps:

- Need recognition
- Information search
- Evaluation of various alternatives
- Choice of product/services
- Post-purchase evaluation

The marketing communicator needs to effectively design the promotion programme in order to help the consumer in making a proper decision.

The good communication strategy should address target consumers needs and wants and help them to choose a particular tourism product. Steps in Developing Effective Market for Tourism Product The marketer needs to address various issues while designing the programme to effectively market the tourism product.

IDENTIFYING THE TARGET MARKET

A tourist organization needs to know their target market consisting of actual and potential customers. The target audience will determine the promotional campaign on what to say, how to say, when to say, where to say and who will say.

DETERMINING THE PROMOTIONAL OBJECTIVE

Once the target market has been identified, the marketer must decide about the purpose of promotional activity.

- *Awareness*: The target market may be totally unaware of the product. The communicator needs to make them aware and knowledgeable about the tourism product.
- *Preference*: If consumers know the product, they need to be made to feel favourably about the product and then moved to the stage of being convinced about preferring such a product to other products.
- *Purchase*: Some members of the target market might be convinced about the product, they need to be taken to the action stage of making an actual purchase of the product. Offering special promotional prices or rebates can persuade them.

DESIGNING A MESSAGE

It is an important step after deciding upon the promotional objective. The communicator needs to develop an effective message to decide what to say and how to say it. "Incredible India' campaign on television is aimed at capturing the attention of viewers about various tourist places all over the India.

CHOOSING THE MEDIA

The communicator must select between personal and non-personal channels of communication.

- Personal communication channels include face-to-face interaction, telephone or mail and are effective channels of influencing the customers of target market.
- Non-personal communication channels include media such as newspapers, magazines, radio, television, billboards, posters and

websites. They are a major source to influence, create and reinforce the image of a product among consumers.

FEEDBACK

After deciding and sending the message, the marketing communicator needs to obtain feedback on its promotional efforts.

They need to know about target consumers' attitudes towards the product and company. Such feedback facilitates changes in the promotion programme or in the product itself. For example, most of the Airlines and 5-star hotels ask consumers about their experience after the flight or stay in the hotel.

THE PROMOTIONAL MIX

After knowing about the main objectives of promotion, let us understand the four main elements of the promotional mix. A company's total marketing communication mix-also called its promotion mix-consists of the specific blend of advertising, sales promotion, public relations, and personal selling that the company uses to pursue its advertising and marketing objectives.

The four major promotional tools of promotion are as follows:

- *Advertising*: Any paid form of nonpersonal presentation and promotion of ideas, goods, or services by an identified sponsor.
- *Sales Promotion*: Short term incentives to encourage the purchase or sale of a product or service.
- *Public Relations*: Building a good reputation of the company with the public by obtaining favourable publicity, good corporate image, and handling unfavourable events if any.
- *Personal Selling*: The sales force of the company makes personal presentations to make sales.

ADVERTISING

Advertising has been defined as any non-personal presentation by an identified sponsor for the promotion of ideas, goods, or services in exchange for value. While in designing the advertising programme, the target audience and message requirements should be analysed carefully. Advertising in tourism has many uses.

They include:

- Creating awareness;
- Advertising a special offer;
- Providing information on seasonal deals;
- Informing about special services;
- Direct selling;
- Soliciting consumer information;

- Overcoming negative attitudes;
- Reaching a new target audience;
- Providing a new use.

DEVELOPMENT OF ADVERTISING PROGRAMMES

Marketing management must make four important decisions when developing an advertising programme:

- Setting advertising objectives
- Setting the advertising budget
- Selecting advertising Media
- Evaluating Advertising Campaigns

SETTING THE ADVERTISING BUDGET

In general, marketing of products can be done with a variety of media options available but certain particular features exist with relation to advertising of travel and tourism in media:

- Tourism has a large and highly fragmented advertising market, consisting of few big enterprises with huge advertising budgets and a large number of small firms with less to spend on advertising.
- Print is the dominant medium in travel and tourism advertising. The higher cost of advertising on TV has made press a more economical medium to reach the target audience.
- Much of the expenditure on travel and tourism is done on brochures, destination guides, and point-of-sales displays. Tourist Boards, tour operators, and tourist information centres provide large amounts of information through printed material to prospective customers.

These specific factors should be kept in mind while setting the advertising budget for a tourism product.

SELECTING ADVERTISING MEDIA

The media planner has to essentially choose the most economical combination of media channels to reach desired target audience. There are various factors to be considered while appraising the media options.

Some of the main factors in media selection are:

- Readership or audience size;
- Geographical reach;
- Repetition and frequency of advertisement;
- Segment target market size;
- Unit cost and cost per thousand;
- Seasonal/period discounts available;
- Availability of medium;
- Reproduction quality.

SOME ADVERTISING TECHNIQUES IN TOURISM MARKETING

The advertiser creates the message in such a manner that will capture the target market's attention and interest. In tourism marketing some techniques of message presentation have been extensively used by advertisers over the years such as following:

SLICE OF LIFE

This technique shows some characters using or discussing the product's uses/benefits. For example, husband and wife recalling their experiences to a particular destination and decide to visit the place again.

LIFESTYLE

This style shows how a particular product fits in with a particular lifestyle. For example, Uttaranchal Tourism prints advertisement exhorting adventurous people to come for river rafting in Rishikesh.

TESTIMONY

The method of selling the product is through the testimony of satisfied customers. A single person, a number of people or a famous celebrity can do it.

MUSICAL

This method shows one or more people singing about the product. For example, Broadway actors sang the song 'I Love New York' to encourage tourists to visit New York. The tourist organizations often use a combination of the techniques while promoting tourist product.

SALES PROMOTION

Sales promotion can be defined as: Those marketing activities other than personal selling and advertising and publicity that stimulate purchases such as exhibitions, shows, and demonstrations. In a way they refer to short–term incentives offered to the consumer to induce a booking, reservation or sale.

OBJECTIVES OF SALES PROMOTION

The sales Promotion in tourism is done with the following objectives:

- *Creating awareness*: Sometimes companies devise special promotions like two or more companies join or tie up together to build awareness. For example, an Airline and hotel group tie-up to promote a particular destination.
- *Encouraging early bookings*: Tour operators often offer discounts at the start of the season to generate immediate bookings. For example, Deccan Airways providing airline tickets at auction to Pune, Bombay or Goa if booked in advance.

- *Increase trial*: The tourists are encouraged to try the product by giving incentives like free stays or trial coupons at much discounted prices.
- *Enhanced repeat buy*: Some promotions are done to encourage repeat stays or visits. For example, Indian Airline offers of multi-coupon discounts to frequent flyers.
- *Combating competition*: Tour operators or hotels may cut down their prices to combat any price cut by competitors or may be done to block competitors' moves in advance.
- *Promote use of tourist product during off-season*: When demand is low for hotel rooms, during low season, special season offers are used to attract customers. For example, Goa hotels offer special discounts during the rainy season; Jaipur and Agra hotels offer discounts during the summer season.
- *Motivating sales force*: The travel agencies give commission to travel agents for selling a certain number of tickets. The agents are also provided coupons, free offers, sales aids and training materials.

TECHNIQUES OF TOURISM SALES PROMOTION

Some of the sales promotion activities used in travel and tourism are as follows:

- *Rebates*: The tourist product is made available at special price less than original price for a limited period of time.
- *Discounts*: Certain percentage of price is deducted as discount from the original price to induce them to buy or buy more. For example, hotel stay for two children at discounted price for a particular package.
- *Refunds*: The seller offers to refund a part of the price paid by the customer on previous purchase of the product.
- *Contests*: These are another form of promotion. In these consumers are required to participate in some competitive event involving application of skills and winners are given some reward.
- *Quantity deals*: The tourist operator provides special package in which buyer is offered additional product at lower or no price. For example, a tourist operator coming out with the offer in family package 'two children for the price of one'.

  Some other techniques of sales promotion are:
  - Vouchers,
  - Competitions,
  - Prizes,
  - Gifts and premium,
  - Additional night stay,
  - Slide shows,
  - Point of purchase displays, and
  - Posters.

9

Selling Adventure Tourism

The central governments of nation states together with the global multilateral institutions are the last of the key players in this analysis of tourism. It is governments that have a pivotal role and possess the potential power to control, plan and direct the growth and development of tourism. And it is largely through governments that tourism-related international investments and loans and overseas aid is agreed and channelled. As such, it is widely agreed that for tourism to assist in development, a favourable national policy environment is required.

It has already been argued that tourism has come to represent a considerable attraction to many Third World governments. It has been widely promoted both within the Third World and by First World 'experts' as a means of economic diversification and an important mechanism in producing foreign exchange. There can be little surprise that in Third World countries characterised by indebtedness and by primary industries (such as agriculture and mining) adversely affected by world market prices, tourism has come to represent something of a panacea.

In this chapter we take global governance as a further way of exploring the politics of Third World tourism development. By governance, we mean the web of institutions and agencies that are central players in the political environment, and the focus of our discussion is on national governments, bilateral development agencies and the supranational institutions (such as the World Bank, IMF and United Nations). As already argued, the consideration of politics has been a poor partner in tourism analysis. The assessment of government activity has tended to focus on strategies, policies and programmes of national-level planning. While such analysis is an essential part of assessing the approaches of Third World governments to tourism, it tends to minimise broader consideration of the inherently political nature of tourism development.

In other words, the pressures that governments face from external influences such as lending policies, First World foreign policy or the activities of international NGOs tend to be bypassed; similarly internal forces may also be overlooked. In short, the politics of tourism is another way of exploring unequal and uneven development. In the first half of this chapter, politics is established as a critical factor in Third World tourism analysis. Most importantly, the need to acknowledge that tourism is not a neutral factor that can be assessed as just another government economic activity is established. Tourism is used for a variety of political purposes and there is a wide range of external influences.

The structural adjusment policies of supranational institutions such as the World Bank and IMF, for instance, are considered along with the policies promoted by the World Trade Organisation (WTO/OMC), World Tourism Organisation (WTO/OMT) and the World Travel and Tourism Council. This provides the opportunity to reflect on the political globalisation outlined and in particular to consider the nature of sustainability promoted by such institutions.

The second half of the chapter uses a number of case studies to illustrate the development of new forms of tourism and the ways in which these are intimately related to sustainability. In particular, we analyse sustainability and sustainable tourism as part of a political discourse. Throughout this chapter, the ways in which politics is reflected through the power jigsaw are considered.

THE POLITICS OF TOURISM

We are constantly reminded by the media of the hazards of travel in the Third World and by implication the critical nature of the politics of tourism. At its most dramatic are the newsworthy events, the killing or kidnapping of western tourists often by political factions eager to further their causes. For these factions, tourism becomes a means to an end: access to the system of global communication.

To First World populations, such events provide a succession of countries - Algeria, Cambodia, Colombia, Egypt, Indonesia, India, Morocco, Peru - which, we are told, are plagued by fundamentalist groupings and where terrorism is rife. The most dramatic of these events was the September 11, 2001 terrorist attacks on the USA.

This event clearly had an immediate impact on the perception of travel security of First World tourists. The international airline and hotel industries were hit hard with the bankruptcies of airline companies of significant size and hotels all over the world reporting dramatic falls in visitors and revenue in September, October and November 2001 over the same period a year before. Lay-offs of workers involved in the tourism industry became commonplace in these same months.

Although this was an incomparable event, evidence from another traumatic event suggests that the effects on international tourism may not be long-lasting. In November 1997, 58 foreign tourists were killed by terrorists at the Temple of Hatshapsut at Luxor in Egypt. Tourism to this part of Egypt, and to most of the rest of the country, dried up overnight.

The livelihoods of a majority of the population of the town of Luxor came to an abrupt end.

The effect was also generalised to some extent to other countries in the Middle East. In 1998, international tourist arrivals to Egypt fell by 14 per cent, and tourism receipts by 45 per cent. However, by 1999 international tourist arrivals were back to a level that might have been expected had the yearly rate of increase up to 1997 continued without the terrorist interruption. It is by no means certain that international tourism after September 11, 2001 will recover as rapidly and as thoroughly as it did in Egypt after the 1997 Luxor killings.

But ten months after the attack on the USA, signs of recovery in international flight bookings were already apparent and it seemed appropriate to conclude that perceptions of danger can change very quickly. Then in October 2002, the bombing in Bali occurred and once again it became easier to see the short-term effects of the politics of tourism than to analyse the long-term impacts of such events.

Western government presentations of supposedly dangerous countries have been one of the principal ways in which our geographical imaginations are filled out, and show how tourists and the tourism industry decide where, and where not, to visit and invest; for example, it was suggested that 'dangerous' regions may actually act as a bonus for some adventurous 'new tourists'. As Richter (1994) demonstrates, the USA has dozens of countries for which *DON'T GO* warnings are provided, of which over 80 per cent are in the Third World. But such warnings, Richter continues, appear to be based as much on ideological reasons as on potential security risks to US tourists. Countries to which the USA is more kindly disposed, such as Israel, Brazil, Mexico and Egypt, appear to require much higher levels of danger to tourists before travel advisories are made against them.

For example, up to 1994, although tourists had been signalled as potential targets for attack by Islamic groups in Egypt, this large-scale receiver of US foreign aid had not been mentioned in State Department advisories. Similarly, despite the seeds of a civil war in southern Mexico, this country too has escaped travel advisories: a reflection, some would argue, of Mexico's 'integration' into NAFTA.

At the other extreme, countries to which the USA considers itself ideologically opposed, such as Cuba and North Korea, remain off-limits to US tourists. The notion that *tourism is politics* is forcefully expressed by Conrad Hilton (of Hilton Hotels), who is reported as saying 'each of our hotels is a little America' and 'we are doing our bit to spread world peace, and to fight socialism'. Conversely, tourism is used by some Third World governments to gloss over glaring social inequalities and in some cases, as discussed later in this chapter, the systematic abuse of human rights.

Of course, for many Third World countries, political stability is one of the principal keys to securing steady stream of First World tourists. The case of The Gambia shows how profoundly political instability, or just the First World's judgement of such instability, can affect a country's tourism fortunes.

The Gambia experienced a period of economic restructuring with two major IMF-instructed economic reform programmes (1985 Economic Reform Programme and the 1990 Programme for Sustained Development) which attempted to diversify the economy. As Thompson *et al.* report, 'Both programmes emphasise the important role played by tourism in the development process'. Tourism made a substantial contribution to the Gambian economy, estimated to be 12 per cent of GDP by the end of the 1980s and became the principal source of foreign exchange.

In 1994, Captain Yahyah Jammeh seized power in a *coup d'état* and established the Armed Forces Provisional Ruling Council (AFPRC). A failed counter-coup in November 1994 resulted in the British Foreign Office issuing travel advice not to visit The Gambia.

As a result of this advice, air charter arrivals (December to March, the peak of high season) dropped from 45,733 in 1993/4 to 8,363 in 1994/5. There was an estimated 60 per cent reduction in the contribution of restaurants and hotels to the GDP and an estimated direct job loss of around 10,000. The indirect or knock-on effects are estimated at least double this impact. Overall, tourism contracted by 60 per cent and the economy shrank by 6.2 per cent. The Gambian tourism industry all but collapsed. Despite the lifting of the formal travel advice for the 1995/6 season, the Economist Intelligence Unit identified what appeared to be further pressure applied by the British Foreign Office: 'the UK appears determined to maintain pressure for an early return to full democracy and civil freedoms, and this position is likely to influence other trading and aid partners' (Economist Intelligence Unit, 1995:17). 'Tourism, accounting for around 12 per cent of GDP, has yet to pick up after the most recent season, ruined by European governments' advice to their nationals to stay away'. Teye has argued that the perception of political instability arising from the liberation wars and frequency of *coups d'état* after decolonisation in sub-Saharan Africa has seriously stunted tourism development in some states. The perception of political instability is not the only likely deterrent to new tourists. After Hurricane Mitch hit Honduras, Nicaragua and El Salvador in October 1998, the tourist money on which many Central Americans depended dried up.

In Honduras the effects were so dramatic that in spring 1989 the Honduran Institute of Tourism, in concert with a number of US tour operators and tourism service providers on the country's Caribbean coast, promoted a type of 'disaster tourism', attempting to attract wealthy North Americans to witness the devastation caused by the natural disaster and to assist in the recovery programme.

Clearly, then, it is not only the actual occurrence of political and civil instability that is of critical importance, but rather the way that it is perceived, constructed and represented in the First World.

These are perhaps dramatic examples, but they help to emphasise the inherently political nature of tourism development and the way in which power is transmitted through tourism. Countries promoting tourism (both mass and new) can be influenced by a range of factors, from the decisions of First World institutions and tourists, to the way in which particular Third World destinations are perceived in the First World. Consequently, Third World governments are also eager to control the way in which their tourism image is projected. We must therefore ask whether the messages we receive reflect truly what is happening in reality.

ASSESSING THE POLITICS OF TOURISM

Although the size and scale of the global tourist industry would seem to suggest that tourism is a hot political issue, so far we have argued that the politics of tourism has remained relatively underexplored. In terms of assessing the activities of Third World governments, the majority of analyses have been policy studies focusing upon national tourism policies, including both individual case studies and comparative policy analyses between countries.

A good deal of this work is also focused upon the identification of relevant and appropriate methodologies for planning and implementing tourism policy. Clearly such discussion is of interest and use, and has a wide appeal to practitioners.

Its weaknesses, however, lie in both its often prescriptive nature and its formulation from within the First World and, in many cases, the failure to set policy and action in a broader and more critical framework which acknowledges that there are competing interests. It was argued that the political economy approach is one of the few attempts to illustrate the way in which control of tourism development is held firmly in the First World.

As Britton argues: 'The World Tourism Organisation, International Monetary Fund, United Nations, World Bank and UNESCO, among others, set the parameters of tourism planning, promotion, identification of tourism products, investment and infrastructure construction policies often in conjunction with metropolitan tourism companies'.

Of course, it is not just external influences that affect tourism policy and development, but internal factors as well. This includes the conflicts between governmental and non-governmental interests, and conflicting interests and priorities within governments themselves. The latter are particularly prevalent where responsibilities over tourism resources overlap more than one government department. In Uganda, for example, there are three separate government departments with responsibilities for national parks, the focus of Uganda's tourism. A similar problem of different outlooks adopted towards its national parks by different government departments in Guatemala. Clearly, it is necessary to avoid the crude suggestion that government policy and action is an undifferentiated whole.

A non-critical approach also tends to assume that there are rational policy decisions that will lead to the surmounting of potential problems. As Hall and Jenkins argue, while 'rationality' represents an influential approach to policy analysis, it is also 'extremely misleading as it fails to recognise the inherently political nature of public policy'.

Take, for example, the approach of Edward Inskeep, a tourism planner who has worked with the WTO/OMT, World Bank and UNDP in many Third World countries: '[the] planning of tourism is necessary not only for scientific purposes and to conserve the environment for the benefit of residents, but also for the protection of long-term investments in tourism infrastructure, attractions, facilities, services, and marketing programs'.

What is important here is to question who benefits from planning and policy formulation and who controls these decision-making processes. If anything the 'benefit to residents' is a poor partner of the need to protect 'long-term investments', but the latter is couched in terms of conserving the environment for local people.

The suspicion that environmental conservation is not really about a concern for local people is confirmed: 'Increasingly, tourists are demanding that their environments be high-quality and pollution-free as well as inherently interesting, and some tourists will change travel patterns if environmental quality expectations are not met'. The results and effects of the Tourism Master Plan for Bali, outlined in one of the case studies given later in this chapter, are also interesting to note in this regard.

Ultimately then, we must ask who controls government policy and planning and what forces drive the processes of its formulation and implementation. Sustainability is a critical consideration here, for Agenda 21 designates national governments as having the lead responsibility for the process.

The overall aim of developing a sustainable tourism programme has been set out by the WTTC, which defines Agenda 21 as the process 'to establish systems and procedures to incorporate sustainable development considerations at the core of the decision-making process and to identify actions necessary to bring sustainable tourism development into being'. We must also ask in whose interests such actions are undertaken and explore how the uneven and unequal nature of development is reflected through this.

The notion of 'interests' is a useful one in focusing attention on which groups, organisations and institutions have influence and power in decision-making. Such influences can vary from the structural adjustment policies of the World Bank and IMF to the campaigns against visiting certain countries.

The differences between the two were technically due, in the main, to INGUAT's inclusion of all the areas whose status as a protected area was only proposed rather than actual. But these differences also reflect the roles and outlooks of the two departments. INGUAT is in the business of enhancing the country's image, of making it look attractive to potential visitors; so it covered as much of the national area as possible with the status of a protected area, with the greenwash of pristine natural areas. CONAP, on the other hand, is more realistic; it was aware that it did not have the resources necessary to oversee those areas which were already designated as protected, still less all those which were proposed.

The infringement of human rights within that country. Our discussion of The Gambia helps to identify different ways in which power is expressed through political processes. It is illustrative of the typical problems faced by Third World countries in their efforts to develop tourism. In this case, the expansion of the sector has been encouraged by the internationally inspired structural reform programmes which have clearly pushed The Gambia along a particular development path. But First World countries also retain the potential to control the tourism industry (especially when much of the industry caters for mass packaged charters, as in this case).

Showed how political economy critiques have revealed the shortcomings of Third World tourism and how tourism is an additional element in uneven and unequal development. However, this has not prevented countries which pursue socialist strategies and ideologies from dabbling in tourism, and in some cases arguing for forms of tourism that are not subordinating and are responsive to the issues of power and control exercised by the First World so heavily criticised in the political economy framework.

As Crick (1989) argues, in some countries this has resulted in seemingly glaring contradictions to the anti-colonial ideologies adopted by newly independent countries. Indeed, some critics suggest that tourism may help to maintain systems of neo-colonial power and control.

Tanzania is a frequently cited example where an emphasis on tourism development in the 1970s ran contrary to the anti-colonial socialism adopted by Nyerere in the wake of independence and the policy of self-reliance pursued by the government.

The Tanzanian intellectual, Shivji, was critical of the separation of politics from economics: 'The justification for tourism in terms of it being "economically good" though it may have adverse social, cultural and political effects, completely fails to appreciate the integrated nature of the system of underdevelopment'.

Other independent countries pursuing socialist ideals have also explored the development of tourism. In Cuba, for example, as much effort has been put into widening the appeal of Cuba as radical chic, with solidarity and study tours, as has been devoted to stemming the foreign exchange leakage characteristic of other destinations in the region. In order to reduce the leakage of foreign exchange, Cuba has established a tourism industry that seeks, if uneasily, to separate tourism spending from the national economy, and forces tourists to buy goods and services in foreign currency (mainly US dollars).

Following a successful *coup d'état* in 1979 in Grenada, a regional neighbour of Cuba, Maurice Bishop, head of the People's Revolutionary Government (PRG), acknowledged the shortcomings of mass tourism as it existed in the Caribbean and started to identify the basis of an alternative type of tourism. Outlining the parallels of tourism with colonialism which we discussed earlier, the socialist Prime Minister argued:

In the early days and even now, most tourists are white. This clear association of 'whiteness' and 'privilege' is a major problem for Caribbean people just emerging out of a racist colonial history where we had been so carefully taught the superiority of things white and inferiority of things black.

Bishop elaborated his ideas further at a Caribbean regional conference on the impact of tourism, where he identified the need to replace 'old tourism' with what he termed 'new tourism'. Along with Jamaica under the socialist leadership of Prime Minister Michael Manley, Bishop attempted to chart the development of a tourism designed to escape the problems that had been associated with 'old' tourism, bound up with 'colonial and imperialist connotations'.

It was foreign-owned and controlled, unrelated to the needs and development of the Caribbean people, and it brought with it a number of distinct socio-cultural and environmental hazards such as the race question and undesirable social and economic patterns such as drug abuse and prostitution.

Bishop's vision was for a 'new' tourism to escape these characteristics. It was to involve all people (as both 'guests' and tourists); it would seek to create linkages between the different sectors of the economy; and above all it was conceived as a tool for development.

However, the construction of Grenada's airport, a key part of the country's attempt to attract tourism, encapsulates and symbolises the political nature of tourism development. Bishop was murdered in October 1983 and with him died this vision of new tourism. Of course, it is questionable whether such a vision was realisable given the context of uneven and unequal development in which Third World tourism operates.

A rather different aspect of the inherently political nature of tourism is the way in which the USA sought to destabilize both Grenada and Jamaica, under Bishop and Manley respectively, through negative publicity and foreign policy statements that were hostile to both countries (Thomas, 1988).

In the case of Grenada this is particularly poignant. Grenada quickly gained an extraordinary international reputation, with Fidel Castro assessing that in conjunction with Nicaragua and Cuba they were representative of 'three giants rising to defend their rights to independence, sovereignty and justice on the very threshold of imperialism' (Clark, 1983, quoted in Thomas, 1988).

As Thomas concludes from the radical agendas pursued in these countries and the reworking of tourism that they advocated, 'they confirmed that any attempt at radical social reorganisation in the region would be met by insistent efforts on the part of the US to destabilise the process (or worse), especially if the proposed reorganisation involved new options for foreign policy and external relations' (1988:246).

The absence of an international airport was a clear weakness in Grenada's tourism plans and a brake on its development, a shortcoming that Bishop readily acknowledged in describing the airport as 'the gateway to our future' (Marcus and Taber, 1983). The majority of capital (US$60 million) and technical assistance for the airport's construction came from Grenada's ideological neighbour, Cuba.

President Reagan, however, claimed that the construction involved a new naval base, a new air base, storage bases and barracks for troops, and training grounds. 'And, of course, one can believe that they are all there to export nutmeg ... It is not nutmeg that is at stake in Central America and the Caribbean, it is the United States' national security' (President Reagan, March 1983, quoted in Ferguson, 1990).

As Ferguson points out, despite the US development agency's (USAID) hostility to the People's Revolutionary Government policies and projects, it was deeply ironic that USAID were financing and administering the completion of the international airport, especially given the initial announcement that the USA had no plans to assist a project that was never intended to promote the development of Grenada's tourism.

After the murder of Bishop and the US invasion of the island, post-revolutionary Grenada provided US technocrats an opportunity for a structurally adjusted blueprint - a 'USAID inspired restructuring and free market deregulation'. Grenada was subsequently a laboratory and showcase of US ideological superiority.

Much USAID/NNP [New National Party] policy and finance was targeted on environmental and infrastructural improvements designed to attract foreign investment and tourism. As Pattullo (1996) states of Grenada, 'mass tourism became entrenched by the 1980s'. Indeed tourism has been one of the principal factors in the US-approved development strategy for the Caribbean. In many other places too, tourism is alluded to as a peace industry, and a way of allowing the expansion of capitalist economies in a stable and peaceful environment. 'The overwhelming majority of USAID funds have ... gone towards dismantling the state sector, encouraging private enterprise and wooing foreign capital - with negligible success'. As Ferguson argues, the failure of the model is all the more significant given the symbolic importance placed on Grenada's development by the US government.

SUPRANATIONAL INSTITUTIONS

Supranational institutions involve a degree of political integration between states but are not subject to the laws of national governments. Such organisations operate in a global sphere of activity and are able to influence, and in some cases determine, economic and political activities in the national sphere.

Supranational organisations exist in many fields of activity. Those described as socio-environmental organisations were discussed. While these may in certain instances influence the policies pursued by national governments, this section deals with those organisations dedicated to direct and deliberate involvement in the formulation of

The International Bank of Reconstruction and Development (the World Bank) and IMF were born at the Bretton Woods conference in the USA in 1944. Their purpose was to provide an order to the global economy to prevent the collapse of international trade and the development of isolationist economic policies, which it was believed had led to the Depression of the 1930s and the rise of fascism. The conference rejected the proposals of John Maynard Keynes to establish a world reserve currency administered by a central bank. Instead, it 'opted for a system based on the free movement of capital and goods with the US dollar as the international currency'.

Initially, a more specific purpose was to provide funds to assist in the rebuilding of war-torn Europe. The European countries objected to the severe loan conditions, so the World Bank worked through the Marshall Plan which provided US finance to re-build Europe mainly through grants rather than loans. Third World countries did not receive the same treatment.

Instead, they were pressured to keep their economies completely open to foreign goods and capital; and in exchange for financial assistance, countries were expected to adopt structural adjustment policies.

Partly as a result of the debt crisis of the 1970s and 1980s, both institutions now exercise enormous leverage over the policies pursued by most governments which require financial assistance. 'That influence is enhanced by donor insistence upon an IMF and World Bank seal of approval as a condition for aid and debt relief' (Oxfam, 1995:8).

As Duncan Green points out, the two organisations are not democratically run: 'decisions at the IMF and World Bank are taken on the basis of "one dollar, one vote", guaranteeing the dominance of both by the US government' (1995:34). In 1995, for instance, the USA had 17.18 per cent of the total vote at the World Bank while the total vote for 23 of the poorest African countries together amounted to 1.58 per cent of the total.

The three most powerful and dominant of these are the International Bank for Reconstruction and Development (known as the World Bank), the IMF and the World Trade Organisation (WTO/OMC), although regional finance and development organisations, such as the European Bank for Reconstruction and Development (EBRD), the Inter-American Development Bank (IDB), USAID and increasingly other bilateral aid programmes also wield very considerable power over the policies pursued by Third World countries. Given the significance of the World Bank and IMF, a brief background to their formation and role is given.

The economic system promoted by these institutions is based on the free movement of capital and goods with the US dollar as the international currency. In such a system, tourism can be seen as much the same as any other cash crop, and pressure exerted by the development banks upon the government of a country to increase its export earnings by boosting production of export crops is as applicable to tourism as it is to sugar, coffee, cotton, bauxite, or other products. Foreign exchange earnings can be boosted by attracting more international tourists and the foreign exchange which they bring with them.

The debt crisis of the 1980s and the First World's reaction to it increased the power of the IMF and the World Bank. Spurred on by the prevailing ideology of President Reagan and Prime Minister Thatcher, the two institutions of the World Bank and IMF embarked on a mission to structurally adjust Third World economies so that they could meet debt obligations and fall into line with the right-wing economic orthodoxy sweeping the globe.

The origins of the debt crisis can be traced back to the huge profit made by members of the Organisation of Petroleum Exporting Countries (OPEC) in the early 1970s. These profits were surplus to requirements within the OPEC countries and much of the money was therefore banked and invested in the commercial banks of the First World. Awash with petro-dollars, the banks sought to make the most profitable use of this money.

One of the ways in which they recycled it was by financing development projects in Third World countries, including tourist resort schemes.

In the rush for 'development', many of the projects financed were ill-considered and poorly planned. Some of the money was spirited away by Third World elites with access to power brokers and decision-makers, and more was paid direct to First World companies taking part in the projects. A proportion of it therefore found its way back into the same First World banks that lent it in the first place.

In the late 1970s and the first half of the 1980s, interest rates on these loans rose sharply, an event that had not been anticipated by the lenders or borrowers in the early 1970s. Many borrowing countries found themselves unable to pay back even the interest on the loans, quite apart from the principal loan itself. First World bankers and politicians became concerned 'that the sheer volume of unpayable loans would undermine the world financial system.

They turned to the World Bank and the IMF, who were to restructure Third World economies so they could meet their debt obligations' (*New Internationalist*, 1994:15); hence, the rise of structural adjustment programmes (SAPs), which since 2000 have become known as poverty reduction strategy papers (PRSPs), and which are produced by national governments themselves.

It should be pointed out, however, that they are produced with substantial input from IMF and World Bank officials and the two organisations retain the power of veto over PRSPs. Critics such as the World Development

Movement believe that PRSPs are merely SAPs containing language about poverty reduction.

From the point of view of our analysis, what is crucial here is that SAPs/PRSPs imposed by the IMF and World Bank on Third World governments effectively force those governments to pursue specific policies not of their own design, although it was precisely in anticipation of such criticism that their means of production and title were changed.

These policies make living conditions for the population harsher and more difficult while supposedly enabling the government to increase its foreign exchange earnings and thereby pay off its debt. The kind of policies associated with SAPs/PRSPs is listed.

It is worth noting, however, that most Third World countries already had little effective control over the direction of their policies before the debt crisis began. Colonial powers of the First World and transnational corporations (TNCs) dictated the main thrust of economic policy throughout the Third World.

The IMF, World Bank and other supranational lending agencies along with the TNCs took over the mechanism of power from the former colonial powers. Moreover, proponents of SAPs/PRSPs point out that once the debt had become a reality, there were no policies other than those given which could realistically be imposed to support global capital accumulation.

The loans which form part of the SAPs/PRSPs are made only on strict condition that the national economy is restructured according to these policies. And this conditionality has meant that the economic and fiscal policies of most African and Latin American countries are now dictated from Washington. In the words of Green:

In the aftermath of the debt crisis, the IMF and later World Bank's use of conditionality allowed the powerful industrialised nations to revamp one Third World

Policies and conditions associated with SAPs/PRSPs

A Increase earnings of foreign capital

- *Boost export production* One implication of this is that the production of goods for local and national needs is relegated in importance as a result of the drive for export production. Tourism is seen as an export product, attracting foreign currency into the country. Many Third World countries which used to be self-sufficient in foodstuffs now have to import basic grains and other foodstuffs. In 1996, for instance, Honduras began to import beans for the first time in its history.
- *Devalue the national currency* Devaluation makes the country more attractive to foreign investors seeking a cheap place to produce their goods. The cheapness of its currency against other currencies also increases its attraction to foreign tourists.

- *Reduce and/or abolish import tariffs* Import tariffs are designed to protect the price of the production of goods for home consumption against the entry of cheaper imported goods. In practice, removing them can have the effect of flooding the country with expensive luxury goods and durables with high value added in production from the First World - for purchase by tourists and the rich elite.

B Reduce state involvement in the economy

- *Privatise state-run enterprises* Tourism is a flagship of the private sector.
- *Cut public spending on activities which cannot be privatised* For example, social services, health provision, education - although increasingly attempts are being made to privatise these services too.
- *Deregulation* Reduction of all forms of controls, especially economic regulations, which inhibit industry's ability to maximise profits.

C Fiscal measures

- *Reduce inflation* This increases security of investment, including investments in tourist developments.
- *Cut interest rates* This increases investment, including investment in the tourism industry.
- *Encourage investment rather than saving* economy after another along free-market lines. Critics believe that in the process, the IMF has systematically put the powerful nations' self-interest before the welfare of the Third World poor.

The initial hope that SAPs/PRSPs may be successful in delivering widespread prosperity through highly dubious mechanisms such as the 'trickle-down' effect and belief in the benefits of economic globalisation is confounded somewhat by the evidence. As Ayesha Imam states:

In most countries in Africa, SAPs have not led to increases in production or investment ... In fact, according to the UN Economic Commission for Africa, production has decreased over the decade since SAPs have been implemented. Investment as a proportion of GDP has fallen too.

Budget deficits have grown and a greater proportion of export-earned money is now used solely to service debts ... The general standard of living has fallen. There have been painfully deep cuts in the provision of health, education and other social services and in the subsidies on basic necessities.

In 2001, the UNDP's *Human Development Report* showed that in terms of control of total world income, the ratio between the richest 20 per cent to that of the poorest 20 per cent had increased from 34 to 1 in 1970 to 70 to 1 in 1997 (UNDP, 2001:16); in other words, in 1997 the richest 20 per cent of the world's population received an income 70 times greater than the poorest 20 per cent, which represents a widening of the gap since 1970.

Even within the World Bank, there is awareness of the effects of these policies. Herman Daly, a renowned and respected economist in the Bank's

Environment Department, has identified some major conflicts between the ultimate goal of international free trade, at which the Bank's policies aim, and national policies pursued in the national interest (1993:124).

Joseph Stiglitz, a Nobel laureate in Economics and former chief economist at the World Bank, has suggested that 'the IMF was run by hard line "market bolsheviks"' (World Development Movement, 2000:6), and that:

The 'invisible hand' of the market is just nonsense. The liberalisation of capital markets has produced more instability but no more economic growth. We knew this fine, economic science did not recommend such a step, but the IMF has gone on promoting it ... the IMF's policies have little or nothing to do with concern for the poor.

In the world of tourism, as in many other industries, this process of structural adjustment effectively delivers control of development to the TNCs and consultancies, most of which are based in the First World.

This relegates the role of the national government to one of providing the necessary infrastructure. For this, it must seek more loans, leaving it yet more indebted than before. Some countries, such as Honduras and Panama for example, are now even offering free trade zones for tourism companies wishing to build and operate resorts. Gonsalves concludes that 'the economies of the so-called Third World are in effect mere extensions of the economic priorities of the First World' (1995:39).

The list of development disasters caused by these supranational organisations in funding such schemes as large-scale dams, roads through sensitive eco-systems, monocultivation practices, infrastructural developments for the promotion of tourism, and many others, is long and well documented. And they have not just been confined to the IMF and World Bank.

During the 1980s, the USAID also gained notoriety for its arrogant and callous disregard for the environments and people affected by its development projects. Organisations such as World Bank Watch, Survival International, the World Development Movement (WDM), FOEI and others have documented these effects, exerted heavy pressure against them, and publicised the events and examples to such an extent that the start of the 1990s saw a growing recognition by the supranational organisations themselves of the effects of their policies.

Both the IMF and World Bank increased their staff who examine the social and environmental impacts of their programmes. The USAID also made strong efforts to green its image and to promote, for instance, community-based tourism schemes rather than grandiose resort projects. A tourism-related example of the mis-direction and failure of their efforts was given on pp. 226-8.

That these efforts to foster a new environmentally friendly image for themselves have failed should come as no surprise, given that their *modus operandi* of forcing national governments to pursue a dictated development path has remained unchanged.

In the wake of the protests at the Seattle trade talks in 1999, arguably the gathering momentum of a global social movement has prompted further attempts at image improvement by the supranational organisations such as the metamorphosis of the structural adjustment programmes into poverty reduction strategies.

With this increasing awareness of the need to demonstrate that they are changing, even if they are not doing so in reality, the IMF and World Bank have acknowledged the role of NGOs and have made attempts to enlist their advice. Despite this, Pierre Galand, Oxfam-Belgium's general secretary, resigned from the NGO working group on the World Bank and its Steering Committee. In his letter of resignation he said to the World Bank:

You have stolen speeches from NGOs concerned with development, eco-development, poverty and popular participation ... The Bank has learned to do excellent analyses and is capable of saying what is important: popular participation - particularly of women - the popular struggle against poverty, and the necessity to protect the environment ... Why are so many beautiful speeches accompanied by such scandalous practices?

More recently, in 2000, Ravi Kanbur, lead author of the World Bank's *World Development Report 2000/2001* (World Bank, 2000), resigned in protest at the Bank's decision to expunge criticism of globalisation from his work (WDM, 2000:6).

In 1995, the Uruguay Round of the GATT gave birth to the World Trade Organisation (WTO/OMC), essentially set up to continue and further the process of international trade liberalisation. The organisation establishes international agreements on rules of trade that are binding on parties to the agreements and it adjudicates in trade-related disputes between member states and between a member state and the rules. It has powers to impose sanctions on member states which break its rules.

To support her claim that WTO/OMC is leading us into an era of 'corporate-led, corporate-driven globalisation' (George in Bircham and Charlton, 2001:14), Susan George cites David Hartridge, director of WTO/OMC Services Division as stating that: 'without the enormous pressure generated by the American financial services sector, ... there would have been no services agreement and therefore perhaps no Uruguay Round and no WTO' (2001:14).

Brookes and Harrison also refer to the WTO/OMC as 'heavily influenced by the interests of big business' (2000:32), and expose the large number of powerful industry associations which influence the WTO/OMC through their positions on consultative committees.

That the WTO/OMC is driven by the corporate lobby is rarely denied, but its proponents point to the need for agreed sets of rules to govern international trade, the need for a body to manage and adjudicate on such rules, and to the fact that: 'The WTO's consensus decision-making means that in theory even the smallest country can hold up a trade deal if it doesn't like what is on the table' (Denny, 2002b: 14).

On the other hand, the perception that the WTO/OMC works solely in the interests of corporations and their profits is the driving force behind the rapid growth and conspicuousness of the anti-globalisation movement. Essentially their arguments are that the WTO/OMC ignores the needs of the poor, the environment and the rights of workers and consumers, and 'locks countries into a system of rules that means it is effectively impossible for governments to change policy, or for voters to elect a new government that has different policies' (Coates in Bircham and Charlton, 2001:28).

The WTO/OMC affects the activities associated with tourism through the GATS. Service industries, of which tourism is a part, now make up the greater part of the world's economic activity and the GATS negotiations would give major new rights to TNCs and reduce the power of national governments to restrict their activities for reasons of environmental protection, labour rights, planning regulations, or similar considerations. It is to the GATS and its effects on tourism that we now turn.

TOURISM AND THE GENERAL AGREEMENT ON TRADE IN SERVICES (GATS)

The GATS is one of several trade agreements administered and controlled by the WTO/OMC. The principal motive for the recent round of economic globalisation, of which GATS is the newest agreement, is arguably to ensure the continued expansion of markets for goods and services produced in and provided from the industrialised nations.

In theory, the WTO/OMC works on a consensus principle to create a rules-based system for the conduct of multilateral trade, and GATS works on the same principle for the same aim. Under the agreement, any signatory country has to accord the same treatment to foreign companies as it does to domestic companies in specified sectors of trade to which they have committed themselves. As Kalisch explains, it

> is designed to ensure that host governments, confronted with powerful transnational corporations who import both their own staff and the majority of goods needed for their tourism operation, cannot compel them to use local materials and products to enhance the 'multiplier effect', or to take special measures to secure a competitive base for their domestic businesses.

The GATS defines import tariffs, subsidies and other measures designed to assist domestic companies as 'trade-restrictive', and thereby effectively undermine the power of governments to legislate in the national interest. In practice, according to a report by the WDM, one of the major UK critics of GATS: 'WTO staff and negotiators openly acknowledge that GATS exists only because of pressure from service multinationals and that this influence has continued since GATS came into effect'. Moreover, the European Commission's website describes GATS as 'not just something that exists between governments. It is first and foremost an instrument for the benefit of business'.

The mechanism of reaching agreement by consensus appears to be given as a major justification for the GATS. But whether a genuine consensus was achieved at the Doha Ministerial meeting in Qatar in November 2001, called to discuss GATS, or at previous similar meetings, is highly debatable: for instance, the 481 delegates from the G7 nations present at the Doha meeting was almost double the 276 delegates from the 39 Least Developed countries, and it is difficult if not impossible to achieve consensus agreement in such unbalanced circumstances.

Indeed, the WDM also reports that widespread pressure is exerted by industrialised countries on Third World country negotiators, including suggestions that aid would be withdrawn. In general, the GATS appears to reflect and reinforce rather than challenge the existing unevenness and inequality in the global economic system.

In GATS, tourism falls into the sector labelled *Tourism and Travel-Related Services* which has four categories: hotels and restaurants; travel agencies and tour operator services; tourist guide services; other (unspecified). Kalisch points out that under GATS:

it would be impossible for a government to impose on foreign companies practices to limit negative environmental, social and cultural impacts in their country, such as restricting the mushrooming of foreign owned development, (including all-inclusive hotel developments, which are highly controversial among local people because they contribute almost nothing to the local economy), and making the employment of local workers, the use of local products and materials a condition of their investment. It could also render a government powerless to stop tourism developments on indigenous land, including sacred sites, in response to community protests.

Kalisch's analysis also suggests that GATS is likely to place fair trade in tourism at a disadvantage since 'the beneficiaries of Fair Trade in Tourism are poor communities, for whom the informal sector (vendors, traders, guides) is an important source of income, as well as small entrepreneurs and workers employed in the tourism industry'.

Representing the UK NGO Tourism Concern, Kalisch (2001) identifies the following concerns about the role that GATS is likely to play in the emerging tourism industries in Third World countries: the manner in which GATS negotiations are carried out in the WTO/OMC disadvantages and marginalises Third World countries and civil society organisations; GATS fails to integrate sustainable development as identified in major international treaties and agreements, such as the Convention on Biological Diversity which includes decisions on tourism; GATS does not address the specific environmental, social, economic and cultural impacts of tourism in a destination; expanding global tourism increases the threat of biopiracy under the guise of ecotourism, when tour operators and clients collect rare medicinal plants from areas inhabited by tribal peoples but without consulting them; and GATS makes no provision for the monitoring and regulation of TNCs.

Of all these concerns of relevance to the activity of tourism, it is perhaps the fear that the GATS will further deepen the increasing poverty and inequities experienced in some

Third World countries that prompts the greatest protest. In the last two decades of the twentieth century, structural adjustment was the major economic policy employed in up to ninety Third World countries under programmes imposed by the IMF and World Bank.

During this time, 'the people of sub-Saharan Africa have become 15 per cent poorer, and growth rates in South Asia and Latin America have stagnated while inequality has risen dramatically'.

The possibility that the GATS will further deepen these effects is feared not just by anti-globalisation protestors but also by the protagonists of fairly traded tourism and propoor tourism. The last of these, pro-poor tourism, is a relatively recent extension of governmental activity into the field of tourism development, and one to which we turn next.

DONOR DEVELOPMENT ACTIVITY AND PRO-POOR TOURISM INITIATIVES

The supranational organisations have had difficulty coming to terms with and adapting their policies to the effects of increasing poverty and inequality beyond cosmetic alteration of names, titles and terms. The need to examine their *modus operandi* in order to reduce poverty and inequality significantly does not appear to have been recognised.

A number of developments in bilateral donor policies, however, have given cause for a little more optimism in this regard, among them the development of pro-poor tourism initiatives.

In one of the few analyses of the current approach of development agencies to tourism, the UK DFID *Sustainable Tourism and Poverty Elimination Study* (Deloitte and Touche, IIED and ODI, 1999) concludes that few agencies regard tourism as a key development sector and yet many agencies, such as the World Bank and European Union, do indeed provide considerable support to tourism related projects, ranging from economic development and employment generation to sector planning and product development. Nevertheless, no agency is regarded as developing and implementing a tourism and poverty elimination agenda.

Reviewing the approaches of the three key agency sectors, multilateral agencies, bilateral agencies and development banks, the DFID report concludes that in general tourism projects respectively involve infrastructure development, tourism master plans and private sector development, community and conservation based tourism, and infrastructure and resort development loans.

In terms of the approach of agencies to tourism as a poverty elimination strategy, the DFID reports two contrasting representations. The first, exemplified by the Danish (DANIDA) and Dutch (NEDA) government agencies is that tourism cannot and should not compete with traditional development sectors (such as education and primary health care).

The second, promoted by the Finnish development agency (FINNIDA) and some multilaterals such as the United Nations Development Programme and EuropeAid, is that as a result of the considerable impact of tourism on poor peoples' livelihoods, intervention is critical.

Such interventions at the local level include the support of small and micro-enterprises, support to rural tourism projects, the development of partnerships between communities and private sector operators, participatory pro-poor planning and a range of measures that have clear benefits for the poor, such as working condition improvements, training and staff development and protected area management.

With the emergence of development approaches focused on the poor, by the end of the 1990s development practitioners had begun to think about the possibility of applying poverty elimination goals to tourism. Tourism had traditionally been viewed as a commercial sector, and considered a 'frivolous or elitist industry' and not a 'serious' development related activity. The DFID has supported a number of studies (including case study research) that seek to elaborate a pro-poor tourism approach and promote tourism as a 'legitimate' development activity.

The emergence and development of pro-poor tourism must be understood and analysed within the global development orthodoxy that economic growth is fundamental to pro-poor development. Ultimately, it is an effort to see if tourism can become more pro-poor and if, in the much repeated sound-bite of its proponents, it can meet the need to 'tilt the tourism cake rather than expanding it'.

Pro-poor tourism is a direct intervention in the debate between the advocates and detractors of tourism. Advocates point to four potential advantages of tourism as an economic sector capable of facilitating pro-poor growth: the high potential of linkage, labour intensity, tourism's potential in poor countries and the ability to build tourism on natural and cultural assets. Detractors are critical of the level of leakage, negative impacts on the poor, displacement and socio-cultural disruption.

Pro-poor tourism is defined by its proponents as tourism 'that generates net benefits for the poor ... [it] is not a specific product or sector of tourism, but an overall approach. Rather than aiming to expand the size of the sector, pro-poor tourism strategies aim to unlock opportunities - for economic gain, other livelihood benefits, or engagement in decision-making - for the poor'.

Pro-poor tourism, it is argued, differs from other tourism types that claim to have some 'developmental' value (principally ecotourism, sustainable tourism, community-based tourism, 'fair trade' tourism and other ethically based tourisms), in that it focuses directly on the needs of the 'poor'.

As such it is premised upon the sustainable livelihoods approach, of increasing significance in discourses of so-called 'people-centred' approaches to development that seek to build upon the capabilities, assets and activities of the poor. However, advocates also recognise that general support for and integration of pro-poor strategies with the mainstream tourism sector (for example, developing tourist boards or the provision of key infrastructure such as roads or water supplies) is essential to complement pro-poor tourism, and that 'interventions do not always need to be poverty-focused to benefit the poor'.

In this way there are clear similarities with other forms of new tourism, in that the success of pro-poor tourism relies on an appropriate policy environment that allows such forms of tourism to grow; and thus, pro-poor tourism initiatives may also include so-called 'top-down' government promoted approaches.

Like other forms of tourism, as an economic activity pro-poor tourism must compete effectively in the tourism marketplace, and access to the market and ability to compete will depend on a number of fundamental factors common to all forms of tourism: the geography of the place of tourism, the level of understanding and knowledge of the tourism function and level of disposable resources, and access to decision-making (much of which is done internationally).

Despite the acknowledged desire of pro-poor tourism advocates to overcome existing problems and encourage new approaches to development through tourism, two key problems arise: the first relates to an understanding of power relationships in tourism; the second to the ability of pro-poor tourism to reduce poverty.

Table. Pro-poor Tourism Strategies.

Issues	Strategies
Barriers to participation in the industry for small and micro-enterprises	• Credit training • Policy reform and planning mechanisms • Partnerships with the private sector
Apparent potential for linkages with other sectors rarely realised of local products	• Improved quality, reliability and competitiveness • Change incentives and attitudes in the business sector towards local products • Facilitate linkage process, reduce transaction costs
The number of tourism the poor limited by their lack of quality of employment in the	• Training in hospitality skills, jobs available to targeted at poor • Development and implementation skills, and of labour people • Initiatives aiming to reverse the industry can be growth of sex tourism and child low standards labour

Tourism can result in lost or reduced access to land and natural resources, or their degradation. Environmental mitigation measures sometimes conflict with, rather than enhance, livelihoods	• Development/reform of planning frameworks • Devolve tenure rights over land or wildlife to local people • Employ appropriate mitigation measures
Tourism can undermine basic services of poor communities by over-burdening water and sewage systems; can result in cultural intrusion and loss of privacy; and has led to a growth of the sex industry Institutions and decision -making processes often structured in such a way that interests of the poor are not taken into account	• Combine investment in basic services for tourism with provision for local needs • Local codes of conduct and local tourism initiatives • Raise awareness of cultural issues among tourists • Participatory planning processes • Local institutional capacity-building • Cross-sectoral coordination • Incentives and capacity for pro-poor tourism
Many governments see tourism as a means to generate foreign exchange rather than address poverty. Where commitment exists, it can be difficult to identify and implement the wide range of policy reforms needed	• Assess and build government commitment to pro-poor tourism • Build capacity to implement pro-poor commitments
The reasons for business to promote the pro-poor agenda are not clear	• Business partnerships promote pro-poor tourism on the business agenda
Pro-poor tourism not currently on the international agenda, yet many international activities have potential to influence pro-poor tourism	• International voluntary codes • Consumer education • Assessment of the impact of • European Union tourism regulations on poor producers • Good practice' guidelines in pro-poor tourism • Promote pro-poor tourism on international agenda

First, the DFID Report is critical of the misrepresentation of tourism as an 'industry where foreign interests dominate', and which directly challenges critiques of tourism that have emphasised the significance of power relationships. However, the authors of the Report themselves point out that 'Developing countries have only a minority share of the international tourism market', refer to the major players in tourism and their 'low level of commitment to any one destination' and point to the significance of 'customer requirements' - the fundamental needs and desires of tourists that must be met for tourism to be a going concern.

And as later pro-poor tourism analysis suggests, 'Most of the critical decisions that affect the sector are made outside of the country or by a few powerful local interests'.

All such elements seem to confirm, rather than question, the significance of the spatially uneven and unequal nature of tourism production, consumption and development. Indeed, this appears to be reflected in advocates' claims that many of the disadvantages that have been attributed to tourism are in fact 'characteristics of growth and globalisation' and that tourism is little different from other economic sectors in that 'negative impacts that arise as a result of tourism development would also occur with development in other sectors'.

While, for the arguments advanced we would stop short of claiming that tourism is no different from other economic sectors, some of the oft-quoted problems of tourism such as leakage or economic volatility or the structure of social relations and power that involve local elites as well as foreign interests, are indeed characteristic of other economic sectors too and that the 'difference between tourism and other sectors might be perceived rather than real'.

For these reasons we have argued that tourism must be understood primarily within an analysis of relationships of power (foreign or otherwise) and that tourism must be considered little different from other economic sectors when assessed within a development context; in this sense, it is a 'prism' for understanding broader global issues and relations.

Our challenge was to try and understand tourism within the context of power and how this affects local livelihoods, and to measure the veracity of the claims that have been made about the ability of new forms of tourism to assist development. A key question is, given the size and strength of growth in tourism, is new tourism capable of facilitating development?

Given the global 'consensus' on the need to dramatically reduce absolute poverty, the second fundamental question centres on the ability of pro-poor tourism to deliver poverty reduction. As might be expected at the initial stage in the development of a prospective approach that is 'relatively untried and untested' and where a blueprint for implementation does not exist, accounts of pro-poor tourism are replete with imponderables (the 'may', 'should', 'likely to') and with acknowledgement that impacts are not easy to measure objectively.

Equally, there has been justifiable caution in extracting too many conclusions from an initial case analysis. While this is certainly no good reason for not embarking on pro-poor tourism initiatives, it does perhaps call into question the confidence invested in pro-poor tourism approaches and the manner in which it has been preferenced and mainstreamed into bilateral development assistance.

Like any other form of activity or approach, pro-poor tourism has needed to capture its unique selling point and appeal to the emergent development policy agendas. In this case the UN poverty reduction targets and the consensus surrounding the needs of the poor as *the* focus for development activities has meant that pro-poor tourism advocates have been careful to define their approach in contrast to other types of tourism, even where the needs of the poor are already being addressed. Inevitably, this has meant trying to rationalise away potential inconsistencies.

So while the UN targets are unequivocally focused on the reduction of the poor living in 'absolute poverty', on less than a dollar a day, pro-poor tourism advocates point to the problems of defining poverty and the 'poor'.

In terms of an intervention in poverty, the DFID report's initial conclusions were that 'tourism probably does not compare with more direct tools, such as investment in health, education and agriculture. But as a strategy for promoting *broad-based growth* (also essential for achieving poverty elimination), pro-poor tourism has good potential', and it is the so-called 'not-quite-so-poor' (55) that are in a better position to be involved in tourism.

On the basis of a review of supporting pro-poor tourism case studies from Ecuador, Namibia, Nepal, St Lucia, South Africa and Uganda, Ashley *et al.* conclude that a 'focus on "the poor" often translates in practice to a focus on local residents or the "community"' (2001:11).

Researchers have highlighted both positive and negative impacts on the livelihoods of the poor through their initial case studies which are all less than ten years old, but show uncertainty about the strength of positive impacts for it is 'difficult to tell how much this is because pro-poor initiatives have fewer negative consequences, or how much it reflects researchers' and respondents' quest for positive results'.

As advocates of pro-poor tourism concur, it is certainly not a panacea: 'it is probably true that the small size of ... initiatives has meant that tourism provides a *minor dent in the national poverty* even when multiplier effects are taken into account'.

Pro-poor tourism is not, therefore, a tool for eliminating nor necessarily alleviating absolute poverty, but rather is principally a measure for making some sections of poorer communities 'better-off' and of reducing the vulnerability of poorer groups to shocks (such as hunger). As the DIFD commissioned research suggests:

Economic benefits generated by pro-poor tourism may not reach the poorest - workers and entrepreneurs are unlikely to be from the poorest quintile. Nevertheless, those with sufficient assets to make crafts, sell tea/food, service the accommodation sector, or work in infrastructure may still be poor by either the international definition or by national poverty lines (particularly where tourism occurs in places where the majority are 'poor').

Additionally, it is difficult to draw conclusions from national aggregate data and analysis that 'shows that in most countries with high levels of poverty, tourism is significant (contributing over 2 per cent of GDP or 5 per cent of exports) or growing (aggregate growth of over 50 per cent between 1990 and 1997)'. While this may well present opportunities for the poor, it must also recognise the geographically uneven and unequal nature of tourism development and activity.

Tourism, and its potential benefits, will not be distributed evenly and may well display sharp regional and social disparities - the Maoist insurrections in areas of Nepal, for example, emphasise the potential volatility of uneven regional growth. As a prerequisite therefore, there needs to be a 'large number of poor people, in areas with tourism assets' and the commitment of government to pro-poor approaches.

It could be argued that in absolute terms the main effort and resourcing should be deployed in addressing the impacts on the poor, reining back the negative impacts of the mainstream tourism industry and seeking to develop mainstream poor-focused initiatives. As tentative analysis suggests, and as conjectured in pro-poor tourism analysis, 'Even if tourism does not directly involve poor people, it may have pro-poor impact, *if* it improves government revenue and *if* that revenue is used in pro-poor ways'.

Equally, given that the implementation of most pro-poor tourism initiatives require subsidies (and this would especially be the case if such initiatives were 'scaled-up' and replicated on a broader basis), and in the light of the need to allocate funds where the impact on poverty reduction will be optimal, Ashley *et al.* (2001) conclude that donors, NGOs and indeed governments, must ultimately consider how cost effective pro-poor tourism is in reducing poverty in relation to other approaches. Of course, there are advantages to the growth of new tourism (and pro-poor tourism) and there is a number of case studies that appear to demonstrate the real advantages and benefits to the poor that arise from tourism.

As advocates of pro-poor tourism understandably maintain, while in absolute terms the scale of benefits may appear small, they can be relatively very significant when viewed from the perspective of the beneficiary groups.

Our tentative conclusions, however, remain the same: given the growth in global inequality and poverty, the benefits to the poor of poverty elimination (however real they may be where they occur) will be marginal within the overall context of tourism. Finally, it is not unreasonable to consider the degree to which pro-poor tourism analysis and promotion is a repackaging of existing initiatives so that they fit within the prevailing development paradigm with an emphasis on poverty reduction, sustainable livelihoods and a focus on the poor and pro-poor growth. The re-adjustment and representation of existing projects and the structure of new initiatives are a key feature of the development merry-go-round in the competition for limited development funds. In addition, it will prove necessary in the long run to consider the cumulative effect of supporting (through multilateral and bilateral aid programmes focused on economic growth) the expansion of capitalist relations and the manner in which this may undercut 'sustainable livelihoods' and exacerbate, rather than alleviate, poverty.

AGENDA 21 FOR THE TRAVEL AND TOURISM INDUSTRY

An examination of the global governance of tourism must include the activities and approach of tourism's supranational agencies such as the WTTC and the WTO/OMT. Together with the Earth Council, these organisations elaborated the role of different tourism interests and their responsibilities following the establishment of Agenda 21 which arose from the 1992 Earth Summit at Rio de Janeiro in a document entitled *Agenda 21 for the Travel and Tourism Industry: Towards Environmentally Sustainable Development* (1995).

Extracts the duties placed upon central and local governments (and national tourism authorities and representative trade organisations such as the WTTC and WTO/OMT) in facilitating 'sustainable' tourism development.

There is a number of observations that can be made about the priorities set out in this document. First, it is clearly set within a framework of environmental sustainability. This is indicated in both the report's rubric, *Towards Environmentally Sustainable Development*, and in the respective forewords of the collaborating bodies:

A key conclusion of the Earth Summit was the importance of harnessing the entrepreneurial drive of the private sector in the cause of environmentally compatible development ... The environment is our core asset, the key component of product quality, and an increasing priority for our consumers.

(Geoffrey Lipman, President, WTTC)

Table. Agenda 21: Responsibilities of Governments.

Priority	Priorities and objectives	Responses and examples of area success
I	Assessing the capacity of existing regulatory, economic and voluntary framework to bring about sustainable tourism, and developing policies to facilitate sustainable tourism	Charge negative externalities to producer; provide cost incentives to companies minimising waste; encourage responsible entrepreneurship through codes of practice. More than 100 codes now exist
II	Assessing the economic, energy, social, cultural and environmental implications of an organisation's own operations	Ranges from a more efficient use of water to encouraging staff to use environmentally benign transport and ensuring the destination's character is truly represented in marketing. Green Globe was established

III	To train and educate all stakeholders in travel and tourism about the need to develop more sustainable forms of tourism	Organisations should work with government departments. The WTO/OMT has establishe a worldwide Network of Education and Training Centres to promote tourism education and training
IV	Develop and implement effective land use planning to maximise the environmental and economic benefits of travel and tourism and minimise environmental and cultural damage	Includes working with government planning authorities on sustainable tourism planning, i.e., transport planning and coastal zone management. Bermuda - one of the world's most affluent countries because of planning regulations?
V	Facilitate information exchange between 'developed' and 'developing' countries	Includes developing partnerships with 'less developed' countries, advising them on sustainable tourism
VI	Provide opportunities for all sectors of society to participate in sustainable tourism	Promote and ensure the participation of women, indigenous people, etc. Develop appropriate training courses. A key example would be the CAMPFIRE project in Zimbabwe
VII	Design new tourism products that are sustainable: socially, culturally, economically and environmentally	Ranges from defining what makes resorts sustainable to using local materials in construction and ensuring government departmentsrealise the benefits of tourism in include conservation. Examplesthe game parks of Kenya and South Africa
VIII	Measure progress in sustainable development by setting realistic indicators at national and local level	Ranges from assessing which data are appropriate to exchanging experiences with other organisations
IX	Develop partnerships to facilitate sustainable development and responsible entrepreneurship	Includes government departments providing a tourism coordinating mechanism for those responsible for sustain able tourism development and

ensuring the necessary infrastructure (e.g., sewage treatment, recycling facilities, etc.) is in place

---

A good deal of our Travel & Tourism activity relies on ... fragile natural or cultural resources, so it is in our interests to protect them for the future ... Travel & Tourism will inevitably continue to increase. Meeting this growth in a responsible, sustainable way, that preserves and enhances the beauty of the attraction, is the challenge we all face.

The overriding concern for the industry must be to seek out ways to enhance rather than degrade its core product, the environment. Reflecting for a moment on some of the words used here to describe the environment: 'core asset', 'core product', 'product quality', 'resources', 'preserve' - the treatment of the environment as a marketable product is clear. It is also clear that the drive 'towards environmentally sustainable development' is a commercial necessity, in order to maintain the marketability and attractiveness of this commodity.

More noticeable is the way in which much, if not all, the discussion bypasses the interests of local people. Where social considerations do appear they are an adjunct. Social development, it is assumed, will be achieved at the same time as improving the environment; the benefits will magically 'trickle down' to local people in the same way as the World Bank and IMF suggest. The ability for local people to choose whether they wish to engage with tourism is not on offer. Rather, it appears to be an agenda for removing the 'growing resentment of residents in some destinations' and allowing for the expansion of the industry.

As the quotations above imply, the report fails to reflect the inherent inequality expressed through global tourism. It is written from a thoroughly First World perspective, where the majority of the tourism industry, tourists and tourism interests are located. The forewords talk of 'our Travel and Tourism activity', 'our consumers', 'our interests'.

The supporting statement for priority (vi), for example, extols the participation of all sectors of society in sustainable tourism and identifies the promotion of the participation of women and indigenous people in 'appropriate forms of tourism development'. But, of course, these remain the receivers of tourism and the report is silent on the gross inequality of who is, and who is not, able to travel. The Third World, so it would appear, is there for our entertainment. It exists to serve us and see to our needs. As the report states, the 'challenge ... is to ensure that tourists don't "love nature to death"'; in other words, to ensure that the tourism product is retained.

Even 'peace' is invoked as an essential prerequisite to successful sustainable tourism development, further reflecting the overall intention of protecting the tourism product while allowing for overall global expansion. Priority (vii) supporting statement urges the use of 'the potential of the tourism industry to promote peace between nations and people', acknowledging that 'Peace is a pre-requisite for a sustainable Travel & Tourism industry and, by facilitating contact and understanding between cultures, well-designed tourism products can make a significant contribution to world peace.' While peace is of course a noble goal, once again there is an insipid suggestion that we need to move towards one happy global community, 'In recognition of economic and social cohesion among the peoples of the world as a fundamental principle of sustainable development' with implicit suggestions about the need for global security, a concern that has been greatly enhanced since the early 1990s.

Not only are Third World populations the receivers of visitors; according to this report they are also receivers of (First World) information. Priority area (v), for example, involving the facilitation of information exchange, more accurately involves advising Third World countries on how to make tourism sustainable.

Rather than exchange, this appears to be information delivery and represents a First World perspective on how certain goals are to be achieved. Similarly, priority (viii) supporting statement encourages the 'exchange' of indicators with other organisations 'especially those in developing countries'. Cynically, many of the priorities and objectives advocating 'training' courses are a further indication of the cycles of dependency and development aid-giving - a 'jobs for the boys' syndrome - that such frameworks maintain.

Participation, so the report suggests, is to be undertaken after key initial decisions have been made. In the wake of the discovery of Mayan ruins near the city of Tekax (in south-east Mexico), and the realisation that this had significant tourism potential, it was agreed that the 'people of the area should participate in the development in order to maximise economic benefits'. The critical point here is that the decision to develop the site and to maximise its economic benefits had already been taken.

Finally, the report offers a Framework for Action, although on the subject of the means of implementation the report is baffling and also reflects the First World perspective. It is difficult to conceive of the processes and procedures set out in the report - that is, securing the commitment of top management to the concept of sustainability, communicating this to all staff, establishing realistic and achievable targets, implementing action programmes, monitoring progress and so on - working in practice.

In short, it amounts to top-draw management-speak: many windy words within a highly ambiguous and inappropriate framework. It is difficult to believe that many grossly under-resourced and under-staffed government departments would be in a position to undertake such a grand scheme. How the report's recommendations are to be implemented in practice represents a serious failing.

The report and its Framework for Action are in effect just one more in a pile of conventions, codes of conduct, declarations and the like weighing down on the governments of Third World countries in respect of tourism development. All these pressures are full of fine words and lofty principles, but few if any of them offer the resources required to enable Third World governments to consider sustainability in the development of their tourism industries.

THE UNITED NATIONS INTERNATIONAL YEAR OF ECOTOURISM, 2002

In November 1998, the United Nations' General Assembly declared the year 2002 as the International Year of Ecotourism (IYE) and invited UN states, members of specialised agencies and pertinent intergovernmental and governmental organisations to participate in the programme, especially regarding ecotourism in developing countries. The UNEP and the WTO/OMT were mandated by the UN to organise events around the IYE. Along with UNEP and the WTO/OMT, TIES was given the role of coordinating the organisation of a series of six regional preparatory conferences in partnership with local organisations, 'to focus on fostering a genuine dialogue among all stakeholders involved, especially local communities and ecotourism practitioners'. These were held in Belize, India, Peru, Thailand, Kenya and Sweden from November 2001 to April 2002, and each preparatory conference presented reports to the World Ecotourism Summit in Quebec, Canada in May 2002, in which TIES was also an active organisational participant.

The IYE was met with enthusiasm by many tourist boards and tour operators, but with varying degrees of scepticism by many NGOs, especially some in the Third World. Most prominent among these was the Tourism Investigation and Monitoring Team (usually referred to as the TIM-Team) of Bangkok, Thailand, with support from the Third World Network based in Malaysia.

Soon after the declaration of the IYE, the TIM-Team called for a fundamental reassessment of ecotourism and for a change of the name to the International Year of Reviewing Ecotourism. In an October 2000 letter to Oliver Hillel, UNEP's tourism programme coordinator, the TIM-Team and a coalition of other groups from Asia and beyond stated:

We, the undersigned NGOs from the South and the North, feel compelled to warn all concerned parties not to skirt the critical issues of ecotourism and the fact that a mountain of money will be spent and a flood of projects initiated around the IYE in order to boost the ecotourism industry. In contrast to advocates who tend to portray ecotourism development as a 'win-win' approach, a means to protect biodiversity and enhance the well-being of local people, we are gravely concerned that this IYE will result in a 'lose-lose' situation for communities and the environment in destination countries.

Citing work conducted on projects including Taman Negara, a national park in western Malaysia, a number of development projects in Thailand and the Greater Mekong sub-region covering six countries, the organisation argued that:

Tourism provides the physical infrastrucure and logistics for freer movement of people and goods within countries and across borders in general and, thus, it naturally has knock-on effects on other sectors. Accordingly, ecotourism development has opened opportunities for a whole range of investors to gain access to remote rural, forest, coastal and marine areas.

There is the observation that the more transportation systems are established into remote areas, the more encroachments, illegal logging, mining and plundering of biological resources occur, including biopiracy by unscrupulous individual and corporate collectors.

Three months later the same coalition of groups sent the same letter to Kofi Annan, UN Secretary General, along with an urgent appeal that the name and focus of the year should be changed. The substance of their appeal and the contrast in the different approaches to the year were reflected in one sentence:

'The new name will convey an unmistakeable message to the international community that the year 2002 is not the time for celebrating the ecotourism industry, but is primarily meant as a period of reflection, stock taking, learning and intensive search for solutions to the various problems associated with ecotourism' (TIM-Team letter to Kofi Annan, 18 January 2001).

The TIM-Team continued to produce regular articles and letters critical of the IYE, culminating in a January 2002 article entitled *UN 'International Year of Ecotourism 2002' in a Deep Muddle - Scrap it!* (TIM-Team, 2002). The UK-based Tourism Concern also expressed its misgivings thus:

How can ecotourism to the Ecuadorian rainforest be taken seriously given the resources consumed to take tourists to the product in the first place? The IYE also seems to be failing to address many critical issues: the fact that people are still displaced from their homes because of tourism, including 'ecotourism', denied access to local resources and losing their livelihoods because of so-called ecotourism; that ecotourism rarely takes on board issues of core labour standards, or gender; or that large environmental NGOs managing 'ecotours' too often behave like large corporations, employing 'top down' methods that rarely support local decision making. Perhaps most crucially of all, Tourism Concern believes that promoting ecotourism means promoting a niche market that does nothing to change the industry as a whole.

A statement presented by a range of indigenous peoples' representatives and NGOs to the Convention on Biological Diversity in Nairobi, Kenya, in May 2000 went further still, naming several of the 'large environmental NGOs managing ecotours':

In our experience, large nature conservation and development organisations do not respect (local peoples') rights. ... several activities undertaken by the [International] Ecotourism Society, Conservation International and IUCN do not respect the rights and interests of Indigenous

Peoples and local communities, particularly in regard to the Year of Ecotourism activities, and often threaten cultural and biological diversity.

Many of the criticisms and dangers of ecotourism raised in the run-up to the IYE have been acknowledged by its organisers. And although the title of the year was not altered, some efforts were made to improve the inclusivity of the events by spreading invitations to participate far and wide. The TIES IYE website is peppered with terms such as 'critical evaluation of ecotourism', 'share the benefits of ecotourism equitably', 'multi- stakeholder consultation', 'active networks of regional stakeholders', 'foster dialogue', and makes repeated references to 'local communities and indigenous groups'.

Nevertheless, as Vivanco points out, 'Since its inception, the IYE has been aggressively marketed as a celebration of ecotourism's role in facilitating sustainable development'. Despite acknowledgement of the criticisms of ecotourism, this celebratory tone is unlikely to be reconciled with the views of those who consider it inappropriate and who would have preferred a more critical approach.

SUSTAINABLE TOURISM AS POLITICAL DISCOURSE

'Beautiful, multi-faceted jewel' (*Financial Times*, 22 September 1992); 'To sea is to Belize'; 'Mounts, mountains and Mayans'; and 'Too good for tourists' - this is how four UK broadsheet newspapers referred to the small Central American country of Belize. Virtually all tourist sources on Belize cite large tracts of 'pristine' rainforest, numerous Mayan archaeological sites, and the second-longest barrier reef (after Australia) in the world. Writers point to a number of successful community-based and conservation projects, including the Community Baboon Sanctuary, Sandy Beach Lodge (Women's Cooperative), the Toledo Ecotourism Association, the Hol Chan Marine

Reserve, the Cockscomb Basin Wildlife Sanctuary (Jaguar Reserve), and Crooked Tree Wildlife Sanctuary. On paper, much of the surface area of the country enjoys some form of designated protection from development.

Up to the late 1980s few would have heard of the former British Colony of British Honduras, which gained independence in 1981. In the post-independence period, tourism has become an attractive strategy for diversifying the economy away from the export of agricultural produce. Belize is an excellent example of how a country uses the notion of sustainability to promote the development of new types of tourism and how a government's use of the language of sustainable tourism is often sufficient to win international accolade, even among academics and environmentalists. In the early 1990s it seemed as if Belize had emerged as the ecotourism capital of the world, hosting a number of international conferences. The experience of Belize provides an example of sustainability as a political discourse.

Unlike its Caribbean Community and Common Market (CARICOM) partners, Belize recognised the need to avoid the negative externalities, foreign exchange leakages and the foreign control of the mass tourism industry developed throughout much of the Caribbean. It also acknowledged the potentially disastrous impact that large-scale tourism development would have on the relatively fragile sub-tropical environment.

In their first term of office, the United Democratic Party (UDP), a right-of-centre and pro-US free market economics party, was the first Belizean administration to focus upon tourism. It approved an *Integrated Tourism Policy and Strategy Statement* in its last year in office, acknowledging the significance of tourism to the government, which had made it the second economic priority next to agriculture. In this way, significant emphasis was placed on the overall potential of tourism, 'its economic stimulus and linkage with other subsectors of the economy' (1989:1), and the guiding objectives stressed the maximisation of economic benefits. This included a particular emphasis on 'long stay and upper income travellers'.

In the 1989 general election the victorious People's United Party (PUP - a nationalist party and like its increasingly indistinguishable rival, a pro-US and free market oriented party) had spelled out clearly the advantages of ecotourism in the party's manifesto in what it also termed *Tourism with Dignity*:

Belize has in abundance what few countries in the world still have left - nature. Ours, for the most part, is still intact. And nature is rapidly becoming tourism's Holy Grail. Belize has so far escaped the most brutal blows of man's destructive hand ... But, we must ask, for how long? The answer is, forever if we safeguard them. The protection of our national environment and development of eco-tourism are compatible goals which will be given high priority. The new PUP Government will place the portfolios of Environment and Tourism in one Ministry.

In the wake of its election victory, the PUP did indeed combine these portfolios and Belize has subsequently enjoyed popular international support and praise for its stand on the environment and promotion of sustainable tourism development and has hosted a number of conferences on ecotourism.

As we argued earlier, however, these conferences hint at the serious deficiencies and contradictions in ecotourism, not least that the conference fees, half the average monthly Belizean wage, ensured that the only local representation was from professionals representing and paid for by government departments and non-governmental organisations. Higinio and Munt (1993) describe two particular conferences held in Belize thus:

Hosted in a new luxury hotel - the construction of which necessitated stripping the protective mangrove cover - on the ecologically fragile outskirts of Belize City, two recent major international conferences on ecotourism highlighted the conflict between environmentally conscious activists and entrepreneurs who have seized upon ecotourism as a convenient marketing tool. The keynote speaker at the First Caribbean Ecotourism Conference in 1991, Voit Gilmore from the American Society of Travel Agents, promised 'millions of Americans just waiting to come'. Howard Hills, a US investor speaking at the 1992 First World Congress on Tourism and the Environment, promised money. Ecotourism, Hills argued, is just like any other business. He boasted that the Overseas Private Investment Corporation would lend up to $50 million to any 'environmentally sound' tourism development, conditional upon a 25 per cent US stake in the project.

Environmentalists consider such sentiments anathema to the very ethos of ecotourism. They argue that a small-scale, locally controlled and ecologically sensitive industry can neither sustain many visitors, nor be a big money-maker. In contrast to the Belizean government's view of ecotourism as a way to develop economically and to earn foreign exchange, environmental activitists see ecotourism as justification for ecological and cultural conservation. An incredulous anthropologist from Scotland's Edinburgh University could only express dismay at Hill's remarks: 'The whole idea of ecotourism,' he said, 'is that it is like *no* other business.'

In the wake of these conferences, commentators began to express concern over the nature of the business of ecotourism and what it had to offer Belize. Despite these concerns, the Belizean government has used its commitment to sustainable tourism to full effect.

At an ecology and tourism symposium in Costa Rica for example, the then Tourism and Environment Minister, Glenn Godfrey, emphasised the relationships between environment, conservation and ecotourism and the fundamental requirement of local control: 'Conservation and therefore ecotourism thrives best where the sunlight penetrates to the lowest levels of autonomous local and community government.' It was a stance he later reiterated at the 1992 Rio Summit, assuring the audience that the Belizean government was committed to 'community-based ecotourism'. But the government's statements have not always matched their actions and a succession of examples from Belize provides a rather less optimistic picture of the use of sustainable tourism.

In 1992 the popular Belizean weekly *Amandala* carried the headline 'Eco-terrorism at Hatchet Caye', following a US resort owner's attempt to blow up part of the ecologically fragile coral reef in order to make his resort more accessible to visiting boats. The developer, Donald McKenzie, was subsequently arrested, fined US$2,000 (for 'dynamiting without a permit') and fled the country.

Of course similar incidents have been reported elsewhere in the world where government rhetoric extolling the virtues of the controlled growth of tourism has been contradicted in practice. In some cases this is a direct result of weak and ineffectual legislation controlling environmental impacts, particularly the inability to enforce legislation. In other cases it reflects the complete absence of necessary controls or the government's willingness to turn a blind eye.

More than environmental damage, however, the Hatchet Caye incident further underlined the unease with the degree and growth of foreign ownership of tourism resources in Belize. *Amandala* reflects these concerns in statements that clearly resonate the political economy of tourism. As Belize struggles to find the balance between the development and conservation of our natural resources, more and more we will run into the Hatchet Caye syndrome: foreign nationals and corporations who do not believe that they are answerable to us ... Belize and Belizeans are beginning to be trampled in the rush by those who regard our laws and traditions as inconvenient at best, and our sovereignty as theirs, bought and paid by their money.

They wheedle, bribe and connive to extract their fortunes. And when all the above fail, they will resort to terrorism; covert campaigns, destabilisation and destruction, to have their way.

The concerns of Belizeans, especially the government's interpretation of what is and what is not ecotourism, were heightened by the announcement of a joint venture with a Mississippi-based company for a US$1 billion development to cover two-thirds of Ambergris Caye, the biggest of Belize's offshore islands.

The Ambergris Caye controversy raised serious doubts about the scale and nature of tourist development. Presented as a major contribution to re-investing in the Belizean people (a reflection of the PUP's 1989 Election spin 'Belizeans First'), the government bought back the northern two-thirds of the 20,000 acre Ambergris Caye from its US owner. It was expected that a newly established Ambergris Caye Planning Authority (ACPA), would have its jurisdiction and planning powers extended over this area of land, known as the Pinkerton Estate.

Without the knowledge of ACPA, however, the government set up a semi-autonomous development corporation, appointed by and answerable to the then Tourism and Environment Minister, Glenn Godfrey (who was also the attorney general). It was planned to earmark approximately half the 20,000 acres for conservation and 2,500 acres for Belizeans. But it was on the remaining 7,500 acres that the corporation proposed a US$50 million 'sustainable development'.

In the relatively fragile ecology of Ambergris Caye, it is difficult to reconcile Minister Godfrey's statement that 'in Belize we must keep tourist developments small' (address to First World Congress on Tourism and the Environment, April 1992) with the claim that the proposed development represents 'an integrated and ecologically sound resort development' when the development was to comprise at least one international hotel, two 'all-inclusive spa hotels', three to five upscale lodges, two golf courses, town houses and villas, a thousand luxury homes, polo fields and stables.

Although the scheme did not progress, it is illustrative of the 'seductions of mass tourism' as Godfrey referred to it, and the manner in which local control is compromised, if it is not entirely absent. Just two days before the contract was to be signed between the developer and the Belizean government, Godfrey presented the document to ACPA for the first time in spite of discussions having proceeded over the two previous years.

A furious member of the ACPA encapsulated the mood of local people arguing that if the proposed agreement of North Ambergris Caye was as good as claimed, why had the minister not let the people know: 'When the government acquired the Pinkerton Estate, we were told in no uncertain terms that we were getting back control of the land and meaningful participation.

To me, 75 per cent to foreigners and 25 per cent to Belizeans is not fulfilling the promise.' As Otis reported in *The Nation* newspaper, one Belize-based diplomat commented, 'There is a latent resentment of foreign ownership. But Belizeans made a devil's bargain. They sold the place' (1992).

A further case in point was the proposed multi-million dollar Belize City Tourism District Project, which would have involved large-scale foreign capital investment or large-scale multilateral borrowing. New Orleans-based architects completed a USAID-sponsored initial study for a waterfront-style regeneration project. The planners hoped to build an exclusive downtown area complete with new hotels and shopping facilities, a promenade with seafront restaurants and cafés, an ethnic crafts and food market and marina for small yachts cruising the Caribbean.

It was, in other words, a mini Miami - the consultants even used Baltimore's Haborplace as an example of good practice and an aim to strive for - designed to transform the seafront district into a vacation *pied-à-terre* for would-be ecotourists, who would presumably feel protected from the urban problems that have become legendary in guidebooks to Belize.

The scheme was also underpinned by the philosophy that the benefits would, somehow, trickle down to the rest of the city's population. This would-be gentrification and a facsimile approach to new developments of certain city quarters globally - aping the style of western water-front developments-is becoming a particularly notable trend.

Not only would ordinary Belizeans gain little from this upscale project, but local representatives were not consulted in the planning process. In a bizarre twist, the city's planning department first learnt of the scheme when a three-dimensional model appeared in the window of the city's supermarket.

In a city of 60,000 where the city council is severely strapped for money and poverty is on the increase, the consultants also lauded the scheme for allowing the authorities to 'concentrate its resources' (and by inference cutting back spending in other, poorer, neighbourhoods) in one area. In this way, it was argued, the district would be a showcase, with cleaning, street lighting and road maintenance, for example, maximised.

Much of this expressed concern over the control of tourism development in Belize is also reflected in the ownership of tourism resources and facilities (a point already emphasised by the *Amandala* quote above). Some commentators have observed that much of the tourism industry is already in the hands of the country's small, but powerful expatriate community. Cater, a delegate at the ecotourism conference in 1991, found that 25 per cent of the registered delegates were US citizens, and more significantly, that among the

43 per cent registered as Belizeans were many expatriate Americans. This is a phenomenon witnessed in many countries with expatriates running bars, restaurants, tour operations, lodges and hotels. Similarly, at the 1992 First World Congress on Tourism and The Environment in Belize City, more than 40 per cent of the 300 delegates came from the USA and Canada, and again, many of the 29 per cent of delegates from Belize were expatriate Americans. And as Linda Baker (2001) has pointed out:

Two decades after it won independence from Britain, Belize finds itself yoked to another kind of colonial enterprise; the foreign-dominated ecotourism trade. ... although Belize is one of the most environmentally conscious countries in the world, a significant percentage of its ecological wealth is concentrated in the hands of expatriates and foreign investors ... In 1998, a Belize Department of Environment report found that foreign-owned resorts and hotels were flouting environmental laws, causing damage to coral reefs and fishing grounds.

In Belize the expatriate community is a resolute and well-represented lobby. Expatriate riverside lodge owners from the western district of Cayo, for example, demanded strict zoning laws to protect their interests from further tourist development.

The depth of expatriate ownership is further reflected through the USAID-initiated Belize Tourism Industry Association (BTIA), an umbrella group representing private interests. In 1992, BTIA was thrown into turmoil when during the annual election of officers, a dispute erupted over whether seats on the committee should be restricted to Belizeans, even though 65 per cent of the membership were expatriates.

It appears, therefore, that the Belizean government's stated commitment to community tourism development is becoming more elusive as foreign control of the industry takes over. It is not just the large multinational companies and developers singled out in political economy approaches, but small-scale, alternative tourism businesses as well.

As Everitt (1987) comments of the post-independence period in Belize, with foreign (mainly Canadian and US) interests in control of the country's most successful tourist facilities, tourism has emerged as a symptom or contributory factor in the creation and aura of neo-colonialism. And it is difficult to escape the impression that Belize is primarily a piece of real estate; an advertisement for Ambergris Caye's Club Caribbean in the US publication *Belize Currents* claims: 'own your own piece of paradise ... Prices start as low as $9,950 ... Values are starting to soar'.

With the importance of tourism growing in the national economy, and the lure of perceived gains from the growth and development of the industry increasing as one of the most positively cited laboratories of successful ecotourism, the Belizean experience must be critically assessed. The government's need for foreign exchange is often in direct conflict with the need to control the scale and content of tourism development.

Expensive new infrastructure projects such as airports, roads and ports require a return on investment. Locally based and controlled tourism projects, while worthy, do not provide the return necessary for foreign investors and multilateral lending institutions. Indeed, a government's aspirations and expectations of tourism development often stand in contradiction to the aspirations of local people.

Sloan concludes that 'Belize is fast becoming one of the most popular ecotourism destinations in the hemisphere. But there's a hitch: All those ecotourists are threatening to trample the place to death - literally'. For others, the problems are considerably more deep-rooted.

As Everitt concludes of tourism, it is 'clear that economic imperialism is rife in Belize despite independence, and ranges throughout the economy which also sells its produce to the United States' (1987:51). Like citrus fruit or bananas, tourism has emerged as another cash crop in the national economy, and one that is challenging the image of small-scale locally owned projects.

Belize is also a perfect example of the complex interaction between a range of interests and why it is problematic to examine individual interests in isolation. In this case the interests of local people, multinational environmental NGOs, aid agencies and the Belizean government are intimately intertwined.

The second and third case studies provide further examples of the relationships between government policy and the discourse of sustainable tourism development. The second case study is from another Central American country, Costa Rica, and the third is from Bali.

Since the 1970s Costa Rica has developed a system of national parks and other protected areas which now cover just over a quarter of the country's land area. Despite severe under-funding for the protection of these areas, this system has formed the base resource of a tourism industry that has relied heavily on the attraction of the country's natural diversity of flora, fauna and landscape.

Consequently, it has become renowned as a destination for ecotourists. Outside San José, the capital city, its tourism industry has been largely based on small-scale, locally owned lodges and hotels which form an integral part of both the communities and natural environments in which they are located. Even within San José, there is a good supply of small hotels and only a limited supply of large-scale, luxury hotels. Partly through the efforts of its ministers speaking at international conferences, Costa Rica also gained an international reputation as a leader in environmental conservation. Whether this was deserved or not is rather debatable given its high rate of deforestation, especially during the 1980s, outside its protected areas.

As the 1990s progressed, however, international admiration of the Costa Rican government's shunning of large-scale, mass tourism developments began to fade as numerous contracts were signed with international consortia to build tourist condominia offering the 'four Ss' of mass tourism but also claiming to be environmentally sensitive and offering nature as part of the attraction. A number of features of these schemes are briefly outlined in the following paragraphs.

In Tambor on the Pacific coast peninsula of Nicoya, a subsidiary of the Barceló Group, a Spanish holiday firm which owns 4-star and 5-star hotels in Tunisia, Mexico, Spain, the Dominican Republic, Costa Rica and the USA, built a 400-room hotel complex within 50 metres of the high water mark. In so doing they stripped a hillside, filled in a swamp, extracted sand from a nearby river, destroyed a hillside to quarry its stone and threatened local species, all without the necessary building permits from the ministries of Housing, Health, Public Works and Transport and Natural Resources.

Additionally, it was reported that white sand was removed from a nearby beach and used to cover the original black sand beach at the complex. The hotel opened in 1992 and has been accused of depositing its sewage in the Rio Pánica.

In 1996 just to the north of Jacó on the Pacific coast of Costa Rica, construction began on the Los Sueños resort hotel, condominiums and marina at the once tranquil village of Playa Herradura. Apart from its negative aesthetic effect on the village, the project altered the extent and ecosystem of a tidal estuary and a marsh that used to stretch along the entire beach. These wetlands were an essential habitat, food source and nursery for a wide range of wildlife. The new yachting marina at the Los Sueños Resort was formally opened by the then President of Costa Rica and the then Minister of Tourism in February 2001.

The massive Papagayo project included the construction of 1,144 homes, 6,270 condohotel units, 6,584 hotel rooms, a shopping centre and a golf course. It formed a large part of the Costa Rican Institute of Tourism's development of Culebra Bay, also on the Pacific coast. The scheme went under the title 'Papagayo Ecodevelopment', but despite the planning which obviously went into it, the 'eco' more appropriately referred to the economic wealth it was intended to generate for its investors rather than to the local ecology it was supposed to save. During the planning of the project, Jeff Marshall, a regular commentator on Costa Rican tourism, said:

The enormous scope of this project is entirely inconsistent with the concept of sustainable and socially responsible ecotourism, which forms the very foundation of the highly successful tourism industry in this country ... It is nothing more than a high-profit real estate scheme designed to make a bundle of money for a few Costa Rican insiders and their foreign corporate allies.

In the mid-1990s, after work on the project had begun, it ground to a halt and people in the region were unsure of its future. Smaller-scale development continued, however, 'with hotels with golf courses being the latest development craze - a seemingly mad idea in this semi-arid landscape' (McNeil, 1999).

Environmentalists expressed concern that the enormous amount of water needed to maintain the golf courses would be taken from wetlands, mangroves and other delicate habitats, while the locals were worried that their water supplies may be curtailed. While the original extravagant plans may not be realised in this case, it appears that the scale of development will still be grandiose and may outstrip the area's carrying capacity.

The Arenal Volcano National Park provides a further illustration of the differences between the Costa Rican government's stated policies and its practices. The Arenal Volcano has two craters which erupt 24 hours a day giving a spectacular exhibition of nature which attracts ecotourists and gave rise to the development and expansion of the Arenal Volcano National Park.

This process of park expansion led to the forcible eviction of some local communities and the formation of an unholy alliance between the park authorities and hotel and resort owners to market the natural environment in an expensive and socially exclusive manner. Isla reports on one example of this process in the Arenal Volcano National Park:

Communities also lost the Tabacon river's hot spring. This spring is highly regarded as medicinal; it has been privatised by Tabacon Resort, which is an international private consortium with the involvement of some 'national' capital.

Tabacon Resort has built 11 swimming pools, using the hot spring water, at the very foot of the Arenal Volcano ... Tourism increased deforestation to build cabins and resort centres ... Forest conversion into resort centres endangers wildlife habitat by provoking mudslides, biotic impoverishment, and species forced migration.

A Tabacon Resort worker, who wishes to remain anonymous, says, 'Before building the swimming pools, we carried hundreds of frogs out of the area. After five years of activity, the frogs disappeared and the toucanos do not stand in the trees any longer. Massive use of chemicals to clean the swimming pools, washrooms, etc. left chemical residuals that force the animals to leave the surrounding areas.'

The link between the burden of international debt and government capitulation to the pressure of transnational companies to develop large-scale tourism projects in order to gain much-needed foreign exchange may be denied in some quarters. But while it may be difficult to prove the direct existence of the link, it is also difficult to refute with any degree of credibility.

The examples outlined above illustrate the subversive power of the pressure exerted by international consortia - baying at the heels of the international lending agencies which stipulate the need for national governments to raise foreign exchange to service their debt. As Michael Kaye, president of Costa Rica Expeditions tour company, has stated: 'the short-term temptations of the fast and easy money from mass tourism development in the context of an economy the size of Costa Rica's should not be underestimated' (1994).

Under such pressure, it should be no surprise that the government of Costa Rica has felt obliged to abandon its previously cautious support for a sensitive and responsible type of community-based tourism development from which it, the government, gained relatively little financial benefit as most of this was received directly by Costa Ricans.

In 1992, Deirdre Evans-Pritchard, an English academic who formerly ran the Eco Institute of Costa Rica, pointed out that the Costa Rican Chamber of Tourism (CANATUR) was under the same kind of pressure as the government: 'the 1992 CANATUR congress championed noble causes and concerns in the name of small scale sustainable tourism development and then, in the final ceremony, awarded prizes to the four largest, most resort-like hotels in the country' (1993:779).

In 1994, the Costa Rican government suffered from another loss of power over its tourism industry which may account, at least in part, for the 1995 reduction in tourist numbers. The then Minister of Environment, René Castro, increased the entry fees to most national parks for foreigners by a factor of ten, ostensibly to further the government's sustainable development programme

by limiting the number of tourists using the country's natural resources. In one sense, his policy 'worked' - between '94 and '96, the nation's parks recorded an overall 26.5 per cent decrease in visits. Castro may have been motivated by more than the principle of sustainable development. The majority of foreign visitors to Costa Rica are 'shoestring' travellers, low-budget backpackers from the US, Europe and Australia. Both Castro and Figueres [then president] ... may have hoped that the tourist industry could recover any losses incurred by the decrease in backpackers through its promotion of Costa Rica as a travel destination for affluent visitors.

In response to the widespread complaints arising from the price increase and the significant decline in tourism receipts, from 1 April 1996, the entry fees were lowered from $15 to $6. Additionally, hotel and car rental companies reduced their daily rates by 15 per cent. CANATUR president, Mauricio Ventura, asked 'Who is the winner in this?' and answered, 'The tourist' (Mesoamérica, 1996).

The Costa Rican Institute of Tourism's (ICT) claim that the country is a model of sustainable development now rings a little hollow. As Jeff Marshall asks:

Instead of promoting massive centralised tourism projects tied to foreign capital, why doesn't the ICT concentrate on the careful planning and development of a network of quality, locally owned and operated, small scale tourism businesses that are compatible with the natural environment and integrated within the existing structures of local communities and economies?

And from her 2001 analysis of land management and ecotourism in Costa Rica, Ana Isla concluded that:

> sustainable development suppresses the human rights of local communities and the rights of nature in favour of the rights of corporations, and vulnerable local nature and local people have

> become connected to the international markets and the world economy on disadvantageous terms. Communities have had to surrender their safe local food system and their role as agricultural producers. Thus, local environments and communities are impoverished.

Sustainable development aggravated poverty and environmental destruction for the short term benefit of capital ... In Costa Rica, these acts of colonisation are called acts of 'sustainable development'. The island of Bali, Indonesia's main cultural tourist draw, has long attracted foreign visitors. Increasing consumer demand has coincided with the Indonesian government's own targets for tourism, which have used Bali as a pivotal marketing tool. At the same time, the special nature of Bali's attractions and the assumed fragility of its cultural life have made it one of the earliest testing grounds for theories about cultural sustainability in the context of tourism development.

National policies to increase tourism were accompanied by a conscious attempt to maximise economic benefits and minimise unwelcome impacts on the island's culture and environment. A tourism master plan drawn up by French consultants and released in 1971 recommended that 'any changes should reinforce not detract from traditional Balinese social structures'. These were based on *banjars*, neighbourhood associations which controlled virtually every aspect of people's lives. As part of the strategy, tourism development was to be confined to the area around the airport, on the southern peninsula.

A new resort, Nusa Dua, was constructed there to cater for the luxury package market and the conference trade. From there tourists are taken to visit famous temples, see craftspeople and artists at work or watch dance performances, with the proceeds going into the treasury of the *banjar* involved. Elsewhere, the largely agricultural life of the islanders was planned to continue.

The plan's formula for sustainable tourism certainly increased visitor numbers and limited the spatial development of tourism. But it 'gave rise to undisguised criticism in Bali ... The Master Plan was a plan for tourism, but it clearly was not a plan for the development of Bali'. In practice, the new hotels needed skills and capital not available locally, thus bringing in outside investors, both Indonesian and foreign, and limiting the projected local employment benefits.

Moreover the planners had not reckoned with the huge popularity of Bali among independent travellers and young people booking flight-only holidays - the 'new' travellers. By 1985, ad hoc, unregulated tourist enterprises of all kinds were flourishing alongside the planned new hotels and packaged cultural attractions.

With tourist numbers exceeding forecasts, international assistance from the UNDP was sought to help with the management, planning and control of tourism on the island. Meanwhile, concern at the growing imbalance of prosperity between the south and other parts of the island led to an apparent *volte face*. The authorities discarded the original vision of a tourist ghetto and instituted a Spatial Arrangement Plan in 1989 which identified sixteen centres for tourism development around the island as part of a dispersal strategy.

This move could be seen as reflecting the agenda of local government, answering local needs, rather than national government, intent as the latter was on preserving the tourism product. In effect, however, the Spatial Arrangement Plan's wider distribution of tourism's economic benefits served to reinforce the kind of power structure that is most damaging to Bali's cultural continuity.

In 1995, an Australian report highlighted disturbing patterns of ownership in new resort developments around the island. It confirmed that these are no more likely to be controlled by local Balinese than the resorts in the southern enclave. Powerful Javanese and foreign investment interests are now firmly entrenched in the island's tourism economy.

Sustainability for these investors is strictly a matter of sustaining profits and their concerns are more about the availability of land for golf courses and condominia than about local needs and the continuation of a flourishing cultural community. The provincial authorities appear helpless to prevent the construction of new attractions alien to Balinese culture; new hotels are sited on sacred land despite local protests; and rural land is transformed into tourist playgrounds.

The Bali Sustainable Development Project undertaken jointly by academics at Canada's University of Waterloo and Indonesia's universities of Gadja Meja and Udayana has attempted to demonstrate an alternative vision to the process of relentless outside manipulation, setting out proposals for integrating tourism into the wider

Balinese economy. Some of its conclusions have been incorporated into the Bali Planning Department's recent five-year development plan, which recognises the importance of maintaining a viable agricultural sector and of supporting village institutions.

Implicit in this is the need to maintain local autonomy. But its effectiveness will depend on the nature of its challenge to the prevailing power relationships, in which outside investors now appear to be dominant.

Aung San Suu Kyi's National League for Democracy (NLD) won 81 per cent of the parliamentary seats in elections in Burma (Myanmar) in 1990. The response by the generals of the SLORC (State Law and Order Council) was to imprison most of the newly elected parliamentarians and to turn the country into what Amnesty International has called 'a prison without walls'.

Since that time, the United Nations Commission on Human Rights has described the country's violations of human rights as:

Extremely serious, in particular concerning the practice of torture, summary and arbitrary execution, forced labour, including forced portering for the military, abuse of women, politically motivated arrests and detention ... important restriction on the exercise of fundamental freedoms and the imposition of oppressive measures directed, in particular, at minority groups. The issue of tourism in Burma highlights a number of points of interest in this chapter. These concern not just the relationship of the Burmese government to the tourism industry, but also the relationship of First World governments and tourism-related TNCs to the Burmese government and the role and responsibilities of tourism more generally.

Since 1990, 'The SLORC has been wooing new investors - especially in the area of tourism and hotel development - with offers of ten year tax breaks and full repatriation of profits'. As Mahr and Sutcliffe point out, such investment from TNCs based in the First World lends the régime political legitimacy, which is confirmed by the arrival of First World tourists - international tourist arrivals increased steadily from 26,607 in 1992 to almost 200,000 in 1998 (WTO/OMT, annual).

The SLORC/SPDC declared 1996 the 'Visit Myanmar Year' and increased its efforts to profit from the tourism industry by aiming at a target of half a million visitors for 1996. To prepare for the expected increase in tourists, the SLORC/SPDC put its people to work - forcibly - as described by Mahr and Sutcliffe:

Whole communities have been forcibly relocated from their homes to make way for foreign hotels and to 'clean up' areas for the eyes of tourists ...

Thousands of people have been forced to work without pay on tourist sites - restoring the moat around Mandalay Palace, for example. Plans have been put into action to relocate the more 'picturesque' ethnic peoples to special villages where they can be visited by tourist groups in what amounts to a human zoo. Model villages for this purpose are under construction near Rangoon and some Padaung people have already been resettled to Inle Lake. There tourists can visit - for a charge - and take photos of 'long-necked' Padaung women.

These human rights violations have been documented in detail by the UK-based Burma Action Group and reported by Tourism Concern and increasingly in the western media. In 1996 Aung San Suu Kyi specifically asked visitors to stay away from her country until the military government hands over power to the NLD. Lonely Planet Publications, however, have been publishing their Burma guidebook since 1979 and have continued to do so since this call for visitors to stay away.

In May 2000, the Burma Campaign UK and Tourism Concern launched a boycott campaign against Lonely Planet Publications because of its Burma travel guidebook written by Joe Cummings and Michael Clark. Under the banner 'There are times when travellers have to take a stand.

This is one: BOYCOTT LONELY PLANET', they asked consumers of travel guides to boycott all Lonely Planet publications until the Burma guidebook are withdrawn. Glenys Kinnock, European parliamentarian, in an article in the UK *Guardian* newspaper summarises the request behind the boycott thus:

Aung San Suu Kyi asks a simple thing ... She's asked for sanctions so that the junta will be starved out of existence. We can impose our own sanctions and not go on holiday to Burma. And we should certainly not buy from publishers that suggest that we should.

In a letter to concerned members of the UK parliament, Tony Wheeler, Lonely Planet publisher, retorted by accusing the two groups of censorship. The debate between the two has been joined with some heat ever since (Wheeler, 2000, 2001; Burma Campaign UK and Tourism Concern, 2000a and 2000b). In response to the boycott campaign's claim that visiting the country is tantamount to approval of the SLORC/SPDC, Wheeler claims that only a tiny proportion of tourist revenues will reach the illegitimate military government's coffers and that the Burmese people want to talk to outsiders.

The cartoon is one of many representations of the boycott campaign's view of the Lonely Planet attitude. Wheeler claims that the NLD voices asking for a boycott are those of NLD members living in exile who are not aware of the current reality in Burma. The debate also reached the UK BBC's Newsnight programme in October 2000 which revealed that the Sittwe Hotel, promoted in Lonely Planet's guide along with other government guesthouses in the area, is included in an International Labour Organisation report (ILO, 1998) as having been built with forced labour. Critics describe Wheeler's approach as one of arrogant defiance and stubborn self-certainty. In the UK *Observer* newspaper Nick Cohen used the debate to describe the attitudes of both the new tourists who are likely to visit Burma and the alternative guidebook publisher who is likely to benefit from sales to them:

The Burma spat has been distinguished by the extremism of the invective of bohemian travellers. Dea Birkett, a travel writer, whined rhetorically in the *Guardian* of all places: 'Aren't holidays supposed to be carefree times for suntans and self-indulgence? Is it really such a crime to seek out somewhere where you can simply enjoy yourself? Tourism Concern and the Burma Campaign's moral outrage is designed to make us feel bad about being good to ourselves. To restrict freedom of movement is the hallmark of totalitarian régimes.'

Forget her wheedling style for a second, and consider the implications of Birkett's words. The opponents of dictatorship, who fight without resources, international support or any military force which might defeat the junta on the field of battle, are totalitarians. Rich western tourists, by contrast, are the true victims even when they stay in Rangoon hotels built on the site of the homes of the Burmese poor - which were bulldozed without compensation - or travel on a moving staircase built by forced labour to catch the marvellous view at sunset from Mandalay Hill.

Only a sadist would want to make them 'feel bad about being good to ourselves' ... Though I'm all for boycotting Lonely Planet, the real significance of the argument is cultural. Discerning liberal consumers are now so self-confident and self-pitying that they pose, without irony, as the victims of Stalin and Hitler when anyone suggests they might make the tiniest moral choice. It says so much about them.

Whatever the pros and cons of the argument, few if any British tour operators can currently be unaware of the debate around the ethical grounds for not visiting Burma. New hotels are being built by TNCs from Hong Kong, Japan, Malaysia, Singapore, South Korea and Thailand, and French and Swiss interests are also involved. Companies such as Voyages Jules Verne, Coromandel and David Sayers Travel all run cultural or trekking tours to Burma. Coromandel describes its relation with Burma thus:

We are probably Britain's leading specialists for Burma, firmly believing that contact with the free world does more good than isolation. In spite of a number of good new private sector hotels and new airlines, Burma remains a destination for the traveller rather than the tourist, but the rewards are great, with splendid scenery, magnificent monuments, and a warm and smiling welcome from the Burmese themselves.

Explore, on the other hand, ceased covering Burma on its tours largely because of UK Foreign Office advice regarding the nature of the régime. Bales also ceased to cover Burma in their main brochure in 1999 for the same reason, although they are still willing to arrange tailor-made tours upon specific request.

Burma represents an attractive Third World destination for the new middle-class tourists. But more importantly from the standpoints of the First World corporate decision-makers, it represents an attractive investment opportunity for tourism businesses. And First World governments can and do assist in these processes of tourism investment and associated human rights violations.

The UK government's stated policy is not to promote investment in Burma because of the SLORC/SPDC's human rights violations. In 1996, however, despite its stated policy, the government's Department of Trade and Industry (DTI) allocated £50,000 travelling expenses to trade missions to Burma for the year. After the first mission at the end of February, in the words of Tourism Concern, the

Shadow Foreign Affairs Minister [Derek Fatchett] asked a parliamentary question about the DTI's plans for future trade missions [to Burma] and the reply was 'we intend to evaluate the results of this mission before deciding on supporting the second'. Civil service speak for 'oops - we've been found out'. It can be assumed that First World governments would not try to cover up public knowledge of such trade missions if they believed that the development to be promoted by these missions could be portrayed as being ethically sound or in the interests of sustainability.

The example of Burma is indicative of the 'reality' to which governments and the industry work. It is a reality which they use to justify their actions and investments. If ethical considerations contradict this reality, then they must be hidden from view. Tourism in Burma gives us an illustration of the way in which investment is used to serve specific interests, those of the Burmese government, First World governments, tourists and crucially tourism-related businesses. Other interests, those of the visited, the resettled, the majority of Burmese people, are decidedly not served by these investments and developments.

But whereas in many Third World destination countries the governments have to be coerced by First World governments, international lending agencies and TNCs, in the case of Burma the SLORC/SPDC actively enlists the assistance of these bodies. Power is still very much based in the First World, but with a willing partner in Burma's military and business elites.

Despite the clarity and documentation of the link between Burma's human rights violations and its exploitation of nature and cultural tourism, the brochures of some new tourism companies still extol its virtues. In such circumstances, then, it is hardly surprising that for many tourists the relationship between travel, tourism and human rights has remained rather nebulous.

Indeed, the occurrence of human rights abuses and their coincidence with perceived danger may actually act as a fillip to tourism in certain circumstances and among certain types of tourists.

It has been argued that an understanding of issues of power is essential to an analysis of tourism developments and the role of governments in this. The necessity for such an understanding is as great for analyses of new forms of tourism to Third World destinations as it is for mass tourism developments - perhaps even more so given the relationship of new forms of tourism to 'development'.

It is commonly perceived, especially from the level of the local community, that power rests with the national government. This may indeed be the case in some instances, but we have suggested that the actions and policies pursued by national governments are often circumscribed at best and are sometimes dictated by the influence of external organisations.

This includes both the inevitability that tourism must increase, as well as the contest over which form of tourism development should take place. It is especially so for Third World governments weighed down by a burden of debt - a burden that was largely foisted upon them by First World banks and governments as well as their own incautiousness resulting from the unseemly rush for western-style development.

For the most part, the outcome of this process of First World influence on Third World development has been government policies which increase the unevenness and inequality of development within national boundaries and which further widen the gap between First and Third Worlds. The policies pursued for the development of tourism are largely those most suitable to the profits and enjoyment of First World investors and tourists rather than those most beneficial to Third World communities and governments. This is not to say that there are no opportunities for positive and beneficial change. Our discussion of pro-poor tourism initiatives, for example, suggests that such opportunities may exist. But given the global analysis and the enormity of global poverty, the ability of tourism initiatives to tackle global inequality is slight.

We have tried to show how, even where governments have attempted to follow environmentally benign, socially and economically beneficial and culturally sensitive tourism developments, forces beyond their control have subverted the policies and have served only to emphasise the seemingly ever-widening gaps. In the process, government attempts to satisfy outsiders' views of the content of tourism have turned sustainable tourism into an item of political discourse.

In order to achieve this broader analysis, a number of key themes (new tourism, uneven and unequal development and the Third World) and key words (globalisation, sustainability and development) were identified. Summarises these positions and seeks to illustrate the relationships between the key words and key themes by drawing some examples from and questions raised by the book. Clearly the relationships summarised in the cells of the table are not exclusive and there is considerable overlap between both the key words and key themes.

Globalisation, sustainability and development, it was argued, were best thought of as key words as each is open to competing meanings and interpretations: to a backpacker the Third World may represent exotic cultures and environments and an endless world of adventure; to mass tourists in the USA, Europe or the Pacific Rim, the notion of the Third World may represent a threat, and a place either to avoid when holidaying or where a holiday needs to be carefully controlled, through all-inclusive enclave tourism, for example.

Arguably, the most important purpose for this book was to establish that these key words are hotly contested and that relationships of power underlie the construction, representation and implementation of these processes. So for example, this helps us understand the way in which new tourism seeks to differentiate and distance itself from mass forms of tourism and how sustainability does not have a fixed and agreed definition that is shared by everyone.

The first of the key themes - unequal and uneven development - was adopted as shorthand for indicating the inequality faced by certain nation states, regions, communities and individuals. The principal focus was on the way in which inequality is expressed globally through the First and Third Worlds, but clearly unevenness is also expressed, for example, in the way certain Third World destinations become tourist magnets while others do not.

This is an explicit recognition that relationships of power must lie at the centre of tourism analysis. This necessitates a more nuanced and extended discussion of inequality and shows that power is transmitted in and through tourism.

This varies from the power wielded by private business consortia such as the WTTC, to the priorities of environmental sustainability, to the way in which new tourism draws in and controls new Third World destinations. As Hutnyk observes: 'social sciences have sometimes been complicit in maintaining distinctions and privileges among different classes of people, and between First and Third World, by choosing to investigate the conditions of "the poor" and "disempowered" rather than pursuing research into power' (1996:216).

We have traced these relationships of power and variable development through the Third World, though we have recognised that in itself the Third World is a socially constructed and contested entity that is inexorably related to development.

Our final theme is new tourism to which we return and recap below. At the outset we argued that this theme was a means or medium for analysing and understanding the broader scope of this book.

We have added 'tourism and geographical imagination' to the themes. The notion of tourism and geographical imagination seeks to emphasise that we are dealing with the nature of representation, how the context and meanings of words such as sustainability and development are socially constructed by host communities, governments, TNCs, smaller operators, environmental organisations and tourists. They are words whose meaning is open to interpretation and are continually contested between different interest groups - a point that is reflected in the examples provided in the final column.

NEW FORMS OF THIRD WORLD TOURISM

As the early chapters of the book argue and portray, they have arisen as a result of a wide variety of economic, socio-cultural and environmental factors. Factors such as a structural economic shift from a Fordist to a post-Fordist mode of production, accompanied by cultural shifts characterised as moving from modernism to postmodernism, and a growing environmentalism, help explain the increase in the number of new forms of tourism.

Independent travel has sought to distance itself from mass tourism, and a variety of benevolent terms (appropriate, alternative, acceptable, responsible, sustainable, and so on) have been employed in an attempt to assert that it is these forms of tourism that provide an ethical and practically acceptable response to 'development' and the structure of disadvantage of the Third World.

We have attempted to demonstrate a tentative link between the economic and cultural shifts in contemporary capitalism and the growth of the new middle classes. We suggested that it is these class fractions in particular (though not exclusively) that can be linked to the growth of new tourism.

Furthermore, these new groups and their motives are more formally represented by the international NGOs which campaign around issues of conservation, ecology, pollution, human rights and cultural identity to which many of the new middle classes subscribe.

These organisations represent the vanguard of this movement to gain a moral base and a justification for their own definition of sustainability, which is often constrained by a restricted association with ecology. The subliminal promotion of a conservation ethic and the assured certainty of one form of sustainability are responsible for the emergence of attitudes which in some cases have been characterised as eco-colonialist.

Index